DAWN OF THE CODE WAR

DAWN OF THE CODE WAR

America's Battle Against Russia,
China, and the Rising Global Cyber Threat

/////////////////////////////

JOHN P. CARLIN
WITH GARRETT M. GRAFF

PUBLICAFFAIRS

New York

PublicAffairs
Hachette Book Group
1290 Avenue of the Americas, New York, NY 10104
www.publicaffairsbooks.com
@Public_Affairs

Printed in the United States of America

Originally published in hardcover and ebook by PublicAffairs in October 2018
First Trade Paperback Edition: 2019

Published by PublicAffairs, an imprint of Perseus Books, LLC, a subsidiary of Hachette Book Group, Inc. The PublicAffairs name and logo is a trademark of the Hachette Book Group.

The publisher is not responsible for websites (or their content) that are not owned by the publisher.

All statements of fact, opinion, or analysis expressed are the author's alone and do not necessarily reflect the official positions or views of the Department of Justice or any other US government agency. This article has been reviewed by the Department of Justice to prevent the disclosure of classified or otherwise sensitive information.

Print book interior design by Jeff Williams.

The Library of Congress has cataloged the hardcover edition as follows:
Names: Carlin, John P., 1973– author. | Graff, Garrett M., 1981– author.
Title: Dawn of the code war : America's battle against Russia, China, and
     the rising global cyber threat / John P. Carlin with Garrett M. Graff.
Description: First edition. | New York : PublicAffairs, [2019] | Includes
     bibliographical references and index.
Identifiers: LCCN 2018020918 (print) | LCCN 2018028431 (ebook) |
     ISBN 9781541773813 (ebook) | ISBN 9781541773837 (hardcover)
Subjects: LCSH: Cyberspace operations (Military science)—United States. |
     Cyberterrorism—History. | Cyberspace—Security measures—History. |
     Computer security—United States. | Computer crimes—United States. |
     Information warfare—United States. | National security—United States. |
     Cyberterrorism—Prevention. | Internet in espionage. | Espionage—United
     States.
Classification: LCC U167.5.C92 (ebook) | LCC U167.5.C92 C37 2019 (print) |
     DDC 327.1273047—dc23

LC record available at https://lccn.loc.gov/2018020918

ISBNs: 978-1-5417-7383-7 (hardcover), 978-1-5417-7381-3 (ebook),
978-1-5417-7384-4 (paperback)

LSC-C

10 9 8 7 6 5 4 3 2 1

*To Sarah, Sylvie, Patricia, and Roy; and to the
men and women of the Department of Justice who
protect our way of life and keep us safe*

Contents

TeaMpOisoN

JUNAID HUSSAIN ORIGINALLY wanted to be a rapper. As it turned out, the Pakistani kid in Birmingham, England, lived life instead on the internet, and at internet speed. In just a decade, from age 11 to 21, he went from gaming to hacking to killing, an arc the world had never seen before, unfolding faster than anyone might have imagined. For the first half of his digital life, the hacker operated with impunity, bragging in an interview that he was many steps ahead of the authorities: "100% certain they have nothing on me. I don't exist to them, I've never used my real details online, I've never purchased anything. My real identity doesn't exist online.—and no I don't fear getting caught."[1]

By 2015, at age 21, he knew different—he was a marked man, hunted by the United States, the #3 leader of the Islamic State of Iraq and the Levant (ISIL) on the government's Most Wanted list. Living on the run in ISIL-controlled eastern Syria, Hussain tried to keep his stepson close by, ensuring that US air strikes wouldn't target him. Inside the Justice Department where I worked at the time, Hussain's efforts made him a top threat. Nearly every week of 2015 brought a new Hussain-inspired plot against the United States; FBI surveillance teams were exhausted, chasing dozens of would-be terrorists at once. We'd pulled agents from criminal assignments to supplement the counterterrorism squads. Inside the government, alarm bells rang daily, but we attempted to downplay the threat publicly. We didn't want to elevate Hussain to another

1

global figurehead like Osama bin Laden, standing for the twisted ideology of Islamic jihad.

We wouldn't even really talk about him publicly until he was dead.

Hussain represented an online threat we long recognized would arrive someday—a tech-savvy terrorist who could use the tools of modern digital life to extend the reach of a terror group far beyond its physical location. In the summer of 2015, he successfully executed one of the most global-spanning cyber plots we'd ever seen: the British terrorist of Pakistani descent, living in Syria, recruited a Kosovar hacker, studying computer science in Malaysia, in order to enable attacks on American servicemen and -women inside the United States.

According to an interview he gave in 2012, Hussain—who went online originally by the moniker TriCk—said he started hacking at around age 11. He'd been playing a game online when another hacker knocked him offline. "I wanted revenge so I started googling around on how to hack," he explained. "I joined a few online hacking forums, read tutorials, started with basic social engineering and worked my way up. I didn't get my revenge, but I became one of the most hated hackers on this game."

By 13, he found the game childish, and by 15, he "became political." He found himself sucked online into watching videos of children getting killed in countries like Kashmir and Pakistan and swept into conspiratorial websites about the Freemasons and Illuminati. Those internet "rabbit holes" led Hussain to found a hacker group with seven friends; they called themselves TeaMp0isoN, hacker-speak based on their old hacking forum p0ison.org.[2] They became notorious in 2011 for their unique brand of "hacktivism," defacing websites, often with pro-Palestine messages, and attacking online key websites such as BlackBerry and NATO and figures such as former Prime Minister Tony Blair—they hacked his personal assistant and then released his address book online.[3] Hussain dismissed other "hacktivist" groups such as Anonymous, saying they symbolized the online equivalent of "peaceful protesting, camping on the street," whereas his TeaMp0isoN executed "Internet Guerilla Warfare." In April 2012, TriCk told a British newspaper, "I fear no man or authority. My whole life is dedicated to the cause."

His online exploits didn't last long: by September 2012, he had been sentenced to six months in prison for the Blair stunt. TeaMp0isoN faded away, but Hussain's anger and resentment at Western society continued to boil. Sometime soon after his release, he made his way to ISIL's territory in Syria and married another British would-be musician-turned-ISIL-convert, Sarah Jones. There, he threw himself into ISIL's online propaganda war, remaking himself as Abu Hussain al-Britani with a Twitter avatar that showed him, his face half-covered by a mask, aiming an AK-47-style rifle at the camera. He turned everything he'd learned about online culture and tools into what one journalist called "a macabre version of online dating," as he quickly gained prominence as ISIL's lead propagandist in the CyberCaliphate, recruiting disaffected youth like himself to the global battlefield. "You can sit at home and play *Call of Duty* or you can come here and respond to the real call of duty...the choice is yours," he announced in one tweet.

Hussain's tactics weren't necessarily new, but he and fellow ISIL terrorists executed them at a level we'd never seen before. Hussain represented, in some ways, the most dangerous terrorist we'd yet seen—a master of the emerging world of digital jihad.

At the time, terrorists were hardly the only ones figuring how to execute their real-world mischief through bits and bytes. We were seeing rising threats across the board from foreign adversaries, organized crime, online activist groups, even lone hackers and vandals. While "cybersecurity" is a frequent topic on the news today, too few people understand the scale, scope, and speed with which the threat online is evolving. My goal with this book is to tell the story of the beginning of America's "Code War," how criminals, terrorists, and spies made themselves at home on a global network that was never designed with safety and security in mind—and how the US government, prosecutors, the FBI, and our international allies have spent a quarter century playing catch-up. What follows isn't just a crime thriller of the good guys chasing the bad guys—it's a warning that we've built our modern society on top of fragile technology, with far too little thought as to the creativity of our adversaries.

My hope in telling this story of the US government's first quarter-century fight online is that it will help demystify a realm that too often seems opaque to outsiders, allow readers to understand this new threat landscape, and raise important questions about how the country should think about the shift of daily life to the internet. Let me be clear: This isn't black magic. We know how to fight cyberattacks. We have built an effective playbook in recent years on how to respond. We know how to target bad guys and build cases against them—and doing so can make a difference. Nearly every case that I discuss in this book has been solved and we've tried to bring the suspects to justice, one way or another.

But there's much more to do in the years ahead.

///////////////

I was born and raised in New York City, and my family still lives there. On September 11, 2001, my father was in a subway car under the World Trade Center, my brother-in-law watched the attacks unfold from his office window nearby, and my wife was in New York for work. At the time, I worked as a junior prosecutor in the Justice Department, and I remember calling around frantically to make sure my family was all okay—on that day, we were lucky, but so many other families were not. For most of the next fifteen years, I had the opportunity to work alongside others to ensure the United States wasn't attacked again like that—first, focused on counterterrorism, and, later, on cyberthreats and espionage.

We knew sooner or later terrorists would turn to the internet—it was too easy not to. I spent much of my time in government watching this rising threat and anticipating when we would first see a "blended attack," one that mixed online operations with a kinetic real-world assault—an attack, for instance, that would see terrorists explode a car bomb at the same time they attacked a city's communication system, multiplying an attack's fear, confusion, and effect. The terrorists saw the possibilities, too: al-Qaeda even released a video comparing the vulnerabilities in computer network security to weak points in aviation security before 9/11.

By the time I arrived at the FBI in 2007, working as a special counsel and later chief of staff to Director Robert Mueller, the threat from al-Qaeda morphed. Whereas Osama bin Laden's terror group originally relied on its own centrally executed plots—such as 9/11 and the 2006 plot against transatlantic passenger planes—the relentless post-9/11 campaign by NATO, Western intelligence agencies, and every tool of the US government severely compromised their ability to organize and direct attacks from afar. Instead, "core" al-Qaeda effectively allowed "terrorist franchises" to continue their mission for them, groups like al-Qaeda in the Arabian Peninsula, and al-Qaeda in Iraq, the terror movement that evolved into ISIL.

Terrorism online presented a unique new twist—never before had the United States been involved in a conflict where the enemy could communicate from overseas directly with individual Americans. In World War II, Tokyo Rose—her real name was Iva Toguri D'Aquino—helped spread English-language propaganda via radio broadcast to US soldiers, just as Axis Sally did in Europe. In Vietnam, there was Hanoi Hannah. The first Gulf War saw Baghdad Betty and Iraqi Jack. But by the end of the 1990s, the internet opened up those broadcasts to a global audience. As *Wired* magazine wrote, "Never before in history have terrorists had such easy access to the minds and eyeballs of millions."[4]

That revolution would only accelerate in the 2000s. As it turns out, the same principles that make the web great for insurgents and niche communities—its openness, ease of use, and global reach—made it useful for aiding and encouraging extremism online. Just months before I moved into my new office on the seventh floor of the hulking J. Edgar Hoover Building on Pennsylvania Avenue, a new online tool named Twitter launched. We had no idea then how much power it would give to online extremists.

Islamic extremism mainly developed in countries with state-controlled media, such as Egypt and Saudi Arabia, so the movement naturally invested heavily in alternative means of communication. The web seemed perfect; in fact, it has helped grow the jihadist movement like no other aid, enabling in many ways the international rise of al-Qaeda. "Core" al-Qaeda relied primarily on in-person lectures and fundraising tours in mosques and community centers around the world—and even, before 9/11, inside the United States—with some brief forays into "Web 1.0" technologies such as forums, bulletin boards, and list servs, to spread its message.

In fact, al-Qaeda specifically shied away from covering the more violent side of its global jihad. It saw the global battle for "hearts and minds" as best won with ideas, not searing images. When its Iraqi affiliate, led by Abu Musab al-Zarqawi, began distributing videos of brutal beheadings, with the then-horrifying but now-too-familiar iconography of hostages in orange jumpsuits, al-Qaeda's top deputy, Ayman al-Zawahiri, wrote a letter warning the Iraqi group to dial back its horror show. "I say to you: that we are in a battle, and that more than half of this battle is taking place in the battlefield of the media. And that we are in a media battle in a race for the hearts and minds of our Umma [Muslim people]," al-Zawahiri wrote, gently chastising his hotheaded Iraqi colleague. "The Muslim populace who love and support you will never find palatable . . . the scenes of slaughtering the hostages."[5]

That difference in approach represented a sign of a coming generational divide, between the older leaders of al-Qaeda, such as bin Laden and al-Zawahiri, and a new tech-savvy generation who understood the power of images online. It mirrored a generational divide that we're seeing play out in every sector of the world. Companies and institutions around the globe are living this divide, between those who remember an age before computers and those for whom using an iPhone is as natural as breathing.

It didn't take long before this new generation began to play a key role for al-Qaeda. In the early 2000s, someone named Irhabi 007 (*irhabi* is Arabic for "terrorist") became something of an online webmaster for al-Qaeda.[6] He emerged as a leader in key password-protected jihadist forums—websites known as Muntada al-Ansar al-Islami (Islam Supporters Forum) and al-Ekhlas (Sincerity)—and helped spread messages from terrorists in Iraq. One terrorism analyst, Evan Kohlmann, labeled Irhabi 007 "the undisputed king of internet terrorism."

No one possessed the slightest idea who he was—or even where he lived—until he disappeared online in 2005, soon after British police arrested a 22-year-old West Londoner, Younis Tsouli, as part of an investigation into a bombing plot. Only later did police realize who they'd caught—and they also identified two associates, Waseem Mughal and Tariq Al-Daour, who helped him. Al-Daour had been the operation's financier; when police arrested him, they discovered his computer held more than 37,000 stolen credit cards, which funded more than $3.5 million in purchases of equipment the men thought would help jihadists, everything from GPS devices to night-vision goggles, as well as upward of 250 airline tickets.[7]*

In Britain, Tsouli and his two compatriots became the first people in Britain to be convicted of conspiring to commit terrorism on the internet. As a Scotland Yard official, Peter Clarke, said at the time, "What it did show us was the extent to which they could conduct operational planning on the internet. It was the first virtual conspiracy to murder that we had seen."[8]

The first, but not the last. Al-Qaeda was undergoing a big shift by the mid-2000s, as relentless American and global pressure—from drone strikes to financial sanctions—reduced the core of the group to a shadow of its previous capabilities. The shift in its tactics accelerated around 2006, after British intelligence stopped a massive plot to down numerous transatlantic airplanes heading west to the United States. It felt like a near miss to us as UK officers swept down on some two dozen suspects on the night of August 9, 2006, but we'd gotten much better at interdicting the centrally directed, organized, spectacular attacks, like 9/11, that al-Qaeda preferred. Instead, al-Qaeda was forced to inspire attacks from afar. It was then we began to see al-Qaeda and its franchises taking the first steps into more creative social media tools.

---

*Irhabi 007's long reach online became clear as police examined his laptop, which included tips on constructing a car bomb and a folder labeled "Washington" with short video clips of key DC sites like the US Capitol and the World Bank building. The videos sent the FBI on a scramble; five months later, in an investigation code-named NORTHERN EXPOSURE, Atlanta's Joint Terrorism Task Force arrested two Georgia teens who had been corresponding with Irhabi and had made the videos. The FBI later determined that the men had been in touch with other terrorism suspects in more than a dozen countries around the world.

Terrorism, after all, is a tactic uniquely focused on attracting media attention. People who turn to terrorism understand that they can never achieve outright military victories; thus, they turn to terror campaigns, meant to destabilize regions and force governments to respond to political pressure and popular uprisings. This has been historically true whether you're looking at the IRA, Black September, or al-Qaeda. Terrorism, as a tactic, is a marginal phenomenon that relies on psychological victories rather than military ones—it can't happen or succeed without public attention and media coverage. By its very name, it seeks to terrorize—to magnify its impact and people's fears.*

One al-Qaeda recruit in particular, an American named Adam Gadahn—who adopted the moniker Azzam the American—began to adopt new media tactics, starring in online videos and serving as something like a public spokesperson for the group. His well-produced videos laid out the group's philosophy and included English subtitles, to ensure as large an audience as possible. Other jihadists followed similar models: In Chechnya, Islamic extremists created a genre of videos known as "Russian Hell," depicting their surprise attacks on Russian forces, a not-so-subtle message aimed at undermining the morale of occupying troops, who never knew where the next attack might come. In East Africa, a twenty-something Alabama-raised Muslim who traveled to join al-Shabaab, Omar Hammami—a.k.a. Abu Mansoor Al-Amriki—began appearing in terrorist videos, becoming, over time, one of the group's best-known leaders. In March 2009, he starred in a 31-minute recruiting video that portrayed the terror group's attack on Ethiopian forces. He pleaded for more recruits: "If you can encourage more of your children, and more of your neighbors, and anyone around you to send people...to this Jihad, it would be a great asset for us." The group's videos were multilingual, featuring cameos from fighters who arrived from around the world, and sought to reach as broad a global audience as possible, with portions in Arabic, Swedish, and Urdu,

---

*Technically, as Title 18 US Code § 2331 defines terrorism, it's "violent acts... intended—(i) to intimidate or coerce a civilian population; (ii) to influence the policy of a government by intimidation or coercion; or (iii) to affect the conduct of a government by mass destruction, assassination, or kidnapping."

among others, as well as with English and Swahili subtitles. Hammami did his best to make jihad look enticing, even releasing rap songs with names like "First Stop Addis," "Make Jihad with Me," and "Blow by Blow." As al-Shabaab's fight continued, Hammami also posted audio messages and uploaded a 127-page memoir to the internet, *The Story of an American Jihadi: Part One*, that traced his path from high school to radicalization to al-Shabaab.[9]

While al-Shabaab succeeded in targeting and luring a handful of recruits—mostly men, largely from Minnesota and the Twin Cities—the online recruitment efforts were never particularly effective; they were to a certain extent ideological spam, the equivalent of the Nigerian scheme email fraudsters who sent out 1 billion emails and hoped 1/1000th of 1 percent of people were gullible enough to think that a deposed oil minister needs help smuggling his ill-gotten gains out of Africa. Yet by blasting across the internet and reaching deep into forums and bulletin boards where disaffected youth hung out, they found some success.

None of these terrorist recruiters online, though, would match the prominence of a onetime American imam, Anwar al-Awlaki. He was born in New Mexico, while his Yemeni father studied on a Fulbright Scholarship, and his family returned to Yemen when he was seven years old. He returned to the United States in 1991 to attend college, and in the years ahead became an ambitious and prominent Muslim imam, first in San Diego and later in northern Virginia. He built a national and then international audience for his teachings, publishing sets of CDs with his lectures for sale through Islamic bookstores and online websites.

The FBI suspected he possessed ties to the 9/11 plot, in part because he ministered to two of the hijackers, Nawaf al-Hazmi and Khalid al-Mihdhar, but nothing had ever been proven. FBI surveillance teams in 2002 observed him regularly soliciting prostitutes. He'd done it before; he'd actually been arrested for that same charge in 1997 in San Diego—and, apparently panicked that the FBI might expose his less-than-pure lifestyle, he fled to the United Kingdom in 2002. In 2004, he returned permanently to Yemen, where he turned increasingly militant and rose to become the public face of al-Qaeda in the Arabian Peninsula (AQAP), the most effective and dangerous of the first generation of al-Qaeda affiliates.

His lectures on Islam—easily found on YouTube—continued to reach a devoted following; he spoke eloquently and charismatically, twisting the ideology of the peaceful Muslim religion into an encouragement for war, and speaking colloquially in English in his lectures—which itself represented an important revelation, expanding the potential audience beyond the normal Arabic-only religious teachings that were inscrutable to most Americans.

Beyond the online lectures, he worked with another American, Samir Khan, to help AQAP reach new audiences and build slick, compelling marketing materials for their cause, including a well-produced PDF magazine called *Inspire* that encouraged extremists from afar to not worry about journeying to distant locales like Pakistan or Yemen to attack the infidels—to stay home and launch what the magazine called "Open Source Jihad," by turning a rented pickup truck into a "death mobile" or, as one article written by "the AQ chef" explained, "Make a Bomb in the Kitchen of Your Mom."

The first issue of the magazine even quoted American officials explaining al-Qaeda's new strategy. One issue of *Inspire* featured a quote from Defense Secretary Robert Gates: "It's pretty clear that people like Awlaki in Yemen and others see any kind of an attack inside the United States, even if it's a small scale attack, compared, say, to the World Trade Center, the Towers, who see that as a success for them. So that makes the challenge for the FBI and the intelligence agencies and the Department of Justice and local police that much tougher. Because you may not have a big, complex plot involving a lot of people that might be easier to detect."

Other articles offered tips on "What to Expect in Jihad" for those who were willing to make the journey overseas. "The open source jihad is America's worst nightmare," the first issue of the magazine promised. The magazine included email addresses that could be used to reach Anwar al-Awlaki or other AQAP recruiters, encouraging would-be jihadists to start a dialogue—as too many did.

In fact, by the late 2000s, Anwar al-Awlaki's fingerprints were on almost every major terrorist plot we found in the United States, including the 2007 attack at Fort Dix, the 2009 shooting at a Little Rock military recruiting office, and the 2010 Times Square bomber—all of which featured attackers who subscribed to al-Awlaki's message and were devoted to his religious lectures. His reach proved long: his death threat against a Seattle cartoonist forced her into hiding, and the Islamic extremist who stabbed a British politician—the first assassination attempt by an al-Qaeda follower in Britain—explained afterward his lectures inspired her.

We also saw him more directly involved in plots: he exchanged emails with Nidal Hasan, the US Army doctor who opened fire at Fort Hood on November 5, 2009, killing 13 and wounding 32.[10] I worked at the time for FBI Director Bob Mueller; it's hard to overstate how greatly that incident, little remembered today, changed our perception of the new terror threat. As the after-action investigation by former FBI Director William Webster found, the shooting revealed gaps in the bureau's counterterrorism efforts—the FBI didn't connect clues that Hasan had contacted al-Awlaki. The director felt responsible. We were in the midst of watching a transformation of the terror threat and hadn't realized the extent to which this new wave wouldn't necessarily involve direct operational instructions—that inspiration from afar proved sufficient.

The FBI was years into a wrenching organizational transformation— one that pushed the FBI, with its deep roots dating back to the 1900s as the country's premier law enforcement agency, to work more as a 21st-century intelligence agency, one that prized careful monitoring of terror threats to not just make an arrest but to understand whole networks. For years since 9/11, the mantra inside the FBI to defeat al-Qaeda's sophisticated operations had been to surveil and watch terrorist suspects, learn who they met, and watch the plot come together before acting. That approach helped guide the 2006 creation of the National Security Division (NSD) at the Justice Department, which I would later lead. Our approach of balancing law enforcement efforts and intelligence gathering only worked if there were, in fact, ties to a larger organization and it was, in fact, a sophisticated operation. In 2009, our focus changed, and we were seeing the propaganda itself as key to inspiring an attack.

Inside the government, there had been until then a running analytic dispute about whether Anwar al-Awlaki had been "operational" or just "inspirational," though the latter certainly proved worrisome enough. That dispute ended weeks after the Fort Hood bombing when we saw Umar Farouk Abdulmutallab, the so-called Underwear Bomber, try to blow up a transatlantic airliner en route to Detroit on Christmas Day 2009. Anwar al-Awlaki, the "sheikh," as he was known in the terror camps in Yemen, personally helped recruit and train Abdulmutallab, even selecting an airliner as his target and helping him record a martyrdom video.[11]

Anwar al-Awlaki's influence and leadership made him one of the prime targets for America's counterterrorism effort by the start of the Obama administration. In 2010, he recorded a full-throated "Call to Jihad." As the New York Times wrote, "In it, with the confidence and poise of a YouTube handyman explaining how to caulk a window, he details just why, exactly, it is every Muslim's religious duty to kill Americans."[12]

A US air strike killed Anwar al-Awlaki in September 2011. Days later, AQAP announced, "America killed Sheikh Anwar, may Allah have mercy on him, but it could not kill his thoughts. The martyrdom of the Sheikh is a new and renewing life for his thoughts and style." Indeed, we saw all too clearly in the years ahead that his tactics were unfortunately here to stay. His lectures helped inspire the bombers of the Boston Marathon in 2013 and even as a new threat arose—ISIL— we continued to see many would-be terrorists devoting themselves to al-Awlaki's online teachings.

For a moment, after his death, it seemed the terror threat in the United States ebbed. In 2011, I moved from the FBI to the Justice Department to be the chief of staff to Lisa Monaco—who had originally preceded me as Mueller's #2—after Lisa was appointed assistant attorney general for national security by President Obama. Lisa's ceremonial swearing-in as assistant attorney general, a pomp-and-circumstance-filled ritual in the department's ornate Great Hall, actually coincided with the day al-Awlaki was killed. Our first job at the National Security Division was to assess together where we stood in combatting the current threat landscape. At that precise moment in 2011, especially after al-Awlaki's death, it appeared we might have turned a corner; I distinctly remember someone telling us as we settled into our new roles on the other side of Pennsylvania Avenue that we should think through what the NSD's strategy should be when terrorism no longer represented the main driving threat facing our country. We felt we already had our answer—cybersecurity and counterintelligence. Little did we know we were about to live through the worst period of terrorism in the United States since 9/11 itself.

///////////////

When "al-Qaeda in Iraq" split from "core" al-Qaeda and evolved into the fighting force known as ISIL, the group's leadership managed to dramatically evolve the multimedia efforts of other terror groups, particularly as use of social media such as Twitter exploded around the world. As ISIL advanced on Baghdad in 2014, social media showed photos of its black flag flying over the Iraqi capital, and the terrorist army tweeted 40,000 times in just a single day.[13]

The group's videos became a horrific staple of our morning threat briefings at the FBI; each morning, the FBI and Justice Department's counterterrorism and national security leadership gathered inside the bureau's state-of-the-art command center at the Hoover Building to review the nation's top threats for the day—everything from geopolitical developments to individual plots and suspects across the country. Too many mornings that included watching the grisly death of a hostage, captured fighters in Syria, or other victims of ISIL. They weren't abstract deaths, either; meeting with the families of ISIL hostages, knowing the pain of their struggle motivated the agents, prosecutors, and other officials. For me, the experience brought back my days as a homicide prosecutor—the raw emotion of a family's loss, as well as the desire to do justice for them and to comfort those left behind.

ISIL's large and sophisticated propaganda arm understood how to command the public's attention: by showing horrific graphic executions of Syrian fighters, hostages, and almost anyone else who crossed ISIL's path. ISIL's brutality was unlike anything the world had experienced; while barbarism has long been part of war, fighters often go to great lengths to keep it secret. ISIL trumpeted its own awfulness wherever it went, elaborately choreographing mass slaughter with multiple camera angles and working so hard to achieve the "perfect" shot that executioners sometimes read their lines off cue cards. The videos were meant to intimidate adversaries, giving the group an air of omnipotence and power often belied by conditions on the ground. According to the videos, every day of combat amounted to victory—and even when the videos showed ISIL casualties, they were carefully posed and celebrated as righteous martyrs. It was an honor to die for ISIL.

The celebration of ground-level warfare—of the actual act of jihad—built on the online videos of groups such as al-Shabaab. Whereas "core" al-Qaeda long celebrated Osama bin Laden, with most of its recruitment and propaganda efforts stemming from his personal messages, and Anwar al-Awlaki's long lectures focusing tightly on a twisted ideological interpretation of Islam, these later incarnations of Islamic extremism celebrated the individual fighters, portraying the appeal of jihad less as a religious experience and more—as Junaid Hussain said in his tweet—as a chance to live out adventure, to move from playing *Call of Duty* to participating in the glories of combat. As *Wired* wrote, the videos "play[ed] like a satanic episode of *Cops*: Videographers with handheld equipment ride along with ISIS death squads as they pursue and assassinate Iraqi security personnel, some of whom are shown begging for their lives. These videos helped persuade police and soldiers in other cities to melt away rather than resist when they heard that ISIS forces were on the march."[14] In fact, one study of 1,300 ISIL videos, conducted by George Washington University's Javier Lesaca, found that one of five of them appeared to be directly inspired by American entertainment like *Call of Duty*, *Grand Theft Auto*, or *American Sniper*.[15]

These graphic and horrific war videos received a tremendous amount of media coverage the world over. ISIL appeared to know precisely how to play the world's media; in fact, the worst atrocities often seemed to coincide with the group's worst battlefield losses—they used their own barbarism to distract the media from setbacks. It almost always worked. But those horrific videos that came to be their global brand for most of the public represented only a small fraction of ISIL's total's multimedia efforts—most videos they produced flew below the world radar, focused instead on providing would-be jihadists an equally distorted view of how lovely it was to join the jihad and live in ISIL-controlled territory. Initially, this other half proved most concerning for us in the counterterrorism world. Fully half of all of ISIL's communications and social media focused on the "utopia" they were creating in the Middle East.[16] Videos depicted a vibrant, socially active, Pleasantville-like atmosphere inside ISIL territory, with thriving economic activity and strict law and order, including religious police patrolling peaceful neighborhoods. The group's very motto ("Baqiya wa Tatamaddad," i.e., "Remaining and Expanding") advanced the narrative that the group represented a stable, secure cause worthy of time and energy.

Fighters posted photos of themselves fishing on the Euphrates, holding up freshly caught fish while wearing masks or with assault rifles slung over their shoulders. Two ISIL fighters were even shown smiling and snorkeling in a bright blue body of water. Other images, shared in recruitment efforts on the messaging app Telegram, showed how the self-declared "caliphate" strived to depict the sheer ordinariness of daily life: rainbows over beaches, fruit hanging in trees, flowers blossoming.[17] One video showed a masked terrorist playing with a kitten in one hand and holding an AK-47 in the other. Even terrorists know the internet's one universal constant: cat videos sell.[18]

Both streams of videos were meant to help attract new recruits—offering both heartwarming stories for those unhappy in their regular lives back home and battlefield inspiration for those who wanted to belong to a larger cause and help shape history. The sheer breadth of ISIL's online efforts was breathtaking, especially given the sophistication of its branding. Researchers noted, at one point, that all of ISIL's materials switched to a new logo at the same time. Charlie Winter, a counterextremism analyst, documented 1,146 different pieces of ISIL propaganda in just a one-month period during the summer of 2015— that works out to be nearly 40 unique pieces of digital media a day from across ISIL's various components—including "a mixture of photo essays, videos, audio statements, news bulletins, posters, theological essays, and so on."[19]

ISIL used cutting-edge cinematography whenever they could: in one video, *The Meaning of Stability #2*, ISIL for the first time used a drone to record a suicide bombing, following a man driving a truck wired with explosives through a Libyan city until he detonated his deadly cargo. It was a camera angle right out of a Hollywood movie like *Zero Dark Thirty*, but this time, told from the terrorists' point of view. As *Wired* wrote, "The Islamic State has long taken pride in its flair for developing content that is innovative and repugnant in equal measure."[20] Just like any global marketer, they developed sophisticated microtargeting efforts; in the United States, they literally distributed videos featuring terrorists and lollipops or cotton candy, while in Europe, they pushed videos with terrorists and Nutella. They knew what appealed in what market and which language.

The propaganda was meant to be just one part of a suite of digital tools ISIL deployed—they saw it as a way to begin a conversation with would-be recruits the world over. Those interested in joining the jihad could then contact ISIL recruiters and sympathizers on Twitter or other social media platforms or internet forums. From there, the conversations often moved to secure, encrypted messaging platforms, such as Signal, Telegram, or WhatsApp.[21] At one point, ISIL even created its own messaging app, known as Amaq Agency.[22]

Our experience behind the scenes showed "lone wolves" didn't really exist. Individuals who pursued radicalization online—I'm always careful to not say "people who were radicalized online," because it's rarely that simple—were deeply challenging for law enforcement and intelligence agencies to identify. Often, would-be jihadists were in touch with extremists online—sometimes even from their own community. Mohamed Abdullahi Hassan, a Somali-American from Minnesota who joined al-Shabaab in Africa, was a key contact and conduit in luring other Somali-American youths from the Twin Cities. That approach turned out to be common: there simply weren't regular people who woke up one morning, read a Twitter thread, and decided then and there to kill Americans. There's not one track to radicalization, and the web doesn't provide some magical radicalization potion. Radicalization is a process, a journey, but online propaganda and dialogue drastically lower the barriers and complications of recruiting would-be terrorists from far away. Terrorists overseas can communicate directly, intimately, and in real time with kids in our basements, here.

The videos deeply concerned us in government, but at first we viewed them primarily as a recruitment effort for foreign fighters rather than as a domestic terror threat. As a recruitment drive, it certainly proved successful, as we began to see hundreds of Americans and Europeans make their way toward ISIL's territory; originally, we feared that those fighters, just like the al-Qaeda recruits who traveled to Afghanistan and Pakistan in the 1990s and 2000s, would learn new skills and then return to their homelands to plot attacks, but ISIL's evolving threat proved even more pernicious.

We became very good in the years after 9/11 at successfully interdicting plots and identifying would-be terrorists through spotting their "signatures"—the path they traveled to Pakistan, Afghanistan, Yemen, or other terror havens, the routes through which money was funneled to them from overseas, the way they made phone calls or sent emails to known terrorists overseas, the way they attempted to purchase the ingredients for explosives or procure rare, high-powered weaponry, and so forth. Yet as the world intelligence community got better at disrupting the physical movement of would-be fighters to Syria or places like Yemen, the threat morphed again and the groups began to push recruits to just "kill where you live." It was amazing to see the speed of this shift; changes that took the better part of a decade in al-Qaeda happened in just months with ISIL.

The new tactics from al-Qaeda and ISIL eluded all of our well-placed trip wires; by switching to encouraging would-be recruits to remain at home, in the United States or Europe, and carry out attacks there, terror recruiters made it nearly impossible for us to spot typical behaviors that would indicate a looming attack. There was no way to know who might download a PDF of al-Qaeda's magazine *Inspire* and use it as a roadmap for an attack; in one issue, the group published an 18-page guide for how to derail trains using cardboard, a plastic container, a rubber tire, cement, and other tools—none of which would have raised the slightest eyebrow as a would-be attacker acquired them. There was no "signature" for such would-be terrorists. They wouldn't travel overseas; they didn't get explosives training in the tribal areas of Pakistan; they didn't meet bin Laden or al-Awlaki in person. The terror groups effectively had no investment, in time or money, in most of these guys, so they didn't care if nine out of ten of them—or ninety-nine out of one hundred—weren't successful. "Someone can do it in their pajamas in their basement," FBI Director James Comey told Congress in the fall of 2014. "These are the homegrown violent extremists that we worry about, who can get all the poison they need and the training they need to kill Americans, and in a way that is very hard for us to spot."[23]

In some ways, though, as I looked at the problem, the situation was even more grating than that. We were, as a country and a society, providing technology to our adversaries—technology developed with our creativity and through our national investments in education; technology that allowed them to communicate securely and instantly among themselves and potential recruits; technology that was specially designed to allow them to keep their conversations private and prohibit law enforcement from listening even with a valid court order; technology that allowed them to reach into our schools, our shopping malls, and our basements to spread poison to our children, tutor them, and provide them operational directions and supervision to kill fellow Americans. And we'd given it all to them for free—available for an easy download in the app store, just a few clicks away. It was as if we developed game-changing military command-and-control technology at the height of World War II and just handed it over to Tokyo Rose and Axis Sally.

In the midst of this already threatening environment, we began to hear the name Junaid Hussain.

///////////////

Working among a dozen cyber jihad recruiters, Hussain and his fellow terrorists declared themselves the head of the CyberCaliphate and applied some of his old TeaMp0isoN tactics to ISIL, defacing websites and seizing control of home pages and social media accounts.[24] He played a constant cat-and-mouse game with Twitter, which suspended or deleted his accounts only to have him pop up with a new one. He promised online that the ISIL flag would fly over the White House and called for the murder of Israelis. In February, ISIL hackers accessed accounts belonging to *Newsweek*, among other sites, and tweeted out threats against First Lady Michelle Obama. They were trying hard to enable and inspire attacks far from the Middle East, posting in March 2015 a "kill list" of 100 airmen from two US Air Force bases.

Throughout, Hussain was in steady contact with dozens of would-be ISIL recruits and adherents the world over through his main Twitter account, @AbuHussain_16.[25] According to the *Los Angeles Times*, Hussain "communicated with [at] least nine people who later were arrested or killed by U.S. law enforcement."[26] His online encouragement touched off a violent—and, to his recruits, deadly—spree in 2015, one that overwhelmed FBI agents as they chased ISIL recruits across the country. "The FBI was strapped," Director James Comey said later. "We were following, attempting to follow, to cover electronically with court orders, or cover physically, dozens and dozens and dozens of people who we assessed were on the cusp of violence." The need was so great that the FBI actually pulled agents from criminal squads to work counterterrorism surveillance.[27] For those on the front lines of counterterrorism, it marked one of the darkest periods since the 9/11 attacks themselves.

We often talked about a terrorist's "flash-to-bang," the length of time a would-be attacker took to go from radicalization to attack, a metaphor drawn from lighting the detonation cord of a stick of dynamite, the "flash," to when the stick exploded, the "bang." With the new social media–driven push to "kill where you live," ISIL transformed the problem we faced with al-Shabaab—where a relatively specific geographic population of the Somali diaspora had been targeted for recruitment—into a national one with dangerously unpredictable results. There was no geographic center and often the would-be ISIL recruits weren't religious to begin with. Over the course of 2015, we found ourselves confronting dozens of seemingly half-crazed young men whose flash-to-bang was both short and erratic. There was no larger plot to unravel, no travel to monitor. The threat cut across geography or ethnicity; 35 different US attorney's districts found themselves chasing cases. Half the suspects were under 25, and, a statistic that is burned into my memory, one-third were 21 years or younger. ISIL was targeting our kids.[28] So many cases involved literal children that we issued special guidance to prosecutors about how to handle juvenile terrorism suspects in federal court—not an issue that commonly arose in such cases in the past.

In April, Hussain helped encourage a 30-year-old from Arizona, Elton Simpson, to embark on a homegrown jihad. As court documents later alleged, the two exchanged messages through an encrypted messaging program known as Surespot, and, in early May, Simpson and a friend, Nadir Soofi, drove to Garland, Texas, to attack an exhibit there put on by anti-Muslim agitator Pamela Geller that featured cartoons about the Prophet Muhammad, depictions commonly considered offensive in Islam.[29] Hussain evidently knew the attack was coming—an hour before their attack began, he tweeted, "The knives have been sharpened, soon we will come to your streets with death and slaughter!"

The two men—one of whom used a photo of Anwar al-Awlaki as his Twitter avatar—opened fire on a police car at the event entrance and were killed by police who returned fire. Hussain celebrated the attack on Twitter, saying, "Allah Akbar!!!! Two of our brothers just opened fire."

There was Munir Abdulkader, a 21-year-old from outside Cincinnati, who said online he hoped ISIL would "rule the world." He and Hussain connected online, and Hussain encouraged him to kidnap and behead a US soldier right there in Ohio—even providing a soldier's specific home address—and suggested that the Xavier University dropout should also try to attack a police station.[30] The *Los Angeles Times* later reported, "The FBI initially tracked Abdulkader by secretly monitoring Hussain's Twitter direct messages. But agents were stymied when the suspects switched to apps that encrypt messages so they can only be read by sender and receiver."[31] The FBI relied on an informant to help figure out their plan; Abdulkader conducted surveillance on a police station and, when he went on May 21, 2015, to purchase an AK-47, the FBI arrested him.[32]

The long reach of Hussain's recruitment efforts encompassed the entire country. One of the shortest flash-to-bangs we saw unfolded in Boston: On June 2, 2015, an FBI agent and local police officer confronted 26-year-old Usaamah Abdullah Rahim in the parking lot of a convenience store. Hussain online had also encouraged Rahim to target Geller's exhibit in Garland, Texas—preferring a larger, more spectacular attack—but Rahim grew impatient and decided to just improvise, launching his own attack at home. Hussain had urged him to carry knives in case he was cornered by the "feds," and Rahim bragged about his new acquisition in a telephone call to a friend, saying, "I got myself a nice little tool. You know, it's good for, like, carving wood and, you know, like, carving sculptures—and you know."[33] Indeed, Rahim pulled a knife when the officials approached, and he was killed. Later that month, the FBI arrested Justin Nojan Sullivan, a North Carolina man who promised Hussain online he would carry out a mass shooting attack on ISIL's behalf. When Sullivan, who went online by the name TheMuhahid, texted Hussain, "Very soon carrying out 1st operation of Islamic State in North America," Hussain responded quickly to make sure ISIL got the social media credit for the attack: "Can u make a video first?"

Inside the government, the tide seemed overwhelming. The period of al-Awlaki's inspired plots seemed so bad at the time, and, in most ways, the country's counterterrorism resources were far better organized and far more sophisticatedly structured by 2015, yet we were still barely keeping up. Earlier in my career at the FBI, we thought ten simultaneous terror cases represented a huge number; at this point we faced dozens. We struggled with the balance of not appearing to be alarmist but realizing that we didn't have the resources to confront this social media–inspired wave. Since 2009, the FBI had greatly boosted its surveillance resources; back then, the FBI struggled to simultaneously watch two terror plots, one linked to Najibullah Zazi, who was plotting to attack the New York City subways, and one linked to David Coleman Headley, who helped plot the terrorist attack on hotels and key sites in Mumbai in 2008. Even with the increased resources, the terror threat seemed to overwhelm us. Thorough round-the-clock surveillance requires dozens of people, and we confronted tracking dozens of cases in every corner of the country.[34]

Everyone worked at maximum capacity in difficult circumstances. Beyond the field surveillance teams, prosecutors inside our division raced to arrange court orders to help identify and lawfully monitor developing plots. After our years at the FBI, Lisa Monaco and I had become accustomed to crisp analysis and detailed briefings, but when we moved over to the Justice Department, information seemed harder to come by. The division struggled with the new onslaught of cases because of its antiquated case management system. As the terror threat rose, we tried to wrap our minds around the problem and convince the rest of government that it represented a priority, but we were stymied in compiling the necessary information. Michael Mullaney, the head of our counterterrorism team, appeared to piece together briefings on crumpled-up papers, but he was never one to make excuses so it wasn't until I finally asked him why the tracking seemed so disorganized that he showed me the software they were using—a tool known as CaseTrack that the rest of the department had moved away from years earlier. NSD's software was never updated from what it had been using when it broke away from the Criminal Division nine years earlier. In effect, he hand-counted the nation's terrorists each day.

It felt like we were just waiting for the next terrorist attack. Too often, it seemed like luck kept us safe—that we'd only discover a plot because a would-be terrorist spoke to the wrong person or because his device failed to work. All told, according to a George Washington University analysis, of the 117 people arrested in the United States for ties to the Islamic State between January 2014 and the beginning of 2017, more than half were caught over the course of 2015.

We struggled internally about how to talk about this flood of cases; we wanted to raise the alarm without playing into the terrorists' hands. How do you talk about such an overwhelming—but low-level—threat without giving ISIL a strategic victory? We were genuinely worried about Junaid Hussain's impact on the flood of recruits, but we didn't want to elevate his importance publicly and lead even more would-be terrorists to his doorstep. They wanted our country to be afraid; trumpeting each case—even when we were successful in disrupting it—only helped them achieve their strategic goals.

Privately and publicly, President Obama and Vice President Biden tried to temper the pervasive fear that crept into society post-9/11. By the time we were confronting ISIL, the types of cases we were seeing—individuals launching small-scale attacks—were a far cry from bin Laden's goal of spectacular attacks like 9/11. "Terrorism is a real threat," Biden said at one point, "but it's not an existential threat to the existence of the democratic country of the United States of America. Terrorism can cause real problems. It can undermine confidence. It can kill relatively large numbers of people. But terrorism is not an existential threat."[35] President Obama cautioned staff to put attacks in perspective: more Americans regularly died slipping in a bathtub than were killed by a terrorist.[36] To the extent that we, as a country and a government, stopped reacting dramatically to each threat, we would rob ISIL and terrorists of achieving their goals. It was a delicate balance. I never shared the view that we'd convince Americans that their bathtub was a bigger threat than terrorism. The country simply wasn't prepared to think that rationally about terrorism; the media was too alarmist, and Obama was criticized for being too publicly blasé—the lack of public government alarm actually seemed to make people feel less secure.

At the same time, agents in the field were living with the fallout from Edward Snowden's leaks in 2013. The leaks all but destroyed any trust and relationship between the US government and Silicon Valley, the companies whose websites housed this new wave of social media–inspired terror. We lived with almost daily examples of what was known as the "going dark" debate; terrorists were adopting encrypted messaging apps such as Telegram, WhatsApp, and Signal so that law enforcement couldn't intercept their conversations even with a valid court order. Sleepless, stressed FBI agents cried out in frustration as they saw would-be jihadists move their conversations with terrorists like Hussain into a digital realm they couldn't read. *What was being discussed? Where was the next target?* The problem couldn't have arisen at a worse time. For two years, the revelations from Edward Snowden salted the relationship between intelligence agencies and technologists, causing our requests and alarms to be met with instant skepticism and suspicion. These Silicon Valley companies built powerful, well-intentioned tools, and terrorists turned them against the American people. Yet those companies were so disillusioned with the government that initially they were barely willing to listen when we asked for help.

Through 2015, we lived what amounted to tactical success but strategic failure—interdicting plots one by one, but failing to stem the tide of social media inspiration emanating from ISIL. Junaid Hussain and his fellow online recruiter terrorists constituted the key link in almost all of them. We debated in our daily briefings how public we should be about his role—we needed to focus government resources on him but didn't want to make him 10,000 feet tall, a hero to his own cause. The battle against Anwar al-Awlaki's work had elevated him to global prominence, increasing his power, and we didn't want to repeat that with Hussain. We pressed the Pentagon to focus its attention "in theater" on hunting Hussain and the other online recruiters. Sure, they weren't major operational figures on the ground for ISIL, but they were having an outsized impact far from the battlefield.[37] Hussain was no longer "just" a recruiter; he was an operational figure, attempting to direct attacks against the homeland.*

The summer of 2015 brought perhaps the most troubling case of all. On August 11, 2015, Hussain posted a series of tweets that, at first, seemed just his normal bellicose rhetoric. He announced, "soldiers... will strike at your necks in your own lands!" Then he followed up with a surprise: "NEW: U.S. Military AND Government HACKED by the Islamic State Hacking Division!" He linked to a 30-page document that made instantly clear this was something different.

Hussain's document began with a warning designed to chill: "we are in your emails and computer systems, watching and recording your every move, we have your names and addresses, we are in your emails and social media accounts, we are extracting confidential data and passing on your personal information to the soldiers of the [caliphate], who soon with the permission of Allah will strike at your necks in your own lands!" The subsequent pages of the document included the names and addresses of 1,351 members of the US military and other government employees, as well as three pages of names and addresses of federal employees and even Facebook exchanges between members of the US military.

The posting set off a scramble across the government to determine where the information came from—and to potentially protect the affected servicemen and -women. After all, given the cases we'd already seen in Boston, Texas, North Carolina, and elsewhere, it appeared Hussain possessed the capability to execute his threats. We'd been waiting for just this type of scenario, running table-top exercises to prepare for a threat we assumed would arrive. But, just like most cyberthreats over the last decade, this particular case arrived via an unlikely target.

One week after Hussain's tweet, a US online retailer in Illinois received an angry email from someone using the email address

---

* One of the key lessons we learned in the fight against al-Qaeda was that we needed to deny terrorists safe havens overseas where they could plot and plan the death of Americans. Hussain, even from far away, presented an imminent threat. The Pentagon agreed; they understood that the fight against ISIL was one that took place on many different battlefields.

khs-crew@live.com. On August 19, the writer, who identified himself as an "Albanian Hacker," complained that the company deleted malware from its servers that he used to illegally access it. "Hi Administrator," the email began. "Is third time that your deleting my files and losing my Hacking JOB on this server ! One time i alert you that if you do this again i will publish every client on this Server! I don't wanna do this because i don't win anything here ! So why your trying to lose my access on server haha ?" The system administrator wrote back the next day, "Please dont attack our servers," at which point the hacker demanded a payment of two Bitcoins—then worth about $500—in exchange for leaving the server alone and explaining how he'd accessed it in the first place.

The FBI was able to trace the internet address of the sent email to Malaysia, where they began to piece together a picture of the prime suspect: Ardit Ferizi. An ethnic Albanian, Ferizi came from Gjakova, Kosovo, a region deeply affected by the war there in 1999. "On the second night of the NATO airstrikes, Ardit was in the fourth year of his life," his mother wrote later. "The street was full of Serbian army and people wearing black uniforms and masks. They came screaming, shouting and shooting, burning houses and killing people."

As a teen, Ferizi formed a group called the Kosova Hacker's Security (KHS), a pro-Muslim, ethnic Albanian collective that—much like TeaMp0isoN—attacked Western websites, targeting computers in places like Greece and France, as well as companies like IBM and organizations like the National Weather Service. In 2011, they compromised Microsoft's Hotmail servers, and in January 2012 the KHS posted online some 7,000 hacked Israeli credit cards. Ferizi taunted his targets online from his Twitter handle, @Th3Dir3ctorY.

In early 2015, just after he turned 20, Ferizi journeyed to Malaysia on a student visa, both to study computer science at Limkokwing University and, we later understood, because the country's broadband offered better opportunities to carry out cyberattacks. We had seen would-be terrorists mix jihad and cybercrime before: the man who orchestrated the deadly bombing of a Bali nightclub in 2002, a blast that killed 202 people, financed part of his attack through online credit card fraud; his jailhouse autobiography, released in 2004, included a chapter entitled "Hacking, Why Not?"[38]

Ferizi, using his account @Th3Dir3ctorY, volunteered to assist ISIL in April, offering help with their servers and also communicating directly with another Twitter account, @Muslim_Sniper_D, which belonged to Tariq Hamayun, a 37-year-old car mechanic who was fighting with ISIL in Syria and went by the name Abu Muslim al-Britani. Ferizi sent @Muslim_Sniper_D screenshots of credit card information that belonged to 67 American, British, and French citizens—including not just names and addresses but birthdays and card security codes. Hamayun expressed his pleasure at the credit card details and told Ferizi that Hussain "told me a lot about u," an indication the Malaysian hacker had already been in contact with the British ISIL recruiter. Hamayun encouraged Ferizi, "Pliz [sic] brother come and join us in the Islamic state."

Then, on June 13, Ferizi hacked into that online retailer's server in Phoenix, Arizona, stealing credit card information of more than 100,000 customers. He set up a user account, "KHS," and used a hacking tool named *DUBrute.exe*—the malware that he later complained the system administrator deleted. He culled through the stolen information to identify people who used either a .gov or .mil email address, ultimately assembling a list of 1,351 military or government personnel, and passed their information to ISIL. That became the basis for the kill list Hussain tweeted in August with his warning "we are in your emails and computer systems." What started out as an attempt for criminal extortion ended with a chilling terror threat and a plot to kill.

As investigators traced Ferizi's actions and his ties to Hussain, I knew this was a case we could prosecute. It was, in some ways, the culmination of years of work to transform the way that we approached cybersecurity threats at the Justice Department and in the US government. We'd spent years pushing to raise the profile of these threats, to train prosecutors and agents to pursue them, and fought dozens of small battles behind the scenes to ease the secrecy that surrounded so many of America's activities in cyberspace. We convinced the White House, the National Security Council, and other intelligence agencies that cybersecurity needed to move out of the shadows—that we needed to use the traditional tools of the legal system to prosecute and publicize cyberthreats in the same way that we tackled terrorism threats. Now we saw a case that constituted both.

In September, Malaysian police closed in on Ferizi, catching him with the Dell Latitude and MSI laptops he'd used to hack servers. In announcing the charges, I said, "This case represents the first time we have seen the very real and dangerous national security cyberthreat that results from the combination of terrorism and hacking. This was a wake-up call not only to those of us in law enforcement, but also to those in private industry."

It was a message I'd echo to businesses and organizations many times in the years to come: *you need to report when your networks have been attacked because you never know how your intrusion, however seemingly minor, might impact a larger investigation.* This was an incident where a network administrator might very well have simply paid Ferizi to go away or not bothered to report the hack to authorities. For years, businesses viewed cybersecurity threats as regulatory problems—how did a hack impact privacy rules or Wall Street standards about "material controls"? The government long complicated this equation with conflicting messages and a poor organizational structure; some arms of government tried to hold companies to account for breaches, with sticks, while others tried to promise help, with carrots. It's often hard—even today—to know who to call in the government for help. Today, though, businesses and institutions confront a broader risk; a sea change puts the private sector on the front lines of national security threats, from nation-state adversaries to terrorists. In this modern threat, you can't know as a business what your real cyber risk *ex ante* is unless you're broadly—and quickly—sharing information. What to you might be a minor inconvenience could, with broader intelligence, represent a terrorist, a global organized crime syndicate, or a foreign country's sophisticated attack.

In court proceedings, Ferizi came off as a confused youth—like many of the would-be ISIL recruits we saw. He explained that in the spring of 2015 he had been angry that a Kosovar journalist falsely accused him of joining the Islamic State—and so he retaliated, confusingly, by stealing the personal information from Phoenix, Arizona, and actually giving it to the Islamic State. "I was doing a lot of drugs and spending all day online," he explained later.

The judge in his case didn't buy the argument. "I want to send a message," US District Judge Leonie M. Brinkema said. "Playing around with computers is not a game."[39]

Hussain, too, met his own kind of justice. In Syria, he was far beyond the reach of American law enforcement, living in an ungoverned space. As part of the new post-9/11 approach to counterterrorism, the government had moved to what we called an "all-tools" approach, bringing to bear on the threat everything from criminal prosecution to financial sanctions to kinetic military action. The goal was that no one across the world should be free from consequences if they sought to attack the United States. Hussain's actions clearly made him an imminent threat to the American homeland, and since we couldn't reach him with handcuffs, he was a top priority for the military.

Just weeks before we arrested Ferizi, on the night of August 24, 2015, Hussain was alone as he left an internet cafe. As US Central Command confirmed publicly the following day, US military forces operating far overhead fired a single Hellfire missile at his vehicle while it was at a gas station in Raqqa, Syria.[40]

The blast killed him instantly.

The Code War

My first interaction with Barack Obama's presidential campaign in 2008 was explaining to them that their computers had been hacked by the Chinese government. Eight years later, one of my final cases as assistant attorney general for national security was chasing Russia's attempts to influence the presidential election through hacking the Democratic National Committee and Hillary Clinton's campaign. In between, I was privileged to serve with those on the front lines of the international fight to secure the internet, helping to combat online not just China and Russia, but also Iran, North Korea, terrorists, organized crime groups, and even lone hackers. Yet even as I left office in 2016, it was clear that the nation's efforts against hackers remained insufficient.

We thought the nation had awoken to the cyberthreat after North Korea's attack on Sony; we thought it had happened after the hacking of 22 million of the federal government's personnel records. But even in those final months of the administration in 2016, the national security apparatus debated what it should say publicly about the Russian hacks—and how soon it should speak. The answer—unfortunately— was too little, too late. And even now, after the damage and the effect are clear, there's no sign that the hacks caused any policymakers in Washington to change course as radically as we need to ensure our security going forward. That practiced ignorance is hardly a new invention. Way back in 2012, one of my Justice Department colleagues, Christopher Painter, who had dedicated years of his life to fighting cyberthreats, grew frustrated with the number of "wake-up calls" he'd lived through. He said then that cybersecurity was infected by "a wake-up call with a snooze button." As he explains it, "You would have, at least early on, a number of incidents which people would get very excited about. There would be a lot of publicity around them. They make an impact for a short period of time and then they would fade away."[1]

That pattern continues. In the year following the attack on the 2016 election, we saw the hacking of Equifax—wherein the personal, intimate life details of effectively every adult American were stolen—and word came, too, of a new type of security vulnerability in the Intel chips that power today's technology that affects nearly every device manufactured since 1995. The scale of these problems should make it clear that ignoring or wishing away cybersecurity concerns cannot be the answer. This game is being played under the table every day by governments, criminals, and other online adversaries—yet it's one that increasingly is having an impact on our daily lives and our personal security.

Cybersecurity isn't just a wonky IT issue. Poor security online represents a genuine threat to the American way of life—one that will only accelerate as more of our day-to-day lives move online, into the cloud, and into the digital world. Cybersecurity, it turns out, is key to modern life. It's essential to the way we bank, shop, learn. Increasingly, it's a necessity for the way we drive, heat our homes, and even vote. There is no longer such a thing as *e*-commerce, only commerce. Protecting our digital lives is no longer just about ensuring we don't lose our family pictures—it's about protecting our values, our health, our culture, and our democracy. The attacks of the last decade by nation-states, organized crime groups, and even individual hackers threaten to undermine trust not just in our institutions but also in the very information that powers our society, from financial and medical records to the news that informs our society.

/////////////

Cyberspace got its start on a street in Vancouver. In the early 1980s, writer William Gibson was walking down Vancouver's Granville

Street, the Canadian city's neon-lit, undersized version of the Las Vegas Strip. Gibson had started writing science fiction just a few years earlier and had been trying to evolve his thinking and the genre past the outer space fascination of his youth.[2] The spaceship didn't capture his imagination. "I was painfully aware that I lacked an arena for my science fiction," he recalled later. His early work to that point had focused on the interactions of humans and technology—so-called cybernetics, the science of how communications and automatic control systems work in both machines and living things.

As Gibson proceeded down the brightly lit but seedy Granville, past the fading theaters, the pizza stores, strip clubs, and pawnshops, he passed a video arcade—and inspiration arrived. Looking inside, he realized he was staring into another world; the kids were totally enveloped by the blinking lights and beeping of their primitive plywood arcade games. "I could see the physical intensity of their postures, how rapt the kids inside were," he later recounted during an interview with *Whole Earth Review*. He felt he could see the "photons coming off the screens into the kids' eyes, neurons moving through their bodies, and electrons moving through the video game." Sure, it was only *Pac-Man* or *Space Invaders*, but these machines transported the players to another dimension. As Gibson said, "These kids clearly believed in the space games projected. Everyone I know who works with computers seems to develop a belief that there's some kind of 'actual space' behind the screen, someplace you can't see but you know is there."

Yet the moment when computers would be a real part of daily life still seemed far away; the computers he knew at the time were the "size of the side of a barn." Then, Gibson passed a bus stop with an advertisement for Apple Computers, the upstart technology firm led by wunderkind Steve Jobs. He stopped again and stared at the life-sized businessman in the ad. As Gibson recalled, the businessman's neatly cuffed arm was holding an Apple II computer, which was vastly smaller than the side of a barn. " 'Everyone is going to have one of these,' I thought, and 'everyone is going to want to live inside them,' " he recalled. "Somehow I knew that the notional space behind all of the computer screens would be one single universe."

But what to call this new thing, this new place where we would live our future lives? Gibson sat down with a Sharpie and a yellow legal pad to brainstorm. He hated his first two ideas: infospace and dataspace. Then on his third try, inspiration hit: cyberspace. It was perfect—it meant something and also nothing. "All I knew about the word 'cyberspace' when I coined it, was that it seemed like an effective buzzword. It seemed evocative and essentially meaningless. It was suggestive of something, but had no real semantic meaning, even for me, as I saw it emerge on the page," he recalled. The term appeared in his short story "Burning Chrome" in 1982 and hit the mainstream when he used it in 1984 in his debut novel, *Neuromancer*, a book I devoured as a child.

In *Neuromancer*, Gibson introduced the term by writing, "Cyberspace. A consensual hallucination experienced daily by billions of legitimate operators, in every nation, by children being taught mathematical concepts....A graphic representation of data abstracted from the banks of every computer in the human system. Unthinkable complexity. Lines of light ranged in the nonspace of the mind, clusters and constellations of data."

Over the coming years that was almost exactly what cyberspace came to define—a world where the virtual and the physical met and, increasingly, reshaped the other. The collective hallucination that would drive so much of society by the turn of the century could be glimpsed in children of that era. Many of us who ended up on the leading edge of cybersecurity and cybercrime issues were first hooked by science fiction and video games as kids. I, for one, was almost literally one of the kids in Gibson's Vancouver arcade. Taken on a family ski trip to Canada around the same time, I ended up with $10 worth of quarters and lost the afternoon immersed in video games at an arcade rather than on the slopes. For Shawn Henry, who later led the FBI's Cyber Division, it was the magic of computers on display on *Star Trek*. For Steven Chabinsky, a lawyer who later worked alongside me at the FBI, it was when a cousin got a Radio Shack TRS-80 in 1979 and let him start playing a then cutting-edge text-based game, *Adventure*, a game all but forgotten today that figures prominently in the memories of many early computer pioneers. As Chabinsky recalls, "There was no graphics, of course, back in these days. You had to type out directions to turn right. And then it says: 'A nasty elf has come at you: What do you do?' And you say: 'Fight elf.' And it says: 'Elf killed you.' I just thought this was remarkable. It was, to me, artificial intelligence."[3] Later, in high school, Chabinsky worked every day after school to save money to buy an Apple II+.

Gibson's definition of a new world also helped establish one of the consistent trends of this new world: it was the science fiction writers, the fantasists, who pointed the way toward the future we were building in the real world. From *Neuromancer* and *The Shockwave Rider* to the movie *WarGames* to TV series like *Black Mirror* to the novel and 2018 movie *Ready Player One*—about the coming world of artificial intelligence—we saw the threats and challenges that would someday end up on the government's plate first played out in fiction.

As it turned out, I devoted much of my career to securing this amorphous, evolving space—trying to figure out how to impose the laws and rules of the physical world on the ever-shifting virtual one. The answer wasn't always obvious; how, after all, do you police a place you can't see but you know is there?

///////////////

Today, it's impossible to truly capture the cost of cybercrime. It's not like the early days of the FBI when you could just total up the cost of the nation's stolen cars or add up the amount of money that walked out the front door with bank robbers like John Dillinger. Instead, there's both a real cost—the actual dollars stolen from bank accounts, businesses, and individuals—and a more subtle cost—the value of the ideas, designs, and intellectual property compromised and stolen by hackers and used to their own advantage. There's also an enormous amount of lost productivity as tens of millions of people are forced to cancel and change credit cards and deal with the hassles that arise from the theft of their personal information. Any way that you calculate it, almost any even conservative estimate ranks annual cybercrime losses in the hundreds of billions of dollars—particularly when you start to factor in the cost of destructive attacks that "brick" computers and force companies to replace sometimes thousands or even tens of thousands of machines.

In February 2018, the Center for Strategic and International Studies and the security firm McAfee said they calculated cybercrime's annual cost at around $600 billion a year—a number larger than the GDP of all but about 20 of the world's countries, larger even than economic powerhouses such as Sweden (about $500 billion), Thailand ($410 billion), or Poland (about $500 billion). Put another way, cybercriminals steal more than all of the work that all 95 million Egyptians create over the course of a year. Globally, economists believe that the internet generates between $2 trillion and $3 trillion a year of the world's GDP. That means that perhaps as much as one-fifth of the internet's total value is disappearing due to cybertheft each year.[4] It's a number that we would find unacceptable in any other sector of the economy—and we should find it just as unacceptable in the digital economy.[5]

My own experience in two particular cybercrime cases—the takedown of the GameOver Zeus botnet and the indictment of Chinese army officials for economic espionage—perfectly illustrated the challenges of understanding the impact and total losses from cybercrime.

We knew that the Russian and Eastern European hackers running the GameOver Zeus botnet had stolen tens of millions in actual money; the FBI had stopped counting when they calculated 100 million US dollars and 100 million euros; we could see where the money was missing—including a single theft of $6.9 million on November 6, 2012, and a single US bank that lost $8 million over just 13 months. We talked with the small businesses that had been crushed by their losses. FBI Special Agent Sara K. Stanley, who interviewed a dozen GameOver Zeus victims across Iowa and Nebraska, recalls that her conversations were heartbreaking. "It made it so much more human," she says. "When you're talking about a bank or a business in rural Iowa, that really affects you. For a lot of people, their trust in the banking system was really affected." For those smaller businesses, the GameOver Zeus losses were crippling. While the government protects individuals from being responsible for losses stemming from bank fraud, no such provision exists for businesses. The thefts easily wiped out a year's profits or more.

Most Americans have little understanding of the dramatic economic rise of China, nor how much of that growth was powered by the theft of American secrets—both in basic technologies, like computing and solar panels, and in the military's adoption of cutting-edge fighter and naval technologies. In barely two generations, China has leapfrogged from effectively a 19th-century agrarian economy to a cutting-edge, 21st-century powerhouse that, depending on the measurement, is either the largest or second largest in the world. American technological research-and-development dollars have unintentionally given China a leg up on almost every facet of that transformative economic growth.

American workers are already competing against Chinese versions of the very same products they originally invented, and if someday the United States and China end up in a military conflict, America's soldiers, sailors, airmen, and marines will find themselves fighting against their own technology. General Keith Alexander, who once headed the National Security Agency (NSA) and US Cyber Command, has explained for years that China's electronic pillaging of US trade secrets represents the "greatest transfer of wealth in history," totaling upward of $250 billion a year. It's a staggering number, and one that has been playing out inside our corporate, university, and military computer networks for more than a decade. "It is clear that China not only is the global leader in using cyber methods to steal intellectual property, but also accounts for the majority of global intellectual property theft," said Dr. Larry M. Wortzel, a former US Army intelligence officer and member of a commission that advises Congress on Chinese–US economic and security matters.[6]

But what were the long-term costs of the Chinese thefts? What about the costs for the companies that find themselves undercut in the Asian market—or even find lower-priced goods dumped back in the American market? What about the long-term price of China building up its own economy on the shoulders and backs of American innovation? What about the ultimate cost in lives of American servicemen and -women if we find ourselves in a military conflict and have our own stolen technologies used against us? Ever since the industrial revolution and Eli Whitney's invention of the cotton gin, the US economy has thrived because we innovate faster—and better—than any country on earth. Over the last two decades, though, we've seen that lead, our nation's core spirit, threatened and undermined by foreign powers stealing digitally that which they would never dare to steal in real life. It's paramount to America's economy that we ensure that countries around the world compete on an even playing field—that countries are competing based on their innovation, not benefiting by robbing others.

We do know that cumulatively cyberthefts come at a real cost to Americans, especially, because the United States is the most connected and most advanced economy in the world. Studies have calculated that we lose about 200,000 jobs a year due to cybertheft, roughly an entire average month's worth of job creation in 2016.[7] That's the entire population of Des Moines, Iowa, or Birmingham, Alabama, going unemployed or losing their job each year because of digital theft, piracy, and espionage. Europe faces its own large losses, perhaps as many as 150,000 jobs a year, the entire population of Oxford, England. The security cost for companies in today's environment is not minimal either; Greg Rattray, a former air force officer who helped pioneer the fight against nation-states online, today serves as the head of cybersecurity at JPMorgan Chase, where he oversees a sprawling effort that spends more than $2 million *each day* on digital security.

The United States remains uniquely powerful—and uniquely vulnerable—in cyberspace. For now. Thanks to the government's original investment during the Cold War in building a decentralized communications network that, it hoped, could help survive a nuclear war, much of the original internet and computer revolution happened in the United States.

What we think of today as the rise of the computer really was two separate evolutions: one focused on large-scale corporate and government computer use, centered on the East Coast among defense companies and early tech giants such as IBM, as well as a more organic personal computing revolution, centered on the West Coast around Stanford, Berkeley, and what would become Silicon Valley.

The two computing revolutions came with vastly different philosophies. The ethos of East Coast computers was solidly establishment, with deep ties to MIT, Harvard, and the Pentagon, whereas the West Coast was solidly 1960s counterculture.* It was a movement that was deeply distrustful of governmental power, a reaction of an era that saw the exposure of J. Edgar Hoover's domestic spying, Watergate, the Church Committee, and the passage of the 1974 Privacy Act to restrict government information gathering. Another key West Coast voice, Stewart Brand, of the *Whole Earth Catalog*, gave his colleagues a rallying cry: "Information wants to be free."

Those two revolutions blended together online in the 1980s and exploded in the 1990s as the World Wide Web began to transform the way Americans gathered information, shopped, traveled, and led their daily lives.

Even well into the 2000s, the United States continued to dominate online: in 2007, Director of National Intelligence Mike McConnell was shown a chart from the internet company VeriSign that traced how 80 percent of the world's digital traffic passed through US wires and servers. That four out of every five bits and bytes came through America in 2007 actually represented a marked decline from the earlier days of the internet. In the 1990s, Richard Clarke, then the White House cyber coordinator, was told that 80 percent of the world's internet traffic passed through just two *buildings* in the United States: known as Metropolitan Area Exchanges—MAE West and MAE East—the two little-known coastal buildings brought together internet connections from around the world. They had been created in the 1980s and 1990s as the US government transitioned the backbone of the internet to the private sector; little forethought had been put into where they went, and their creators little understood how critical they'd become. The eastern one had been planned by a group of engineers over lunch in 1992 at a Mexican restaurant and originally located in a walled-off corner of an underground parking garage in Vienna, Virginia.[8] It outgrew

---

* The first Vietnam "draft dodger," the first person to burn his draft card, Fred Moore, helped pioneer the personal computing movement.

the parking garage quickly—it soon handled fully half of the world's entire internet traffic—but remained effectively hidden in plain sight, moving to the fifth floor of a nondescript office building in nearby Tysons Corner. The western exchange was located inside the 15-story Market Post Tower in downtown San Jose, California.

Few of the original creators of the internet understood just how integral it would become to modern life—that the decisions they made in setting up a primitive network among a small group of trusted and known colleagues would lead, down the road, to a technological transformation that would become ubiquitous in daily life, with first hundreds of millions and then billions of users. The rise of the "internet of things" will only accelerate these connections: by 2020, there may be as many as 20 *billion* devices connected to the internet.[9]

During the early era of the internet, security often remained an afterthought and authentication procedures were almost unheard of. The early internet connected a small community of like-minded engineers and scientists who intrinsically trusted each other. At every stage of the internet's growth, we have systematically underestimated the future threat for these systems to be exploited by unethical players.

Partly that gap was intentional. Securing things correctly can be slow, expensive, time-consuming, and annoying to users. "The fundamental problem is that security is always difficult, and people always say, 'Oh, we can tackle it later,' or, 'We can add it on later.' But you can't add it on later," recalled Peter G. Neumann, who has tracked computer security problems since 1985. "You can't add security to something that wasn't designed to be secure."[10] Too often, programmers simply push a product quickly to market and then update holes and vulnerabilities as they're pointed out. It's so common that it has its own name: patch and pray.

David D. Clark, who was the internet's chief protocol architect in the 1980s, recalled that when he recorded the seven key goals of the original internet inventors, they outlined that the system must support multiple types of communication services and networks, be easy to use, and be cost-effective. But "security" was nowhere on the list.[11]

Yet even as the wonders of the internet led to the frenzied dot-com bubble of the late 1990s, we began to see the cost of early shortcuts. The Y2K bug—a problem that arrived just as I came of age as a lawyer—was a conscious decision made early in the history of computer programming to save an extra two digits in date codes. It made sense back during an era when punch cards could only store a limited number of characters, and, even though it was identified as early as 1958 as a future problem, the practice continued through the 1970s because memory remained expensive, costing as much as $1 a byte. For each individual company at the time, the trade-off seemed worth it in the moment. "It was the fault of everybody, just everybody," said computer pioneer Bob Bemer, who was one of the first to identify the looming glitch.[12] Ultimately, fixing the Y2K bug cost US companies and the US government an estimated $100 billion.[13] Twenty years after Clark's original paper on the internet's goals, he'd revised the list. When in 2008 he was asked by the National Science Foundation to imagine a new internet, he put at the top of his list of goals one thing: security.[14]

America's early lead online allowed us to remain at the forefront of technology; the world's technology titans—and the largest companies of the last ten years—are, for now, still mostly US companies—Facebook, Google, Amazon, Apple, and others. Apple's iPhone and Google's Android operating systems dominate nearly all of the world's cell phones. Yet, today, the internet is increasingly global—two out of every five users today are in Asia, with hundreds of millions more in China and India still waiting to be connected. By 2008, China could lay claim to being the internet's largest online user base, with nearly a quarter million new Chinese users joining the digital age each day; in 2017, official estimates held that over 50 percent of the country, about 731 million people, had access to the internet.[15] China's online shopping powerhouse Alibaba did $25 billion in business in 2017 on the country's Singles' Day, its equivalent of Black Friday.[16] China is leading aggressively on new just-around-the-corner technologies, such as artificial intelligence and quantum computers, each of which will herald both new economic opportunities and huge security risks.

We've experienced a huge transformation online over the last decade—a transformation reshaping the lives of every American—as the world shifts from analog to digital. We stand on the cusp of a societal transformation no less profound than the one at the turn of the last century, which saw the industrialization of an agrarian economy and the shift from the horse-driven buggy to the motorcar. It's an era that has already begun reshaping the global economy in ways that we're only just beginning to understand, yet it's one that's happening faster and more broadly in society than we realize.

The United States faces an inflection point when it comes to the internet's effect on daily life. What has enriched our economy and quality of life for the past several decades may start to hurt us more than help us—unless we confront its cybersecurity challenges. In a speech I helped research and craft when I worked for him, FBI Director Robert Mueller said in 2007, "In the days of the Roman Empire, roads radiated out from the capital city, spanning more than 52,000 miles. The Romans built these roads to access the vast areas they had conquered. But, in the end, these same roads led to Rome's downfall, for they allowed the invaders to march right up to the city gates."

The technology revolution that powered the nation's growth for the last forty years turned the United States into the envy of the world. Just like the Roman road network of two millennia ago, the internet connects us to the world. Empowered by advances in technology such as cheap storage, increased bandwidth, miniaturized processors, and cloud architecture, we're rapidly extending internet connectivity throughout our lives.

This expansion carries risks we have not adequately addressed. Increased connectivity makes our critical infrastructure—water, electricity, communications, banking—and our most private information more vulnerable. We invested an enormous amount over the past few decades to digitize our lives, but we made these investments while systematically underestimating risks to our digital security. We can't afford to make the same mistake with our nation's infrastructure that we made when we moved our information from analog to digital. As I said in speeches during 2016, "You saw what one terrorist with one truck could do in Nice. What happens when you can have a fleet of driverless trucks?" Today, there is no internet-connected device that's safe from a determined and advanced adversary, so thinking about security online needs to focus not just on building stronger defenses but also on creating methods of deterrence through policies and law enforcement, as well as emphasizing risk management and resilience techniques that will help a victim bounce back when the inevitable attacks occur. We must think creatively about how the internet of the future should be constructed and connected; there's no reason, with automated cars, that the computer system that runs your car stereo should be connected to the one that runs your brakes.

I sometimes use the analogy that we're living online in a house of straw, yet even as the wolf approaches the door, not only are we not seeking shelter in a stronger house, we're continuing to cram ever more stuff into our straw house. We've spent the last 25 years moving almost every piece of valuable data in our society online, and now we're rapidly accelerating the pace of moving our stuff online, too—our homes, our cars, our medical devices. We know the wolf is there, but we're putting ever more of our life into the vulnerable house. A lot of the book that follows is about chasing that wolf, but catching the wolf will not fix the problem as long as we continue living in the straw house. Another wolf will always come along.

///////////////

What worries me most is that we can already see the flaws in the world ahead. Online attacks from our adversaries have underscored a decades-long failure of imagination, where the United States has systemically underestimated the risks of digitizing our economy, our information, and our daily lives. Attacks have almost always come in unexpected places—and in unexpected ways. None of us could have predicted that the first destructive online attack to affect US soil would come against a Las Vegas casino company; we wouldn't have placed a Hollywood movie studio at the top of the list of North Korea's targets;

and we certainly didn't expect Russia to first attack us by using Twitter and publishing John Podesta's risotto recipe.

Understanding how we go forward from where we are—with cybercrime and bad actors threatening the future of the world's greatest economic engine—requires understanding how crime developed online and the unique challenges that were presented by our adversaries online, as well as the lessons each of these incidents imparted on the government and the private sector.

Law has been a long time coming to cyberspace—some of which was by design. The internet was originally designed to be borderless, open to the world beyond, free of the tyranny of even the most democratic of governments. That proposition ultimately proved impossible—even in those early days of the internet, as you'll see, people struggled with trust problems—but the original, open-minded ideology, designed specifically to ease the spread of information for research purposes, today ends up undergirding systems from banks and stock markets to nuclear facilities, dams, and electrical grids, and, in the years ahead, will increasingly guide all aspects of our personal communication, transportation, and medical care as well.

In reexamining the history of the internet, today's mess of a world is utterly predictable. The flaws of the internet and today's digital world were present at the creation—in fact, today's flaws were originally seen as the strengths of the new world. As the former head of the Defense Intelligence Agency said decades ago, "We were not technically surprised about the capability in the past. We were surprised about the way in which or the circumstances in which this capability was put to use."

A generation after the end of the Cold War, we find ourselves today in a Code War. And much like the Cold War, it's not a war at all. It is a complicated, multidimensional, international period of tension that requires resources and attention across government and the private sector. In some ways, it's far more complicated than the Cold War— whereas there we confronted a single, locatable adversary with a defined ideology, today we confront online a world beset by anonymity and vulnerabilities, evolving adversaries who on any given day could be nation-states, terrorists, criminals, hacktivists, or single individuals seeking fun, profit, or destruction.

To confront this problem, we must be creative and rely on multiple instruments of power, from criminal prosecutions to international sanctions to offensive cyberattacks. Just as we did in the Cold War, we must build relationships and alliances with like-minded countries and emphasize our shared belief in the rule of the law. We must establish an international regime of deterrence, to ensure that bad actors don't feel like they can attack with impunity. We must bring these discussions and this intelligence out of the shadows. This Code War will never be as neat and easy as the Cold War—which, to be fair, was neither neat nor easy. We face an inherently asymmetric threat, a landscape where we are far and away the most vulnerable target.

We have struggled to define this threat, partly because the very term *hacker* has morphed over time to encompass a dizzyingly wide variety of behaviors; organizational gurus celebrate "life hacks" and large Silicon Valley companies continue to embrace the freewheeling ethos where their technologies began; the address of Facebook's corporate headquarters is One Hacker Way, in Menlo Park. This multi-sided nomenclature has complicated efforts to police cyberspace. The law—and the media—prefers clear, easily definable terms. A terrorist is a terrorist no matter what tools he or she is using. A criminal can exist online or offline. But hacks and hackers can be good or bad, welcome or invasive, a noun or a verb, a person or a tool.

Although hacking is a skill that requires knowledge and experience, hackers don't need (and often don't have) formal training. Computer skills can be honed anywhere, using materials publicly available on the internet, and the equipment needed to engage in malicious activity and evade detection is inexpensive and widely available. As a result, we face cyberthreats driven by an array of groups—from Russian criminal syndicates, to al-Qaeda and ISIL, to foreign intelligence services and their proxies. As scholars Benjamin Wittes and Gabriella Blum have noted, cyberspace is a world of distributed threats, easily available weapons, and universal vulnerability.

Robert Mueller in 2012 said that "there are two kinds of companies out there: those that have been hacked, and those that don't know it yet." Recent years have seen a tidal wave of stolen user information from online databases—including one hack of Yahoo's accounts that saw the theft of a billion users' information—and these too often insecure corporate databases are steadily compiling ever more data on Americans.

That trend is equally true on the government side. During the near decade I worked on these issues in the government, almost every government agency faced a cyberattack. The FBI and CIA websites were both knocked offline by hacktivists. Both the House and the Senate on Capitol Hill suffered data breaches. The Department of Agriculture saw the information of 26,000 employees stolen in a 2006 theft; the Department of Commerce actually had to disconnect from the internet in 2012 after a malware attack; the Defense Department saw some of its most valuable weapons systems stolen; the Department of Education had a database of grant reviewers raided; the Department of Energy and the national laboratories faced regular attacks on their nuclear information; the Departments of Transportation and Treasury both had their websites knocked offline; and even the Veterans Affairs Department saw a major data breach.[17] And so on. I was personally involved in the government's crisis response to perhaps the biggest theft of all: the theft of records on every federal employee from the Office of Personnel Management.

Attackers stole dossiers of professional, financial, medical, and personal details of 21.5 million federal employees—including some employees working at the highest levels of our government. The information stolen was invaluable—helping both to target and identify current US intelligence officers, as well as to help target other US employees for future espionage recruitment. Rob Joyce, who served as President Trump's first White House cybersecurity coordinator, said that he's had his Social Security number stolen six times in different data breaches.

This was the landscape we confronted over the course of the Obama administration: a broad panoply of threats—China, Russia, Iran, North

Korea, non-nation-states like ISIL and the Syrian Electronic Army—
each of which represented different motivations, different abilities, and
different threats to the national security and well-being of the United
States. In each of the cases we wanted to prove we could figure out who
did it, provide that proof openly to the American public, and then have
a demonstrable consequence imposed by the government—whether
it was international sanctions, diplomatic punishments, a military response, or an indictment (or, even better, an arrest and a guilty plea).
We hoped this new approach would help transform cybersecurity from
a world filled with secrets to a world where we could reckon publicly
with threats.

This book tells the story of how we began to impose costs using every tool we could, from handcuffs to international sanctions. The story,
though, is far from over—and, in many ways, it's actually still getting
worse. And what follows is not by any means my story alone; in fact, it's
quite the opposite.

When you work for the Justice Department as a prosecutor, the first
thing you learn is that the job is bigger than you. Almost every prosecutor remembers the moment: the time you first introduce yourself
to a court as appearing on behalf of the United States of America. I
was in court within weeks of being sworn into the bar, prosecuting a
misdemeanor domestic violence case. I practiced the line beforehand:
*Good morning your Honor, I am John Carlin appearing on behalf of the
United States of America.* Even the rehearsal resonated. The sense and
the responsibility that what you say—and how you conduct yourself—
represents a mission bigger than yourself inculcates itself over years,
shifting the way you see yourself and bear the mission of the department and the government. Many years later, as chief of staff to then FBI
Director Mueller, my job included reviewing all of his public speeches,
internal and external. Mueller believed the mission of service to the
United States at his core. He was almost fanatical about that ethos: the
use of the pronoun "I" was banned; it was almost always replaced with
"we." If we missed one, his scrawled red *X* would catch it.

"I" lived much of this story—but "we" worked this threat together,
a sprawling team of agents, analysts, lawyers, officials, and even

numerous private sector partners worked together—beginning long before I joined the Justice Department and continuing now after I've left it. This account of how America learned to attack cyberthreats is based on my own experience and on dozens of interviews with other participants and thousands of pages of court documents, industry research reports, and news articles. (And, consistent with normal procedures, the Justice Department has reviewed this text to ensure that it doesn't compromise classified material.) Together, it's the story of a dedicated group of public servants—prosecutors, federal agents, and intelligence community officials—who, working alongside an equally dedicated set of private sector security researchers, talented network engineers, and internet pioneers, have sought to impose law and order on the space originally designed to be ungoverned that now undergirds our daily life.

<hr />

Any response to hacking includes two equally important halves: attribution and deterrence. It's the equivalent of any criminal justice process: there are the investigators who solve the crime and then those responsible for the prosecution.

In cyber, the United States has long been better at the first than the second. Government reports known as "National Intelligence Estimates," which represent the collected and agreed-upon thinking of the nation's intelligence apparatus, had long identified and named the four major nation-state adversaries the United States faced online: China, Russia, North Korea, and Iran. Altogether, there are approximately 108 foreign intelligence services that target the United States, but the top four represent a threat greater than any other.[18] Yet it was a long time before we took any public action against them.

I often find that people who aren't steeped in cybersecurity still believe that solving cybercrimes is nearly impossible, that it's all just anonymous bits and bytes moving invisibly across wires around the globe. But the truth is that, with persistence, resources, and work, we're able to solve many—sometimes even most—cyberattacks. It's certainly an uphill battle—especially because so many attacks and crimes are carried out by suspects overseas where governments refuse to cooperate or prosecute. There are key cases over the last decade, such as the cyber-attack on the Sands Casino, that remain frustratingly uncharged—but the United States is much better about "attribution" than is publicly understood. Much of my goal inside the government was to help take that secret success and understanding out of the shadows, to make public what we knew in ways that would discourage future attacks and under-score vulnerabilities to the American public.

Years of experience investigating and prosecuting online threats have highlighted for me that hackers are far from superhuman—in fact, they're ordinary people who lead lives online and offline. They exhibit online all the frailties and flaws we see offline: they can be arrogant, careless, and forgetful; they leave unnoticed traces of themselves behind—the digital equivalent of footprints or fingerprints; they reuse passwords, rely on old technology, or cut corners when they're in a hurry or think no one is watching. Investigating cybercrimes can't just rely on technical bits and bytes; cybercriminals make mistakes offline, too, and you need all available tools to bring someone to justice.

Hackers have social media accounts and cell phones just like the rest of us, which they use to connect with friends and family and to share professional news. As FBI Agent Elliott Peterson, who has put together some of the biggest cyber cases of the last decade, says, "They're criminals all the time. They're real people all the time. You can exploit their seams." In one of Peterson's cases, the FBI identified a Russian hacker because he used the same password both to run his online spam empire and to log in to sites like Apple iTunes.[19] In another case, Peterson and his colleagues uncovered photos of another hacker in leopard-print pajamas—a hacker who had led an online financial fraud that netted hundreds of millions of dollars—because they were able to trace him back to social media sites where he used his own name.

Hackers' own malware is often sloppy, containing its own clues or vulnerabilities. In 2011, a team from the Republic of Georgia laid a trap for a hacker rummaging through its network: they hid an intriguing document, titled "Georgian-NATO agreement," that actually contained malware of its own that, once exfiltrated and downloaded, allowed the Georgian team to turn on the hacker's camera and photograph him sitting, wearing a yellow shirt, hunched over his computer examining his stolen take.[20] In 2018, researchers announced that they'd been able to trace a particular attack to North Korea in part because the hacker had infected his own computer with his own malware.

Similarly, most of the methods hackers use aren't fancy so-called zero-day exploits, hidden and unknown flaws in software or hardware that can fetch top dollar in online marketplaces. In fact, little in the cyberworld relies on sophisticated black magic.

Most hacks—even the most damaging ones—have come through relatively unsophisticated means exploiting obvious vulnerabilities: software patches that haven't been installed, weak or default passwords protecting sensitive data, or "phishing" techniques where a user has clicked a nefarious link in an email and allowed hackers access to an account. Defending against cyberattacks doesn't require some advanced form of voodoo or witchcraft—in many ways, these threats prey on obvious human frailties, laziness, and predictable behaviors. As Rob Joyce said in one of our conversations, "It really comes down to doing the basics. So much of this—these intrusions—can be handled by addressing the basic blocking and tackling of security, whether it's patching, having a good architecture, understanding in advance where the threats are, having logs, monitoring, watching, and dealing with it."[21]

It's important for us—as a society, as companies, and as individual web users—to understand that most of these attacks are preventable and avoidable. And that when they happen, we can often determine who the perpetrator is.

Once we do, the challenge becomes that second half of the equation: deterrence. It's taken the United States the first quarter century of the digital age to begin to understand how to take judicial action in cyberspace. The delay was not for a shortage of tools—we possess powerful carrots and sticks, from leveling sanctions on nation-states, entities, and individuals to freezing bank accounts to filing criminal charges that make it nearly impossible to travel internationally. In the short time since we moved to using these strategies, we've had more success than many might think with actually returning hackers to United States courtrooms in handcuffs to answer for their crimes. Through cooperation with governments overseas, we've captured many of our most wanted hackers—arresting Chinese and Iranian spies, Russian criminals, Islamic terrorists, and hacktivists around the world.

Yet we're still today in the early stages of sorting out a coherent policy for responding to bad actors online, just as we're struggling to answer large questions about what the internet means for geopolitics. "Cyberspace challenges all historical experience," Henry Kissinger argued. Whereas the original techtopian view of the spread of the internet was that it would break down national barriers and allow the free flow of information around the world—and, to a certain degree, it has, over the last decade—it's also become all too clear that cyberspace does not exist independent of politics. In fact, we increasingly see that as the digital world becomes the prime driver of economic power and cultural influence, the internet is deeply and complexly intertwined in national ideologies and international geopolitics. To paraphrase Carl von Clausewitz, the internet is politics by other means.

///////////////

When fighting adversaries online I learned that there really is little difference between the virtual and physical worlds. When it comes to geopolitics, cyberspace is clearly an extension of the real world. Countries behave online the same way they do in the rest of their policies: They deploy similar tactics and pursue similar interests. They all spy, and they all have unique flavors.

If Vladimir Putin's Russia viewed democracy as an existential threat and its battle against the West as a zero-sum game, that view carried forward to the digital world. Russia specialized in mischievous actions that attempted to exploit the online seams of Western democracy. At the beginning, Russia—our country's oldest adversary—was quiet inside computer networks, the equivalent of a submarine searching quietly beneath the surface, and very carefully focused on achieving its political aims. At first, Russia acted as a more traditional intelligence collection effort, as you would see from a nation-state offline.

It deployed highly sophisticated efforts online, largely focused on traditional nation-state interests. And it didn't like to get caught. Then, quickly, as Russia's real-world politics evolved and the state became increasingly tied to the organized crime empires that thrived under Vladimir Putin, we saw Russia begin to cross confusing lines, with criminals conducting espionage, and intelligence officers committing crime.

Iran, which has spent decades as one of America's most lethal adversaries, with its state sponsorship of terrorist groups such as Hezbollah, was pointed and destructive, yet careful to ensure we were never sure how closely their activities were linked to the government. Just as, for years, it used small, fast torpedo boats to target large naval ships in the Persian Gulf, it relied on cyberassaults to provide an asymmetric advantage. Iran used different online proxies to advance geopolitical goals—just as in the real world it relied on and funded Hezbollah to target adversaries around the globe—and focused its cyber activities on intelligence collection and on helping the country evade international sanctions.

The bombastic North Korea, which spent decades locked in a heated war of rhetoric that occasionally flared up into fatal but low-level showdowns around the Korean peninsula, was both noisy and destructive online—pursuing targets with only the vaguest conceit of deniability and, seemingly, daring the United States to retaliate. Online, it cared about defending its leader's reputation and about making—stealing—money. Unlike, say, the US budget process, where Congress carefully and specifically allocates money to various agencies, North Korea, starved for hard currency, has long let its military and intelligence agencies pursue an "eat what you kill" strategy. In North Korea, you can spend what you steal or earn overseas, which is why the country has traditionally been one of the world's leading drivers of counterfeit currency.

China was noisy online—seemingly pillaging without concern for who might notice—but careful never to cross into a destructive attack and deeply embarrassed when their activities were made public by another government. China was almost solely focused on economic and military gains—trying to speed the country's technological advancement and knowledge. If China wanted to accelerate and innovate in a given sector, you were sure to see that it targeted Western companies who excelled at the task. Deeply concerned about its domestic political stability, China also turned to the internet to surveil and target human rights activists and conduct state intelligence operations.

Those approaches evolved as the geopolitics evolved. For example, as Russia overseas became more aggressive offline—with real-world attacks in places like Georgia and Ukraine—it became more aggressive online, too, a pattern we saw come together in a sophisticated and multifaceted manner with its efforts to influence the 2016 presidential election. As we saw Vladimir Putin's government solidify control, becoming effectively a mafia state where the political apparatus, the intelligence world, and organized crime all blended together into a single inextricable, multiheaded octopus, we saw the same behavior online—as sophisticated criminals and organized crime groups who had focused on financial theft and fraud suddenly redeployed those same tools to help Russia gather geopolitical intelligence. Inside the United States, they moved online from thefts to active intelligence operations, like that against the 2016 election.

Over time, these adversaries have grown—and even learned from one another. Over the last fifteen years, we've seen three distinct epochs of evolving cyberthreats, and we are clearly moving into a fourth.

At the start, we saw China engaging online in simple economic espionage—the direct theft of corporate and government secrets. The Chinese government—and its ruling and deeply intertwined Communist Party of China—is a big, complex bureaucracy with various competing interests and factions, just like the United States. Similarly, China is a rational actor on the world stage. Since their thefts were done with the express purpose of economic advantage, it was a carefully calculated cost-benefit analysis for them; for years, the gains and economic opportunity from the thefts clearly outweighed the costs imposed on them from afar. The challenge China presented to us was straightforward: How do we change that cost-benefit analysis? How do we manipulate the levers of government to impose costs on what had, until the late 2000s, been a consequence-free burglary spree?

Iran in the late 2000s began doing destructive attacks—beginning with an often overlooked plot to take action inside the United States, attempting to assassinate the Saudi ambassador at a restaurant in Washington. Then—after they themselves had suffered a digital assault—they moved into digital attacks against foreign countries, first against Saudi Arabia and then against the United States, targeting a Las Vegas casino owner and the Wall Street financial sector. Their actions raised a fresh question for us as policymakers: What do you do with an adversary who is using asymmetrical warfare deliberately—and they're not yet doing the most damaging stuff that they could do?

The struggles with Iran played out against a much larger geopolitical backdrop, both in the Middle East and with the United States as Iran pushed for a deal on its nuclear program. Iran, too, traditionally has been more of a state actor—there's usually geopolitical logic to their actions—but given the complexity of the power struggle inside the Iranian government, its military, and its intelligence agencies, we weren't even sure as events unfolded how much of the attacks were being encouraged or directed by Iran's leadership.

The attack by Iranian actors on the Sands Casino was arguably the first destructive nation-state cyberattack inside the United States—even though its distributed denial of service (DDoS) attacks against Wall Street caused monetary damages, I put it in a different category, as I'll explain later—but the Sands Casino attack came and went with nary a blip on the national radar.

The third epoch was begun by North Korea, a notoriously unpredictable state actor. Its hackers had long been focused on robbing banks, relying on infrastructure outside of the country, in places like China. But then North Korea launched a destructive attack and used social media to amplify it—its attack on Sony was in part a communications attack.

In the years since, I've spoken to dozens of groups assessing cyberthreats, and almost everyone points *not* to the Sands Casino attack in early 2014 as the first destructive cyberattack in the United States; they point instead to the attack on Sony. Why do people remember Sony? Sony was as destructive as Sands, but we don't remember it because of the malware that was used to wipe the company's computer drives. Sony involved the theft of intellectual property—millions of dollars' worth of intellectual property—but we don't remember it because of the stolen intellectual property. We don't even remember Sony as an attack on free speech and American democracy, which it was, just like Iran's attacks on Sands and Russia's attack on the 2016 election also were.

We remember Sony today because of how hackers hit the softest part of the system—emails—and weaponized that information through the use of social media. Then North Korea got the mainstream media to pick up on those leaks and do the hackers' bidding for them, causing reputational and financial damage to the company by airing their innermost secrets.

Unfortunately, that part of Sony's legacy—so obvious now in hindsight—didn't sink in with the government and the private sector. We learned the wrong lesson; we focused on deterring destructive attackers and hardening our network systems. Russia, meanwhile, watched the Sony hack and learned the power of stolen information to influence public opinion and undermine confidence in an organization. And Russia saw how American society had been quick to blame and isolate the victim, Sony, rather than unite against the perpetrator.

The Sony attack, as it turned out, represented the Rubicon: coupled with the experience of media and global reaction to WikiLeaks and Edward Snowden, North Korea knew that media organizations—some reputable, some not—would rush to cover the leaks, amplifying the thefts with little self-reflection. If North Korea simply sent a stolen spreadsheet of a company's executive salaries to reporters, they'd publish it quickly. Particularly in the sped-up news cycles of the digital age, the media had decided that the "newsworthiness" of purloined internal secrets outweighed any ethical dilemmas raised by how that material was obtained.

The tactics pioneered by the attack on Sony were exactly the same tactics that the Russians later used to influence our election in 2016. We saw these tactics build on one another. As Russia considered whether to weaponize the emails they'd stolen from the Democratic National Committee, they knew from the North Korea attack on Sony that the media would lap up—and publish without delay—purloined emails.

Today, we face the fourth epoch, one I fear will see adversaries—both nation-states and non-state actors such as ISIL—combine cyberattacks with real-world "kinetic" attacks. In places such as Georgia and the Ukraine, we've already seen Russia mix a physical military attack with online efforts to target critical cyber infrastructure, shutting off power grids, blocking access to government websites, and more, all in an attempt to paralyze and slow the reaction from the target of an invasion. We feared at the National Security Division a similar so-called blended terror attack, where a terror group might knock offline emergency communications or cause a power outage at a local hospital at the same time they carried out a bombing or attack. We've already seen in the United Kingdom hospitals paralyzed by ransomware attacks, with emergency rooms closed and operating procedures cancelled because malware has frozen out the computer systems. In the financial world, we've seen sophisticated hackers hit a one-two punch of their own: stealing millions in cash through fraud-focused malware and then hitting the bank's servers with a DDoS attack that distracts bank officials until after the money is safely gone. We know, too, where the next threats will come: adversaries are already beginning to target so-called Internet of Things devices.

Moreover, as we're beginning to see, cyberattacks target a particularly nefarious vulnerability in our society. While we've spent the last decade primarily thinking about cybersecurity as the theft or leaking of data, increasingly the threat comes from the alteration and destruction of data. Cybersecurity's next great fear is about undermining confidence—banks unsure their records are correct, military commanders unsure their positions or radars are correct, citizens unsure their votes are correctly tallied. We've seen this in the real world with Stuxnet, a piece of malware targeting Iran's nuclear system that made machines go haywire and led its scientists to think they made errors, and now with Twitter and Facebook, where the efforts of groups like the Russian Internet Research Agency have made us wonder: Is that voice online a real human and is that a real news story or headline?

Meeting, responding to, and countering these new threats requires new tools and new approaches—and new ways of thinking about the way that we traditionally use geopolitical tools.

~~~~~~~~~~~~

The rise of the internet has presented the world with a complex and unprecedented threat; it has blurred—and will, over the coming years, even further blur—our understanding of the world in six fundamental ways, ways that make the internet particularly challenging to governments and to the legal frameworks that we've carefully built up around our societies over centuries.

First, it has blurred the line between peace and war. War, over recent decades, has increasingly become the province of lawyers, especially as so many modern adversaries—from al-Qaeda to ISIL—are not clearly defined nation-states. Lawyers review proposed drone and air strikes, sit in the room as covert raids are approved, and provide detailed instructions to officers and soldiers in the field about when they can shoot and when they should hold fire; we have entire manuals, such as the 180-page US Army *Laws of Land Warfare* and the Pentagon's 1,176-page *Law of War Manual*, that lay out America's collected obligations under international law, treaties, and agreements to minimize war's impact on civilians and control war's utter brutality.[22] As the Pentagon's general counsel wrote in the introduction to the 2015 edition of the Pentagon guidebook, "The law of war is of fundamental importance to the Armed Forces of the United States. The law of war is part of who we are. George Washington, as commander in chief of the Continental Army, agreed with his British adversary that the Revolutionary War would be 'carried on agreeable to the rules which humanity formed' and 'to prevent or punish every breach of the rules of war within the sphere of our respective commands.'"

In the years since, our government—and governments around the world—have developed a complex bureaucratic framework and clear set of policies that recognize a black-and-white distinction between peace and war. But the internet has delivered nations—and non-nation groups—the ability to engage in actions that appear to step well past the line of peace but fall short of actual war. Today, according to a count by cybersecurity expert Adam Segal, at least 41 countries have cyberwarfare doctrines and at least 17 have offensive capabilities in cyberspace.[23] We don't really understand how to define these tools. If Chinese military officers had invaded the headquarters of the Solar-World manufacturer in Hillsboro, Oregon, we would know that was an act of war, just as if the North Korean Air Force had bombed and destroyed Sony's offices in Los Angeles, we would recognize the act as one of war. If Soviet KGB agents had broken into the headquarters of the Democratic National Committee in Washington in the midst of the Cold War, there wouldn't have been any doubt that the United States would have taken punishing, bipartisan retaliatory action. But what happens when all of these things happen virtually?

Second, the internet has blurred the line between public and private. Through the Cold War—and for centuries before then—national defense has been the sole province of the government itself. In fact, perhaps more than anything, defense has been the main responsibility of a government, ensuring its citizens are free from marauding invaders and able to live their lives coercion-free. Yet, online, most of the responsibility for protection falls to private companies, requiring a new partnership and a sharing of national intelligence to which our government has struggled to adapt. We didn't ask major companies, such as Campbell Soup or Ford Motor Company, to build their own air forces or missile defense systems to respond to Soviet bombers during the Cold War, but today the private sector—both large companies such as Boeing and small ones such as boutiques in Iowa and SolarWorld in Oregon—represents the front line of cyberthreats. As President Obama said in Silicon Valley in 2015, cybersecurity "has to be a shared mission" because "so much of our computer networks and critical infrastructure are in the private sector, which means government cannot do this alone."

Third, the internet has blurred the line between nation-state and individual. Geopolitical and military strategists have steadily marked the trickle-down effects of weaponry in the 20th century, as technological advances put tools of war and weapons of mass destruction that had long been deployed only by well-financed and technically capable nation-states into the hands of well-organized terrorist and rebel groups. Even more recently, we've seen that it's possible for highly capable individuals to manufacture and deploy chemical and biological weapons. Online, the situation is even more fraught. Today, weapons of mass destruction can be deployed online by individuals even accidentally—the first "internet virus," the Morris Worm, was unleashed by a graduate student who didn't understand the destruction his program would cause. Terror groups, hacktivist groups such as Anonymous, and "patriotic hackers" can today unleash tools and disruptions online that a few decades ago would have been the sole capability of the world's most powerful nations. It's not always clear—certainly not immediately and sometimes not ever—why a particular online target was attacked and by whom, which challenges governments to know who they're facing in a digital battle. As Henry Kissinger has argued, "When individuals of ambiguous affiliation are capable of undertaking actions of increasing ambitions and intrusiveness, the definition of state authority may turn ambiguous."[24]

Fourth, the internet has blurred the line between physical and virtual. We used to be able to draw clear lines between the digital world and the real one; your car was a car, and your computer was a computer. A spreadsheet existed online, but your most valuable possessions were hidden in a safe deposit box locked inside a vault inside of a sturdy brick or stone bank downtown, protected by armed guards. Cyberspace today includes a complicated set of parts: physical hardware (the computers and infrastructure that run networks), software (the code that runs on computers), and information (the data created and saved inside that software and hardware). Each part impacts the others and would cease to be useful without the full constellation. With today's technology—and even more so in the future—it's difficult to tell clearly where the physical world ends and the virtual begins. Money today exists almost entirely virtually, with cash a rarity—and the rise of cryptocurrencies like Bitcoin presage an era when there is no physical money at all. As security expert Bruce Schneier says, "Your modern refrigerator is a computer that keeps things cold. Your oven, similarly, is a computer that makes things hot. An ATM is a computer with money inside. Your car is no longer a mechanical device with some computers inside; it's a computer with four wheels and an engine. Actually, it's a distributed system of over 100 computers with four wheels and an engine. And, of course, your phones became full-power general-purpose computers in 2007, when the iPhone was introduced."[25]

Fifth, the internet has blurred the line between borders, between domestic and international. One of the greatest strengths of the internet and the digital age has been how they have opened up the world—in Thomas Friedman's famous phrasing, "The world is flat." The internet has allowed instant access to far corners of the globe, allowed people sitting at their desks in one country to chat via video with people a continent away, and given anyone with internet access the ability to reach as many readers or viewers as the *New York Times* or CNN. This trend has provided all-new challenges to governments and nation-states. Governments today are organized bureaucratically to make clear legal distinctions between foreign and domestic. The State Department is prohibited from publishing "propaganda" aimed inside the United States; the CIA operates overseas, while the FBI is responsible for security domestically. Yet these distinctions appear increasingly meaningless; terrorists from the Middle East can communicate directly with American citizens without ever setting foot inside our country, and robbers can pillage Wall Street banks from places most people couldn't even find on a map. The person on the other end of a cyberattack could be a teenager down the street, a terrorist overseas, or a military officer in uniform at a desk in an adversary's capital—and you often don't know which it is until you've solved the case.

Sixth, and finally, the internet has blurred the line about what's worth protecting—what's a "secret" and what's "critical infrastructure." Our government used to have a very clear understanding of what secrets it was trying to keep—our original classification system arose to lock down the details of the nuclear age and atomic weapons. In the years since, it has primarily focused on military secrets, the work of the intelligence agencies, and diplomatic efforts around the globe. Yet we've seen in the last decade the weaponization of information in places we never considered a "national secret": the internal communications of a political party, the seemingly boring old personnel records of government employees, the health insurance details of millions of Americans, and, even, the Amazon shopping list of a movie executive.

For individuals, whereas a decade ago we had a good understanding of what personal information we should try to protect—our checkbooks and our Social Security numbers—today we worry about "personally identifiable information" we'd never previously considered: the GPS records on our cell phones that could tell someone every place we've been for years, the intimate details and photographs of our lives that flow through our email accounts on a daily basis, and the details of our personal health collected by Fitbits and other health-focused devices.

At the same time, government and industry officials have spent years warning about a "cyber 9/11" or a "cyber Pearl Harbor," a devastating attack on our nation's critical infrastructure. We've fretted about attacks on our power grid, on our water supply, on hospitals, or on our air traffic control computers. Yet, in 2016, when Russia hit us with what was our first true cyber Pearl Harbor, they attacked a soft spot we'd never thought about.

Russia attacked America's confidence in America. They sought to undermine our belief in our own government, our ability to participate in our own democracy, our own unique American mojo. America's can-do attitude has long been central to America's future, but Russia realized that our national confidence was more delicate than it had been in years—and they exploited this insecurity online. They amplified our own messages attacking each other, they stoked our own anger, they weaponized our own hyperpartisanship. It was easy for Russian trolls and bots to hide among the many Americans angry with their present—and worried about their future. America was, as one friend of mine said, "dry tinder for the Russians."

And over the last year, those who have sought to exacerbate these divides have continued to advance the work of the Russian government. You only need to log on to Facebook or Twitter these days to see that our hatred for ourselves—our distrust of each other—is leading us to doubt proud historical traditions, to question bedrocks of our democracy and long-standing principles about America's role in creating a better world. The very online tools that a decade ago we hoped would usher in a new era of openness and participatory democracy have instead been turned into tools of hate that spread disinformation and stoke anger with ease. As one columnist recently put it, "Companies that are indifferent to democracy have acquired an outsized role in it."

Together, the combination of these six blurred lines has presented the United States—both its government and us as citizens and individuals—an unprecedented challenge. I've spent the last decade of my professional life helping the US government navigate these six sea changes—and I know we, as a government and as a society, are not close to where we need to be to tackle this future. The internet, a tool that was once created to help the US government survive a war, has now become a central point of global tension and a lurking threat to our daily lives. It doesn't have to be that way—but we as a society and as a government need to commit to changing the trajectory.

In a single week in March 2016, we demonstrated to our adversaries online that the tide was beginning to turn. The indictments and cases we announced were the result of a strategy years in the making—together, they represented a radical change in how the US government was approaching cybersecurity threats.

On Tuesday, March 22, 2016, the Justice Department announced charges against three members of the Syrian Electronic Army, a hacker collective supporting dictator Bashar al-Assad, who targeted American media websites. In April 2013 the hackers had managed to send a tweet from the Associated Press saying that President Obama had been injured in a bombing at the White House, a panic-inducing event that briefly caused the stock market to drop by $136 billion.

The following day, on Wednesday, the Justice Department announced that a Chinese national, Su Bin, had pleaded guilty to hacking into Boeing's computers to steal sensitive military information.

Then, on Thursday, the biggest bombshell yet: the United States indicted seven hackers associated with the Islamic Revolutionary Guard

Corps who had targeted American financial institutions and had gained access to a hydroelectric dam outside New York City.

We had three messages that we wanted to communicate that week—all of them a long time coming. It was the culmination of years of effort to adapt to a three-pronged approach for cybersecurity threats. Inside the government, we saw it simply as the need to figure out who was behind an attack, default to making that attribution public, and then impose consequences to shape online behavior. Finally that three-pronged internal approach was being translated into what we hoped were three strong messages for the public.

First, an internal one: We wanted to demonstrate clearly to others across the US government that national security law and the normal criminal justice system could be applied to cyberspace. The internet wasn't an anonymous black hole. We can prove in a court of law that a specific actor was behind a specific action.

Second, a message to the private sector: For years, we had heard that companies felt they were fighting cyberthreats alone, without sufficient help or backing from the US government. We knew that they wanted stronger action—and the one-two-three punch against Chinese, Iranian, and Syrian hackers was meant to underscore clearly that we would pursue a more aggressive course of confronting bad behavior online.

Third, a message to our foreign adversaries: This behavior was unacceptable. It was a simple message, but an overdue and all-too-necessary one. We wanted to establish a clear set of acceptable behaviors online—just as, over decades, countries have (mostly) come to consensus through treaties, agreements, and international bodies about what constitutes acceptable behavior in the physical world. We needed to draw clear lines online between "traditional" accepted behavior, such as state espionage, and that which is done for either direct economic benefit or to cause real-world effects. We wanted there to be clear lines and "norms" online, just as there are in the physical world.

For too long—much of the first 15 years of the information revolution—cybercrimes were cost-free, for both criminals and nation-states. Despite how high-profile many of these thefts were, there was almost nothing that the US government did about them. It was an odd incongruence: Actions that took place virtually escaped punishment; had they taken place in the physical world, they would have provoked obvious and clear retaliation based on established precedents and international law. Whereas if the Chinese military had snuck into Boeing at night and loaded hundreds of cartons of documents into a tractor trailer, or if Russian intelligence officers had tried to rob Bank of America of $10 million cash, we would have known almost instantly and America would have almost instantly taken military action in retaliation, for years we struggled to figure out first the scope and then the response to similar actions conducted electronically.

At the beginning of the Obama administration, the US government had never publicly accused a foreign nation of cyber intrusions. Over those next eight years, the United States publicly pointed fingers at what we considered the country's four major foreign threats online. We indicted Chinese military hackers for industrial espionage and Iranian hackers for launching disruptive attacks on our financial sector, and we publicly accused North Korea of hacking Sony's computer system and Russia of interfering with the 2016 presidential election by leaking Democratic operatives' hacked emails. We also prosecuted organized crime figures who tried to undermine our financial system from afar and brought to justice terrorists who tried to use the internet to kill American servicemen and -women. This is the story of how we tried to take cyberthreats out of the shadows and used the criminal justice system to shine light on cyberattacks from nation-states and foreign adversaries such as terrorists and the Syrian Electronic Army. That change happened amazingly fast for government time, but not fast enough to meet the threat.

It wasn't enough then. And there's much left to do in securing our digital lives.

But it was a start.

CHAPTER 1

The Rise of the Hackers

My first in-depth exposure to computer crimes came in 2004, when I helped prosecute what became the government's first copyright case against a peer-to-peer file-sharing network, a case known as Operation Digital Gridlock. In the way the Justice Department then thought about such cases, prosecuting the masterminds behind an online network sharing illegal files didn't really "count" as a computer crime; it was considered an intellectual property case. The same unit oversaw both halves, computer crimes and intellectual property (IP), but mostly kept itself busy in court enforcing IP laws. At the time, there weren't enough computer crimes to keep a squad in business.

In 2004, peer-to-peer file-sharing represented one of the most high-profile problems online—the industrial-scale sharing of illegally copied music and movies had been made all too easy by applications like Napster. The file-sharing network, started in 1999 by Shawn Fanning and Sean Parker, had grown to tens of millions of users—it was adding 300,000 new users a day by 2001—and nearly all of them were trading songs, movies, or software files illegally. It was copyright infringement on a mass level never before seen; industry and law enforcement seemed powerless to stop it.[1]

The recording industry had filed suit against Napster and other file-sharing sites, such as Grokster, arguing that the standards that would define theft or copyright infringement in the real world should also be applied online. Illegal file-sharing wasn't an embrace of the internet's openness, it was robbery from the artists and innovators who created music, movies, and software. Industry groups, increasingly desperate as services such as Napster took hold on college campuses, were intensely noisy and encouraged the government, both at the Justice Department and on Capitol Hill, to focus resources on the problem.

We had long devoted such resources to physical goods—pursuing, for instance, knock-off designer purses and seizing warehouses full of goods—but the digital world represented new territory for us. It felt a strange shift to me as a federal prosecutor, going from investigating homicides, rapes, and big narcotic conspiracies to going after bits and bytes of MP3s and .MOV files. In one sense, though, the movie and recording industries were correct: theft was just theft—and we had an important role in enforcing and shaping that norm. In a landmark case, *Metro-Goldwyn-Mayer Studios Inc. v. Grokster, Ltd.*, Justice Stephen Breyer had written, "deliberate unlawful copying is no less an unlawful taking of property than garden-variety theft." It was our job to help enforce that standard, shape the societal norm, and ensure ordinary people recognized illegal file-sharing as bad behavior that they shouldn't participate in. We wouldn't look away as people shoplifted CDs from malls, so we shouldn't look away if it happened online.

We were very deliberate, though, about choosing our targets and cases; while the recording industry had been filing lawsuits and protests against thousands of people who were only downloading illegal files, we went after those actually sharing and hosting the files. None of the people we targeted were downloaders only; these were, in the words of one attorney, the "kingpins" of file-sharing.[2] The file-sharing site we targeted in DIGITAL GRIDLOCK was known as The Underground Network. It relied on a peer-to-peer (P2P) protocol known as Direct Connect, where users could set up their own "hubs" to share files, and we investigated hubs with names such as Achenon's Alley, MOVIE-ROOM, PROJECT X/THE ASYLUM, and SILENT ECHOES. The network required users to share at least a gigabyte of files themselves to participate—the equivalent of at least 250 songs. Many users, though, shared far more; all told, there were about 40 terabytes of stolen files available on the site on any given day, a mass of content equivalent to about 10.5 million songs or four times the print collection of the Library of Congress.

On August 25, 2004, the FBI executed six simultaneous search warrants in Texas, New York, and Wisconsin, collecting computers, software, and evidence from five residences and one internet service provider. Contrary to the public perception that all these peer-to-peer "copyright pirates" were broke college kids who didn't know any better, the hub hosts we targeted were in their forties and fifties. "P2P does not stand for 'Permission to Pilfer,'" then Attorney General John Ashcroft said in announcing the case. "Illegal distribution and reproduction of copyrighted material is a serious criminal offense. Today's investigative action sends a clear message to online thieves who steal the hard work and innovation of others. And it sends a clear message to those who think nothing of downloading those stolen goods to their computers or MP3 players. You can pay the fair value for music, movies, software and games like every other consumer, or you can pay an even higher price when you are caught committing online theft."[3] The following year, the first two of ultimately four defendants were convicted of federal felony copyright piracy on P2P networks.[4] One of those convicted, a 42-year-old user who went by the name Axeman, shared an average of 6.72 terabytes of data a day, roughly equal to 6,000 digital movies.[5]

The cases were considered successes, but a lesson I learned was that the criminal justice system was not always the right tool to solve a problem. At a great investment of time and resources, we'd nabbed four people from a massive community illegally sharing files online. It felt like we were fighting a rearguard action to protect a dying business model; we were helping to enforce horse-and-buggy standards as Henry Ford's Model Ts were rolling off the assembly line. All of the prosecution in the world wasn't going to bring back the recording industry's profitable days in the 1990s of selling full CD albums for $17.99. The landscape had shifted—and industries needed to shift with it. Government can only do so much, and the justice system is often a blunt tool if relied upon to achieve societal goals.

The solution to peer-to-peer file-sharing required the industry to look at their business model and figure out a way to use new technology to provide people what they wanted at a reasonable price and with a reasonable ease of use. What ultimately helped address—at least to an extent—the scourge of peer-to-peer networks was the arrival and growth of the iTunes store, a new tool that allowed users to securely buy music, television shows, and movies digitally with confidence that they were getting what they paid for. It's a lesson that I carried forward over the next dozen years as I continued on in cybercrime and cybersecurity. It's also a lesson that we as a society need to keep in mind even today: no matter what we do as a government, changing technologies require changes in businesses and ways of life. I don't know anyone at the Justice Department who thinks we can prosecute our way to a safe, reliable internet. Cybersecurity and cybercrime are evolving threats and there's no easy fix to securing our technology. Prosecutions and criminal investigations are just one tool, among many, that we need to be using to create and enforce norms and shape the 21st century online. For too long, we didn't chase the wolf—and we need to—but technology needs to change, too, so we're no longer living in that straw house.

At the same time, the justice system is a particularly effective tool to draw clear boxes around accepted societal behavior: the tools the internet provides are value-neutral; they can be used for good and for evil. Peer-to-peer technology can be a powerful tool for sharing files among companies or individuals, but it's also a "vector" to encourage sharing illegal files. We can support one use while condemning another. It's up to us as a government and a society to draw those lines, to define what's acceptable behavior in cyberspace.

///////////////

Joining the Justice Department had been an almost lifelong dream of mine. I'd always wanted to serve in government—and specifically to try cases in courtrooms as a prosecutor. But like many of the prosecutors and FBI agents who joined the government in the 1990s, fighting crime to me did not mean cybercrime—and it certainly didn't mean "national security." I'd joined to fight street crime, fraud, and corruption. I could have hardly imagined where my career would lead, but perhaps I should have learned to expect surprises: after all, my first job at the Justice Department—prosecuting tax cases—was in a division both far from what I expected and far from where I would later end up. At the time I accepted that job, I had not yet even taken my "Tax" course in law school.

As corny as it may sound, I wanted to be a prosecutor because I felt that defending the rule of law was the cornerstone of American history. Growing up a history buff, I'd been influenced by James Thomas Flexner's biography of the first president, *Washington: The Indispensable Man*, a portrait of how a flawed man had helped launch a democratic country, a first-of-its-kind experiment of a nation fundamentally governed by laws, not men. "In all history few men who possessed unassailable power have used that power so gently and self-effacingly for what their best instincts told them was the welfare of their neighbors and all mankind," he wrote. Washington's work led, Flexner argued, to "the very ideals many of us more admire: the sanctity of the individual, the equality of all men before the law, government responsive to the people, freedom for all means of communication,... [and] the self-determination of people everywhere."[6] My college admissions essay focused on Washington and the importance of the rule of law. Looking back, it's an embarrassingly apple pie topic—almost literally—but America has always represented to me the fight for the principle of a nation of laws, not men, a people guided by the foundational principles of self-determination and the rule of law, and this guidance makes us unique in history and is where we have taken the lead in changing the world. It's a principle that leads to peace and economic prosperity and values civil rights and civil liberties.

Growing up in New York City, coming of age as I did in the 1980s during an era when crime appeared rampant and maybe intractable—a permanent condition of the country's largest city—was a big part of what motivated me to become a prosecutor, too. There is a famous *Saturday Night Live* (SNL) skit from 1991, just after New York City had set another annual record for homicides, teasing the city's reputation as a "rotting, crime-infested hellhole." Kevin Nealon played a radio host interviewing a city official, played by Joe Mantegna, and they listened to callers' tales of woe, dismissing each in turn as the victim's fault. When one caller reported being mugged on the subway, Mantegna shot back, "It's 1:15 a.m. on the subway, what do you expect?" When another caller reported being mugged in Midtown in the afternoon while carrying groceries, he queried, "Did you make eye contact?" When the victim replied affirmatively, he said, "Can you tell me why someone in 1991 would make eye contact with a stranger on the street? Why not just wear a T-shirt saying 'I'm an idiot, stab me'?" Crime was just a natural condition of such a large city, the SNL characters said. "That's the price you pay for living in the most vibrant city in the world."[7] The city official then handed out pamphlets with the "I love NY" logo entitled "What to do when you've been shot," "What to do when you've been doused with gasoline and set on fire," and a New Yorker's guide to avoiding eye contact.

It was a skit that rang all too true to my childhood: I vividly remember when Officer Friendly came to school and taught us to be streetsmart, not make eye contact, cross to the other side of the street if someone seemed suspicious, and look for the yellow signs designating "safe havens" at local stores and bodegas on our walk home from school in case we were threatened. Those daily threats seemed normal. I didn't realize how strange my childhood was until I arrived at college in bucolic Massachusetts farm country and realized most of my non–New York classmates had never feared making eye contact on the street. The tactics that I'd learned to get home from school safely became strange and antisocial in a community where the most threatening encounter was with a cow.

To a certain extent, that same mentality fits the world of cybersecurity right now; the hopeful days of the early internet materialized into a scary, seemingly ungovernable space populated by all manner of evildoers preying upon hapless victims. When victims get hacked, you can hear the echoes of that SNL skit: "Well, did you run your software updates? Did you change your password every hour and use a unique 30-character mixed-case, alphanumeric password on each of the 45 websites you browsed today? Well, what do you expect—it's the internet." That's not the mentality we need today. Laws can be enforced online. "Normal" behavior can be shaped. Governments and decent citizens can't cede the space to criminals and predators—and the expectation shouldn't be that each internet user needs to be a highly trained cyber equivalent of a Navy SEAL to send email, make purchases, or install a thermostat that can be run from an iPhone.

I am optimistic that the mentality and expectations around the internet can be changed precisely because I saw that change happen in New York. A mix of social changes, law enforcement efforts, and smart leadership managed to radically transform the city; crime today is down nearly 90 percent, to effectively the lowest recorded levels ever, and the city is thriving economically. You don't have to define deviancy down—and the expectation is not that it's your fault you were robbed if you made eye contact with someone. President Obama made famous a Martin Luther King Jr. quote—which actually was first said by a 19th-century minister, Theodore Parker—about how "The arc of the moral universe is long, but it bends toward justice." I've always believed that—and I believe it still today. With work.

////////////

After college and before heading to law school, I spent a year working at Freedom House, a nonprofit group dedicated to measuring and helping with the transformation of countries around the world toward democracy and free elections. It works diligently to define the characteristics of a democracy and what is meant by "free." One of the lessons of our history—and the experience of democracies around the world—is that you can't take freedoms for granted. Democracy has always been a constant fight against forces that seek, through evolution or revolution, to twist the institutions that allow for the peaceful transfer of power into ones that entrench power. If you don't protect your institutions, they can't protect you as a citizen. I didn't realize at the time that this fight would prove so central to my life. Over two decades, I went from working on the evolution side of that fight from Freedom House in the mid-1990s, during an era of hope at the end of the Cold War, to watching from a front-row seat in government as the revolution side of the fight played out in Russia, as it retrenched from a fledgling democracy to a criminal autocratic state led by Vladimir Putin. And I devoted my energies, later, at the National Security Division to combatting Russia and three other countries with a very different set of values: Iran, North Korea, and China.

We took that moment of hope in the 1990s for granted, as Francis Fukuyama's *The End of History and the Last Man* made it appear that ideological struggles were over and democracy would reign supreme.* At the time, the rising digital world seemed to take freedom even one natural step further, allowing for a place that can be without rules and completely unfettered. The same year, 1996, that I worked at Freedom House, John Perry Barlow—a former lyricist for the Grateful Dead who been an early participant in the web—authored and posted online a "Declaration of the Independence of Cyberspace," writing, "Governments of the Industrial World, you weary giants of flesh and steel, I come from Cyberspace, the new home of Mind. On behalf of the future, I ask you of the past to leave us alone. You are not welcome among us. You have no sovereignty where we gather."

Barlow—who with two like-minded digital pioneers, John Gilmore and Mitch Kapor, founded the Electronic Frontier Foundation—believed that the virtual worlds of cyberspace existed beyond the reach of any pedestrian earthly government. "Cyberspace does not lie within your borders," he wrote. "I declare the global social space we are building to be naturally independent of the tyrannies you seek to impose on us. You have no moral right to rule us nor do you possess any methods of enforcement we have true reason to fear.... Your legal concepts of property, expression, identity, movement, and context do not apply to us. They are all based on matter, and there is no matter here."[8] Barlow's view of a techtopian libertarianism was hardly an outlier; the view seemed so dominant in fact that the outcome seemed preordained—the only question was, how would the world accomplish it? UCLA's Kenichi Ohmae argued that the "modern nation-state itself—the artifact of the eighteenth and nineteenth centuries—has begun to crumble," and MIT's Nicholas Negroponte, another early digital ideologue,

---

*We might have known better, though: the similarly iconic book of the 1980s, Paul Kennedy's *The Rise and Fall of Great Powers*, had hinted we would all be speaking Japanese by now—the American system turns out to be more resilient than we often believe.

said, "Like a mothball, which goes from solid to gas directly, I expect the nation-state to evaporate."

It didn't quite work out that way.

///////////

For the law school set, working for the government was not career path number one. Our professor, Alan Dershowitz, joked in our Criminal Law 101 class at one point that none of us would ever see the inside of a courtroom. I proved to be one of the exceptions: I joined the Justice Department right out of law school, starting as a trial attorney in October 1999.

I basically ended up working cybercrimes because I knew how to set up my coworkers' printer and how to use email. The tax division, where I was first assigned, wasn't any special interest of mine, but one of my Harvard Law professors, Phil Heymann, had suggested it was a good place to start if I wanted to get into a courtroom quickly and wanted to try big cases. I knew my classmates who went into the private sector might spend years buried in menial tasks before they ever worked a case firsthand, and I was eager to get there faster than that. The point of the Attorney General's Honors Program is to bring promising graduates straight into the heart of the Justice Department—it's basically the only way to get hired into the department right out of law school—so I was often a good two decades younger than the other prosecutors in the tax section.

Which meant that I knew how to use email—and, just as importantly in an office setting, I knew how to make the office printers work. Coming into the Justice Department, I was part of the first generation of prosecutors who grew up with computers—or at least some of us had. Technology fascinated me growing up.

The first computer we had in my house when I was growing up in New York was a giant, person-sized box my older sister had won in a raffle. It was huge. I remember being amazed how the printer was built right into the machine. Later, we graduated as a family to an Apple IIe and an Atari, which I proudly taught my grandfather how to use. When a knee condition one summer kept me out of camp, I spent my days indoors learning to code in BASIC—coding was a revelation to me, a choose-your-own-adventure where you could make the computer do what you commanded. Later, in high school in New York, I was part of a small group of students picked to help build an early CD-ROM "textbook" on the Civil War, weaving together primary sources, oral histories, music, and more in what was then an exciting multimedia advance on the staid printed textbook, an attempt to harness the new power of technology to put the reader, rather than the author, at the center of the experience. The CD-ROM textbook reader could follow their own path, engage with primary sources, and explore the history at their own pace.

I have vivid memories of early games like *Questron*, where you gained experience and "leveled up" through the game, and of mastering video games such as *Pac-Man*. It seems unremarkable to a generation raised with smartphones and social media, but the early computer experience seemed to open the window to new worlds. Early on, our collective guide to these new worlds was science fiction writers, who were simultaneously imagining the era—sometimes all too presciently— we would all soon inhabit. Because computers and the digital realm remained so much the province of fantasists and geeks, these authors were in some ways the only people doing deep thinking about the world ahead. When I was nine years old, I devoured the *Lensman* series by E. E. "Doc" Smith, an early pulp sci-fi series about cops and robbers playing out in space that focused on what we would later identify as an artificial-intelligence system that becomes self-aware. Isaac Asimov, in his famous *Foundation* trilogy, imagined a world where you had the ability to analyze bulk data predictively and essentially have what we now call AI, artificial intelligence.*

It was not a world that translated naturally or easily to the all-too-real world of murders, rapes, and all the other crime that crossed a prosecutor's desk. Figuring out how to translate the new world of bits and bytes to a world dominated by centuries-old legal traditions that

---

*As we begin to imagine the legal implications of robotic consciousness, we could do worse than start with his three laws of robotics.

dated to stone tablets and paper scrolls was not easy. For decades we struggled to broaden the universe of people who understood cyberspace and tried to get ahead of the trends we could see coming. That failure of imagination and failure to translate repeatedly stymied the government's response to digital challenges from the lowest levels of the Justice Department right up to the table in the White House Situation Room. What constituted a crime in the digital age? It wasn't always easy to say.

⁂

When I arrived in the federal government, big technological and societal changes were just beginning to take hold; as I scouted for my first apartment in DC in the summer of 1999, I remember walking down 17th Street and seeing people talking on big clunky cell phones. In our work space at the US attorney's office, we relied on computers with WordPerfect, which elicited a lot of office jokes about Microsoft and the Justice Department's groundbreaking antitrust case against the technology giant that was then working its way slowly through the courts.

The tax unit where I was assigned was in the midst of its own massive case, investigating a multilevel marketing scheme known as the Institute of Global Prosperity, which ran informational seminars and sold people "research" on how to avoid paying taxes. It offered all manner of false and discredited materials that tried to convince its victims that if they filled out a few forms, they could live tax-free for life. Not surprisingly, the people behind the scheme were practicing what they preached. It was, as tax cases go, a relatively straightforward case, but the company was not only bilking victims of their money for worthless information, it was also exposing them to legal jeopardy with the government if they followed the advice.

What made the scheme new at the time, though, was that the marketing was done largely online—which meant that the veterans in the tax unit turned to me, the guy who helped them set up their printers, to help gather the necessary digital evidence. As part of my digital evidence work, I'd attended trainings by the Justice Department's Computer

Crime and Intellectual Property Section (CCIPS), and met Orin Kerr, a pioneer who later wrote the first textbook on computer crimes and brought a prosecutor's eye to the era of the techtopia that still dominated public thinking. At the time, the whole area of computer crime was a small field—the Justice Department only had 18 attorneys working it in 2000. The security world online was quite cloistered. Even two decades after the first cybersecurity cases began to arise, the world of computer threats remained—on both sides—effectively the exclusive province of small groups of fantasists and geeks, many of whom were deeply reluctant to welcome others into their realm.

The team, originally known as the Computer Crime Unit, had been started in 1991 by Robert Mueller, when he had been the assistant attorney general overseeing the criminal division during George H. W. Bush's presidency. Mueller had been intrigued by the book *Cuckoo's Egg*, which had been published in 1989 and told the story of how Clifford Stoll, a computer manager at the Lawrence Berkeley National Laboratory in California, had almost single-handedly identified an intrusion into his network and traced it back to West Germany and a hacker employed by the KGB. The book heralded a new wave of threat and, over time, became a classic. Looking back now, it's incredible to see how primitive the technology was at the time—the self-assembled Sinclair computers that inspired the West German hackers came with tape cassettes—not even floppy discs—and their dial-up modems plugged along at only 300 bits a second, barely an eighth of the 2,400 bits the primitive dial-up of the 1990s would deliver.

His early interest, though, inspired a tradition at CCIPS, where all new attorneys were given a copy of *Cuckoo's Egg* to read when they started. I remember at one point being given my own copy after being led into a dusty closet at the Justice Department filled with cartons of the book. It was not exactly a stellar endorsement of the FBI's early cyber efforts: the first time Stoll tried to report that a hacker was rooting around in the national laboratory for military information, the FBI demurred and told him to call his local district attorney. They didn't think a cyber case was worth the effort. It would, in the real world, take years to change that mentality—to help agents and prosecutors understand that just because a case started small didn't mean it didn't present a big threat. As my Justice Department colleague Chris Painter recalled years later, that shift came as agents began to focus not just on what had already happened but on what might happen: "Recognizing that you've got critical infrastructure that could be affected, where the damage is not obvious but the threat against them [is]," Painter said later. "You don't want to give constantly free bites at the apple, right, so the next attack might be the one that brings down the whole system. We don't want to wait."

Mueller's early interest helped jump-start the Justice Department's efforts in computer crime, but in those early years, few really understood the rules of the new road. No one yet understood how laws written for an age of telephones built on a network of copper wires could be translated to account for digital bits and bytes.

"Hacking" has been a core part of the internet's ethos since its creation—an improvisational, tinkering spirit in a decentralized, anti-authority medium with only the loosest of rules and much room for experimentation. As a term, *hacking* derived from the good-natured pranks central to the culture of places like MIT, where students delighted in practical jokes and collegiate stunts such as surreptitiously placing an old Chevrolet, painted like an MIT police car, atop the school's iconic Great Dome, or writing a computer program that calculated the most efficient way to travel over all of New York City's subway system. The school even hosted a website, hacks.mit.edu, recounting its proud history of "good hacks." By comparison, MIT labeled devious computer- or phone-related endeavors as "cracking." As Steven Levy wrote in his 1984 book *Hackers*, which began to popularize the term, computer programmers and designers were "adventurers, visionaries, risk-takers, artists, and the ones who most clearly saw why the computer was a truly revolutionary tool."[9] Levy described a "Hacker Ethic" that held that "essential lessons can be learned about the systems—about the world—from taking things apart, seeing how they work, and using this knowledge to create new and even more interesting things.

They resent any person, physical barrier, or law that tries to keep them from doing this."[10]

Success in the hacking world of the 1950s and 1960s came only through experimentation, and computing's egalitarian culture believed that information should be free and decentralized—hoarding of time, data, or learning threatened the ability of the enterprise to advance. The first generation of computers were massive room-sized machines that offered an almost religious and magical experience, carefully tended by teams of workers like they were totems in a mystical shrine of a forgotten society. "To a hacker, a closed door is an insult and a locked door is an outrage," Levy wrote, as he documented life at computing hubs like MIT.[11]*

At Stanford's AI Lab (SAIL), the system did not require passwords and all files were open by default, unless a user took extra steps to hide them. But then SAIL's hackers simply wrote a program to identify hidden files and then worked diligently to unlock them. "Anybody that's asking for privacy must be doing something interesting," SAIL's Don Woods explained.[12]

The curiosity and imagination central to early institutional computers blended the professional and personal, and as technology steadily advanced, the teams of lab staff gave way to a more personal, more intimate relationship that encouraged even more experimentation. Early personal computers were often ready-to-make kits or homemade assemblages as likely to be cobbled together by hobbyists as by professionals. Sold through small ads in the backs of magazines, the homebrew computers involved long hours of soldering, circuit arranging, and wiring.

"Phone phreakers," who stole free telephone calls by circumventing AT&T's long-distance system, played an integral role in early

---

* The teams of computer scientists spent their days working to advance knowledge and technology, then spent nights devoting hours to literally picking locks across campus to ensure that they could always get access to whatever tools they needed. "There was another side of the world where people felt everything should be available to everybody, and these hackers had pounds and pounds of keys that would get them into every conceivable place," recalled David Silver, who worked in MIT's AI Lab.

computing—including, most famously, Steve Wozniak and Steve Jobs, who founded Apple Computer. The phreakers used gadgets known as "blue boxes" to mimic the specific 2,600-hertz tone AT&T used to control its switches, allowing them to bypass billing systems and dial for free. In 1971, an *Esquire* magazine article, "Secrets of the Little Blue Box," brought the practice out into the mainstream, celebrating the counterculture and making a celebrity out of John Draper, an early phreaker known as Captain Crunch, nicknamed after the red plastic captain's whistles that came in the eponymous cereal boxes that happened to hit that perfect 2,600-hertz note.[13]* "Phreaking," Draper explained, wasn't about theft, it was about "learning about a system. The phone company is a system. A computer is a system. Do you understand? If I do what I do, it is only to explore a system. That's my bag."[14] Teens also built their own simplistic programs, like the one seen in the movie *WarGames*, which dialed numbers at random searching for new computers, exploring the breadth of the internet long before search engines made it easy to navigate.

Systems, by and large, were wide open, with security measures turned off by default. Network technicians could turn on security systems such as passwords if they wanted, but doing so went against the spirit of collaboration. "We didn't focus on how you could wreck this system intentionally," recalled one of the original inventors of the networked age, Vint Cerf, who, with others, spent years tweaking the system to work, often literally sketching on paper how computers could talk to one another. "You could argue with hindsight that we should have, but getting this thing to work at all was non-trivial."[15]

ARPANET, an early network founded by the Pentagon as a place for scientists and engineers to share information, started in 1969 at UCLA; additional "nodes" were soon added at places like UC–Santa

---

*Authorities knew well enough what to do with telephone-related crimes; shortly after that *Esquire* article on phone phreakers was published in 1971, John Draper was arrested and charged with toll fraud. He received probation, but had continued his phreaking, and the FBI stayed on top of him—surveilling him and arresting him again. The second time he went to prison. When he was released, he was hired by a new start-up named Apple Computer.

Barbara, the Stanford Research Institute, the University of Utah, MIT, and Harvard. No one really understood what they were building at the time—the connections they were creating seemed like they could be important and useful, but for what? "No one had any answers, but the prospects seemed exciting. We found ourselves imagining all kinds of possibilities—interactive graphics, cooperating processes, automatic database queries, electronic mail—but no one knew where to begin," recalled Steve Crocker, one of ARPANET's pioneers.[16] The entire network was an indulgent experiment for the computer research community, irrelevant to most other scientists and technology researchers.

Years were spent on the basics like establishing common protocols guiding how information could be transmitted and translated between different types of machines. The conceptual leap at the foundation of ARPANET, known as packet switching, spent years in development. Rather than relying on the way a telephone operated—with a fixed line open between a transmitter and a receiver—the online network didn't transmit a message in its entirety, but instead broke it down into tiny pieces of data, known as packets, that could each race independently across the network via whatever route at that moment seemed fastest. Then, at the other end, the packets were reassembled together.[17]

In 1973, ARPANET had swelled to 25 machines. The machines, often made by the defense giant Honeywell, were behemoths, room-sized institutional computers to be shared among an entire faculty—ARPANET connections cost as much as $250,000 annually—but they were, certainly by modern standards, primitive and not all that powerful. Early machines even had voice headsets installed, so researchers could double-check by voice that their computers were transmitting as intended. "I'm going to type an 'L,'" a researcher at UCLA would shout to a researcher at the Stanford Research Institute. "Did you get an 'L'?"[18]

"To be at a site connected to the ARPANET was to be among an elite," a journalist observed. "In its early days and even into its middle years, the ARPANET had the feel of a private club.... Getting into the club wasn't easy, but once you were in, you were given free rein."[19] Among such a small group, security wasn't even an afterthought—it defeated the very purpose of the network. Carnegie Mellon prided itself on having every file on every computer open to everyone else on ARPANET, unless a user sought to explicitly protect it. That mindset was partly what contributed to the lack of security—there was, for years, even decades, so little worth stealing or damaging on any of the computer systems. "People don't break into banks because they're not secure. They break into banks because that's where the money is," explained Janet Abbate, the author of *Inventing the Internet*. As she said, "They thought they were building a classroom, and it turned into a bank."[20]

Trust was inherent and expected on ARPANET—and yet as the network grew, the costs of that approach were becoming more clear. In December 1973, Robert Metcalfe, one of the system's early creators, sent out a message warning that most sites had inadequate security protections—fundamentally, the network and its users were just too trusting. The phone numbers to dial up ARPANET were widely known and, once a user dialed in, the system required "no user identification before giving service."[21]

Whereas hackers were professionals who subscribed to a shared online code and were focused on openness, the decentralization of information, and a collective responsibility to never harm data—the data was the treasure they shared together—malicious network users were known as "network randoms," "net randoms," or simply "randoms," a reference to their uncertain online origins.[22] The presence of "randoms" online undermined the network's collective spirit.

MIT, which left its network wide open—no passwords necessary—was notorious for allowing "randoms" online, much to the consternation of others at more buttoned-up institutions.[23]* As one writer recalled, "net randoms" were often users "who stopped by and rummaged through the systems just to see what all those crazy MIT hackers were up to."[24] But they could, either accidentally or on purpose,

---

* Richard Stallman, one of the early computing pioneers at MIT, advocated for users to adopt a simple carriage return as their password—when the login screen appeared, just hit Return and log in. "It's much easier to type, and also stands up to the principle that there should be no passwords," he told other users. At one point, he was able to get nearly a fifth of the lab's users to forgo passwords entirely.

cause trouble for legitimate users—pulling pranks like sending fake emails telling users their accounts were about to be deleted from the network. "There is a collection of hosts on the east coast at a well-known institute, that seems to give out accounts/logins and pass-words to just about any ol' random who requests them," email pioneer Geoff Goodfellow complained in a March 1980 bulletin board post-ing, pushing for system administrators to crack down on such un-restricted guest accounts. "Allowing the randoms to get on the net in the first place allows them to then have run-of-the-ARPANET-backyard, and try their sharp hands as cracking and breaking into the various systems around the net—fun fun fun!"[25] The Pentagon grew so concerned about "randoms" that they threatened to disconnect MIT from ARPANET.[26]

As computing power increased, researchers sought to harness the collective memory of the wider network. The first generation of "com-puter worms" actually started benevolently—though the phrase al-ways grew from a dark meaning, coined from a 1975 science fiction novel by John Brunner, *The Shockwave Rider*, about a dystopian future government that controls the flow of information through a powerful computer system.* The world is freed from tyranny by a savant who can program through the cutting-edge technology of a push-button tele-phone and designs a "data-net tapeworm" that forces the government to unplug its master computer.

Four years after the publication of Brunner's novel, two researchers at Xerox's Palo Alto Research Center, Jon Hupp and John Shoch, de-signed the first real-world computer worms in an attempt to improve efficiency, creating a program that slipped onto idle computers across the network and used their spare processing power to speed up com-plex calculations. The "Vampire Worm" was designed to activate at night, when researchers went home, and then shut down in the morn-ing when they returned. They also designed a "Town Crier Worm" that moved through the network sharing announcements. Yet their

---

*In a twist that does seem prescient, people in Brunner's novel are so overwhelmed by the constant pace of information that they take sedatives.

research quickly proved problematic: one defective version of the vampire worm repeatedly crashed the Palo Alto network.

When things did go awry online, either on purpose or accidentally, it wasn't at all clear whose problem it was. In December 1980, engineers at the San Francisco–based company US Leasing found their computers acting up; the machines were sluggish and sometimes unresponsive. The following day, employees arrived to find that the company's printers had spent the night spewing gibberish—a message, printed hundreds of times, that declared: "THE PHANTOM, THE SYSTEM CRACKER, STRIKES AGAIN. SOON I WILL CRASH YOUR DISKS AND BACKUPS ON SYSTEM A. I HAVE ALREADY CRASHED YOUR SYSTEM B. HAVE FUN TRYING TO RESTORE IT, YOU ASSHOLE." Other messages, scattered throughout, declared "REVENGE IS OURS" and made reference to various names. The company's head of data processing noticed a reference to MITNICK and wondered if it was a sign that the intrusion had grown out of an MIT prank—but it was hardly as innocent and fun-spirited as a normal MIT hack.

The company called the FBI, who promptly dispatched three agents. They carefully interviewed engineers and examined the evidence, vulgar printouts lying all over the floor. *They saw a crime, sure, but not a federal one.* The federal government had no law against computer intrusions.

As far as the agents who arrived at US Leasing could tell, the hacker had dialed in from a California number, which meant there was no way to pursue him or her for violating interstate telephone laws. Maybe, the agents suggested before they left, US Leasing could try the local police? California, after all, had a year-old state law against unauthorized computer access.[27] It would be years before the company figured out that the break-in had been tied to Kevin Mitnick, who in the 1980s and 1990s became the first well-known hacker; at the time, he was still in his teens. He had started as a phone phreaker and then graduated to cracking computer networks.[28] "My friends and I thought it would be cool to get everyone's password," he wrote later, explaining the appeal of hacking. "There was no sinister plan, just collecting information for the hell of it."[29] Confronted by an FBI agent at one point in his early career, Mitnick later recalled, "He told me, 'You can get twenty-five years if you keep messing with the phone company.' I knew he was powerless, just trying to scare me."[30]

Similarly, FBI agents in Connecticut were summoned by a company called National CSS Inc., which helped oversee time-sharing on computer systems—someone had stolen the company's main password directory, enabling access to some 8,000 customer accounts. The company had only figured out the theft when customers began to complain their accounts had been billed for computer time they'd never used. In writing about the case, the *New York Times* tried to define a "hacker," writing, "Hackers are technical experts; skilled, often young, computer programmers, who almost whimsically probe the defenses of a computer system, searching out the limits and the possibilities of the machine. Despite their seemingly subversive role, hackers are a recognized asset in the computer industry, often highly prized."[31]

⁂

By the early 1980s, the network protocols that had guided ARPANET—protocols that limited the network to only 256 machines—were remade to allow for the growth of desktop computers. On January 1, 1983, ARPANET shifted over to a new system protocol known as TCP/IP, the transmission control protocol/internet protocol, that allowed multiple regional and national networks to be stitched together in a common language, encompassing people far beyond the clubby world of higher education and professional research, and leading the user base to soar into the hundreds and then thousands. The internet had arrived. Vint Cerf and Robert Kahn and the others who designed the TCP/IP system had considered including encryption in the foundation of the internet, but it proved too complicated—and, besides, the National Security Agency had made clear it wasn't all that thrilled for the network to have cryptography baked into its transmissions. Instead, the internet's core functions would all take place in the clear, unencrypted, and would be easy for anyone with the right know-how to intercept.[32]

The decentralized nature of this new internet reversed the paradigm of the monopolistic Bell Telephone Company. AT&T had built a national network with an "intelligent core"—the network was run by the phone company with smart switches, centralized protocols, and user authentication systems—and "dumb edges," where users just plugged a basic telephone handset into a wall; all of the technology standards and functions were centrally controlled, with users able to do little more than choose the color of their telephone handset (and that, only after decades when the only choice was black). The internet, by design, was the reverse. The core was "dumb," just wires carrying information back and forth without a care for who was sending what, and the edges were "intelligent," with users able to make complex decisions about the use and performance of each computer terminal. It made the system easy to expand, but inadvertently established at the core of the internet a security flaw: each user was responsible for their own protection. There was little a centralized authority could do to protect each individual edge. "We were afraid a smart switch would get in the way of our experiment," early pioneer Larry Roberts recalled.[33]

The goals of this new wider community fundamentally changed the network's purpose: what had once been used primarily for calculating complex math problems and sharing laboratory results came instead to be dominated by email and electronic bulletin boards covering seemingly every topic imaginable. As computers grew more powerful, the focus of hacking shifted from the hardware itself to the software that ran on it—you no longer needed to be soldering circuit boards in your kitchen at night, you could spend your days writing "code" to design new games. In this new era, though, the software appeared just as improvised—sold on floppy discs packaged in Ziploc bags, with simplistic graphics and labels stuck on by hand.[34]

The definition of the term *hacker* morphed, too, as the internet grew large enough—and accrued enough users—that damaging it could cause real harm. In fact, when Steven Levy's book *Hackers* was published in the early 1980s, it was written as an elegy to a lost time and generation, when free-minded thinkers and tinkerers dominated the computer landscape—before the buttoned-up bureaucrats seized control of the digital world. "It is painful for me to bring back the memories of this time," said Richard Stallman in the book, the MIT hacker who had advocated for no passwords. "The whole culture was wiped out."[35]

/////////////////

Computers and the digital world were beginning to capture the imagination of the wider public; my family was one of the millions who first purchased a desktop computer in this era, marveling at how the room-sized behemoths of a previous era had been miniaturized to fit in the family den.

The same year, 1983, that ARPANET was rewritten to be easily expandable, the new breadth of the network caused the Pentagon to grow concerned about its own online security. It split the military systems off onto their own network, known as MILNET. The dangers of connected devices suddenly seemed all too real. And that spring, the movie *WarGames* starred Matthew Broderick as a precocious teen hacker who accidentally nearly triggered nuclear war with the Soviet Union by hacking the military's computers at its NORAD base in Colorado in an attempt to play video games. President Reagan, an avid movie buff, watched the drama at Camp David and returned to the White House with a direct query to his military leaders: "Could something like this really happen?" General John Vessey, the chairman of the Joint Chiefs, was surprised when he went to investigate the answer; he returned to the White House the following week and announced, "Mr. President, the problem is much worse than you think."[36]

That answer to a presidential query about a fictional movie prompted the first serious thinking inside government about securing cyberspace, a secret scramble to begin addressing new vulnerabilities. The work was codified in a classified directive known as NSDD-145, the first White House policy on "cyber warfare," titled innocuously, "National Policy on Telecommunications and Automated Information Systems Security." The eleven-page document laid out in its opening paragraph a new paradigm: "Telecommunications and automated information processing systems are highly susceptible to interception, unauthorized electronic access, and related forms of technical exploitation, as well as other dimensions of the hostile intelligence threat. The technology to exploit these electronic systems is widespread and is used extensively by foreign nations and can be employed, as well, by terrorist groups and criminal elements. Government systems as well as those which process the private or proprietary information of US persons and businesses can become targets for foreign exploitation."[37] The document, though, was quickly forgotten—and, in a situation that would repeat for each successive president, each new administration for the next thirty years had its own wake-up call to the all-too-vulnerable world of cybersecurity.

Underscoring the new digital reality, a real-life version of *War-Games* unfolded publicly at the same time, as six young hackers from Milwaukee—the group, aged 15 to 22, dubbed themselves the 414 Gang after the city's area code—were investigated by the FBI for breaking into government computers and deleting billing records at the Sloan-Kettering Cancer Center to cover their tracks. Their hacking was hardly sophisticated—relying largely upon networks that hadn't bothered to change their default passwords—and was done simply for fun.

Coming so quickly on the heels of *WarGames*, the case of the 414 Gang caught the nation's attention. One 17-year-old hacker, Neal Patrick, appeared on TV network morning shows and testified before Congress about how he'd managed to access sensitive government computer networks from his home in Milwaukee using his family TRS-80 computer from Radio Shack.[38] He explained that his dad had told him to stop exploring online bulletin boards after receiving a long-distance telephone bill for $300, but he'd instead switched over to using "borrowed" credit cards traded openly on bulletin boards to avoid his dad knowing what he was doing. "We did it for curiosity, just plain curiosity," he said. "In hindsight, the illegality does not justify our curiosity. We'd never do it again."

When it caught up to the 414 Gang, the government, though, was stumped: there was at the time no law against hacking or computer crime, and so the FBI improvised and leveled a misdemeanor charge of making obscene or harassing telephone calls.[39] "Government views these intrusions as serious, whether or not there was intent to profit," the assistant US attorney, Eric Klumb, said at the time.*

The incidents caused Congress to begin paying attention; until then, computer security had been at best only a passing concern on Capitol Hill. Individual states such as Florida and Arizona had begun passing anti–computer crime laws in the 1970s, but little attention or progress had been paid at the national level.[40] In 1977, Senator Abraham Ribicoff had proposed a "Federal Computer Systems Protection Act" that aimed to define and criminalize "computer crimes," but the bill never went anywhere. In 1983, six other computer crime bills were introduced; the issue was beginning to attract real attention. The FBI's deputy assistant director, Floyd Clarke, warned in one hearing that computers in the hands of a criminal could be just as dangerous as "a gun, a knife, or a forger's pen."[41]

That fall, Fred Cohen, a graduate student at the University of Southern California, popularized a new term—he designed and demonstrated a parasitic, self-replicating computer program during a security seminar at Lehigh University. The program, which he dubbed a "computer virus," worked all too well, seizing control of the systems he was using in under half an hour. "The experiments were so startling that I wanted to do more," Cohen recalled later. "But what happens to most people who do this experiment, and it happened to me, too, is that as soon as you try one, all of a sudden you get real afraid to try another."[42]

The arrival of threatening programs inside a system that had been founded on the basis of trust and openness heralded a new era. Until then, security had not just been an afterthought during the first decades of networked computers; the very concept ran counter to the entire point of a platform and network that allowed users to share and access files and tools from afar. Computers were meant to help people, not block them.

---

* The fraternity of prosecutors with computer crime experience remains small to this day; years later, in 2007, I replaced Klumb as the coordinator of the Justice Department's special computer crime prosecutors.

Soon, the online community began to differentiate between "white hat" hackers, who worked for companies or government, and "black hat" ones, out for criminal gain. Hacker groups sprouted, like the so-called Legion of Doom and, later, the Masters of Deception in the United States. Their culture was intimately tied into the phone hacking where many had gotten their start; on their bulletin boards, their online guides and tips were known not as "files" but as "philes."[43] Most were teenagers, more inclined to juvenile pranks than criminal acts—they would prank other hackers by tweaking the phone company's computers to think a home phone number was a pay phone. In Europe, a German collective known as the Chaos Computer Club thrived, taking advantage of the fact that European laws were even more out-of-date than American ones, so it wasn't even illegal to crack into a system and poke around. Even as those groups gained prominence online, security remained at best an ancillary topic of concern; it took an explicit warning from one of the field's pioneers to move it toward the center.

In 1984, programmer Ken Thompson, who had codesigned and invented the UNIX operating system, received one of the computing industry's highest honors, the A. M. Turing Award, named after groundbreaking English computer scientist Alan Turing. Thompson had spent his entire career in technology, watching as the online environment evolved, and he felt that the world was at a turning point; he used his award acceptance speech to lay out a devious program he'd once explored writing software code that almost invisibly created its own back door—a back door that would be left open even as new versions of the software were created. His successful exercise pointed to how the technical community needed to begin reckoning with the security holes that lay at the center of the internet and computing in general.

"The moral is obvious," he told the crowd after walking them through his code. "You can't trust code that you did not totally create yourself." That fundamental flaw—one that is still true and persists to this day—pointed to a larger problem, he explained. Hackers, he said, shouldn't be celebrated any longer by media, which often seemed to portray hackers as if they were like the character Broderick played in *WarGames*, well-meaning "whiz kids" and harmless explorers in a new land. "The acts performed by these kids are vandalism at best and probably trespass and theft at worst. It is only the inadequacy of the criminal code that saves the hackers from very serious prosecution," Thompson said. "I have watched kids testifying before Congress. It is clear that they are completely unaware of the seriousness of their acts. There is obviously a cultural gap. The act of breaking into a computer system has to have the same social stigma as breaking into a neighbor's house. It should not matter that the neighbor's door is unlocked. The press must learn that misguided use of a computer is no more amazing than drunk driving of an automobile."[44]

Congress was hearing similar warnings from the government and the business community, and, in April 1986, a New Jersey representative, William Hughes, introduced H.R. 1001, the Computer Fraud and Abuse Act, which assessed penalties for "unauthorized access" to a wide variety of "protected" computers that belonged to the government or financial institutions or were otherwise engaged in interstate commerce; the legislation built on earlier 1984 legislation that had only criminalized accessing of classified information or financial-type records. It was the first major attempt to define a criminal act online as different and distinct from a crime in the physical world—a "digital crime" rather than just an existing crime that was digitally enabled and prosecutable under existing laws. "Computer technology has left us with a new breed of technologically sophisticated criminal," Hughes explained, describing a criminal whose tools "are no longer Smith & Wesson, but IBM and Apple."[45] As the measure passed the House, Hughes argued, "Unless we act now, computer crime will be the crime wave of the next decade." Ronald Reagan signed the legislation in October 1986, and in the years ahead, it became the main cybercrime tool for the government.

The Computer Fraud and Abuse Act sought to define virtual crime akin to real-world crime. It criminalized computer espionage, trespassing, fraud, theft, and threats, as well as attempts to damage computers, traffic in stolen passwords, or conspiracies to do any of the same.

It didn't take long for the act to get its first use.

ͮͮͮͮͮͮͮͮͮͮͮͮͮͮ

November 2, 1988, isn't a date that rings today with any sense of national infamy, but the first national-scale computer crime began that Wednesday evening. Earlier that year, Robert T. Morris Jr.—a talented Cornell graduate student and, awkwardly, the son of the top scientist at the NSA's Computer Security Center—had discovered a bug in the operating system UNIX that then powered much of the entire internet. Morris wrote a short 99-line, self-replicating and -propagating worm that exploited the vulnerability to give him access to other infected computers.

The worm worked in three ways to attempt to break into a new computer. First, it simply asked nicely—exploiting the trust that then existed on the nascent internet and attempting to run a "remote shell" on a new computer, a tool designed to allow users to execute commands across the network if they weren't physically present. If the network administrator had locked down that function, the worm then tried a "buffer overflow" attack, overwhelming the login system with a 536-byte string of characters, the maximum-size entry the system could execute. That command caused the system to freeze up and, in its confusion, to effectively forget what it was supposed to do—and allow the worm to set up a remote shell. Last, if the first two efforts failed, the program tried to break the user password on the mail program.[46]

To Morris, the worm was just another chapter in his proclivity for annoying but harmless computer pranks. As a student at Harvard, he'd programmed the network such that when people mistyped the command for the email program, "mail," as "mial," they instead launched a mini-adventure game—his prank was sophisticated enough to exclude the accounts of senior faculty members, so it continued with little notice for quite some time.[47] With the worm, he'd hoped to just test how many computers he could reach. In mid-October of 1988, he'd sketched out five goals for the worm, all of them more curious than nefarious—he wanted to infect three computers per local network, avoid slow machines and interfering with active users, and use each new infection to try to access more networks and steal new passwords.

On Wednesday night, November 2, he slipped the program onto the internet through MIT's network, to disguise its origin, and quickly discovered, to his horror, that the program was far more effective and destructive than intended. He had intended it to spread slowly and quietly, but Morris had made a couple of critical programming errors and instead thousands of computers at universities, government offices, military bases, and medical facilities ground to a halt as the worm replicated itself at a rate far faster than expected, clogging the system and forcing many users to disconnect their computers from the main network.

Panic set in at computer labs across the country, as systems administrators noted the program deluging them. At 6:30 p.m., the RAND Corporation noted its presence; then, an hour later, MIT's AI Lab saw the worm. Soon, it was infecting computers at Lawrence Livermore National Laboratory, then Stanford, and dozens of others.[48] By midnight, it hit the US Army's Ballistic Research Laboratory and the army made the decision to sever its connection to the internet entirely. Programmers at Berkeley, the home of UNIX, rushed to determine a fix. As the school's computing team assembled to fight whatever this unknown virus was, someone made a crude sign and hung it on the computing lab's door: "Center for Disease Control."

By the next day, more than 6,000 computers were affected nationwide—perhaps as much as 8–10 percent of all the computers then connected to the internet—and news of the event was on the front page of the *New York Times* on Friday morning. "The big issue is that a relatively benign software program can virtually bring our computing community to its knees and keep it there for some time," an official at the Lawrence Livermore National Laboratory explained.[49] It took days for the internet to come back online.

It didn't take long for the worm to be traced back to Morris; in his panic watching the damage unfold, he'd had a friend try to spread the word about how to remediate the problem. By late Friday night, the media was reporting that a Cornell student was involved. Cornell's deans and computer science faculty convened and assembled all the evidence they needed to point the finger at Morris.

The case fell to an Ithaca FBI agent named Joe O'Brien. He had no experience with computer crime—he was an organized crime agent and had mostly used his Apple II computer to write a memoir about infiltrating the Gambino family. At the time, in fact, the FBI had only a single agent who specialized in computer crime, Mike Gibbons. On Saturday morning, O'Brien arrived at Morris's student office, ushered away the gathered reporters, and boxed up the contents of the office.[50] It was normal FBI procedure, but largely meaningless for a computer crime—all the evidence in the case was digital. Then he began interviewing witnesses, Morris's friends, and other faculty.

For everyone involved, it seemed an open question whether an actual crime had been committed. As O'Brien investigated, Morris met with a defense attorney, Tom Guidoboni, in DC. Guidoboni quickly realized that, until arriving at his office, Morris had been oblivious that his actions might constitute a crime. "He didn't know there was even a law to violate—and he certainly wasn't aware of the computer crime statute in particular," one account of the incident recalled.[51]

The Morris Worm wasn't the first program to do damage online; in 1987, at Lehigh University, the first destructive computer virus had been loosed on its network, but engineers were quick to contain it and it never left the campus, and just weeks before Morris's experiment ran amok, *Time* magazine had featured "computer viruses" in a goofy-looking cover story with cartoonish bugs crawling all over a desktop monitor. Yet the Morris Worm was something different—a national digital watershed, not least because it was the first time the word *Internet* was ever used in the *New York Times*.

Everyone agreed that Morris hadn't meant to cause actual damage. The Justice Department struggled with how to appropriately respond. The department's trial attorney overseeing the case, Mark Rasch, recalled that his colleagues were torn about whether the case was a felony or a misdemeanor. As he said later, the Justice Department feared creating a perception that actions like Morris took were cost-free. "If the government treated this as a misdemeanor, a trivial offense, others would go out and do it," Rasch said. "You had conduct that was planned, premeditated, that was deliberate, over periods of months, that caused massive disruption and expense to a wide number of different individuals."[52]

That was precisely the scenario the Computer Fraud and Abuse Act had been created to criminalize. But the case still raised numerous questions that prosecutors continue to struggle with to the present day; the Morris Worm continues today to be a literal law school textbook case about the complexity of computer crimes: How do you draw lines between when someone has "unauthorized" access to a computer system and when they have access but exceed their level of "authorization"? How should accidental destruction be measured against purposeful attacks? In the real world we have clear distinctions between negligent homicide or manslaughter and premeditated homicide—what are the digital equivalents? Should the prosecution of computer crimes lead—helping create and shape norms for cyber behavior—or should it follow, reflecting preexisting societal understandings?*

The government charged Morris with a single felony, the first such prosecution by the Justice Department under the Computer Fraud and Abuse Act, known as Title 18 US Code § 1030, or, as it would come to be known in prosecutor nomenclature, a "1030 violation."[53] At trial Morris freely admitted that he was the worm's creator and that he was sorry. The defense argued his intent: "It was not designed to cause permanent damage. It didn't break any machines. The virus didn't read anybody's private files and didn't steal any information and didn't put one dollar into Mr. Morris's pocket." The jury wasn't convinced—they

---

*Nearly a quarter century later, these questions are still largely unanswered; we'd see echoes of many of these hard questions in the story of another MIT graduate student, Aaron Swartz, who committed suicide in 2013 after being prosecuted under the Computer Fraud and Abuse Act for downloading journal articles from MIT's network.

found him guilty after six hours of deliberation.[54] Morris was ultimately sentenced to a fine of $10,000 and three years' probation, as well as 400 hours of community service.

The Morris Worm also pointed out the challenges in trying to respond to attacks online; Morris, fearful of what his worm had wrought, had tried to anonymously publish tips on how to kill it, but too much of the network had already been hit by the attack for his news to spread. Separately, teams at Berkeley and Purdue had each independently come up with their own ways to respond, but, again, their efforts to spread solutions were hampered by the worm's pervasiveness. Without access to their online networks, most systems administrators had no idea how to contact colleagues across the country; they'd never had a reason to share telephone numbers before. Most had never met each other in person—that was the beauty of the whole internet, after all. The simple trading of telephone numbers marked an early lesson in what would become the hallmark of a cyber response: resiliency, the need to plan for attacks and outages in advance to speed repairs and fixes.* Those frustrations—and the fear of more damaging attacks to come—led the Defense Advanced Research Projects Agency (DARPA) to fund and found the first coordination center for computer problems, a team at Carnegie Mellon known as the Computer Emergency Response Team Coordination Center, or CERT/CC for short.

⁘⁘⁘⁘⁘⁘⁘

The Morris Worm marked, in some ways, the last days of innocence for the internet—not just because of its damage or impact but because of larger technological shifts unfolding at the same time.[55] The online network was quickly morphing, growing with the invention of the World Wide Web in 1989—which both eased navigation for technical neophytes and expanded the graphic design possibilities of

---

* It was a theme we'd see for years, even in cases such as Sony, where the company had to switch to faxes and printed messages to communicate with its workforce. Even today, in advising sometimes even sophisticated organizations on their cyber response plans, I'm surprised at the number that haven't thought through alternate means of communications if their systems are compromised.

the internet—and the rise of dial-up services such as America Online (AOL), CompuServe, and Prodigy, which opened the internet experience up to ordinary families. Because of its original federal funding, it had been illegal for the first decades of its existence to use the internet for commerce, but that law changed in the early 1990s, and companies began to tentatively tiptoe into the digital world. That new energy and commercial interest helped drive a decline in the hobbyist, tinkering ethos. The military began to pay attention too; in December 1992, the Pentagon issued its first, then-classified directive on "Information Warfare."[56]

"Real" criminals hadn't ventured into the internet yet, either. In part that was because even amid the rise of dial-up services, it wasn't entirely clear that there was money to be made online. Yet it was clear to the internet's founding generation that their world was coming to an end. As the average American flocked into their world, hackers embraced their bad-boy image. Defcon was a conference that started in 1993 where first hundreds, then later thousands, of hackers flocked to Las Vegas for an annual trade show that featured numerous opportunities for bragging rights.

The government's role in policing the new digital world remained unclear. *Harper's* magazine hosted an online discussion titled "Is Computer Hacking a Crime?" Over eleven days, people gathered on a popular early online forum, known as the Whole Earth 'Lectronic Link, or the WELL, to debate the ethics and criminality of hacking. Was, in the words of Emmanuel Goldstein, the editor of *2600: The Hacker's Quarterly*, "electronic rummaging…the same as breaking and entering"?[57]* One famous hacker, known as Acid Phreak, declared in the debate, "There is no one hacker ethic. The hacker of old sought to find what the computer itself could do. There was nothing illegal about that. Today, hackers and phreaks are drawn to specific, often corporate systems. It's no wonder the other side is getting mad. We're always one step ahead."[58]

---

* The magazine was named for the 2,600-hertz sound used to fool the phone company's long-distance system.

The government continued to stumble its way through prosecutions and policy debates. The trial of one famous hacker, Craig Neidorf, collapsed when he showed that the file he was being prosecuted for stealing from the phone company was actually available to any member of the public who requested it and paid $14.[59] But government investigators were making tentative progress; as they investigated the hacker group Masters of Deception, who were battling online against Texas-based hackers Legion of Doom, the government for the first time installed what they then dubbed "datataps," wiretaps designed to intercept conversations between computers.[60] They brought high-tech equipment up from Washington and installed it in a special suite inside the World Trade Center, where the New York office of the Secret Service was located. "This is the crime of the future," declared US Attorney Otto Obermeier when he later announced the indictment of five hackers. "This kind of conduct will not be tolerated."[61] Journalists warned that the security problems ahead looked dire; the phone company systems and the online network, Tymnet, that the hackers had penetrated "look[ed] like a fortress" compared to the new World Wide Web, which had "virtually no security."[62]

Through the 1990s, the Communications Decency Act—which tried to severely restrict "indecent" content online—and the Clipper chip debate—where the Clinton administration proposed outfitting computers with encryption that only the government could decode—sparked online uproars among those who felt the government was treading on the inherent freedom that online space provided. As I went through law school, I followed the debates and declarations from John Perry Barlow and others about defending the unique sovereignty of the online space. Barlow, who raised cattle in Wyoming, recalls awakening to the challenges of cyberspace when an FBI agent, Richard Baxter, showed up at his ranch asking about the "New Prosthesis League," which was actually a hacking group known as Nu Prometheus League. Barlow had attended the Hackers Conference with phone phreakers like Steve Wozniak, and the FBI figured someone who had attended that conference might be able to help them track down the group that was stealing code from Apple Computer. "I knew Agent Baxter from before. I'd had livestock stolen when I was still in the cattle business, and he's a pretty good hand with livestock theft. But in this instance, he was at sea," Barlow recalled later.[63] Barlow spent two hours explaining to the FBI agent the crime he was investigating. "It was one of those conversion moments where I realized that here you have, you know, clueless, well-armed, insecure people roaming around in a place they don't understand—and it scares them. And nothing good can come of this." As Barlow said, "America was entering the Information Age with neither laws nor metaphors for the appropriate protection and conveyance of information itself."[64]

The Justice Department created a new role for prosecutors, known as computer and telecommunications coordinators, to work these cases, bringing assistant US attorneys to the FBI Academy at Quantico for training under the leadership of the then heads of CCIPS, Scott Charney and Marty Stansell-Gamm, and by the late 1990s, there was no denying that the gloss had come off the seemingly carefree days of hacking.[65] Hacker Kevin Mitnick, who had become something of a *cause celebre*, was arrested after three years on the run, bringing to an end more than fifteen years of cat-and-mouse games with authorities. "He was arguably the most wanted computer hacker in the world," Assistant US Attorney Kent Walker told the *New York Times* after Mitnick's capture.[66] Yet despite his notoriety, his capture was made possible only through the stubborn determination of private sector researchers, not the government. When he was finally located in North Carolina, the team that found him included a computer scientist, Tsutomu Shimomura, and a *New York Times* reporter, but there was nary an FBI agent in sight. The hacker was held without bail because the judge considered him dangerous when "armed with a keyboard."* Mitnick was ultimately sentenced to five years in prison; at his court proceedings, a plane circled overhead towing a "Free Kevin" sign.

---

*I worked with Walker years later, when he was Google's general counsel. Mitnick was prosecuted by a team that included Christopher Painter, who became one of the Justice Department's top cybercrime experts, a close colleague, and later the Obama administration's top "cyber ambassador" at the State Department.

Foreign adversaries were certainly beginning to realize how much espionage potential might exist online, and the US government was beginning to understand just how tightly its own operations were already linked to the digital world. The internet was a crisis waiting to happen; when the Pentagon organized a team of in-house hackers to test its own networks, they were easily able to hack 7,860 of the 8,932 systems they tried.[67] Almost no one noticed; only 390 users of the compromised machines detected their machine had been hacked—and only 20 actually took action, reporting the hacking.

Officials also raised alarms as the internet morphed from an occasional place of tinkering and exploration to a world powering everyday commerce and communication. Just two weeks after the May 1997 initial public offering of the new commerce website amazon.com, the FBI arrested a hacker named Carlos Salgado Jr., who went online by the name of Smak, and had stolen 100,000 credit cards from an internet provider. Salgado tried to sell them, on a CD-ROM, for $260,000 in cash—only to discover when he arrived at the smoking lounge at the San Francisco airport to make the exchange that his underworld contact was actually an undercover FBI agent. Salgado had been betrayed by an informant; agents were astounded when they realized that he possessed the equivalent of $1 billion in credit.[68] Salgado was perhaps the first hacker to figure out how much money there was to be made online stealing others' data. In a sign of just how new the landscape was, the FBI had the court records sealed to ensure that the customers whose credit cards were stolen would never know—the FBI and the business Salgado had targeted feared "loss of business due to perception by others that computer systems may be vulnerable."[69] The government at the time feared companies would simply cover up thefts rather than report them to the FBI if they thought their business might be at stake.

On January 28, 1998—while Washington was otherwise consumed by the bombshell of President Clinton's relationship with Monica Lewinsky—the US Senate Intelligence Committee convened an overlooked hearing about future threats to the country. Across the spectrum, leaders from the FBI, CIA, and the Defense Intelligence Agency

(DIA) pointed to the digital world.[70] In that hearing, FBI Deputy Director Bob "Bear" Bryant said, "We have a society that's terribly dependent upon computers and the service they perform for this nation. It's helped our economy. We're probably world leaders in computer technology. But it's also a vulnerability, and it could be used and is being used by criminals, by terrorists, by intelligence services and certainly by military services. And we have to basically put in the infrastructure and vehicles to protect this great nation from this type of attack."

The head of DIA, Lieutenant General Patrick Hughes, discussed how the intelligence community assesses adversaries—and how "surprise" attacks rarely actually were. There were, he said, three components to a potential threat: capability, intent, and will. The third was always the hardest to assess, he argued. "That's where most of the surprise actually has come from. We were not technically surprised about the capability in the past. We were surprised about the way in which or the circumstances in which this capability was put to use. We need to focus on that," he said.

It was a warning that proved all too true in the years ahead: in the digital world, capability rarely surprised us. Many of the cyber cases we faced in the years ahead instead were, in fact, all too predictable.

※※※※※

Just a week after that congressional hearing, on February 3, 1998, automated intrusion alarms went off at Andrews Air Force Base: someone had tried to break into an Air National Guard computer system. It was a so-called root-level intrusion, meaning the hacker had gained access to the main level of the system. The attack came at an ominous time. The military was on high alert; weapons inspections in Iraq had collapsed, and the air force was readying air strikes on Saddam Hussein's regime. Thousands of personnel were heading overseas for a potential attack.

Over the coming weeks, the digital attacks spread to Lackland Air Force Base, Kirtland Air Force Base, and others—seemingly every base at the center of the planned air campaign. Was this Iraq launching a preemptive attack or gathering critical intelligence? "It was a wake-up call," recalled Brigadier General Francis "Frank" Taylor, the head of the air force's Office of Special Investigations.[71]* The deputy secretary of defense, John Hamre, warned President Clinton that this might be "the first shots of a genuine cyber war."[72]

The hacking was sophisticated. Utilizing a known vulnerability in the UNIX operating system known as Solaris, whoever was behind the attacks would sneak inside the network, then install a "packet sniffer" to gain additional usernames and passwords, and create a new back door to ensure ongoing network access. Yet there was a twist. The hacker or hackers didn't appear to be doing anything once they gained access— there was no malware left behind.

The Pentagon enlisted the help of the Justice Department's new National Infrastructure Protection Center (NIPC), which had representatives of the FBI, NSA, and the military, among other agencies, and had been a creation of President Clinton's 1998 directive known as PDD-63 that tried to tackle emerging cyberthreats. The NIPC was meant to function as the government's premier cyber task force, "coordinating investigations, analysis, and warning in a multitude of jurisdictions, both domestically and internationally."[73]

The staff at the NIPC's watch center immediately realized what a threat the attack appeared to be. "On the receiving side, it really very much looks like the dot-mil environment is under attack at this point from this other nation-state," recalled Steven Chabinsky, one of the FBI team who worked the case. "Playing it out in real time—and keeping in mind that this is the first time we really saw a large-scale, across-the-board [attack] coming from one area intrusion set—there was

---

*Again underscoring how small these computer circles were inside government, General Taylor and I shared a Senate confirmation hearing in 2014, when I was nominated to take over the National Security Division and he was nominated to be undersecretary for intelligence and analysis at the Department of Homeland Security (DHS). Senator Dianne Feinstein joked at the time about the contrast between me, the very "young-looking" Justice Department nominee, and the "slightly more mature" general, who had had a 35-year career in the military, then had turned to the private sector, and was returning to government. Frank became a great colleague.

obviously the real possibility that we are, quote, unquote, under attack. You see the dynamics play out then between the interagency: If we are under attack, how are you sure of attribution? What is the appropriate response? And then you respond symmetrically."

They dubbed the case SOLAR SUNRISE, and began to trace the suspicious network connections, following some of them back to Emirnet, a United Arab Emirates internet provider that might've been a gateway to Iraq. Yet the investigation then took a surprising turn: investigators located two ISPs that the hackers appeared to rely upon, Maroon.com, in Texas, and Sonic.net, in California. The Maroon.com connection appeared to lead back to Israel, which was an unlikely source for an Iraqi attack. But FBI agents in San Francisco got a big break when they went to Sonic.net's offices: the internet provider explained that in the same time period of the suspicious military network attacks, they'd been contacted by Harvard and MIT network administrators who complained about hacking attempts from Sonic.net against the universities. In that case, the company had quickly identified two customers responsible: local high school students who went online by the nicknames Stimpy and Makaveli.

In mid-February—even as military troops were departing Andrews Air Force Base for operations in the Gulf—the FBI in San Francisco received court authorization to surveil the two high school students online. In an era of dial-up modems, a pen register device recorded the telephone calls from Stimpy's house to the internet service provider, then investigators watched online as the students talked in the Internet Relay Chat with an Israeli hacker who went by the name The Analyzer; the Israeli hacker appeared to be teaching the California teens how to hack in real time.

On February 25, Hamre discussed the SOLAR SUNRISE case at a media breakfast, calling it "the most organized and systematic [cyber] attack" yet seen, explaining that the culprits had been identified as California teens. The remarks, quickly trumpeted by the press, spooked the FBI. "Once the case became public, a lot of thoughts came across our mind. The first one, in particular in California, was to get to the sites as quickly as possible," FBI Supervisory Special Agent Scott K. Larson recalled.*

At 6:30 p.m. that night, the FBI raided both homes, serving search warrants. Special Agent Chris Beeson found Stimpy working at his bedroom computer, amid empty Pepsi cans and half-eaten cheeseburgers. "The individuals were online in chat channels as investigators entered the homes," Larson recalled. The teens quickly admitted their role and pointed investigators toward The Analyzer, a teen named Ehud Tenenbaum.[74] Forensic analysis showed that Tenenbaum might have hacked as many as 400 websites. It was in some ways a relatively innocent example of themes we saw echoes of in later years in a much darker way: young students trained online and radicalized, in a way, by someone unknown and overseas, to carry out attacks here at home.

Richard Clarke warned, "If two 14-year-olds could do that, think about what a determined foe could do."[75] It wasn't long before just that scenario presented itself.

///////////

In March 1998, the military reported a new hack at Wright-Patterson Air Force Base in Ohio, soon followed by another at the US Army Research Laboratory in Maryland. Staff at the Defense Information Systems Agency (DISA), the Pentagon's network engineers, thought the intrusions appeared to be coming from a London server and contacted the internet provider there for more details—only to discover logs that showed both numerous other compromised US systems and links back to a Moscow computer. DISA quickly called the FBI. In the months ahead, the attacker or attackers continued to expand the targets, hitting universities and commercial sites, as well as other government sites such as the Department of Energy's national labs, hacking computers at Los Alamos, Sandia, Lawrence Livermore, and Brookhaven.

---

*Larson and I later worked together at the FBI, where he went on to be chief of the Computer Investigations and Infrastructure Threat Assessment Program at FBI headquarters.

The intrusions found soft targets across the government and continued unabated for the rest of the year; investigators made little progress locating their foe. Whoever the hacker was, he was excellent; the intrusions, the Pentagon said, were "sophisticated, patient, and persistent." The hacker would even edit server logs to remove any sign of his presence. The FBI traced numerous leads through university websites, but in each case found the educational servers had just been a jumping-off point for the attackers. Mimicking the SOLAR SUNRISE case, investigators called the new intrusions MOONLIGHT MAZE. It was a sprawling investigation, involving cases and leads across 19 of the FBI's 56 field offices, pointing toward the coordination challenge that we long struggled with in cyber cases, where infected computers and digital evidence easily crisscrossed the geographical organization of the FBI and the Justice Department.

Circumstantial evidence continued to appear to point toward Russia: the FBI noted that the hacker or hackers worked "European business hours" and had taken off three notable days: Christmas Day 1998 and January 7 and 8, 1999, all Russian Orthodox holidays. The FBI turned to Kevin Mandia, a former air force special agent and one of the country's top digital investigators, for help, and his work showed that the hacker's original code had been written in Cyrillic.* It appeared someone from Russia was stealing government research—and doing it not as recreation, but as their office job. The hacker evidently knew exactly what to get. The modus operandi was consistent—upon entering a new network, the hacker would save the main directory list and then log off, returning hours, days, or weeks later to download apparently carefully chosen specific files relating to the government's advanced emerging technologies. Eventually, investigators came to believe that the hacker was actually working off a public Pentagon document, known as the "Military Critical Technologies List." As one military source later told journalist Thomas Rid, "This document served as the intruders' 'roadmap' through all Army and government systems."[76]

---

* Mandia later led the training session that first introduced me to computer crime at the Justice Department, and he remains a leader in the field to this day.

As the attacks approached the one-year mark, the government created a special coordination group comprising 40 representatives from nearly a score of Pentagon, law enforcement, and intelligence agencies; the team had T-shirts made, with the operation's logo—a moon overtop a blue and yellow labyrinth—on the front and the words "Byte Back!" printed on the reverse. Just days after the creation of the MOON-LIGHT MAZE coordination group, the broad outlines of attacks became public in an *ABC News* report titled "Target Pentagon: Cyber-Attack Mounted Through Russia."

Recently declassified documents show that investigators planted a "digital honeypot" on one of the compromised networks, an attractive-looking document that contained special code that would allow them to trace the path the document took once it was stolen.[77] The honeypot led them to a computer at the Russian Academy of Sciences. When presented with the evidence of Russian involvement, the military officer overseeing the Pentagon's response, Brigadier General John "Soup" Campbell, was left unsure how to respond in this new cyber arena; he asked the intelligence officer briefing him, "Are you saying that we're under attack? Should we declare war?"

The FBI wasn't sure how to proceed, faced with such an unprecedented case involving a foreign nation-state. With White House approval, it decided to walk through the front door and ask the Russian government for help. Amid generally warm relations between Clinton and Boris Yeltsin, cooperation was opening up between Russian and American law enforcement. According to author Thomas Rid, the FBI saw its opportunity in early 1999 when the Russian Ministry of Internal Affairs asked for help identifying the people behind a California website that had defamed Yeltsin's daughter. The FBI took the chance to ask for a favor of its own. As Rid recounts, investigators zeroed in on five specific MOONLIGHT MAZE intrusions, and over a March dinner in Washington, the FBI asked the Russian minister of internal affairs for help tracing them.[78]

A delegation of US investigators boarded a Delta flight to Moscow on April 2, 1999: two FBI agents, a language specialist, as well as a special agent from NASA and two personnel from the US Air Force Office of Special Investigations. Back in Washington, another special team of agents manned the FBI command post to aid coordination, working Moscow hours, from 11 p.m. to 6 p.m. Eastern Time.[79]

The gambit appeared promising at first. After a first night of vodka toasts and camaraderie, the Russians and Americans worked together productively, appearing to confirm that the hacks had been carried out by someone in Russia. But, after that, the FBI team quickly found themselves stymied, shunted off on unwanted sightseeing tours. The cooperative ministry official who had helped that first day disappeared. The new liaisons stonewalled the Americans, and there was no further cooperation from the Russians on the case.

It quickly became clear that this was not a criminal case, it was a national security one. The intrusions were likely carried out by Russian intelligence working under the express permission of the government. The early attempts at cooperation had been an intragovernmental miscommunication. Seeing its role at an end, the FBI shut down the investigation, even as the attackers continued to probe Pentagon networks in the months ahead. The attacks grew so persistent that the Pentagon for the first time required all of its computer users to change their passwords in an attempt to shore up network security. That August, the Pentagon officially inaugurated what it called the Joint Task Force–Computer Network Defense. In opening the new center, Hamre declared, "Cyberspace isn't just for geeks. It's for warriors now."[80]

⁂

Throughout government and the private sector, the arrival of the millennium underscored just how tightly organizations had integrated technology into their systems without realizing the potential downsides. As the final minutes of December 31, 1999, ticked away, Shawn Henry was locked inside the FBI's special Y2K command center. He— and hundreds of others across the government—nervously waited to see whether the millennium bug would wreak havoc. The Y2K problem was that computer programs that had relied on just two digits to display the year ("112189" for November 21, 1989, for instance) were suddenly presented with the prospect of their calculations being off by a century as 1999 ticked over to 2000.[81] People feared that planes would fall from the sky, ATMs would cease to function, and employee records or accounting software would go haywire as programs struggled to account for years of conflicting data.

Shawn had started working public corruption cases and been promoted eventually to be the unit chief of what was then known as the Computer Intrusion Center. It was hardly a glamorous position at the time. "I don't think anyone else applied for the job," he recalls. But at the dawn of the internet, it was a place to do interesting work. He helped usher through approval for the first FBI undercover investigation online. He'd been thrust into the front line of the government's rush to secure its digital infrastructure before the year's end. Billions of dollars went into rushed efforts to make systems Y2K compliant as technology became ever more central to American life.[82]

At precisely midnight, the lights in the command post went off; a gasp arose. Then laughter erupted as the lights flicked back on and everyone realized it was simply a prank. An agent had turned off the light switch. While problems spread the world over as the New Year marched time zone by time zone, most were minor. The world had dodged this one.

Shortly after 2000, new digital threats emerged—and the first mastermind was, again, a teen. Michael Calce had grown up online in the 1990s. "I was a pretty bratty kid. I come from a divorced family. My father had custody on the weekends and he wasn't exactly sure how to preoccupy me so he took a computer from his work and brought it home and was like 'Here, figure out what to do with it,'" Calce explained years later. When he got his first free trial of AOL, at age nine, he hacked the system to let him continue on the early internet service for free.[83] He continued experimenting and adopted the online moniker Mafiaboy. He used commonly available online hacker tools to gain control over loosely protected university networks and harnessed them into a powerful tool.

Early on the morning of Monday, February 7, 2000, at age 14, Calce unleashed a relatively new plague: a DDoS attack, which flooded a target website with traffic from thousands of hijacked, infected "zombie" computers—often without the original owner's knowledge that their computer had been taken over. He'd hoped to make a name for himself in the hacker world. "The overall purpose was to intimidate other hacker groups," Calce said later. "The whole of the hacking community was all about notoriety and exploration."[84]

It worked—all too well. By 10:30 a.m., Yahoo's website was fully clogged; half of users couldn't even access it. In the hours and days ahead, similar attacks hit eBay, Amazon, CNN, ZDNet.com, and other top websites. The high-profile attacks attracted immediate attention from the White House on down, and FBI investigators began to zero in on a suspect when they saw someone boasting in an internet chat about a DDoS target that hadn't yet been made public. "U just pin em so hard they can't even redirect," Mafiaboy said in one chat, then bragged about raising his sights: "I'm thinking something big. Maybe www.nasa.gov."[85]

As the FBI traced the suspect's internet connection back to Canada, they enlisted the help of the Royal Canadian Mounted Police. Within days, Calce noticed a suspicious utility truck parked at the end of his block and he knew the gig was up; soon, the Mounties arrested Mafiaboy. He eventually pleaded guilty to more than 55 charges. His court-appointed social worker testified in court that Mafiaboy "has shown no remorse, is likely to hack again, and needed a more structured life and help to sort out his 'moral reasoning.'"[86]

The FBI and the US government couldn't really believe they'd caught a 15-year-old boy—it had seemed a replay of the SOLAR SUNRISE investigation, as suspicion first fell on a foreign adversary and then settled on a more prosaic homegrown threat. As Chris Painter, who helped prosecute the case, recalled, "The same kind of debate went on—this must be a nation state; this is too sophisticated; it couldn't possibly be anything else—and it turns out to be a 15-year-old. It did show people that we're vulnerable, and I think that did create a lot of questions about how do you deal with these issues?"[87]

The case was serious—market analysts estimated damages topped $1 billion—and was trumpeted as a key, early victory in international law enforcement cooperation. Attorney General Janet Reno, who had been a major booster of early attempts to combat cybercrime and had evangelized the rising threat to the private sector, declared that the case showed "our capacity to track down cyber-criminals wherever they may be."[88]

Even as the attacks were ongoing, President Clinton convened an internet security summit, again repeating the frequent call-to-action that the country faced an imminent "electronic Pearl Harbor" and that the DDoS should be a "wake-up call." A month after the Mafiaboy attacks, the Justice Department launched a website, cybercrime.gov, meant to herald its new efforts online.[89]

Yet at the same time, it seemed hard to get worked up over a tech-savvy teen who wasn't legally old enough to drive. The DDoS attacks underscored the perilous weakness of the internet, even as the dot-com boom drove millions of people to the web and online commerce soared. A 15-year-old boy had knocked the world's top website offline.

"We now know that the internet wasn't designed to shoulder a new economy, and we'll need some fundamental improvements before a teenager will have any problem clogging up web sites," wrote tech journalist Kevin Poulsen two months after the Mafiaboy attacks. "Mafiaboy isn't the innocent child who pointed out that the Emperor has no clothes; he's one of many guilty children who pointed it out by throwing things at the Emperor's privates—a more serious offense."[90]

///////////////

That April, just a couple months into the new administration of George W. Bush and years before I was paying any attention to China—my nose was buried deep in the Institute of Global Prosperity tax fraud case at the time—a US Air Force EP-3 spy plane collided over the South China Sea with a Chinese fighter jet. The American plane, technically known as an ARIES II signals intelligence aircraft, had been on a routine six-hour mission from its base in Japan, monitoring electronic transmissions, when two Chinese fighters began harassing it about 70 miles away from the island of Hainan. One of the fast-moving, maneuverable jet fighters collided with the American plane, a slow turboprop that had been flying flat and level. The fighter crashed, killing the Chinese pilot, and the heavily damaged American plane was forced to make an emergency landing with its 24 crew on Hainan. The collision sparked a diplomatic crisis, as the plane's crew were held for ten days and the US government demanded the return of its sensitive aircraft.[91]

The incident, mostly forgotten today, touched off perhaps the first online skirmish in what would be years of low-grade cyberconflict between the two countries. While the Air Force crew were held as prisoners, a US hacker collective known as PoizonBOX defaced a number of Chinese websites with sayings like "We will hate China forever."

Chinese hackers retaliated.[92] On May 1, May Day—a national Chinese labor holiday—the White House website was knocked offline by a DDoS attack, deluged by a tsunami of malicious web traffic, enough to clog the system and have it grind to a halt. Similar incidents took place across government; a Department of the Interior website was defaced with a message reading, "Beat down Imperialism of American [sic]! Attack anti-Chinese arrogance!" More than 1,000 websites nationwide came under attack—seemingly without rhyme or reason. An Ohio school district's website played the Chinese national anthem as the country's red flag fluttered in a graphic.[93] American hackers, unaffiliated with the government, responded in kind, slapping insulting comments on Chinese websites. The incident seemed a strange novelty. The *New York Times*, which devoted seven paragraphs to the incident, called it the "First World Hacker War."*

We had no idea at the time just how common these online skirmishes would ultimately prove to be—in fact, one of the key players in the online skirmish was a group of patriotic civilian Chinese computer engineers at the Shanghai Jiao Tong University who were known as Javaphile; they had formed the year before to share development tips

---

* It was actually China's second hacker war. In 2000, Chinese hackers had defaced Japanese websites as part of an international dispute over Japanese atrocities against the Chinese city of Nanjing in World War II; hackers targeted more than 300 websites, including that of the Japanese prime minister.

on the programming language Java and had seized the opportunity to enlist in efforts to defend their homeland online in the weeks after the EP-3 collision. The group renamed themselves the Honker Union of China, a phrase that translated roughly as "red hacker," meant to evoke their patriotic motives.

At the time, especially amid the attempts to calm the international tensions after the Air Force crew was returned safely to the United States, the Communist Party appeared to distance themselves from the Honker Union, decrying the attacks on both sides as "web terrorism" and "unforgivable acts violating the law." It was years before we understood who was behind the Chinese attacks—and also years before we realized just what a harbinger of the future the incident was.[94] Within a decade, the Chinese government had a very different approach to cyberattacks.

///////////////

That spring, in May 2000, the "I Love You" virus hit, cascading across the internet as people clicked on email messages that purported to be a love letter from a friend but actually installed malware on their computer. "Of course, everybody wants to know who was enamored with them, so they all click on it and of course their computers were all infected with this virus," recalled Shawn Henry, the FBI computer crimes leader. The case challenged the FBI's organizational structure. "One of the things was in the past when there was some type of a criminal act, it was relatively clear where [the] venue was. It was in a particular city where the act took place," Henry recalled. Yet the "I Love You" virus had victims across all 50 states and all of the FBI's 56 Field Offices— each of which could then claim to have "venue." It fell to him as the FBI's computer intrusion unit chief to choose one; he settled on Newark, but then the case took an even more complicated turn. Following an intense investigation, agents traced the infection back to a young man in the Philippines. They were able to actually direct authorities in the Philippines right to the hacker's home to put handcuffs on him. "At the end of the day, the Philippine government had no law against what he did. So even though he was identified, even though he caused great monetary damage—and this got worldwide attention—nothing happened to him. They arrested him and then they let him go," Henry recalled. "What I got from that is that this is not merely a United States problem. This is a global problem."

That message resonated at the Justice Department. Even as the United States itself wrestled with how to tackle cyberthreats, Chris Painter and Justice Department colleagues began to push international partners to toughen computer crime laws—not just to bring their laws up to the US model but in some cases to actually go further, to push forward legally where US law still seemed too anemic for the challenge of cybercrime. Within months, the Philippines had updated its laws—and other countries followed suit.

Increasingly, though, the government seemed to be playing catch-up. As the dot-com boom transformed American life, bringing the internet into the daily routines of millions of people both at home and at work, hacking professionalized, too, morphing from a hobbyist's playground into a criminal's profit center. Gone was the era of the "roguish" phone-phreaker hackers like Kevin Mitnick; they were replaced by aggressive criminals focused not on exploration but on exploitation. The growing importance of email in daily life and the explosion of websites created new "attack vectors" and gave rise to spam, and the online commerce boom created opportunities for theft as well as the use of stolen credit cards.

///////////////

By 2001, when I transferred from Main Justice over to the US attorney's office in DC, just a couple of blocks away, I quickly became my team's go-to person on digital forensics and digital evidence. The DC US attorney's office is unique because the capital isn't a state but a federal district, which means that we had responsibility for prosecuting both typical federal crimes and the run-of-the-mill crimes that would normally be prosecuted elsewhere by local or state prosecutors. Over the years ahead, I rotated through prosecuting domestic violence cases, violent crime, and, eventually, homicides. Working as a DC assistant US attorney meant a near-constant flood of cases; I worked with an incredibly talented group of highly motivated lawyers—a class that has since gone on to the federal bench and leadership roles in government and the private sector. We first prosecuted misdemeanor cases—the prosecutorial equivalent of going through boot camp—but we must have been prosecuting the best prepared misdemeanor cases in the country.

The lofty mission of the Justice Department is about more than just imprisoning criminals; an early lesson I learned as an assistant US attorney was that a big part of the job is *not* prosecuting every case; the criminal justice system can be too blunt an instrument for many desired solutions. Much of being a prosecutor is meeting with victims, talking with them, and making sure to understand what "justice" represents for them—what remedies or solutions do they want? This applies to domestic violence victims, victims of drug addicts, and victims of gun crimes. You have to treat a scourge not just case by case, but by examining all the various tools the federal government could bring to bear on a given issue. I found this approach, sometimes called "community policing," also applied in cybercrime and intellectual property cases.

Chris Painter, who was one of the Justice Department's early leaders on cybercrime, recalled how long it took for the FBI to wrap its mind around how to approach such cases. In the early days, the FBI would come into a business that had been hacked like a bull in a china shop, paralyzing business operations in order to collect evidence. "Even in the late '90s we had sporadic instances within the bureau where we'd hear stories of the FBI going in, and in order to preserve the data they would, basically, seize the machines of the victims—take them offline for a long time. We took care of that right away," he recalled. "That didn't end up repeating itself. The stories repeated themselves, but fortunately we were able to make sure that we were protecting the victims, we recognized them as being ongoing concerns. We were trying to get the information that we needed while at the same time being able to allow the business to proceed."

⁄⁄⁄⁄⁄⁄⁄⁄⁄⁄⁄⁄⁄⁄⁄⁄

Digital evidence was increasingly part of every case, not just "computer crimes." We were learning how to gather information on criminals' habits online, track cell phone records, search emails, and read a browsing history. I'd always kept up my interest in digital crime, and in 2004 I received a call from Stevan E. Bunnell, who headed the office's fraud unit, asking me to become the office's computer hacking and intellectual property prosecutor.

The new role gave me a front-row seat to the rising threat. I traveled down to the National Advocacy Center, a stately Georgian-style building on the campus of the University of South Carolina, which runs most of the Justice Department's training exercises. There, I attended one high-energy training led by a cybersecurity expert name Kevin Mandia; he was wearing an oversized Paula Abdul–style headset, animatedly moving around the room as he led this group of buttoned-up government prosecutors in exercises combatting computer hackers. He gave us all hacker software and led us through various criminal schemes, variously playing the hacker or the digital forensics investigator. None of us left South Carolina expert hackers, but we at least understood the technology well enough to translate it into legal documents and, eventually, courtrooms.

As federal prosecutors, we were handed cases from across the government. At the time, the FBI was still totally consumed by its post-9/11 counterterrorism push and hadn't yet begun to pay much attention to cyberthreats. Instead, many of the best cases we worked came from other agencies, such as the Secret Service, which had responsibility for financial crimes, the postal inspectors, the Pentagon's inspector general, and the Air Force Office of Special Investigations, where Mandia had actually gotten his start as a special agent.

The web had turned out to be a great organizing tool for criminals themselves; hacking forums such as Counterfeit Library, CarderPlanet .com, and ShadowCrew proliferated, sometimes gathering thousands of members who shared tips, traded tools, and sold purloined identities and credit card numbers. A "full info"—which included a name, address, Social Security number, and mother's maiden name—could be had for about $30.[95] These "carders" saw their work very much as businesses and even organized themselves into a trade conference: they marked the first birthday of CarderPlanet by hosting a few dozen criminals, out of more than 400 who had applied, at the first world-wide carders conference in Odessa in 2002.[96] These online bazaars of stolen goods were highly sophisticated, offering Amazon-style reviews of products, escrow services, and even the ability to test stolen credit cards to ensure you were buying legitimate, usable stolen data—all tools meant to instill confidence in marketplaces where, by definition, everyone involved was a criminal.

Much of early cybercrime focused on so-called carding schemes, stealing credit card numbers, counterfeiting cards, and identity theft scams that allowed criminals to make illegitimate purchases. US customers were particularly susceptible because American credit card companies had been slow to adopt the card security measures prevalent in Europe. Plus, their model of passing along fraud costs to the affected merchant meant that Visa and Mastercard managed to turn a profit even on stolen cards.

Many Russian online crime forums were located in a small number of what were known as "bulletproof hosting" facilities, data centers that specifically touted their willingness to flaunt the law and embrace criminal or controversial online content; these sites, mostly located inside Russia or in Eastern Europe, charged exorbitant fees—ten times or more the price of legitimate hosting sites—but the fees were part of a business model that often involved payoffs to corrupt local police or government officials who looked the other way at the hosting facility's criminal links.[97] In a pattern that has persisted straight through to today, most online criminals were left alone by the Russian government as long as they focused their activities outside of the country—stealing from foreigners and robbing banks overseas. Besides, many Eastern European nations either didn't have computer crime statutes at all or didn't enforce them, meaning that the crimes were almost risk-free. The best known of these bulletproof hosts, notorious to investigators and webmasters online, was the Russian Business Network (RBN), a group based in St. Petersburg that was the vanguard of a new type of Russian organized crime. "The Russian mafia is behind RBN, and they have big guns and small morals," one observer said at the time.[98]

Russian and Eastern European organized crime was markedly different than the Sicilian Cosa Nostra; rather than based on family or community ties, it was driven by an entrepreneurial spirit that saw criminal organizations come together to seize interesting opportunities. Bitter rivals one day might very well be found in business together the next if the money and risk were right.[99]*

In the early days of online crime, these digital criminals ran sophisticated and ambitious but unimaginative enterprises. They focused on offline crimes transported to the digital world—the trading of child pornography or financial "scare" schemes that had long plagued people on the telephone, like when a fraudster called claiming to be from the electric company and insisting to be paid for an overdue bill right then or the resident's electricity would be shut off.

These cases were often known as "1029s," a reference to Title 18 US Code § 1029, the statute that dealt with "fraud and related activity in connection with access devices," or identity theft.[100] The statute had grown out of the same efforts in the 1980s that led to the Computer Fraud and Abuse Act and then was further refined in the "get tough on crime" efforts of the early 1990s, a little-noted provision included in the massive 356-page 1994 Violent Crime Control and Law Enforcement Act that famously included funding for 100,000 new cops, the assault weapons ban, the creation of sex offender registries, the Violence Against Women Act, and the expansion of the federal death penalty. Later revisions and expansions of the law accepted that local and state authorities struggled with the expertise to prosecute computer crime and recognized that such investigations should increasingly be the primary jurisdiction of the federal government, specifically the Secret Service.[101]

The bulletproof hosts powered an online scourge of spam email in the late 1990s and early 2000s; at its peak, more than 90 percent of the world's email was unsolicited junk. Spam encouraged recipients to purchase penny stocks in pump-and-dump schemes or to illegally

---

*In the early days of online crime, the competition between rival gangs regularly turned violent; in 2004, one Russian gangster, who ran an online payments system aimed at facilitating child porn, kidnapped a rival payment operator and demanded a million dollars in ransom.

purchase pharmaceuticals online, such as erectile-dysfunction drugs like Viagra and Cialis or even lifesaving cancer medications. Far from fly-by-night organizations, these knockoff online pharmacies operated sophisticated customer-service centers that helped ensure satisfied customers and stayed off the radar of payment companies such as Visa and Mastercard. The online tide of spam was powered by malware installed unwittingly on tens of thousands of computers around the world that had been harnessed together into botnets controlled by criminals. One such botnet, built through the spreading of the Storm Worm, had been single-handedly responsible for one out of every five spam emails globally.[102]

Over time, these organized crime groups realized that running the botnets could be lucrative in and of itself—allowing them a platform that they could rent out to other criminals to facilitate all manner of schemes online or to spread specific pieces of malware for a price. One spam king, Peter Yuryevich Levashov, also known as Peter Severa, or Peter of the North, rented his botnet out for between $200 and $500 per million pieces of spam, and then also took a cut of the referral traffic his spam emails generated; such schemes netted him upward of $600,000 over a three-year period, according to records that leaked online.[103]*

The scourge of Eastern European cybercrime presented us with interesting lessons about criminality and the elasticity of these online crime markets; many of the carders and hackers working in places like Russia were talented engineers who had little legitimate opportunity to use their skills. The former Soviet Union countries had excelled in technical education, but the collapse of most of their economies in the 1990s and the lack of mature business climates meant there were far more computer scientists than there were high-tech jobs. Many hackers were actively seeking legitimate, well-paying opportunities for work. More than one Russian hacker was uncovered by investigators through undercover operations that had them apply for

---

*Levashov, perhaps the world's most notorious spammer and a master of botnets, was finally arrested in 2017 while on vacation in Spain and was extradited in 2018 to Connecticut to stand trial.

legit jobs; agents or informants inside these criminal forums simply told a target that they had a lead on a possible job, and the hacker happily sent over a resumé listing his actual name and professional background.[104]*

Hacking efforts often amounted to an old-fashioned shakedown: a criminal accessed a company's network, then demanded a "security consulting fee" to tell the company how he got inside and to keep it quiet. Maksym Igor Popov broke into the network of eMoney, a payment processor, and Western Union, in July 2000 and then tried to charge the companies "fees" that ranged up to $500,000.[105] When the FBI finally arrested Popov, Special Agent E. J. Hilbert, himself a former (noncriminal) hacker who had used the moniker Idolin, realized he might be the perfect person to infiltrate these crime forums. "I truly respect your skill set," Hilbert told the Ukrainian hacker.[106] As Kevin Poulsen re-created for *WIRED*, they partnered for years in an operation, code-named ANT CITY, where Popov spent hours a day in an FBI conference room plying the online forums, talking with other hackers, and gaining intelligence—and then each night returned to his prison cell. The operation came to an end only when Popov finished his sentence and went home to Ukraine.[107]

The FBI was learning cybercrime the hard way, realizing how exposed its systems could be. According to Poulsen's reporting, Agent Hilbert got word on New Year's Eve 2004 that a gang called X.25 had penetrated some AT&T servers in New Jersey that ran the FBI's network. The hackers had stolen documents that included a spreadsheet of more than 100 of the FBI and Secret Service's top cybercrime targets, including compromising notations like "cooperating with the government." Inadvertently, the FBI paid Popov, who was already back in

---

* The money in crime, meanwhile, was steady and lucrative—competitive even with the private sector at the time, ensuring that talented engineers in Russia or Eastern Europe could be lured away from legitimate jobs for an easy life of crime. Botnet owners and spam empires even advertised jobs online, writing postings like, "local office in Moscow (benefits package included), full-time (9 hours per day, 5 days a week)" with "the salary for a probationary period $1.5K (1 month), after $2K+."

Ukraine, $10,000 to try to recapture the information, without realizing that their informant was actually one of the people who perpetrated the hack.[108]*

//////////

The rising insecurity of the digital world was on display as authorities struggled in 2003 and 2004 against the rise of damaging computer viruses—known as SoBig and Bagle, each version more virulent and effective than the last, the latest iterations of the threat made famous by the Morris Worm 15 years earlier. In its first two days in the wild in August 2003, SoBig caused an estimated $50 million in damages in the United States, interrupted operations at Air Canada, and crippled computers at Lockheed Martin. "Bagle had the distinction of being the first truly commercial virus," Joseph Menn wrote in *Fatal System Error*.[109]

Viruses and worms obviously weren't new; the Morris Worm and the Melissa virus in 1999 had marked the arrival of mass-market computer infections, but whereas in both of those cases the inventors were arrested and sentenced, the minds behind SoBig and Bagle remained stubbornly at large.

The viruses burrowed into unsuspecting computers and harnessed tens of thousands of infected computers for massive spam email campaigns. Spam had long dogged the internet, predating, in fact, even the broad use of the World Wide Web; the term, a reference to a Monty Python skit that mocked the canned ham, was first used in 1993 when a software bug in Usenet forums led to the accidental posting of 200 copies of the same message.[110] In subsequent years, its meaning broadened to include all the get-rich-quick schemes and scams offered in unwanted emails. But the new generation of viruses allowed criminals, often from Eastern Europe, to supersize their spam empires, causing millions in damages to infected computers, even as US authorities seemed powerless to stop them.

---

* The main target for the hack, Leonid "Eadle" Sokolov, indicted in New Jersey, remains at large today.

The FBI appeared unable to make progress against the viruses. Not even a $250,000 reward from Microsoft led to any breaks in the SoBig case; private security researchers collected evidence and turned it over to the FBI, but months went by without action. Finally, those industry researchers took some tentative steps toward the strategy we would later adopt at the Justice Department, a "name and shame" approach that, even if the creator avoided prosecution, might cause him to alter future behavior. They pointed a finger publicly at Ruslan Ibragimov, a Russian who ran a spam service called Send-Safe. In a blog post and nearly 50-page technical treatise titled "Who Wrote Sobig?", they published evidence linking him to the virus and the subsequent spam. The anonymous paper compared Send-Safe's software with the code for SoBig, concluding the similarities "should be considered as significant as finding a fingerprint on a murder weapon."[111] Even as he publicly denied the allegations, the researchers urged his hosting company, MCI, to dump him as a client—it did, along with the next two companies Send-Safe tried to restart with.[112]* It was one of the first vigilante-justice movements to police the web in the absence of formal government charges.[113]

————

While agents like Chris Beeson had pioneered many of the FBI's computer crime efforts in the 1990s, the pool of talented agents focused on cyberspace remained tiny inside the bureau. Particularly in the face of the constant, grinding terrorism threat, cybersecurity remained not exactly a career backwater but certainly an area that wasn't capturing a lot of high-level attention. In its own way, though, that meant dedicated agents could put together fascinating cases with little attention from headquarters.

The star of the bureau's cyber efforts in the early 2000s was J. Keith Mularski, who grew up around Pittsburgh and whose bubbly and gregarious personality stood starkly at odds with the traditional stoic

---

* Privately, the authors of the paper said they suspected that the "real force" behind SoBig was a customer with "special needs," i.e., a Russian government operation.

G-man persona. He spent his first seven years in the FBI working espionage and terrorism cases in Washington, DC, but put in for a transfer back to his hometown as soon as he saw a 2004 posting for a new cyber initiative in Pittsburgh.

At the time, he knew little about computers and taught himself as he dove deeper into a two-year undercover investigation deep in the online forum DarkMarket, chasing identity thieves. He'd realized early on that hackers were the mafia of the 21st century—that there was an organization and hierarchy to what seemed like a chaotic shadow world online.

During the case, Mularski—using the online identity Master Splyntr, a name plucked from his son's fascination with the Teenage Mutant Ninja Turtles—impersonated an Eastern European spammer with the pseudonym Pavel Kaminski. He partnered with the antispam website SpamHaus to "backstop" his online identity; SpamHaus tracked for industry and investigators the world's top spammers, who all feared the attention that came with an entry on SpamHaus's ROKSO, the Register of Known Spam Operations, the private sector's equivalent of a Most Wanted list. Mularski asked for "Master Splyntr" to be entered on the list, labeled one of the world's worst, which would help establish his bona fides for other criminals online. Then, for months, he explored the world of carding from his computer in Pittsburgh, guided by strict Justice Department regulations that governed how he could interact with others online. As he got deeper into the world of carders, he applied to FBI superiors for greater latitude to interact with the criminals online in an undercover capacity. First, he received permission for what's known as Group II operations, which allowed him to have increased contact with the criminals on DarkMarket and other forums, and later, he successfully sought authorization for what's known as Group I operations, a category reserved for highly sensitive operations that must be approved at FBI headquarters.[114] The ploy worked. Each day, a simple FBI computer script crawled the online forum and identified stolen credit cards and passed their details along to Visa and Mastercard to be canceled. Mularski sat at home in the evening, his laptop open, chatting with criminals the world over.[115] Over time, he gained the trust of other members of the criminal forum and, in an incredible coup, ended up becoming DarkMarket's administrator, access that helped investigators make international arrests of 60 people across three continents. The case demonstrated the power of studying a criminal community and establishing relationships within it, instead of just arresting the first bad guy you saw.

From there, Mularski and his Pittsburgh colleagues, drawing upon local resources such as Carnegie Mellon, grew the city into one of the top cybercrime centers in the country; the US Secret Service squad in Pittsburgh investigated and ultimately prosecuted other major crime forums, including the site CardersMarket, where its leader, Iceman, whose real name was Max Butler, received the longest sentence yet for a cybercrime, 13 years in prison.

Such cases inspired Mularski, who has remained at the forefront of the FBI's cyber efforts to the present day. A decade after his first cases in Pittsburgh, Mularski—along with his Pittsburgh colleagues, such as Luke Dembosky, who prosecuted Iceman—became a critical leader in our fight against China and also went on to be a major part of our efforts at the Justice Department to pursue national security cyberthreats. As he recalls, "[Pittsburgh] was the place to be."

※※※※※※

Not long after DIGITAL GRIDLOCK, I ended up in the midst of another computer case when the FBI's Computer Intrusion Squad in the Washington Field Office reported a breach of seemingly monumental proportions. It appeared that the FBI's entire computer network had been compromised. The investigation quickly zeroed in on Joseph T. Colon, an IT support contractor for BAE Systems in his mid-20s who worked at the FBI's Springfield, Illinois, Field Office. At first glance, the case seemed a worst-case scenario: Colon, who had arrived at the FBI in December 2003, had cracked the passwords of every FBI employee, including FBI Director Robert Mueller himself.[116] Little noticed at the time, the case showed the threat from a trusted insider and in many ways foreshadowed Edward Snowden years later—a young, frustrated contractor who used his legitimate network access to rampage through sensitive systems in ways never intended.

As we discovered in the investigation, in March 2004, just months after he arrived at the FBI office, Colon had penetrated the classified network with two easy-to-use hacking programs downloaded from the internet—*Pwdump3.exe* and L0phtcrack, a well-known tool created in the 1990s by one of the nation's first hacker groups, a so-called hacker think tank in Boston. It was a great example of the gray area in which many pieces of what is commonly lumped together as malware exist, a piece of software that was written by "good guys" and used regularly by network security teams to analyze their own networks, but that could also be easily repurposed to nefarious ends.

Its original creators, L0pht Heavy Industries, had become famous in the 1990s as "gray hat" hackers, existing online somewhere between the "white hat" good guys and the "black hat" bad guys, and had been warning for years about the vulnerabilities that permeated the internet.

The group of about seven hackers worked in IT security by day and found themselves frustrated by the lack of attention most companies paid to their network protections. Their name "L0pht," sounded phonetically, came from the fact that two of the founders shared a loft space with the hat business that their wives ran. In that space, decorated with the *Battlezone* arcade game and cast-off computers collected from across Boston, they teased big companies such as Microsoft for what they called "kindergarten crypto," easy-to-break encryption that was supposed to protect users.[117]

They'd become in some ways the US government's stand-in for the world of hackers; White House Counterterrorism Coordinator Richard Clarke traveled to Harvard Square to meet with them and learn about this new digital underworld. He watched in awe as at their warehouse gathering spot they showed him how they cracked passwords and intercepted satellite communications.[118]

In May 1998, the seven of them actually testified before the US Senate Committee on Governmental Affairs; committee chairman Fred Thompson introduced them by reading off their seven hacker names—the first people to testify before Congress under pseudonyms other than people in the Witness Protection Program: Brian Oblivion, Kingpin, Tan, Space Rogue, Weld Pond, Mudge, and Stefan von Neumann.[119] They warned just how vulnerable the internet was to nefarious actors—too many companies didn't pay enough attention to security up front, too many companies didn't adequately protect their own systems, too many companies undermined their already weak security measures with shortcuts or by allowing easily guessable passwords. One network L0pht studied had 700 users all with the same password: "CHANGEME." Neumann told the senators that "until high-visibility disasters occur, few people are willing to admit that something drastic needs to be done. It may take a Chernobyl-scale event to raise awareness levels adequately." At the hearing, Senator Joe Lieberman called them the Paul Revere of the digital age. Unfortunately, those warnings from 1998 continued to sound familiar to those of us who worked on these issues over the next twenty years.

The hackers released L0phtcrack as a way to demonstrate how easily crackable most passwords were. When it was released in 1998, L0phtcrack could crack an eight-character password in about 24 hours using a standard Pentium II computer.[120] It only got easier as computing power increased. By 2004, when Joseph Colon downloaded it, L0phtcrack had become a standard online tool for hackers, as was *Pwdump3.exe*, which had been written in the late 1990s, too.*

At the FBI, Colon had launched a brute-force password-guessing attack, overwhelming the system with guesses until he was able to access the Security Account Manager (SAM) database that held the passwords for the FBI's 38,000 computer users. The SAM database encrypted the passwords using a 128-bit algorithm to translate each user's password into a long string of apparent gibberish known as a "hash."

Once inside the database, he used *Pwdump3.exe* to extract all of the "hashed" passwords into a file he could download and store himself. Then, with all the time in the world, he ran L0phtcrack to decrypt the

---

* The tools are also good illustrations of how little hacking has changed in decades; to this day, L0phtcrack and *Pwdump3.exe* remain central tools for hackers, and I run across them all too often in hacks I'm working on even as a private sector lawyer in 2018.

hashed passwords; the program would crack the encryption algorithm by relying upon techniques like dictionary word comparisons, lists of common passwords, and character substitutions to decipher what each password actually was. It didn't take long before he had the plain-text computer password for every single person in the FBI and the ability to access every file saved on the FBI system. Since the FBI then required users to change their passwords every 90 days, Colon repeated the feat in May, again in July, and once more in November.[121] For nearly a year, Colon had "God-level access" to the FBI's system.

As we realized what Colon had accomplished, we wondered: Did we have a spy in our midst? The answer was stranger and more banal than imagined. As the investigation made clear, Colon actually intended to use his access for good; as he'd started his IT work, he'd become frustrated with the FBI's bureaucracy—routine tasks, from setting up a computer to adding a new printer to migrating a computer's operating system, all required an "IT ticket," in writing, and authorization from the FBI's DC Field Office. But by stealing the passwords for more powerful users on the system, Colon was able to bypass the normal network restrictions and do such wild and crazy things as add a new printer to the network. "It was motivated by a desire to do a good job for the FBI and see the [computer project] completed in time and under budget," his lawyers wrote later in a court filing. "Other than congratulations for a job well done there was nothing in it for Mr. Colon. His motivations though misguided were pure."

Colon had inadvertently exposed just how vulnerable the bureau's network was—the system was relatively flat, meaning that it was easy to move among the different units, and little was compartmented for security purposes. There was a lot we could learn to prevent a future incident. The FBI ultimately invested thousands of hours and millions of dollars to secure the vulnerabilities that Colon demonstrated.*

---

*These were odd cases to work as a prosecutor; we were learning how broad a set of "actors" we faced in cyberspace—and how you never knew who was on the other end of the keyboard until you solved the case. There was a certain letdown that came from discovering, late in a case, that you weren't chasing sophisticated terrorists, spies, or criminals, but some teen out for the digital equivalent of a Saturday joyride.

In my role at the US attorney's office, I was only responsible for the criminal side of these cybercrime cases; whenever we traced a computer intrusion overseas, the case disappeared from my desk. If we suspected a nation-state was behind a particular intrusion, it was transferred over to a special unit of investigators who focused on cases related to national security and foreign counterintelligence. Even though we supposedly worked for the same office, the investigators in that unit worked entirely apart, behind a locked door, inside of what was known as a Sensitive Compartmentalized Information Facility, a SCIF in government parlance, which was protected against electronic eavesdropping. I never learned what happened to the cases that disappeared behind that locked door into the SCIF—and, given how much was on my plate, I didn't really care.

The false dividing line between the "intelligence" world and the "criminal" world had long been a problem in the Justice Department, the FBI, and the US government writ large. In fact, Justice Department rules that drew the same false distinction in terrorism cases had deeply complicated efforts to chase and stop al-Qaeda in the years before 9/11. The so-called Chinese wall between intel and law enforcement meant that the CIA refused to share all it knew with the FBI, and even within the FBI, agents were often reluctant to share what they knew with each other. Agents sitting right next to each other would refuse to share their information, making arrests and surveillance more difficult.

The distinction between "intelligence" and "criminal evidence" had grown out of the post-Watergate reforms, as the Church Committee recommended that the government take active steps to rein in wiretapping and surveillance powers after a series of scandals. Those powers should be tightly grounded in the Justice Department, the commission led by Senator Frank Church declared, saying that the attorney general "as the chief legal officer of the United States" was "the most appropriate official to be charged with ensuring that... intelligence agencies conduct their activities in accordance with the law."[122] As part of that answer, Congress passed in 1978 the Foreign Intelligence Surveillance Act (FISA), a law meant to provide a clear roadmap—and the only roadmap—for conducting electronic surveillance to obtain foreign intelligence information within the United States. The CIA had much greater leeway overseas, but inside the United States, intelligence gathering was the sole purview of the FBI and it would be tightly controlled by a series of checks and balances that include all three branches of government. To gain permission to conduct surveillance in an intelligence matter, the FBI—through the Justice Department—had to apply for a "FISA warrant" with the newly established Foreign Intelligence Surveillance Court (FISC), staffed by federal judges (currently 11 of them) who are appointed to the FISA court by the chief justice of the United States and who rotate through the court on a part-time basis. This new regime would be supervised by strict oversight by Congress and inspectors general.

The balance between civil liberties and security is a constantly swinging and shifting pendulum in a free society. As originally drafted, the FISA law had required that national security officials swear, when seeking a warrant, that "the purpose" of the application was to obtain "foreign intelligence." Over the 1990s, the FISC interpreted that phrase narrowly, drawing a firm line between "intelligence" and anything that might actually be a criminal prosecution—even if that prosecution was aimed at a spy or a terrorist. Those court rulings and subsequent Justice Department procedures created a culture where intelligence information was kept separate from law enforcement—a culture that hurt law enforcement's ability to advance national security by taking criminals off the streets.

The catastrophic intelligence failures that enabled 9/11 proved the folly of such a distinction; after it happened, Congress and the Bush administration worked to break down the "Chinese wall" between law enforcement and intelligence—while maintaining the underlying protections for civil liberties. Through his years as director, Robert Mueller always hammered the theme that these reforms didn't come with any compromises in terms of civil liberties. The FBI had suffered dark chapters in its past, to be sure, but Mueller always believed that core to the FBI's culture was that it could do its job while respecting the Constitution. As he said at the FBI's 100th anniversary, "While it is a time of change in the FBI, our values will never change. It is not enough to stop the terrorist—we must stop him while maintaining his civil liberties. It is not enough to catch the criminal—we must catch him while respecting his civil rights. It is not enough to prevent foreign countries from stealing our secrets—we must prevent that from happening while still upholding the rule of law. The rule of law, civil liberties, and civil rights—these are not our burdens. They are what make us better."[123]

The reforms—marrying up the intelligence side and the law enforcement side—had been enormously successful on the counterterrorism side, helping the country fight terrorists with a united front. The FBI came up with constitutional and legal procedures to access and share intelligence with other agencies, to know how to "connect the dots" better, and to understand better how the terrorism threat was evolving at speed. The combination of reforms, renewed focus and vigilance, and new emphasis within the FBI had worked, too; the whole-of-government "all-tools" approach to terrorism had kept Americans safe for years since 9/11.

However, the same problem was unfolding in the cybercrime area—we falsely divided the world between cyber intelligence and cyber law enforcement. From my desk on the law enforcement side at the US attorney's office, I didn't understand precisely how bad the information-sharing problem was and just how much intelligence I was never seeing. Then, in January 2007, I transferred back to Main Justice to be the national coordinator for computer hacking and intellectual property crimes. I finally began to see the intelligence side.

And that's when I first realized just how much of a problem China was.

CHAPTER 2

Comment Crew

EARLY ONE MORNING in August 2006, FBI Agents Kevin Moberly and Bill Baoerjin snuck down Grovewood Lane in Orange, California. The dark suburban neighborhood outside Santa Ana still slumbered. They used flashlights with red filters to preserve their night vision as they covertly approached the target house. As glamorous as being an FBI agent might seem, investigatory work isn't always fun—and on this particular morning, they had an unpleasant task: rooting through their suspect's two trash cans. First one—remaining as quiet as possible while rooting through a week's worth of household detritus—and then the other. They didn't have enough time—or light—to look closely, so anything interesting went into a bag to take back to the office. It wasn't until later, when they untied a stack of Chinese-language newspapers back at the FBI office, that they knew what they'd found.

There, plain as day, tucked carefully between the newspapers, lay documents that clearly belonged to Rockwell and Boeing, the massive government contractors that had employed their suspect, Dongfan Chung, until his retirement.

The next month, the agents returned to formally search Chung's house; inside a room in the home's unfinished basement there were thousands more documents from Chung's former employers. As FBI agents later pieced together, Chung had been giving away technical details of America's aviation projects since 1985, when he'd returned from a vacation in China with an eight-page list of questions provided by the Nanchang Aircraft Manufacturing Corporation. Months later, he delivered the answers—including 27 engineering manuals—to the Chinese consulate in San Francisco, where they were sent out of the country via diplomatic pouch. His work continued for years and—despite appearing to only have a modest salary from his employer, Rockwell—Chung amassed a small real estate empire, including an auto-repair shop, three rental apartments, and two houses.[1] While the money from the Chinese government certainly was one lure, Chung was also ideologically committed to his homeland; as he wrote in one letter, "I would like to make an effort to contribute to the Four Modernizations of China," referring to the government's effort to improve the country's agriculture, industry, science and technology, and national defense. In turn, an aviation ministry official wrote to Chung, "It is your honor and China's fortune that you are able to realize your wish of dedicating yourself to the service of your country."[2]

By the time they arrested Chung, FBI agents had excavated more than 150 boxes of engineering reports and related material, collecting over their searches a total of about 250,000 sensitive documents relating to programs like the B-1 bomber, the F-15, the B-52, the Chinook helicopter, and even the space shuttle—as well as other critical defense projects. It was a massive, logistical nightmare for someone looking to hand over those documents to a foreign government in terms of both sneaking them out of a workplace undetected and delivering such a physical volume to dead drops or a handler.

Chung's trial marked a significant milestone: he became the first American in history convicted of economic espionage, and the court sentenced him to more than fifteen years in prison. Yet it would be just the first of a growing wave of such cases—in fact, it was just one of more than a dozen cases of Chinese espionage that unfolded in 2006 alone.

The theft shifted dramatically even as Chung faced trial; it might have been the last classic espionage case of the 20th century. The problem of 21st-century espionage that I would confront in the months and years ahead became evident in a related case: a few months earlier, the FBI had arrested Chi Mak—the man who ultimately pointed agents toward Chung. Another defense contractor, Mak had been passing

secrets, primarily about the US Navy, for decades. At trial, federal prosecutors called him "the perfect sleeper agent," arguing that Mak had
been an active Chinese intelligence officer, dispatched to the United
States in the 1970s with the hope that he'd establish himself and gain
access to our country's secrets.[3]

He represented just one part of what one US official told the *Washington Post* was China's "intellectual vacuum cleaner," a network of intelligence officers, engineering students, and advanced scientists who
specifically targeted economic and defense secrets that would help
China rapidly catch up with America's technological lead.

Brett Kingstone, a businessman who had faced Chinese-sponsored
theft at his own company, told one newspaper, "There are over 3,500
operatives in the US masquerading as students or on H1B visas [spe-
cial work visas] for the sole purpose of getting jobs in American manufacturing or defense industries for the sole purpose of stealing secrets
for the Chinese government."[4] Together, they formed a highly coordinated, advanced, and persistent effort to grow China's domestic capacity. China in ancient times had been one of the world's most innovative
forces, the country behind everything from paper to gunpowder to
the invention of the compass. Yet by the late 20th century, its brand
had become synonymous with cheap, knockoff manufacturing. China's leadership knew the growth they needed, and their ambitions for
their country required China to regain its superiority in innovation.
As one US intelligence report concluded, "Chinese leaders consider
the first two decades of the 21st century to be a window of strategic
opportunity for their country to focus on economic growth, independent innovation, scientific and technical advancement, and growth
of the renewable energy sector."[5] The fastest way to accomplish those
goals wasn't to innovate at home—it was to steal our more advanced
technology.

It was an effort so widespread that they were even literally stealing
vacuum cleaners. James Dyson, the inventor of the eponymous bagless
vacuum cleaner, complained to the UK government that he'd spent
millions of pounds combatting Chinese trade thefts—and still suffered
losses to IP theft of as much as £40 million. He'd even hired private

detectives who had seen his appliances being dissected and reverse-engineered inside Chinese factories. As he said, "If you develop a fan and make a success of it, if Chinese companies just pile in and copy it, they ride on our coat tails. They have not had the development or patenting costs, they have not taken any risks. It is just a Chinese habit of copying and making a great export success out of other people's property."[6]

In the cases of Chung and Mak, the FBI had almost literally had a front-row seat on how such schemes worked: they'd installed a surveillance camera over Mak's dining table and then watched him repeatedly load CDs into his computer, copying documents onto the discs. Agents listening to a covert recording device overheard Mak's brother, Tai, talking with his wife, Fuk. She asked if on their upcoming trip to China they'd have to carry another heavy load of documents from Chi. Not at all, Tai reassured her—everything they were smuggling could now fit on a CD. And, indeed, when agents stopped the couple at the Los Angeles airport and searched their bag, they were carrying just the CDs that Mak had carefully burned for them at his dining room table.[7]

A single CD could have held all of the hard-copy documents dug out of Chung's basement; in fact, every single thing Dongfan Chung had taken over decades would have fit on a single CD-ROM. And within a few years, there wouldn't even be a need for a physical CD-ROM at all—nor would there be a need for them to actually dispatch a spy to the United States in the first place.

China's vacuum cleaner was getting an upgrade.

///////////////

I had the opportunity to move back to Main Justice in early 2007, a couple of months after those FBI agents searched Chung's garbage, amid a massive reassessment of how the country was confronting China in cyberspace. I became the national coordinator for the Justice Department's CHIP program, the network of specially trained "Computer Hacking and Intellectual Property" prosecutors who were scattered across the country.

My new job was based inside CCIPS—the unit that oversaw computer crime at a national policy level—and represented a drastic change from the pace of trying crimes in the field. By that point, I had tried some 40 cases and had worked on many more that never made it to trial and were settled with plea deals. For years, I'd felt that I'd spent most of my days in reactive mode. Working inside the computer crime unit was totally different. There weren't many former trial prosecutors there. I was surprised, arriving at CCIPS, to realize how many faces I recognized from my early days as an assistant US attorney—many of the people working computer crimes were the same ones I had learned digital search-and-seizure procedures from years earlier. They had a deep—and valid—sense of ownership over the issue.

CCIPS was in many ways an odd duck in the Justice Department— more visionary than perhaps its day-to-day workload appeared; discussions there tended toward long-running conversations about evolving technology and legal trends. For years there hadn't been much "computer crime," the double-C in the unit's acronym, and so prosecutors had stayed busy with the "IP" portion of the name, intellectual property cases that often focused on physical goods. The prosecutors who did work computer crimes kept busy with cases that were far afield from nation-state threats—prosecuting email spammers, click-fraud and adware cases where criminals were attempting to defraud online users and advertisers, and copyright violations, as well as helping prosecutors with digital evidence rules.

Whereas many line prosecutors out in the field distrusted Main Justice in general—it's easy to see the bureaucrats in Washington as attempting to stymie or steal cases from the field—CCIPS actually had a decent reputation for cooperation. The prosecutors in CCIPS were supportive, smart on technology and a rapidly evolving area of law, and not "turf-y" at all. I'd worked with some, such as Chris Painter, on DIGITAL GRIDLOCK and Joseph Colon.*

---

* Colon, in particular, had been a hot case inside CCIPS because it represented the first time the Justice Department had ever considered charging someone with an offense known as "1030(a)(1)," which was the national security charge of the Computer Fraud and Abuse Act (known as "1030"). We'd looked long and hard at the charge and ultimately decided to stick with a simple "1030" charge—computer fraud without the national security component.

Inside CCIPS, we knew China presented a problem long before we did anything about it. But at the start, China wasn't *my* problem—which, as I came to understand it, was a big part of the problem. The government is often terribly bad about sharing its own information internally, and China's rampant economic espionage existed just between the seams of a government that still treated theft and spying as if they were two entirely different things.

To the extent that CCIPS focused on China, its work aimed at collaboration with Chinese officials to combat the lawlessness of IP inside China, meeting with counterparts overseas, working through business groups and traditional international law enforcement channels. Beyond economic espionage, software piracy ran rampant in China, and illegal bootleg DVDs and music CDs were sold openly on streets in major cities. In these bilateral discussions and the internal CCIPS conversations, the focus was not on nation-state activity. Just as we had when I was a prosecutor working in the field, when information came in that a nation-state might be involved in theft, we sent it behind the locked doors of the Justice Department's office of intelligence or the FBI's counterintelligence division.

I'd only been at CCIPS for a few months when I began talking with Lisa Monaco, who I had worked with previously when we were both prosecutors in the DC US attorney's office and who was now Director Robert Mueller's special counsel. She was poised to become Mueller's chief of staff and was looking to fill her current position, as special counsel, and Mueller always liked that role to be filled by someone who had a prosecutor's background. As our conversations continued, she explained that Mueller thought the FBI should be doing more on cybersecurity, particularly on figuring out how to tackle the nation-state threats. I'd already seen firsthand that CCIPS treated its mission as the prosecution of criminal enterprises, not the prosecution of nation-state threats. Across Pennsylvania Avenue from Main Justice, as the bureau continued its post-9/11 evolution from a domestic law enforcement agency to a national security–focused intelligence service, it was beginning to realize that cyber was the next international threat on the horizon—and the FBI was already behind the curve. Lisa said one of my first projects would be to help the bureau figure out how to approach the threat.

We didn't need to look far at that time for a real-life example of what the risks could be. As I was beginning to talk to Lisa and others at Mueller's office about the FBI's need to improve its cyber capability, the Baltic nation of Estonia weathered what appeared to be the first wide-scale cyberattacks on a country's infrastructure.

In late April 2007, the Estonian government had removed a six-foot statue of a Soviet soldier that had long stood in the capital, Tallinn. Riots broke out as ethnic Russians protested. Then a massive botnet attacked, drowning nearly every major website of the country, from newspapers to government servers, with a deluge of nefarious traffic. ATMs went down. Government services ground to a halt. "The attacks were aimed at the essential electronic infrastructure of the Republic of Estonia," Defense Minister Jaak Aaviksoo said later. "All major commercial banks, telcos, media outlets, and name servers—the phone books of the internet—felt the impact, and this affected the majority of the Estonian population. This was the first time that a botnet threatened the national security of an entire nation."[8] The attack went on for days; much of the malicious botnet traffic seemed to be emanating from servers and IPs that appeared to belong to the Russian Business Network, the St. Petersburg–based den of online criminal activity. There was never much doubt that the attack came from Russia—but to what extent it was government-sponsored remained a public mystery. The attack caught global attention and raised difficult questions. Estonia was a member of NATO: Could they invoke "Article 5," declaring themselves under attack, and rally Europe and the United States to their defense? Just how much of a real-world response could you mount in retaliation for a cyberattack? In the United States, the news of the Estonia attack also served to make the intelligence community take a second look at the foreign hackers who constantly probed US critical infrastructure; one of the challenges in cybersecurity was that the groundwork you laid as a hacker in advance of a retaliatory strike—an attack you would launch only if attacked yourself—looked identical to the preparations for a preemptive, first strike. Just how worried did we need to be?

///////////////

What I most remember about meeting Robert Mueller for the first time was the short interview. After hearing stories for years about his intense cross-examinations, I prepped and steeled myself for a lengthy interview long before I wound my way to his seventh-floor suite in the Hoover Building.

Robert Mueller was a legend among assistant US attorneys; I'd followed his career since my days in law school. He'd risen through the Justice Department's ranks in the 1980s to become the head of the Criminal Division under President George H. W. Bush. Then, when the administration ended, he only lasted about a year in private practice before he called the then US attorney in DC, Eric Holder, and asked to come back as a line prosecutor. It was the rough equivalent of a three-star general retiring and then reenlisting as a second lieutenant; Mueller, though, had dedicated his life to public service, volunteering to join the Marines and go to Vietnam in the 1960s, and he never seemed happier than when he was prosecuting a case. He'd tried homicides in DC in the mid-1990s, a job that I also had years later, then he became US attorney in San Francisco, then acting deputy attorney general during the first months of the George W. Bush administration, before being named FBI director in the summer of 2001. He'd started just one week before 9/11. In the years since, several of my friends and former colleagues had had the chance to work for him, including not just Lisa but Ken Wainstein, who hired me as an assistant US attorney while he was US attorney in DC, and later went on to be Mueller's chief of staff, and Matt Olsen, an old friend who had been Mueller's special counsel and later served as the head of the National Counterterrorism Center. All four of us came to the same opinion: Mueller seemed like he stepped right out of a history book—dedicated, decent, humble, and honest about the role of the FBI. In a city sometimes too focused on ego and flash, he had kept his head down for decades and let his work speak for itself.

Sitting in Mueller's office that day, we launched right into the interview. Mueller was never big on small talk, but he knew that he was supposed to make the effort, so he barked in his brusque prosecutorial style, "Married?" *Yes.* "Kids?" *Nope.* Then he moved on—small talk was over. And after a few more questions, so was the interview. I stood up and realized I was going to be working for this legend in a legendary organization.

In June 2007, I showed up for work for the first time at the hulking Brutalist concrete monolith that was the J. Edgar Hoover Building, and walked into the seventh-floor suite that housed the offices of the FBI director. My task: figure out how the FBI should be tackling cybersecurity. I spent months in briefings, visiting key sites, and talking with the small cadre of agents, analysts, and technicians who had been investigating computer threats.

All of a sudden, I finally understood what had been happening on the other side of that locked door in the US attorney's office in DC; I had been granted access to the other half of the picture. And it was far, far worse than I imagined. Lisa had been with Director Mueller when he went to what was known as the National Cyber Investigative Joint Task Force (NCIJTF) in Northern Virginia, the bureau's still-evolving attempt to create a national multiagency team similar to its success with the Joint Terrorism Task Force. Its name, NCIJTF, was a mouthful, and Mueller would always struggle to get it correct in speeches; normally he'd just call it the "cyber task force." It had been modeled on a cyber team that Shawn Henry had helped get started at the Washington Field Office, a model that bureau leaders hoped might be able to turn national.

Lisa and the director had an eye-opening briefing as analysts and agents walked through the two main nation-state threats they saw on the cyber landscape: China and Iran. Iran was a rising power online, but China was mature and sophisticated. "That's what the intel folks were beating the drum on," Lisa recalls. "China was the big dog."

Meetings like that had helped launch a small group of agents and bureau leaders, including Lisa and Lee Rawls, then the director's chief of staff, to begin reevaluating every aspect of the FBI's commitment to computer crime—from the resources dedicated to digital forensics to the very structure of the teams who tackled the threat.

On the seventh floor, Lee Rawls had been pushing hard for the bureau to become more engaged in cybersecurity, and his voice carried a great deal of weight. He was Mueller's closest confidant; their friendship dated back to their college days at Princeton and, in the decades since, he'd become an experienced Washington operator—a veteran lawyer, onetime assistant attorney general, and the chief of staff to the Republican Senate majority leader, as well as heading government affairs for Pennzoil and teaching at the National Defense University. Mueller had brought him to the FBI in the mid-2000s to help navigate the bureaucratically treacherous evolution of the FBI in the years since 9/11. Rawls was a dyed-in-the-wool Republican, but at the bureau he played an apolitical role—helping use his calming influence and long history with Mueller combined with his knowledge of DC's political world to keep the FBI out of politics. (Lee was one of the few people who spoke to Director Mueller as a peer—and wasn't afraid to confront the director. Mueller used to tell a story about a particularly heated senior staff meeting, where Mueller was, in his telling, a "wee bit impatient and ill-tempered," and Rawls interrupted the meeting to ask, out of the blue, "What is the difference between the director of the FBI and a four-year-old child?" The room grew hushed, and Rawls delivered his pointed rebuke: "Height.")

By the time I joined the team, the FBI was years into a substantial transformation that had begun in the hours after 9/11. In those first days after the attack, Robert Mueller had received a very specific order from President Bush: "Never again." The way Mueller told the story, he'd gone in to brief President Bush soon after the terrorist attacks and begun ticking through the rapid progress the FBI was making on identifying the hijackers and tracing their connections. The president interrupted him and said that it was all well and good that the FBI was investigating the attack—he was sure the FBI would do a great job at it—but his question for Mueller was simple: What are you doing to stop the next attack? It was a startling comment, one that upended the FBI's entire 90-year history up until that point. The FBI focused on fighting crime by investigating it after the fact—catching bank robbers after they'd robbed the bank. But in the world of terrorism, the catastrophic consequences of a large-scale attack and, on 9/11, the arrival in the United States of suicide attackers, made after-the-fact investigations necessary but not sufficient. The FBI—and indeed, all of the tools of the US government, including its intelligence agencies and its military—needed to be brought to bear to stop terrorism before it happened. Success would no longer be viewed as solving the case afterward, when families were grieving. Success was preventing the attack from occurring in the first place.

It was a story Mueller told regularly for the 12 years he ended up serving as FBI director. It felt like I must have heard it myself 150 times. But his repeated—and unending—emphasis on the story and its message drove home to me how to make a successful cultural change: while details matter, you can't ever lose sight of the big picture—the culture and the mission—and as a leader, you have to empower people throughout the organization to creatively solve the problem in ways you couldn't possibly imagine.

None of this was easy for the FBI—it wasn't a minor cultural change or a small bureaucratic battle. In fact, even when I arrived, years after 9/11, the FBI was locked in a nearly existential fight. In the wake of the attacks, numerous Capitol Hill leaders and intelligence veterans had proposed breaking apart the FBI to form an "American MI5," a domestic intelligence agency that was focused on fighting counterterrorism and espionage like the British MI5. Mueller, a lifelong Justice Department veteran, believed it was critical for the FBI to remain intact, that the nation was stronger and safer precisely because of the way that the FBI married law enforcement and intelligence and because it was grounded in the Justice Department, reporting to the attorney general, the government's designated protector and enforcer of the Constitution. But if Mueller failed at his transformation, the entire structure of American law enforcement would change.

The FBI's mantra at the time, as part of its post-9/11 transformation, was "threat-driven, intelligence-led," meaning that the bureau was focused on particular, definable threats as driven by the information it and other three-letter government agencies were able to gather.

The number-one threat was clear: al-Qaeda. Fighting terrorism was still nearly all-consuming. When I worked for Mueller at the FBI, much of my day—much of nearly everyone's day at the FBI—was still focused on terrorism; it's easy to forget today just how different the threat picture looked back in 2007 when I arrived at the bureau. The 9/11 attacks had occurred just a little over five years earlier, and the previous summer of 2006 had been perhaps the most tense period inside the national security world since the months immediately following those 9/11 attacks. Western intelligence agencies had desperately chased a potentially devastating plot to down multiple transatlantic aircraft using peroxide-based liquid explosives.* Ultimately, British police arrested 26 people across the United Kingdom in early August. News reports and government briefings outlined how authorities had disrupted the plot in its final planning stages—a series of coordinated attacks involving as many as a dozen or more suicide bombers targeting anywhere from three to ten aircraft simultaneously en route to the United States. The death toll would have easily reached into the thousands; the toll to international travel and commerce would have easily reached into the billions.

Yet even as real and present as the al-Qaeda threat remained, an increasing number of voices—such as that of then Deputy Assistant Director Shawn Henry—inside the FBI were telling us the bureau also needed to be looking forward, anticipating the rise of the cyberthreat and directing resources to tackle it. We'd waited too long to focus on international terrorism; their argument was that we shouldn't make the same mistake with cybersecurity. Another of the leaders of the transformation inside the bureau was Steven Chabinsky, the lawyer who had been captivated as a child by the text-based game *Adventure*. At the FBI in the 1990s, amid the early cyber initiatives by President Clinton,

---

* This was the plot that led to the long-term ban on carrying more than three ounces of liquid in carry-on bags.

Chabinsky had helped organize a bureau-led effort known as the National Infrastructure Protection Center. "It was an incredible concept then, and today that strategy is still sound," he recalled later. "The concept was that multiple government agencies and the private sector have to work together to combat cyber." I originally met Chabinsky when I was a prosecutor and sought his advice on digital cases before I moved over to the FBI.

Chabinsky and Henry—with the support of Lisa Monaco and Lee Rawls—had been fighting to bring organization to the FBI's cyber efforts. The bureau at that point was terrible at even understanding what the FBI itself knew. In one cyber case, Henry and Chabinsky realized that multiple field offices had opened a total of 200 cases into a similar threat. "It turned out when you started to look at all the intelligence, when we started to collate it all, that it was one group of people—it wasn't 200 separate groups," Henry said later. "You think about the resources that are being employed in 200 separate cases administratively, operationally, and there's not a lot of cross-correlation of data. If you have an infrastructure set up both internal to the organization and within the government, you can start to look at this type of information and really get a better understanding of who that adversary is."[9]

The FBI had formed an official Cyber Division in 2002, recognizing both that traditional crimes—such as child pornography, identity fraud, and intellectual property theft—were migrating online and that the internet opened up new avenues for new crime as well. "This encompasses 'cyber terrorism,' terrorist threats, foreign intelligence operations, and criminal activity precipitated by illegal computer intrusions into U.S. computer networks, including the disruption of computer supported operations and the theft of sensitive data via the Internet," explained Jana D. Monroe, the new assistant director of the Cyber Division in a July 2003 congressional hearing. "The FBI assesses the cyber-threat to the U.S. to be rapidly expanding, as the number of actors with the ability to utilize computers for illegal, harmful, and possibly devastating purposes is on the rise."[10]

Until then, digital crimes had been handled almost piecemeal across the bureau with little national coordination, as small groups of computer-savvy agents pioneered new investigative techniques and pushed the domestic law enforcement agency's role further overseas. But those agents had already determined there was no shortage of troubling cases to be found online.

Despite being intensely hierarchical in its quasi-military structure, the FBI's culture was heavily decentralized. Each of the 56 offices was overseen by a special agent who supervised every aspect of investigations in that territory. For decades, cases were run by Field Offices that claimed "office of origin," making them the central repository for knowledge no matter how big a case it got. That model was pressured by the rise of global threats like terrorism; the New York Field Office had claimed "office of origin" investigating al-Qaeda, for instance. Mueller had begun to try to shift that after 9/11, centralizing the investigation of large, global threats at headquarters to ensure that national cases got national attention. The shift hadn't been entirely successful; dots hadn't been connected in the Nidal Hasan case—the Fort Hood shooter— in part because of the complexity introduced by the "office of origin" model and how information still wasn't being shared thoroughly across government.

In 2007, we were seeing the problems crop up in cyber cases. It didn't make sense for any one Field Office to run the "China" case. At the same time, though, Mueller thought that the bureau's key strength was the agents on the front lines; it's possible that nowhere in government could a person make as big of a difference as a single dogged FBI agent pursuing a case. The FBI had succeeded in this way for decades— one dogged agent at a time. How do you preserve that creativity and strength, at the local field level, while directing resources against a central threat?

The FBI originally created Cyber Division in 2002, after years of rising government warnings, both public and private, about behavior that investigators were seeing online, attacks that spanned the spectrum from individuals to nation-states. It wasn't a given that a separate division should exist, though: there were long-running debates throughout the 2000s, up through when I arrived at the FBI, and that continued even through the start of James Comey's time as director in 2013, about how distinct "cyber" crimes really were. Was "cyber" actually just a tactic or tool for criminals—like a gun or a ransom note—or was it something different? Ultimately, through many organizational reshuffles and evolving conversations, the theory of the Cyber Division's focus developed: "normal" crimes, such as child pornography, that happened to be done digitally would be pursued by the FBI's Criminal Division—the team that investigated such crimes in the physical world—whereas the Cyber Division would focus on the "new" crimes that were only possible because of the interconnectivity of the internet, cases such as hacking and network intrusions.

The FBI was woefully behind the curve given the scale of the threat; most of the major cyber cases had come out of just a few squads, primarily in Atlanta and Pittsburgh. We needed to take the lessons from the bureau's transformation in the area of counterterrorism and move to the same approach in cybersecurity. For too long, we'd treated "cyber" as a technical problem, one where you just followed bits and bytes through wires. Hackers were humans, too. And to catch them, we needed to understand them as humans—what motivated them, what they hoped to accomplish, who their bosses were, and who those bosses' bosses were. To tackle China, for instance, we needed to develop new squads of people—agents, analysts, and prosecutors—who knew the politics and the military, and not just rely on people who could track IP addresses and penetrate firewalls.*

---

*At the same time, there was also a need to update the laws for the types of crime we were seeing; the Computer Fraud and Abuse Act had originally required a "loss" greater than $5,000, but fixed monetary losses were incredibly challenging to prove in many cyber cases. How do you calculate the loss to a specific computer user if their computer is hijacked unknowingly for a botnet? For each individual victim in a botnet of thousands or tens of thousands of computers, the impact might be trivial, but collectively, there's been real damage to the internet ecosystem. Moreover, the $5,000 threshold provoked possible technical factual disputes—encouraging defendants to litigate based not on their underlying guilt but on whether the dollar mark had been hit. In 2008, the Justice Department successfully pushed Congress to amend the act to remove the specific monetary figure—a case still had to prove damage or loss to a victim, but it no longer needed to reach a specific identifiable threshold.

/////////////

At the FBI, my day always began early. Mueller arrived at the office between 6 and 7 a.m., and his senior staff needed to be there before him—we needed to be ready to start discussing the day and the threats as soon as his motorcade pulled into the basement of the Hoover Building and he was whisked up a special elevator to the seventh floor. By that point, he'd always read the day's intelligence briefing—any last-minute updates or breaking news would have been waiting in his armored Suburban for him to review on his way in to work.

Mueller and our team would walk down to the FBI's command center, known as the Strategic Information and Operations Center (SIOC), for the morning threat briefings with the attorney general and his deputy. The SIOC, deep in the heart of the Hoover Building, had been an invention in the 1990s, after the Oklahoma City bombing, to help the FBI manage and respond to unfolding crises. It had workstations for dozens of personnel from across the government, as well as a number of high-tech but drab conference rooms for briefings.

We spent the first hour of each morning discussing the most dangerous threats facing the country. More and more, they were in the realm of cybersecurity. I began to fully understand how rampant China's hacking of American industry and government was. The same month I moved to the FBI, the Pentagon discovered that the Chinese military had successfully penetrated a computer inside the office of Defense Secretary Robert Gates; it wasn't a sensitive computer, but the Pentagon was forced to take that specific network offline for more than a week to determine the damage.[11]

We regularly heard similar stories about Chinese hacking when we spoke to industry leaders or trade associations as part of the Justice Department's normal private sector outreach. We heard—consistently—immense frustration from companies, not about China's thefts, but about the FBI's behavior in investigating cybercrime. *What's the point of even telling the FBI,* they'd say, *our information just disappears into a black box and we never hear anything back. The information is only ever a one-way street. Besides, we're not even sure that we want to go through the process of pressing charges—would the FBI disrupt our operations to collect evidence or would China cut us out of the market entirely?* The companies could see the nuisance—and the long-term risk—of such economic thefts, but they weighed that against the near-term success and expansion possibilities of doing business with China. Being cut out of the Chinese market entirely, after all, seemed much more of an existential risk than whatever was being stolen from their networks in the present moment.

Those stories—and our own intelligence—led us to be increasingly concerned there was a wave of espionage and theft pillaging American business. We knew, though, how reluctant most corporations and boardrooms were to do anything about it.

I remember visiting a company on the West Coast and receiving a briefing about how they had carefully weighed the pros and cons of confronting China. Their charts showed that their China business was currently in the black. They knew they were having their intellectual property stolen by Chinese hackers, and they'd projected out the profit curve, showing clearly that in seven or eight years the stolen IP would kill their business model. At that point, a Chinese competitor would be able to provide their product at a lower cost using their own stolen information. But that day, the general counsel explained to me in their executive conference room, they were still in the black—and didn't want the government to step in and upset the apple cart.

We tried to persuade them of the folly of this way of thinking. With frustration evident in my voice, I pointed out how their own calculations showed their own eventual death. "You're showing me—you've done the projections—that it's going to be too late by then to turn your business around," I said.

The general counsel actually agreed with my assessment, but he explained that the company's boardroom imperative was to improve shareholder value at that moment. Who knew what might happen down the road? The company's leadership might change, there might be some new industry innovations. At that moment, though, they wanted to maintain the status quo. He finished with a statement that left me shaking my head: "We are going to be coming back to you and complaining, but we're not there yet."

Over multiple conversations in Lee Rawls's office, just down the hall from Director Mueller's suite, Lee, Lisa, and I, along with others, discussed the folly of the government's approach to China in cyberspace. China already represented the world's second-largest economy, racing to catch up to the United States. To do so, it pillaged our economic advantage, building up its own industry and economy at a furious pace at the cost of our corporate trade secrets. Unlike the Soviet Union during the Cold War, China knew it couldn't compete against us militarily— so it instead relied on quieter threats and opportunities to advance its interests. China's approach to espionage was guided by a philosophy known as a "thousand grains of sand," the geopolitical intelligence equivalent of "death by a thousand cuts." Its largest resource, its people, was directed at assembling many tiny incremental thefts that together could be transformative.

America's continued silence didn't make any sense. It was not going to get easier to confront China after its economic power grew, especially if and when their economy overtook America's. Every day wasted gave them an extra advantage—an illegal one that came at the cost of US jobs, innovation, and productivity. We were in a desperate fight whether we admitted it or not.

What China appeared to be doing went far beyond the espionage generally tolerated between nations. While US intelligence agencies did everything they could to learn about the economies, militaries, and politics of other nations, the US government did not participate in espionage meant to benefit the private sector—we didn't help Boeing get a leg up by learning what Chinese aviation firms were doing or help Monsanto learn about Chinese agricultural systems. China, though, was using the power and assets of the government to create an unfair playing field for businesses; it was helping to pick winners in the private sector.

The history of government-directed economic espionage was long and checkered. Russia and even France, for example, had over the years turned their state efforts toward helping the private sector and key national industries. Notoriously, business executives were warned in the 1990s that Air France's first-class cabins were believed to be bugged as a way to help French executives learn the game plan of visitors before they ever sat down to negotiate—as Motorola learned when they traveled to Paris to pitch French Telecom (now known as Orange SA), only to discover that the French delegation appeared to know everything about their plan.[12] But this kind of economic espionage was not something that the United States did—and, in modern times, it wasn't something brokered by Western nations.

Ultimately, we understood that China's economic espionage—like all espionage—was a cost-benefit analysis: Did the economic gains China was gathering outweigh the geopolitical costs it faced for that activity? And, in 2007, it was an easy decision for the Chinese: we weren't imposing any costs at all. Rawls thought it was high time for a change. We needed to figure out a way to disrupt China's epidemic of economic espionage.

Understanding what we could do to challenge China's operations in cyberspace—and ultimately what would be effective in reshaping their behavior—required first understanding what the rising Asian superpower hoped to accomplish with its online activities. China had long used the internet as a tool to hasten its rise, growth, and modernization, even as it had warily eyed the freedom of communication and information that comes with being online.[13] Ensuring economic stability at home—and thus, in turn, ensuring political stability and the future of the ruling Communist Party—drove almost every other Chinese decision on the world stage. The Communist Party demonstrated a remarkable resilience and adaptability, outlasting the Soviet Union by decades, even as its modernization efforts allowed it to avoid the economic paralysis experienced by other authoritarian regimes, such as North Korea and Cuba.

Mao's disastrous collectivization efforts had decimated the country economically in the 1960s, and the resulting famine killed upward of 30 million, leaving the country poorer than North Korea.[14] By 1979, the Communist Party changed tactics, loosening economic restrictions and allowing some semblance of a private market economy again. "Let some people get rich first, and gradually all the people should get rich together," Deng Xiaoping decreed. Evan Osnos, a staff writer for the *New Yorker* who covered China, wrote that the country's subsequent rise is "a transformation one hundred times the scale, and ten times the speed, of the first Industrial Revolution."[15] In 1978, the average Chinese income was just $200, and as late as 2005, a quarter of a billion Chinese—a population only slightly smaller than the entire United States—still lived on less than $1.25 a day, and its per capita income was still under around $3,000.[16] But by 2014, per capita income had leapt to $6,000, doubling in just ten years.

The internet and digital world were key drivers in that growth; in many realms, digital advances have helped China leapfrog generations of technology and industry in the Western world as it industrialized and modernized with stunning rapidity. The internet arrived in China in January 1996, at a time when the country had just five telephone lines per hundred residents.[17] By August of that year, China was beginning to restrict certain online content, and just a year later *Wired* coined the term "Great Firewall," denoting the system through which China throttled open access to the world beyond and prohibited certain types of potentially threatening political content.[18*]

China has no formal equivalent to the American term *cyber*. Whereas we tend to refer to *cyber* as encompassing both online offense and defense, both propaganda efforts and covert measures, Chinese strategists define the online realm in a subtly different—and broader—way, speaking of "network strategy" to refer specifically to technical online protections and "information security" to refer to a wide range of tools and operations aimed at influencing others online.[19**]

---

*Ultimately, Chinese censors settled on 11 categories of forbidden content, ranging from pornography to information "detrimental to the honor and interests of the state" to "information inciting illegal assemblies, association, demonstrations, protest, and gatherings that disturb social order."

** The term *hacker*, meanwhile, translates into Chinese as "dark visitor," an apt descriptor of the shadows online.

Operation Allied Force, NATO's air war in Yugoslavia, is largely forgotten in the United States, but it dramatically changed the approach of the Chinese military. On May 7, 1999, American B-2 stealth bombers accidentally hit the Chinese embassy in Belgrade, killing three, after US targeters mistook it for a warehouse. The bombing outraged the Chinese government, which decried it as a "barbaric attack," and the incident stoked international tension; US diplomatic personnel in China faced days of sometimes violent protests, and hackers defaced the website of the American embassy in Beijing. More broadly, the incident prompted the Chinese military to speed its efforts at modernization; the military had watched nervously earlier in the 1990s as US forces easily routed the Iraqi military from Kuwait in the Gulf War. "China's leaders realized that without incorporating information technology into their weaponry and equipment that the PLA risked being left behind," one US military theorist concluded.[20] "China believes it can keep up with other countries by utilizing a multitude of information engineers and citizens with laptops instead of just soldiers." The People's Liberation Army (PLA) began to focus on what it called "acupuncture war," the targeting of specific nodes and key network hubs of an adversary's command systems and infrastructure.[21] Soon after the bombing campaign in the former Yugoslavia, Chinese President Jiang Zemin declared the internet was a "political, ideological, and cultural battlefield."

"Strategically, the objective of war in the information age is to destroy the enemy's will to launch a war or wage a war. Tactically, the aim is to paralyze the enemy's power system," explained Shen Weiguang, a leading Chinese information warfare strategist. "The essence of [information warfare] is that it targets the human heart with the weapon of information. It attacks the will of the nation, the morale of the troops, and the resolve of the commanders."[22]

To combat this new weapon, the FBI—and the US government as a whole—needed a new strategy. Rawls and Director Mueller tasked me with researching it; we didn't have long to organize one. Mueller wanted quick results and wanted to announce a new approach that fall.

During his time as director, Mueller rarely spoke in public. Unlike many in Washington, he had no love of the spotlight. But those rare high-profile speeches were a critical part of his learning process, giving him a chance to go deep on an issue as he and the staff crafted what he was going to say and how he'd say it. As a speech approached, we'd have briefing after briefing. A lifelong prosecutor, Mueller relentlessly cross-examined those briefing him, delving deeper, becoming comfortable with the nuances of a particular issue, and developing his own point of view. He meticulously prepared, devouring briefing memos and the reading packets we sent home with him every night. Once we knew what we wanted him to say, we'd go through draft after draft; he prepped as if each speech was the closing argument of a trial.

To start figuring out what Mueller would say in 2007, I went to Pittsburgh.

///////////////

Pittsburgh, at first glance, doesn't seem the likeliest place for the US government's top cyber detectives, yet over the last quarter century a unique constellation of computer science resources had grown up around the industrial hub, including Carnegie Mellon—which is home to the Software Engineering Institute, a federally funded research center, as well as the country's first Computer Emergency Response Team, CERT/CC, which dated back to the first scary day on the internet, the unintended explosion of the Morris Worm.

In the years since, Pittsburgh developed a whole ecosystem of key cyber resources, including the National Cyber Forensics and Training Alliance (NCFTA), which since its own founding in 1997 emerged as perhaps law enforcement's most important clearinghouse for computer crime. NCFTA was part of the city's dramatic transformation from a dying steel town to a thriving, hip technology hub—the very city, years later, where Uber would first deploy its self-driving cars.

On paper, according to government charts at least, public–private information sharing is supposed to be the purview of groups like the

Department of Homeland Security's National Cybersecurity and Communications Integration Center, a 700-person, billion-dollar-a-year, state-of-the-art operation based in Arlington, Virginia. Yet in practice the close partnerships that developed inside the industry-funded NCFTA since its founding on the banks of the Monongahela River in 1998 had put it at the core of many of the FBI's biggest cybercrime cases of the last decade.

The low-budget research team, a mix of investigators, researchers, and engineers—effectively a national teaching hospital for cybersecurity efforts—has become a key forum for private companies like Microsoft to share information on potential criminal cases, allowing the FBI agents assigned to NCFTA to collect and parcel out cases.

Often the cases stay right in Pittsburgh, and when they do they end up on the desk of FBI Supervisor J. Keith Mularski—the pioneering cyber agent who took on the identity of Master Splyntr and helped build the Pittsburgh team into a powerhouse.

As I listened to FBI agents talk about their window into the China threat, I realized that not everyone thought we'd succeed with a new approach. In fact, many of my colleagues thought we might never confront China publicly over its hacking—the intelligence we were gathering about China's behavior was highly classified and deeply sensitive, given the complicated geopolitical relationships between the US, the world's only superpower, and the rising Asian superpower. The politics of cybersecurity were just too fraught. One FBI section chief told me that he didn't think anyone would care enough to risk antagonizing China.

Mueller had also been driving each of the FBI's 56 Field Offices to focus on what he called "domain awareness," ensuring that the special agents in charge of each office understood the threats in their particular corner of the country—and how they differed from other corners. There was plenty else in the world besides al-Qaeda to keep us worried; in addition to long-standing threats like South American drug cartels, we were seeing the rise of transnational organized crimes from places like Eastern Europe.

While that "domain awareness" worked at the field-office level, I soon realized that we didn't really understand the international portrait of cyberthreat. I'd seen the threat in my own cases and others had their own piecemeal understanding, informed by whatever cases they'd seen in their own territory, but the FBI—and the US government writ large—didn't have a global, easy-to-digest portrait of what was happening. The FBI's cyber capability was still nascent; the intelligence reports we got on cyberthreats weren't anywhere close to as sophisticated or analytical as the ones we routinely saw around terrorism threats. What exactly were the cyberthreats to American companies and individuals?

To answer that question, the FBI built a really big television screen—a wall-sized monitor at NCIJTF—that brought streams of data together to watch cyberthreats unfold in real time. I remember staring in awe at the screen, watching a Chinese hacker sneak into a university, then leap from there into a private company, and then from that network penetrate a defense contractor's server. I literally watched the data begin to stream back to China.

The screen was a technological marvel—itself a significant intelligence success, marrying numerous data sources into a single, easy-to-understand visual presentation. But it was hard to look at the screen and think of it as a success. In fact, it seemed quite the opposite: a very pretty picture of a losing battle.

Once the government and the FBI had this portrait, the next logical question arose in our world: What do we do with it? How do we disrupt and deter this threat? Again, we were looking to the lessons that the FBI had learned in the terrorism world. The same approach needed to happen within the cyberworld. As Director Mueller continually instilled in us: it wasn't enough to just solve cyber incidents after the fact; we also needed to stop incidents from occurring. Both tasks were hard and required a lot of luck. Often, the attackers were far beyond our reach, hidden overseas in unfriendly countries where our extradition treaties didn't touch, and, as we were learning, often the attackers were government agents themselves. Not only did we need to identify and help disrupt attacks as they unfolded, but also we needed to use every tool available to the government to raise the cost of hacking for our foreign adversaries.

Success on both fronts would be a long time coming. In fact, we wouldn't get there for seven years.

ⲙⲙⲙⲙⲙⲙⲙⲙ

On November 6, 2007, I traveled with Mueller back to Pittsburgh, where he was set to take the stage at Penn State and articulate, for the first time, the FBI's approach to national security cyberthreats. Before the speech, we toured some of the local computer labs; at NCFTA, the director received a demo of *Second Life*, the massive online free-form world where millions of people had created avatars and built virtual lives. The idea baffled him; he couldn't understand why anyone would devote time to such an unnecessary exercise. We began to talk, too, about longer-term threats—such as, could someone launder money through the virtual in-game currencies of a world like *Second Life*? Was it possible for someone to cause psychological or "physical" harm to an online avatar, virtual persona, or virtual world that could be grounds for a criminal prosecution?* The conversations then presaged the rise of virtual currencies, such as Bitcoin, and, as it turned out, the virtual harm question didn't stay theoretical for long: soon China prosecuted hackers who had pillaged *World of Warcraft* accounts.[23]

Then, Mueller took the stage and laid out the cyberthreat as he saw it. "There is an old saying that all roads lead to Rome. In the days of the Roman Empire, roads radiated out from the capital city, spanning more than 52,000 miles. The Romans built these roads to access the vast areas they had conquered. But, in the end, these same roads led to Rome's downfall, for they allowed the invaders to march right up to the city gates," Mueller said. "The internet has opened up thousands of new roads for each of us—new ideas and information, new sights and sounds, new people and places. But the invaders—those whose intent

---

* These debates are probably close over the horizon in the United States, as we advance in virtual realty keep moving toward more sophisticated and persistent online personalities.

is not enlightenment, but exploitation and extremism—are marching right down those same roads to attack us in multiple ways."

Mueller had launched our new mantra: we had to build the legions that would protect our Rome. It wasn't the first time that the government had turned to Roman metaphors to confront new threats—nearly a decade before, in 1998, the secret White House plan to tackle Osama bin Laden had been known as DELENDA, a reference to "Carthago delenda est," the Roman vow to destroy rival city-state Carthage.

///////////////

None of these were problems for the FBI alone; all across government, officials were trying to wrap their arms around cyberthreat—and the opportunities it presented for targeting adversaries overseas. As 2008 arrived and the Bush administration took stock of what it would be leaving for the next president, cybersecurity was at the top of the national security agenda. The outgoing director of national intelligence, Admiral Mike McConnell, pushed for an executive order that reorganized and refocused the government's cyber efforts. McConnell, who had led the National Security Agency in the 1990s, had come back into government from the private sector in 2007 to be the nation's director of national intelligence, a post held previously by John Negroponte and created in the wake of 9/11 to coordinate and wrangle the country's 17 intelligence agencies. As one of his first major efforts, McConnell had pushed for—and received—permission from President Bush in May 2007 to authorize the National Security Agency to bring sophisticated cyber weapons and tracking techniques to bear against insurgents in Iraq. General David Petraeus had credited the cyberoffensive as "being a prime reason for the significant progress" by US troops during the surge, responsible ultimately for "the removal of almost 4,000 insurgents from the battlefield."[24]

But on a daily basis, McConnell tended to be much more concerned about what adversaries were doing to the United States in cyberspace. In that same May 2007 meeting, McConnell had argued to push that cybersecurity was increasingly the nation's top risk. Earlier that year, the

Idaho National Laboratory had run a scary experiment—purposefully hacking a generator and causing it to spin out of control and destroy itself. In real life, such an attack could leave a power plant knocked out for months; the United States had limited capability to manufacture generators (most came from China or India) and new machines often took 18 months or longer to procure. Inside government, we debated how public to be with such warnings: When was it necessary and good to make people aware of such threats versus just giving ideas to our adversaries and scaring people?

In his meeting at the Oval Office, McConnell pressed the president on a scenario where the 9/11 attackers had targeted cyber vulnerabilities rather than aviation—such as by deleting financial data on stock markets. Bush turned to Treasury Secretary Hank Paulson and asked if such a scenario was possible: "Hank, is what Mike is saying true?"

"Not only is it true," Paulson replied, "but when I was in charge of Goldman, this is the scenario that kept me up at night."

"Mike," President Bush said, "you brought this problem in here. You've got thirty days to fix it."[25]

As director of national intelligence, McConnell had invented a neat party trick: he would sometimes try to underscore to Cabinet secretaries the cyber problem by pulling a memo out of his briefcase in a meeting and handing it across the table. As journalist Fred Kaplan recounted, McConnell would say, "You wrote this memo last week. The Chinese hacked it from your computer. We hacked it back from their computer."[26] That got a Cabinet member's attention, but we were all still struggling with the next step: Then what?

McConnell's efforts eventually led to one of the most significant steps forward in the US government's efforts to tackle cyberspace: a little-known but important task force led by Melissa Hathaway, who had worked alongside McConnell in the private sector at Booz Allen Hamilton. Hathaway led a groundbreaking interagency task force—normally a phrase that seems an oxymoron in government, as interagency task forces are too often the government's way of pretending to solve a difficult problem while doing very little.

At the first meeting, Hathaway announced the task force's marching orders: those involved would have to clear their calendars—they would meet from 10 a.m. to 2 p.m., every Tuesday and Thursday. No delegates or deputies were allowed. Shawn Henry, the FBI's representative at the meeting, was stunned—it seemed impossible that such senior firepower would be locked into such an expansive and inflexible series of conversations. These were all important government officials—they didn't have time to trek out to Northern Virginia to meet twice a week. And yet Hathaway was entirely serious. "A week from today, I want each team to present what you think your authorities are, your capabilities are, and to identify your authorizations—executive orders, legislation, and so forth," she commanded. Henry looked around the table. "Everyone's staring at each other—no one trusts each other," he recalls. In this case, it worked. Hathaway convened the task force—again and again and again—until it had come up with a stronger, more unified government approach for cybersecurity, an approach that embraced what she called "one team, one fight."

In January 2008, President Bush launched what came to be known as the Comprehensive National Cybersecurity Initiative (CNCI), a push to mature the government's approach to cyberspace, both in terms of protecting its own networks and in terms of better coordination across the government and private sector. At the time, its very existence was classified. The document describing it read, in part, "The United States must maintain unrestricted access to and use of cyberspace for a broad range of national purposes. The expanding use of the Internet poses both opportunities and challenges. The ability to share information rapidly and efficiently has enabled huge gains in private sector productivity, military capabilities, intelligence analysis, and government effectiveness. Conversely, it has created new vulnerabilities that must be addressed in order to safeguard the gains made from greater information sharing."[27]

The new order made clear that the FBI's NCIJTF, or the "cyber task force," as Mueller always called it, would be the central coordinating body for the government's cyberthreat investigations, and created a new Department of Homeland Security center for sharing information with the private sector. Moreover, it laid out clear roles and lanes for each agency and department with a role in the issue. The new CNCI was coupled with an extensive set of revisions to what are known inside government as "twelve-triple three," that is, Executive Order 12333, a Reagan-era order that serves as the charter for the intelligence community, explaining who does what, how, and why. The order helped delineate and define that the CIA was the lead agency for overseas human intelligence, the NSA was the lead agency for overseas signals intelligence, and the FBI was the lead agency for all kinds of domestic intelligence.

In a rapid, intensive process over the spring of 2008, the White House and McConnell pushed forward reforms that ensured the various intelligence agencies would better share their knowledge and, notably, worked to better coordinate the collection of foreign and domestic intelligence between the FBI and CIA.[28] The revisions also embraced a new concept known as "national intelligence," a term meant to capture information useful across the government, beyond simply, say, the military's battlefield intelligence or routine law enforcement intelligence gathered by the FBI, Secret Service, Drug Enforcement Administration, or Coast Guard. It was an important step toward what we had been seeing in our own cyber quest—that while information sharing was routine and critical in the counterterrorism sphere, the government hadn't been thinking equally creatively about how to assemble the many puzzle pieces it was collecting about cyberthreats.

The combined efforts of the CNCI and the 12333 revisions marked an important step toward developing an "all-tools" approach to cybersecurity. That "all-tools" approach had been one of the critical advances in the counterterrorism arena: a recognition that the government needed to look holistically at a problem. There were a wide variety of carrots and sticks available to solve an issue or disrupt a threat, from criminal prosecutions to immigration enforcement to export controls to diplomatic or financial sanctions to military kinetic attacks. But in order to bring that full toolset to bear, the government needed to share information quickly and ensure that everyone was defining and understanding a threat similarly. In government parlance, we needed to share intel at speed and pace and then consider together: How can we creatively disrupt this threat? In the years since 9/11, we'd gotten quite sophisticated about such efforts when faced with national security threats on the counterterrorism side—but we had barely scratched the surface on the cybersecurity side.

//////////////

The improvements in the government's posture were critical; the attacks and crimes we were seeing boggled the mind. In one incident, hackers managed to stage a coordinated bank robbery against the Royal Bank of Scotland in 2008, stealing $9 million in just 12 hours.[29] "The barrier to getting more was that the ATMs actually ran out of cash," recalled Shawn Henry, one of the leaders of the FBI's cyber efforts at that time.

Then, a year after the apparent Russian cyberattacks on Estonia, we saw a new twist: when the Russian military invaded the Republic of Georgia, the bombers and tanks were married for the first time with widespread cyberattacks.[30] Through the summer of 2008, botnets targeted Georgian websites with DDoS attacks. While Russia tried to shrug and blame the DDoS assaults on unknown vandals, the targets lined up a little too neatly for the government to not have played a role. DDoS attacks focused early on the Georgian city of Gori, hitting just before bombers began attacking it from the sky. "How did they know that they were going to drop bombs on Gori and not the capital?" asked one security researcher afterward.[31] The arrival of cyberattacks on a battlefield hardly surprised anyone. "It costs about 4 cents per machine," internet researcher Bill Woodcock told the *New York Times*. "You could fund an entire cyberwarfare campaign for the cost of replacing a tank tread, so you would be foolish not to."

That same year, in November and December 2008, the Conficker Worm rampaged across the internet, becoming the largest infection we'd seen in years. Millions of Windows-based computer systems in a total of 195 countries were affected by year's end, and the real-world impact hinted at the increasing risks of cyberattacks: French fighter planes were grounded because they couldn't download flight plans;

the UK city of Manchester saw over $1 million in damages as its city network was disrupted. The worm malware was highly sophisticated, leading to industry speculation that it was the work of a group of criminals or even a nation-state, like China. "There were simply too many levels of expertise involved; no single villain could be that proficient in so many obscure disciplines," wrote Mark Bowden in his book on the outbreak, *Worm*.[32] The estimates of infections ranged from a low of 8 million computers to as many as 25 million, providing a powerful botnet for whoever was behind the attack. Ironically, the botnet grew too large to be useful to whoever started it—it was never really monetized, likely because too many researchers and investigators were watching it too closely—but the costs were still all too real. Globally, Conficker cleanup cost as much as $9 billion.

The incident underscored how poorly the government and the private sector were collaborating on cybersecurity incidents—which is to say that they weren't really cooperating at all. Microsoft had formed an industry working group to combat the worm and offered a $250,000 reward for information about the perpetrator, but they'd received almost no help from the government at all and, as the worm mutated and spread, always seemed to be the ones informing high-ranking government officials of the new threats. In fact, one of the leaders of the working group, Rodney Joffe, had tried to brief government officials, only to discover that his own PowerPoint had been classified by the US Computer Emergency Response Team (US-CERT) and presented to the White House without his knowledge. To industry, it was a clear example that when working with the government, information only flowed one way. As Joffe says, "The government was isolating itself from the private sector, because it was just a one-way street. It had a very arrogant view of the private sector's ability to understand what was going on and respond to attacks." The Conficker Worm was a clear case where the private sector's knowledge was far ahead of anything the government possessed. The working group later summed up its view of the government's contribution: "Zero involvement, zero activity, zero knowledge."[33] As Joffe says, "Conficker was the inflection point. That was the point that proved that the private sector had its act together and the government really had to change the way it was organized."

/////////////

One of McConnell's other efforts was to push for the creation of a new military organization to oversee hacking efforts. The effort received an extra boost when, in the fall of 2008, the Pentagon realized that one of its classified networks had been hacked—the first time an adversary was ever known to have penetrated a classified network, which by their very design were supposed to be "air gapped," entirely disconnected from the normal internet.* According to journalist Fred Kaplan, "a detailed analysis, over the next few months, confirmed" that a malware-infected thumb drive had been inserted into the classified network. According to Kaplan's reporting, Russia had seeded infected thumb drives at kiosks in Kabul, including those near NATO's military headquarters, in the hopes that a cheap American would buy one and then use it at work.[34] The effort to defeat the malware on the network, known by the code name BUCKSHOT YANKEE, helped make clear the challenges the military had in securing cyberspace.

McConnell's idea, championed in the subsequent Obama administration by then Defense Secretary Robert Gates, led to the creation of US Cyber Command—announced finally the following summer, in 2009, and originally headed by NSA Director General Keith Alexander—a military unit that would harness unique digital expertise and ensure better coordination across the different branches. It had three primary prongs: protecting the so-called .mil environment—the military's own computer networks—aiding troops in combat, and offensively deploying cyber weapons.

As the year unfolded, it was clear that China was the top threat—and that it wasn't just a US problem. During a private 2008 meeting at Ramstein Air Force Base in Germany, US officials compared notes with security leaders from Germany, France, the Netherlands, and the

---

*The Pentagon actually runs four entirely separate networks: the open internet, an unclassified network known as NIPRNet, a "secret"-level classified network known as SIPRNet, and a "top-secret"-level classified network known as JWICS.

United Kingdom. Germany's representatives reported that Chinese-based cyberattacks had hit every sector, including "the military, the economy, science and technology, commercial interests, and research and development," and that they were able to notice a specific increase in hacking activity "before major negotiations involving German and Chinese interests," *Reuters* later reported.[35] The French, meanwhile, said that they "believed Chinese actors had gained access to the computers of several high-level French officials, activating microphones and Web cameras for the purpose of eavesdropping."

The efforts, the United States believed, were part of a sophisticated group of government hackers that researchers knew by the moniker Comment Crew. (Different firms or researchers also called it the Shady Rat or a half-dozen other monikers.[36]) That group specialized in a highly sophisticated version of phishing, where fraudulent emails that purport to be from a reputable sender are actually aimed at convincing a recipient to divulge confidential information such as usernames, passwords, or bank accounts. Often phishing emails contain links or attachments that appear to be legitimate but that either lead to fake websites or, when clicked, launch and install malware on the recipient's computer.

Whereas most online phishing attacks are marked by sloppy spelling, obviously suspicious links, or too-good-to-be-true invitations—the classic example is the "Nigerian scheme" that explains how an African leader needs help smuggling large amounts of money—these Chinese attempts were meticulous, more targeted and individually researched, aimed at either specific users or specific target sets, and were known in the industry as "spear phishing." They even got right the unique way US military personnel usually sign their emails, with a "V/R" followed by their name and email signature, an abbreviation that stands for "very respectfully." The Chinese hackers also carefully researched social networks to understand who might be a useful person to impersonate online; in 2009, five US State Department employees who were involved in climate change negotiations with China received an email that appeared to be from Bruce Stokes, then the international economics columnist at *National Journal*, an insider DC magazine, and the husband of Wendy Sherman, a top State Department policy official.[37] Entitled simply "China and Climate Change," the spoofed email's body contained convincing-looking comments on China, and then an attachment with hidden malware that, if clicked, would have delivered the hackers access to nearly every corner of the user's computer.

That approach, researchers learned, was a favorite of the Chinese hackers. They often tried to deploy malware known as the Gh0st-Net remote access tool (RAT), which allowed the hacker to snoop on keystrokes, covertly snap screenshots, activate and record sound and video through the infected computer's webcam, and also install and manipulate files.[38] The technology itself wasn't anything special—any sophisticated hacker at that point could deploy similar malware—but the sophistication and simultaneous precision and breadth surpassed many other threats we saw at the time.

The Chinese hackers also understood the psychology of office workers—they knew what it would take to get someone to click quickly on an infected document. According to the *New York Times*, for one successful attack, Chinese military hackers based in Shanghai used an email message with an attachment titled "salary increase—survey and forecast." It yielded them more than fifty megabytes' worth of email messages, as well as a complete list of names, accounts, and passwords for the computer users of an entire US government agency.[39]

In addition to targeting people of policy interest, such as the State Department climate negotiators, among many others, the hackers targeted corporate executives. As *Bloomberg* later reported, in the midst of Coca-Cola's research about acquiring China's largest soft drink company, the China Huiyuan Juice Group, one of its executives, deputy president of Coca-Cola's Pacific Group Paul Etchells, received a targeted email that appeared to be an innocuous message about energy efficiency from Coca-Cola's CEO.[40] He clicked, activating the malware on his computer and opening a back door that the Chinese government used to snoop through Coca-Cola's network for more than a month. *Bloomberg* reported that the hackers uploaded more than a dozen different malware tools to allow them greater and greater access to Coca-Cola's network, including targeting one of Coca-Cola's Hong Kong executives with a so-called keylogger, a piece of software that allowed them to record every keystroke she made on the computer. Once they had control of her computer, they searched for emails related to the Huiyuan deal and forwarded them to an anonymous Gmail account, presumably controlled by the hackers. Later, and much to the surprise of Coca-Cola, which had believed the deal would sail through the Chinese government's antitrust review, the Chinese government blocked Coca-Cola's acquisition.[41]

Coca-Cola, though, was just one of numerous Western companies that saw their business in China come under digital assault. The lead executive overseeing China for the European steel company Arcelor-Mittal was hacked by a team that rooted through a folder named "China" and downloaded draft PowerPoint presentations; the British energy giant BG Group saw hackers target its geological maps and drilling records; the Chesapeake Energy Corporation saw information about its natural gas leases stolen, even as the company was engaged in conversations with the Chinese energy leader Sinopec.[42] Among the files stolen? Two files named "Sinopec CA—Executed.docx" and "General—China SHG\deals\STA."

Bloomberg reported that Coca-Cola wasn't even aware they had been targeted until the FBI showed up and warned them on March 15, 2009.[43] That was true in far too many instances, we found. The FBI had been watching China's intrusions across many sectors—and unfortunately we had some firsthand experience, too. I had traveled to China with a delegation that also included FBI Deputy Director John Pistole to discuss law enforcement cooperation; we had expected to be watched carefully while in the country, but were still surprised at how flagrant the surveillance was. We returned to our hotel rooms at one point to find our luggage clearly rifled and lying in the middle of the room. Later, when we returned to Washington, Director Mueller's assistant, Wanda, was targeted with a sophisticated, near-perfect spear-phishing email that appeared to be from me. It caused the FBI to rethink and harden our own internal defenses, too.

As we learned more, much of China's electronic spying represented the work of the Third Department of the PLA. At the time, China focused the PLA's intelligence efforts on what they called the General Staff Department and this was broken down into the Second Department (focused on overt and covert human intelligence efforts, so-called HUMINT), the Third Department (focused on signals intelligence, so-called SIGINT), and the Fourth Department (focused on electronic warfare and intelligence, so-called ELINT).[44]

The Third Department, the rough equivalent of our NSA or the British General Communications Headquarters (GCHQ), devoted an enormous amount of resources to their cyber surveillance and espionage. The Third Department, though, actually had a wider mission than its Western counterparts—all-encompassing missions that belonged in the United States to the Defense Language Institute and the Defense Information Systems Agency, the Pentagon's IT administrator.

As best as US researchers could determine, there were at least six Chinese technical reconnaissance bureaus that targeted foreign networks—including units based in Lanzhou, Jinan, Chengdu, Guangzhou, and Beijing.[45] By the late 2000s, they had been at work for years; US researchers suspected the so-called Third Department had begun working on "information warfare" activities as early as 1997, winning at least five military excellence awards in the intervening years for its "research in information warfare theories."

The clean-and-neat analysis that we saw in intelligence, though, often belied the messier situations we saw as we dove into the hacker networks themselves. The macroanalysis of the US government and international community didn't accurately reflect how fungible the lines were on the Chinese side. We came to understand that many government hackers, for instance, worked their own side projects—sometimes in the evening, sometimes even during the workday or during their lunch hours—doing criminal financial attacks or taking bribes to go after specific targets or to meet certain performance metrics that would reflect well on their bosses. Hackers used the technical infrastructure set up for military hackers, which existed outside of the Great Firewall, to further their own projects on the open web—smuggling and laundering money out of the mainland or simply using their own social media profiles outside of China's normal restrictions. Such mixing of activity, especially when it overlapped with the Chinese workday, made it difficult to determine how much of what we were seeing was a sanctioned government-directed operation and how much was freelance opportunism.

That problem swung both ways: plenty of espionage activity came from civilian hackers, who either out of a sense of patriotism or a desire for profit were working to further China's economic and military goals—perhaps even tens of thousands of Chinese hackers who mixed their computer skills with national service. Just as technology entrepreneurs were celebrated in the United States, Chinese culture celebrated its hackers. One study in 2005 by the Shanghai Academy of Social Sciences compared hackers to rock stars, finding that two out of five elementary school students in China "adored" hackers, and fully a third said they hoped to grow up to be one themselves.[46] As one Chinese hacker explained in a 2005 Hong Kong *Sunday Morning Post* article, "Unlike our Western [hacker] counterparts, most of whom are individualists or anarchists, Chinese hackers tend to get more involved with politics because most of them are young, passionate, and patriotic."[47]

Websites such as chinahacker.com and cnhacker.com offered courses for those who wanted new skills. On the surface, it wasn't dissimilar to the cult of technologists we saw in American culture—as Silicon Valley entrepreneurs and start-ups were celebrated and feted in TV shows, movies, and websites—but these Chinese hackers were being turned, en masse, against our own economy, undermining American jobs and companies through skilled international thefts. A Hong Kong professor, Jack Linchuan Qiu, explained, "Chinese hackerism is not the American 'hacktivism' that wants social change. It's actually very close to the state. The Chinese distinction between the private and public domains is very small."[48]

The government, initially at least, hadn't gone to great lengths to hide the military's involvements. Some of the websites that the Comment Crew hackers relied upon had been created in the city of Chengdu—the capital of the central Chinese province of Sichuan—by an individual named Chen Xingpeng who registered them using the exact postal code used there by the PLA's First Technical Reconnaissance Bureau.[49] And there weren't great efforts made to hide the links between the government and the companies benefiting from the espionage: we saw companies write thank-yous to the government for their aid in stealing specific pieces of intellectual property—and we saw government hackers receive performance awards noting their success in certain heists and the extent to which their work contributed to the country's economic growth. We even saw companies come to the government to pitch hack targets—saying they needed X piece of intellectual property or Y trade secret in order to accelerate their growth and could the government find it for them?

Cybersecurity researchers believed that they had even been able to trace some of these Gh0st RAT intrusions back to a specific Chinese hacker: Yinan Peng, who led a group of what the US government believed were civilian hackers working on behalf of the government, a team known as Javaphile. The group traced its origins back to the downing of the US EP-3 Air Force plane in 2001, and Peng appeared to have remained quite active. Peng, who went online by the moniker Coolswallow and Ericool, had delivered a lecture at the Shanghai Jiao Tong University entitled "Hacker in a Nutshell," where he had been identified as a consultant to a public security bureau. He was a Buddhist scholar, publishing essays on the religion online and explaining how Buddhism provided a window on the life of hackers. He had also published two articles in 2008 about computer network exploitation techniques, identifying himself as a researcher affiliated with Shanghai Jiao Tong University's Information Security Engineering Institute, which was headed by Peng Dequan, a former science and technology director at China's lead foreign intelligence service, the Ministry of State Security.[50]

We knew a seemingly incredible amount about Yinan Peng—we had even seen him receive an email from known Chinese government hackers who were part of one of the related Comment Crew teams.[51]

But, at that time, even being able to trace back the attacks to an individual meant little to the US government—there was no tool in our toolbox to do anything with that information. However, the Comment Crew group was the primary focus of our efforts in the years ahead—an elite Chinese team that was known by a number of monikers, including APT1, for "Advanced Persistent Threat 1"—APT being industry jargon for a nation-state-sponsored group of hackers.

We knew we needed a lot of pieces to come together to make a case work. We needed to be able to prove in an unclassified setting the identity of the hacker behind a specific Chinese government–directed theft and tie the theft to specific economic gain by a private company. Each part of that process represented a challenge; several of our most intriguing cases we weren't able to re-create in an unclassified manner that could be used in open court. And, perhaps most critically of all, we needed a willing and cooperative victim, someone who wouldn't feel traumatized by taking matters public. But no matter how challenging the process was, I knew we needed to start imposing costs on China. If we didn't, there'd be no reason for them to change their incredibly lucrative and successful behavior.

The theory was simple—but it would take years of diligent, often frustrating work to get there.

As the summer and fall of 2008 unfolded, I found myself in the midst of a very different type of Chinese espionage operation. Shawn Henry called me one day in midsummer and explained that the bureau had seen evidence that Chinese hackers had successfully penetrated the computer network of Democratic presidential nominee Barack Obama; what the campaign had originally thought was just a run-of-the-mill computer virus was actually malware that had allowed the Chinese to begin exfiltrating policy documents and learn the internal debates of the campaign. We had experience providing so-called defensive briefings to politicians and candidates when the FBI felt they might be targets of intelligence operations by foreign powers, but this was the first time we'd seen a hack in the middle of a presidential campaign. Lisa called Denis McDonough, the Obama campaign's foreign policy advisor, whom she'd never met, and told him that a man named Shawn Henry would soon contact him and that McDonough should take the briefing. An FBI agent then visited the Obama campaign's Chicago headquarters to provide a warning, and White House Chief of Staff Josh Bolten called the campaign's head, David Plouffe. "You have a real problem," Bolten said. "It's way bigger than you guys think and you have to deal with it." Days later, we realized that Republican challenger John McCain's network had also been penetrated. In some ways, the fact that both had been targeted made it easier for the bureau to step in—we could provide equal information and assistance.

The bureau tried hard to stay out of partisan politics, so Mueller was adamant that we provide the precise same briefing to both campaigns—there couldn't be any hint that we were favoring one side over another. I spoke with both campaigns, and they sent representatives to Washington: Obama sent two members of his national security team, Denis McDonough and Mark Lippert; McCain sent his foreign policy advisor, Richard Fontaine. We met separately in the FBI's command center and explained that a "foreign organization" had targeted their networks, but stopped short of telling them it was China.[52]

Both campaigns had an immediate concern: Was this material going to be used against them? Our assessment, based on China's typical behavior, was that it was only an espionage operation—that is, they wanted to study and learn from the stolen documents, not to use them in any way publicly. The tech-savvy Obama campaign devoured the information we provided, asking numerous follow-ups and questioning how to strengthen their defenses; they had a top-flight cybersecurity firm, Kroll, cleanse their network. The McCain campaign, which had struggled to embrace technology, took in the briefings, but asked little in the way of follow-up. The hack came and went without public notice and the documents never surfaced publicly, though the McCain campaign fielded an odd complaint from the Chinese government: the hackers had accessed an unsent letter from McCain to the president of

Taiwan, sympathetic to Taiwan, and a Chinese diplomat complained to the campaign.[53] It was, to us, a particularly brazen complaint.

Ultimately, the 2008 presidential campaign hack was another missed alarm bell, a missed chance to understand the importance of cybersecurity on the geopolitical agenda.

CHAPTER 3

Operation Aurora

ON A BLUSTERY January day in 2009, Barack Obama took the reins of the US government, stepping into the deepest economic crisis the country had faced since the Great Depression. The mythology, already quickly settling into his team's psyche, held that the optimistic, grass-roots power of technology and social media had both delivered him to the Oval Office and would help lead the country out of the economic doldrums. The situation was dire; at the time, the country was shedding 600,000 jobs a month and unemployment was on its way up to 10 percent.[1] "The state of our economy calls for action: bold and swift—and we will act not only to create new jobs but to lay a new foundation for growth," Obama told the massive crowd at his inauguration.[2]

For many of the new appointees flooding back into government in 2009, at the White House, Main Justice, and across the national security apparatus, their last stint in government had been during the pre-9/11 Clinton years. Much had changed since that time—including the addition and reorganization of an entirely new Cabinet department, the Department of Homeland Security, that itself comprised a quarter million government employees. The arrival of the new administration presented a moment to take stock of the FBI's transformation on terrorism issues—as well as to realize how much more work still needed to be done to get the Justice Department and the bureau on the same page on cybersecurity.

"I remember maybe the most surprising thing to me during [the] transition, because I had been in national security work from 2000 to 2003 and then took a break for a while and came back, was the incredible degree of cooperation that existed between NSD and the bureau," recalled David Kris, who served as Obama's first assistant attorney general for national security.[3] During his earlier stint, both before and after 9/11, the Justice Department and the FBI had often been at odds; the relationship between FBI Director Louis Freeh and Bill Clinton had been poisonous. The two didn't speak at all for the final years of the administration, and the FBI was largely sidelined from national security conversations. Yet the intense period after 9/11 had seen a sea change in that relationship, with the FBI becoming a tightly integrated part of the national security establishment on terrorism issues. At the beginning of 2009, though, the success of that trust and integration on the counterterrorism side made clear that we needed a similar approach against the rising cyberthreats.

The president visited the FBI in April, as part of his tour of the federal workforce, addressing the bureau's employees in the courtyard of the Hoover Building. "The challenges of the 21st century have called on us to think anew, and to act anew. And in recent years, the Bureau has undergone a profound transformation to keep pace," Obama told assembled FBI employees. "With the spread of new technologies, you increasingly confront adversaries in unconventional areas—from transnational networks to cybercrimes and espionage. And through it all, you must continue to stay one step ahead of all who step outside of the law."

Barack Obama arrived in office as a new-generation leader, years younger than his predecessor, more tech-savvy than any president before. There seemed much promise in the new administration's ability to tackle technological challenges. President Obama fought to be able to keep his BlackBerry as president, refusing to be shut off from the world as commander in chief. In his first months in the White House, he hosted an event and speech on cybersecurity that even included a reference to "spoofing and phishing and botnets," terms that were still unfamiliar to nearly all of the country's top decision makers. "We meet today at a transformational moment, a moment in history when our interconnected world presents us at once with great promise but also great peril," he said. "It's the great irony of our information age, the very technologies that empower us to create and to build also empower those who would disrupt and destroy."[4]

Despite the high hopes for a more aggressive and tech-savvy approach to cybersecurity, the change of parties and administrations slowed the government's gears; just as it seemed like we were working up momentum on cybersecurity, the incoming administration wanted to take their own time to study the issue and propose solutions. Bush's carefully planned Comprehensive National Cybersecurity Initiative, the result of untold hours of work, was put on pause. "[The CNCI] was the very best of what the government did—$10 billion in funding, signed off on by six Cabinet secretaries—and the very worst of what the government did—when the administration changed, it all went back on the shelf," explains Shawn Henry. "That kills me."

Beyond the normal delays of bringing a new administration and appointees up to speed on long-running conversations, economic challenges devoured the administration's bandwidth. Each day a historic crisis appeared, and long-term strategic challenges such as cybersecurity fell aside. With the Obama administration, we ran into a unique challenge, too: the very tech-savviness that helped propel them into office led some to embrace technology more as an answer than a problem. In some ways, the grassroots-powered mythology surrounding the 2008 Obama campaign was more akin to the heady days of the mid-1990s, when people saw the freedom and openness of the internet as an all-but-unalloyed good. Its dark side was not something that the administration seemed particularly keen to dwell on.

One of the biggest internal debates at the start of the Obama administration was whether the White House would appoint a new cyber czar to coordinate efforts across governments—and, if so, would that person be at the White House, at the Office of the Director of National Intelligence, or at the Department of Homeland Security? Each model reflected a slightly different role and emphasis. More than twenty years into the challenge, the government was still trying to make sense of the patchwork of roles and responsibilities that agencies had assumed as the world shifted from analog to digital.

The prefix *cyber-*, originally drawn from William Gibson's book, had entered the government's nomenclature in the 1996 report of President Clinton's Critical Infrastructure Working Group, a team originally tasked with examining the post–Cold War terrorism threat in the wake of the Oklahoma City bombing and the vulnerability of the nation's key facilities and networks. Yet rather than just focus on the physical safety of buildings, airports, and government offices, half of the working group's final report dealt with emerging digital threats. One Justice Department lawyer assigned to the team, Michael Vatis, knew Gibson's book and recommended the group adopt the term. During a Capitol Hill hearing after the final report was produced, Deputy Attorney General Jamie Gorelick warned, "We have not yet had a terrorist cyber attack on the infrastructure. But I think that that is just a matter of time. We do not want to wait for the cyber equivalent of Pearl Harbor."[5]

In the years since, the government made repeated attempts to bring coherence to its efforts at digital defense—a defense that increasingly involved not just the government but business leaders far removed from Washington and geopolitics. In 1997, a presidential commission concluded, "Just as the terrible long-range weapons of the Nuclear Age made us think differently about security in the last half of the 20th Century, the electronic technology of the Information Age challenges us to invent new ways of protecting ourselves now.... National defense is no longer the exclusive preserve of government, and economic security is no longer just about business."[6]

In the first year of the Obama administration, Melissa Hathaway—who had led Mike McConnell's push on cybersecurity—helped lead the government's transition team on digital defense. The new Obama team ultimately embraced many of her team's conclusions, focusing a strategy around building partnerships with the private sector and working collaboratively to share information better. As Rob Knake, one of the Obama team's National Security Council staff on cybersecurity, quipped, the new administration's goal was to adopt the "Home Depot model" of working with the private sector: "You can do it, we can help."

Understanding, though, precisely who did what in cyberspace remained all too challenging. There was no "cyber 911," no clear government agency or clearinghouse to call if and when a company found that it had fallen victim to a cyberattack, either an intellectual property theft or a financial fraud. Instead, different agencies all had different roles, different legal authorities, and different approaches to cyberspace.*

The government broke its roles down into three broad categories: the Defense Department and the National Security Agency (NSA), the FBI and the Justice Department, and the Department of Homeland Security (DHS). Particularly early on in the cybersecurity debate, the NSA possessed the technical competence but people worried that it would overly militarize cyberspace and that it lacked the necessary trust with the private sector. Legally, too, its mission was only outward-looking: the NSA was prohibited from spying on Americans domestically.

DHS, still new, badly lacked for actual authority and also for technical expertise. While the Secret Service, which had been moved from the Department of Treasury to the new DHS, had long been the nation's expert on investigating cybercrimes, they had only a narrow window into the issue since they had only a "criminal" mission, not the "national security" mission of the FBI. They could pursue crooks, but they couldn't chase spies and nation-states. Overall, DHS was meant to be the public face of government cybersecurity efforts—DHS Secretary Janet Napolitano opened in October 2009 a new National Cybersecurity and Communications Integration Center, which was supposed to be a central repository for information sharing—but it conflicted at times with the FBI's NCIJTF, which worked closely with the private sector.

In the Obama administration, turf battles too often continued to rise up over the handling of information, threats, specific hacks, or relationships with the private sector, and the National Security Council began again to study the various agency roles. Finally, Robert Mueller

---

*In the final days of the Bush administration, Homeland Security Advisor Ken Wainstein—my former boss from the DC US attorney's office and another alum of Mueller's staff—tried to establish the Justice Department as the lead cyber agency during the revision of Executive Order 12333, but codifying that had erupted into a turf battle and he'd punted it to the next administration. It was a preview of more turf-jockeying to come.

had had enough of interagency conversations, working groups, and study commissions. The process was too bumpy, too slow, and not enough. He called Napolitano and NSA's leader, General Keith Alexander, and suggested the three hash out a cybersecurity agreement in person. "This is too complicated—for every example there are five exceptions," he said. "What's the simple explanation about who does what? Let's just hammer this out."*

The three of them met and, more or less on the governmental equivalent of a napkin, sketched out what came to be known as "the bubble chart," delineating in three bubbles the roles of DHS, NSA, and the Justice Department. The new approach laid out a lead role for each agency: DHS would be responsible for fixing, mitigating, and preventing attacks through information sharing and also for aiding with remediation after an attack. The FBI and the Justice Department would be responsible for the investigation and prosecution of an attack, as well as for deterrence. The Pentagon and NSA would focus on overseas disruption.

Even though the "bubble chart" became a running joke in government circles, that model held as an agreement among the agency leaders about how to do business.**

///////////////////

On a daily basis, the broken trust between the private sector and the public sector proved immensely frustrating. At one conference, the

---

*A similar battle had played out in the early 2000s over the respective roles of DHS and the Justice Department in the terrorism arena; DHS had been created to "prevent" terrorism, but it hadn't been given many operational resources to do that, and the primary investigative counterterrorism agency, the FBI, had been left at Justice—so exactly what was DHS supposed to do? Eventually, through many meetings, arguments, and working groups, a somewhat clear dividing line emerged: the FBI would be in charge of investigating and disrupting terrorism, while DHS would be in charge of "hardening" targets, protecting infrastructure, and strengthening recovery and response operations. It seemed to Mueller that we should be able to work out a similar division of labor on cybersecurity.

**Much later, in July 2016, toward the end of the Obama administration—a lag that shows how these efforts slowed in the early years of the administration—that model was codified in what is known as Presidential Policy Directive 41, PPD 41, on "United States cyber incident coordination."

speaker before me—a former Securities and Exchange Commission (SEC) official turned private defense attorney—warned about voluntarily sharing any information with the government. "Anyone who tells you to voluntarily share something with the FBI, they're the ones who should end up in handcuffs—and it's likely you'll end up in handcuffs, too," he told the crowd in his final line. As he returned to his seat, the announcer's voice boomed, "And our next speaker is John Carlin from the Justice Department on why the government's here to help." The audience sat stone-faced that day.

To change the private sector's perception, we began a quiet outreach campaign to corporate general counsels to hear their concerns—and, in response, implemented low-profile initiatives we hoped would change the threat landscape. To ensure that companies at least were warning their peers, the Justice Department and the Federal Trade Commission (FTC) clarified antitrust guidance to make clear that companies could share threat information within their own sector. Relatedly, we issued a white paper giving companies more leeway to share threat information, explaining that as long as it was in "aggregate" form it wouldn't violate privacy laws.[7] Then, to assuage liability concerns, we had the FTC and SEC state publicly that not turning information over to law enforcement could be used against a company in deciding whether its response to a breach met a reasonable standard of care—but that going to law enforcement would be considered beneficial. These were all seemingly minor changes, far off the public radar, but important nudges to help us assemble a better picture of what foreign actors were doing to American business.

We continued warning target companies and conducting outreach across industries, but continued to meet with reluctance. We showed one US company's leadership that their Chinese partner in a joint venture had been simultaneously stealing intellectual property and using it to accelerate their own technological advances. The company was shocked, rightly feeling betrayed by their Chinese partner, but resisted making that concern public; while they scaled back the joint-venture partnership, they worried that embarrassing the Chinese regime might lead to larger problems for them across China—and potentially cause trouble to their employees inside the country.

Change would only come if we could start a virtuous cycle: our prosecutors had to see that we would actually bring a case, then companies would feel more free to come forward as victims, providing more cases for prosecutors to bring. Everyone needed to see that there was a point to sharing information and that it led to solid, tangible results.

We could identify multiple different Chinese hacking teams, working against multiple different objectives and targets, each with its own preferred tools and level of tradecraft. Economic espionage was not China's only online effort. The Chinese government and military also carried out more traditional espionage aimed at groups considered enemies of the regime. In 2009, one cybersecurity firm released a detailed study of China's cyberespionage aimed at Tibetan groups, including malware aimed at the Dalai Lama's private office.[8] The attacks featured convincing spear-phishing emails that purported to be documents from the Tibetan Freedom Network but actually contained malware that fed the computer's location back to a Chinese-controlled server. It had proved successful, allowing Chinese hackers to exfiltrate documents on the Dalai Lama's negotiation positions. The Chinese closely monitored those involved in the Tibet movement; one woman, returning to her family village from Nepal, was arrested and confronted by Chinese authorities with years of transcripts of her online chats.

We also saw much more traditional targets of espionage: the US-China Economic and Security Review Commission, which was created by Congress to monitor China's rise, reported that in 2010 officials reported Chinese attempts to "infiltrate the e-mail accounts of top U.S. national security officials, including then Joint Chiefs of Staff Chairman Admiral Mike Mullen and then Chief of Naval Operations Admiral Gary Roughead."[9]

While properly executed and well-researched phishing attacks could be quite sophisticated, many of the hacks we saw weren't all that advanced. Yet since most companies and government officials still hadn't yet put real money or training into cybersecurity, a surprising number of even senior corporate executives and government officials weren't all that tech-savvy, and they fell for fake emails and relatively basic schemes. Our intelligence consensus was that few of our online adversaries were being forced to bring their A game to cyberattacks. They were succeeding just fine with second- and third-tier-level attacks. Later, FBI Director James Comey compared Chinese hackers to "a drunk burglar. They're kicking in the front door, knocking over the vase, while they're walking out with your television set. They're just prolific. Their strategy seems to be: 'We'll just be everywhere all the time—and there's no way they can stop us.' "[10]

As we carefully studied the infrastructure China used in its attacks on the United States, we zeroed in on the servers they commandeered, often without the owner's knowledge, to obfuscate their activity. These hubs, known as hop points, became a key investigative tool. Hop points, in general, are of little interest—they're just rest stops between a hacker and a victim, a run-of-the-mill computer that's been exploited by a hacker but has no real purpose other than to help obscure the hacker's origins.* Most of the hop points we saw the Chinese hackers use were actually based in the United States, although some were overseas. If a hop-point victim was inside the United States, we could get permission directly from them to monitor the network, but if it was overseas, we were required to get a court order. "A large amount of China's hacking [at the time] against U.S. companies is done through U.S.-based servers acting as the 'hub.' Meaning, China breaks into a computer in the United States and from there moves out along spokes and breaks into hundreds or even thousands of other victims," Steve Chabinsky, the former deputy assistant director of the FBI's Cyber Division, explained to Foreign Policy in 2014. "The FBI oftentimes establishes visibility on these 'hubs'—typically by getting consent from the victim company whose computer is being misused."[11]

---

* This is one reason I'm quite wary of the so-called "hack back" debate, allowing private companies to take retaliatory action against the sites that they think are hacking them—unless you're incredibly careful and sophisticated, it's all too easy to not realize online who is the ultimate person attacking you—and if you do correctly identify the ultimate target, to reach them you often have to transit back through multiple innocent victims along the path.

From those hop points, the Chinese hackers began their malicious activity: scanning for vulnerable computer ports, launching spear-phishing attempts, deploying remote access malware, and so forth. We traced both upstream—to see the IP addresses the hackers were coming from, IP addresses that could even be traced to a physical location in the world—and downstream—to understand what networks they were targeting and what documents and files they were trying to steal.

But security researchers noticed something else when they examined hop points: the hackers used these hop points for a lot of mundane activity, too, stuff that perhaps they didn't want to be traced right to their work computers. They checked email, monitored their stock portfolios or investments, and, of course, looked at porn and other not-safe-for-work content. They also ran a lot of "side projects" off the hop points, engaging in criminal frauds or schemes through the hijacked network. Hop points were a good way to save money, too: sometimes you could even catch a hacker using them to conduct activities like Bitcoin mining, relying on the processors of the hijacked computers to earn cryptocurrency and force someone else to bear the cost of the electricity, making the Bitcoin for the hacker pure profit.

Most importantly for our case, though, from sitting atop these hop points we were able to begin to see some very interesting data—for example, photos of the hackers dressed in the uniforms of their day jobs, with the Chinese Army. We were even able to trace some of the hackers back to their homes, because they were sloppy and used their work IP credentials at home, too.

This realization became a mantra of ours: exploit the seams. Hackers were humans offline and online.

*

Google's "legal discovery portals" represent some of the company's most valuable tools, helping to track and monitor Google's contacts with law enforcement—if a hacker was able to crack them, it provided a "who's who" of spies, hackers, and criminals. A nation-state could check, for instance, whether US or foreign law enforcement was monitoring its spies or intelligence officers. Given their value, the company closely tracks activity on their portals and in so doing flagged one user who appeared to be querying a long list of Chinese names. When the company's security department asked why, she was puzzled—she hadn't done anything of the sort. Alarm bells started to go off inside the company, and experts began examining her computer—the beginning of what ended up being one of the most consequential breaches until that point.[12] Google took the threat and the penetration deeply personally; Sergey Brin, one of the cofounders, relocated his desk to sit with the security team, and the company went on a high-priced hiring spree, even offering $100,000 signing bonuses to top security personnel.

In January 2010, VeriSign's iDefense publicly accused the Chinese government of stealing the source code—the crown jewels of a tech company, the secret back-end recipe for how a website works—for at least 33 companies, including the tech giant Google, as well as Yahoo, Symantec, Northrop Grumman, and Dow Chemical.[13]* The hackers had relied upon previously unknown vulnerabilities in both Microsoft's Internet Explorer and Adobe's PDF reader—so-called zero-day exploits—to deliver malware onto targeted computers.[14]

Zero-day exploits represent the crown jewels in the cyber realm, incredibly rare and valuable commodities to both regular hackers and, especially, nation-states, which rely on zero days to conduct high-level espionage and prepare military attacks on unsuspecting targets. They were not used routinely, but instead were hoarded and stockpiled for special access or emergency situations. Tech companies were often willing to pay big money privately for zero days, as were governments interested in using them for future hacking. Inside the US government, there were often intense philosophical discussions about when and whether companies should be made aware of zero-day vulnerabilities to issue software or hardware patches; often the FBI or DHS preferred to let companies know quickly, to help them harden their systems, while intelligence agencies might prefer to hold on to them

---

* Ultimately, with time, the United States came to believe that the attacks had targeted thousands of companies worldwide, far more than the initial 33 identified.

to exploit in their own work. This debate, which continues to this day, led to a formal system known as the VEP, the Vulnerabilities Equities Process, which brought together government agencies to weigh in on zero days to industry. The high value of a zero day meant that spotting one in the wild was exceedingly rare—upward of 90 percent of hacking efforts didn't involve exploiting any unique vulnerabilities—which meant that someone had really wanted the information they were after if they were willing to burn one or more zero days on the attack. It indicated a talented, highly capable adversary going after a high-consequence target.

The use of the Adobe PDF reader underscored how hackers were moving beyond the core internet applications that powered the internet and were finding softer targets in the tools that users relied upon without a second thought.[15] Together, the attack represented an impressive—and important—evolution in the way hackers were thinking about their private sector targets, utilizing complicated malware with multiple pieces and at least three layers of encryption to obfuscate its real intentions. Once inside a victim's computer, this malware opened a hidden back door to the hackers' control server that appeared to be a normal secure sockets layer (SSL) connection, a routine type of secure portal that's used dozens of times a day browsing the web.

"We have never ever, outside of the defense industry, seen commercial industrial companies come under that level of sophisticated attack," McAfee's then head of threat research, Dmitri Alperovitch, said afterward.[16] The hackers also appeared to not just be after trade secrets: Google reported that the attacks had also targeted Chinese human rights activists using its platform. Similarly, Microsoft reported that its own surveillance database had been targeted by Chinese hackers. "What we found was the attackers were actually looking for the accounts that we had lawful wiretap orders on," Microsoft's David Aucsmith told one Washington audience.[17] "If you think about this, this is brilliant counterintelligence. You have two choices: If you want to find out if your agents, if you will, have been discovered, you can try to break into the FBI to find out that way. Presumably that's difficult. Or you can break into the people that the courts have served papers on and see if you can find it that way. That's essentially what we think they were trolling for, at least in our case."

It was another indication of how, in the cyberworld, private companies were increasingly on the front lines of national security, facing sophisticated foreign adversaries intent on penetrating their secrets.

Security researchers at McAfee had determined that two of the malware files the hackers had used had the word *Aurora* in file folders that stored the malware and came to believe that it was the code name that the hackers used themselves. The hack, thereafter, was known as Operation AURORA. AURORA appeared reminiscent of an attack six months earlier that also exploited weaknesses in Adobe products, including Reader and Flash, and targeted more than one hundred companies. VeriSign reported the IP addresses used in the Google attack were just six addresses away from those used in the earlier attack—a suspicious proximity given the vastness of the web—and a hint, the company said, "that it is possible that the two attacks are one and the same, and that the organizations targeted in the [recent] Silicon Valley attacks have been compromised since July."

The government and private sector researchers scrambled to trace the attack, initially meeting a stone wall on a Taiwanese server; eventually, though, they were able to untangle the attack further and trace it directly to two Chinese universities, Shanghai Jiao Tong University and the Shandong Lanxiang Vocational School. The schools had close ties to both the Chinese military and Baidu, the Chinese search engine that was perhaps Google's top global competitor.[18] When the *New York Times* interviewed a professor at Jiao Tong, he said, "I'm not surprised. Actually students hacking into foreign Web sites is quite normal."

The crisis made real to Silicon Valley what we had been seeing across the board: China was pillaging our nation's networks, exploiting them for both traditional espionage and economic advantage. It also crystalized the challenge for American businesses expanding into China that sought to balance profit with values: if China was willing to attack Google in order to target human rights activists, maybe you couldn't do business there and be consistent with your company's values.

The attack made Google reconsider its own relationship with China. As word of the attack spread, Google took the strong step of announcing that it would no longer comply with a five-year-old agreement that it censor search results inside of the country. Until then, if Chinese users using the native language search engine, google.cn, sought information on topics such as "Tiananmen Square massacre," "Dalai Lama," or even criticism of senior Chinese leaders, they would find no results. China had also pressured Google to obscure key government sites on its Google satellite views. But that, it appeared, wasn't enough for Chinese leaders; according to the *New York Times*, Chinese leaders like Li Changchun—a Politburo member who led the country's propaganda efforts—discovered that they could still turn up unflattering stories about themselves by conducting searches in Chinese on Google's main search engine.[19] The search engine, in Li's mind, also didn't do enough to censor information about Chinese leaders and their families—a fact Li confirmed by Googling his children. According to news reports, Li Changchun and other senior party leaders directed that hackers attack Google. As part of his escalating campaign, he also ordered China's three major state-owned communications companies to cease doing business with Google.

The combination of cyberattacks and official Chinese pressure was too much for the Silicon Valley giant. "We have decided we are no longer willing to continue censoring our results on google.cn, and so over the next few weeks we will be discussing with the Chinese government the basis on which we could operate an unfiltered search engine within the law, if at all," David Drummond, the company's chief legal officer, said in a statement the week the attack became public. A few months later, Google effectively pulled out of the country entirely—no small decision, given that the fast-growing market represented a key area of future growth and that Google's operation there already employed about 700 people and had around $300 million in annual revenue.[20]

Just days after the AURORA hack was announced, Secretary of State Hillary Clinton called for an internet free of censorship. "Virtual walls are cropping up in place of visible walls," Secretary Clinton said in Washington at the Newseum, a museum dedicated to First

Amendment rights, including freedom of speech and freedom of the press. "With the spread of these restrictive practices, a new information curtain is descending across much of the world."

Secretary Clinton directly chastised China's AURORA attacks on Google—particularly focusing on reports that human rights activists using its tools had been targeted as part of Chinese attacks. "Countries or individuals that engage in cyber attacks should face consequences and international condemnation," she said. "By reinforcing that message, we can create norms of behavior among states and encourage respect for the global networked commons."[21]

The public criticism highlighted a particular challenge for the United States as we encouraged the growth of the internet worldwide. Fundamentally, we want an internet free of censorship, one that empowers human rights activists and advocates for free speech. To enable that freedom, in the past the government has promoted—even helped fund in certain instances—sophisticated communication tools and encryption that allow prodemocracy groups to share information, collaborate, and document abuses without fear that their authoritarian regimes could spy on them. The US government has supported tools like Tor, free software that helps internet users anonymize their network connection, making it impossible to trace where they're accessing the web from and also lets them access content prohibited by local censorship (e.g., the Great Firewall in China). Yet even as we support those technologies for their ability to support freedom overseas, we have also long worried that those technologies in our own society can be used by terrorists, criminals, and child predators to disguise their actions and to plan attacks and plot against our citizens knowing that not even a legal court order for surveillance can access their communications.

The duty of internet companies to comply with the laws of the countries where they do business is a complicated one. In 2004, an editor at a Hunan Province business newspaper, Shi Tao, used his Yahoo email address to anonymously send a Chinese-language prodemocracy website in the United States the restrictions the Communist Party had decreed for the approaching fifteenth anniversary of the Tiananmen Square protests. Just days later, Yahoo complied when the Beijing State

Security Bureau demanded the company turn over details of the anonymous email, including the name and location of the sender. The government informed Yahoo that the sender was suspected of the "illegal provision of state secrets to foreign entities."[22] After Yahoo complied, Shi Tao was promptly arrested, found guilty in a two-hour trial, and sentenced to a decade of forced labor.

The case quickly became an international cause—and Yahoo faced immense pressure from critics, especially as it became clear that Yahoo had acted similarly in other cases, including another dissident who had been sentenced to seven years for sharing online articles about government corruption. "American technology and know-how is substantially enabling repressive regimes in China and elsewhere in the world to cruelly exploit and abuse their own citizens," said US Congressman Chris Smith in 2006. "Yahoo said that it must adhere to local laws in all countries where it operates. But my response to that is: if the secret police a half century ago asked where Anne Frank was hiding, would the correct answer be to hand over the information in order to comply with local laws?"[23]

By the following year, Yahoo conceded, settling a lawsuit on the family's behalf out of court. In another congressional hearing, its cofounder Jerry Yang faced withering criticism; Representative Tom Lantos, a Holocaust survivor, told Yang, "While technologically and financially you are giants, morally you are pygmies."[24] Shi Tao's mother testified, as well, and Yang bowed three times to her in apology, saying, "I want to personally apologize." Yet at the same time, the company's general counsel, Michael Callahan, told House members that he wouldn't guarantee that Yahoo would not do the exact same thing in the future: "I cannot ask our local employees to resist lawful demands and put their own freedom at risk, even if, in my personal view, the local laws are overbroad."

The AURORA case highlighted this tension and how hard it was to broker even routine international law enforcement cooperation with a country like China. In many places around the world, the FBI and federal law enforcement have been able to work with their local foreign counterparts even if the respective countries have rivalries in other areas; the United States and Russia even managed to cooperate on traditional law enforcement efforts at some points in the 1990s and early 2000s. Yet even though US and Chinese law enforcement had shared common problems—organized crimes, narcotics, child pornography—that might under different circumstances be areas where our law enforcement could cooperate with theirs, the fact that cracking down and silencing human rights activists remained near the top of China's law enforcement priorities made it nearly impossible to cooperate on other issues. Both sides lacked the trust to encourage information sharing.

///////////////

In early 2011, Lisa Monaco—my former colleague both in Mueller's office and as a prosecutor—was nominated to be the assistant attorney general for national security. Lisa had been involved in some of the most significant cases of her generation and had a broad breadth of experience; she'd worked for Janet Reno, then was part of the elite Enron Task Force, which led the prosecution of the energy giant in the early 2000s, and then had been tapped to be a special counselor to Mueller and later chief of staff. Smart and a careful speaker who eschewed the spotlight—like much of the team Mueller assembled around him— she'd seen firsthand the way Mueller had pushed to transform the FBI to confront the terrorism threat and, more recently, to begin to address cyberthreats. At the start of the Obama administration, she'd been quickly tapped to be a top national security aide to the deputy attorney general and then, ultimately, became his principal deputy, working across a broad range of issues at Main Justice.

Two years later, she was the administration's uniform and uncontroversial choice to lead the department's National Security Division, a little-understood creation of what was known as the WMD Commission. The 2005 group, officially known as the Commission on the Intelligence Capabilities of the United States Regarding Weapons of Mass Destruction, and cochaired by Senator Chuck Robb and Judge Laurence Silberman, had been tasked with examining the intelligence failures that had led to the conclusion that Iraq possessed weapons of mass destruction, but it had interpreted its mandate broadly and examined the US intelligence community in thoughtful depth. The problem, the WMD Commission concluded, wasn't necessarily that the nation's multibillion-dollar intelligence apparatus wasn't gathering the requisite information—it was that the intelligence agencies weren't doing a good job telling each other what they knew. Among its conclusions, it noted that while the CIA, FBI, and Department of Homeland Security had accomplished sweeping reorganizations following 9/11 to ensure better, faster information sharing, the Justice Department had not changed at all—its three primary national security units, the Office of Intelligence Policy and Review, the counterterrorism section, and the counterintelligence section, all reported to different leaders. "If there is method to this madness, neither we, nor any other official with whom we spoke, could identify it," the commission concluded.[25] The WMD Commission recommended creating a new assistant attorney general for national security who would oversee all three, streamlining the Justice Department's reporting and ensuring that a single set of eyes—and a single philosophy—guided both terrorism and espionage cases.

Silberman, who had once served as deputy attorney general and had also worked on the court that oversaw FISA cases, had come to believe that there was a fundamental difference between law enforcement cases and those focused on counterintelligence or counterespionage. "They were different kinds of skills," Silberman had concluded, in part because the focus of a counterterrorism or counterintelligence case wasn't always aimed at a criminal prosecution—it was often about deflecting or disrupting a case and there were lot of different tools agents and investigators could bring to bear on a terrorism or espionage suspect short of putting them in handcuffs.[26]

The new National Security Division (NSD)—the first litigating division of the Justice Department created since the Civil Rights Division in 1957—ended up being part of the 2005 USA PATRIOT Reauthorization Act. "It will help our brave men and women in law enforcement connect the dots before the terrorists strike," President George W. Bush said as he signed the legislation.[27]

It was more than a reshuffling of the deck chairs: the new assistant attorney general was required to approve any indictment and prosecution that charged a suspect with more than 20 specific, de-lineated criminal statutes dealing with counterterrorism, espionage, export controls, and other related crimes.[28] "It was supposed to be a national view for national security," Lisa says. That gave the assistant attorney general a unique ability to help shape the national prosecu-tion strategy for the Justice Department; whereas each US attorney could mostly follow their own whims on traditional criminal and civil prosecutions, national security cases had to be coordinated with Main Justice.

By the early years of the Obama administration, NSD numbered around 300 lawyers, all working side by side on terrorism and espio-nage cases. Each of the first three so-called AAGs for NSD put his own stamp on the division: Ken Wainstein launched the division with a la-ser focus on counterterrorism, the primary fear at the time; J. Patrick Rowan broadened its portfolio and boosted the prosecution of export control cases and nonproliferation issues; and Obama's first appointee, David Kris, worked to grow the division's appellate work and integrate the Justice Department's Office of Intelligence. Lisa's job, in addition to everything already on the division's plate, was to prioritize and tackle national security cyber cases.

I saw the tremendous value of the NSD during my time at FBI; day to day, the bureau possessed great trust in the terrorism prosecutors and the lawyers who appeared on its behalf before the Foreign Intel-ligence Surveillance Court. The trust across Pennsylvania Avenue be-tween the FBI and NSD on terrorism cases appeared almost unique in the government, helped no doubt by the fact that four of the first five NSD leaders actually worked first for Mueller at the FBI: Ken Wain-stein, Pat Rowan, Lisa, and—eventually—me. The "operators" really connected on a shared sense of mission. While there were certainly some policy tussles with the FBI's general counsel office, there was pri-marily great agreement and cooperation at the field level. I had seen this in action during two major terrorism cases in 2009, the cross-country chase of would-be New York City subway bomber Najibullah Zazi and the long-term investigation of David Coleman Headley, an American who helped plot the 2008 Mumbai attacks. The cases brought together both routine law enforcement resources and special international intelligence to successfully stop both individuals in a way that the FBI never could have done before 9/11.

Yet as strong as that relationship was on counterterrorism issues, Lisa and I both could tell at the FBI that we didn't have the same relationship when it came to cyber: we didn't line up well with NSD's work. There was plenty of cooperation on the intelligence side, among those collecting information about the cyberthreats to the United States, but precious little led toward action. Much of the disconnect appeared organizational; while the two aligned well on counterterrorism, the FBI's efforts on cybersecurity were more split—the bureau had a separate cyber branch, apart from its National Security Branch—and there was also frustration between the counterintelligence division at the FBI and the Justice Department's own counterespionage section inside NSD.

Lisa, who had been serving as the principal associate deputy attorney general—the top deputy to the Justice Department's deputy, a position that involved liaising with all of the country's US attorneys—received a vivid illustration of the challenges of prosecuting cybersecurity when the Nasdaq stock market had been hacked in October 2010. Two different offices jockeyed for the control of the investigation; the Secret Service, who prosecuted financial crimes, tried to assert control of the case in New Jersey, where the Nasdaq's main data center was located. At the same time, the FBI's Cyber Division in New York City—where the Nasdaq was headquartered—also tried to assert control. "This is exactly the problem," Lisa recalls. "They were so focused on the bureaucracy, they were missing the fight—it wasn't criminal versus cyber, it was US versus Russia."

I had lived the same fight: After Lisa had moved across to Main Justice in 2009, I'd become Mueller's acting chief of staff—and after his typical, laborious, tortured weighing of personnel choices, he made me the permanent chief of staff. As the Nasdaq hack unfolded, I remember the head of the FBI Cyber Division coming into my office to complain he didn't know who to call at the Justice Department about the Nasdaq case; for years, terrorism cases had been run through a central team, coordinated nationally, but cyber remained piecemeal.

When Lisa took over at NSD, she felt the same challenge existed at Main Justice—the unit was constructed for the threat as it existed after 9/11. Even the unit's nomenclature seemed outdated: the very name of the NSD's section—counterespionage—evoked an era of spies in trenchcoats meeting in dark alleys, whereas the FBI had long since moved to counterintelligence, a broader term meant to capture more asymmetric nation-state threats. "NSD needed to see the new threat vectors," Lisa says. "We needed to understand who's who at the zoo. We needed to understand how old and new threat actors were using our technology—namely the internet—against us, to steal our secrets, our technology, and R&D and weaponize it against us."

She told Robert Mueller she was going to ask me to join her for the transformation as her deputy and chief of staff, and I soon moved back across Pennsylvania Avenue to Main Justice.* As Lisa jokes, "It's the only time I won a wrestling match with Mueller." On the back of an agenda for a meeting with Mueller, we sketched out what her vision for an updated structure for the division would be—we understood from our time at the FBI that it sat on a trove of data about Chinese economic espionage that never made it to prosecutors. Instead, at Main Justice, prosecutors still focused on traditional computer hacking cases and intellectual property violations, even as nation-states became a primary threat. Cases fell through the cracks between the divisions.

Early on at NSD, Lisa held an all-hands meeting and laid out her vision for the next evolution of NSD. Counterterrorism, of course, remained a top priority, but NSD needed to lead the way on two rising threats: counterintelligence and cyber.

To help understand the latter problem, we recruited Anita Singh, a tough and loud former CCIPS attorney who had worked at the National Security Council for John Brennan and had a good understanding of

---

* My departure from the FBI was delayed by a few months in the spring of 2011 when President Obama unexpectedly asked Mueller to stay as director for an additional two years; Mueller—who had already become the longest-serving director since J. Edgar Hoover himself—agreed to stay in part because he felt the FBI's transformation was still a work in progress and that the extended term would help him solidify some of the cultural changes. The unprecedented extension required a special act of Congress, and I stayed on to help manage his reconfirmation for the job, which passed the Senate 100–0.

the classified side of the cyberworld.* Anita had worked at one point at the Boston Consulting Group, and we tasked her with studying the strategic orientation of the National Security Division.

After weeks of interviews and meetings across the Justice Department, Anita came into my office, plopped down on my couch, and told me her unsurprising conclusion: our impression was correct. Cyber cases against China fell through the cracks, because neither the criminal side nor the national security side felt ownership. The criminal side handled traditional economic espionage, but the national security side handled cases against foreign adversaries. Each side knew a great deal, but they stopped pursuing leads when a case seemed to stray into the other's lane. "The department wasn't set up to look at theft," Anita recalls. NSD just wasn't doing that much in cyber. NSD had great expertise on hacker tactics and techniques, but had not been trying to translate that information into prosecutable cases. "It was actually surprising how much was happening across criminal [division] and NSD, but the puzzle pieces weren't being connected. It wasn't all being looked at together," Anita recalls. Much of her early work on the issue was simply inviting the Justice Department's various teams to sit together and share information. "It was a literal bringing to the table, gathering everyone to share what they knew. That hadn't really happened in an organized way." Before I'd ever gone over to NSD, I knew from my time at the FBI that we could assemble enough information and evidence that we could bring a criminal case. As our charging documents later showed, we would even be able to make public photographs of specific Chinese hackers traced to individual hacks. On the strength of our confidence, Lisa was willing to work the phones to find us a partner in a US attorney somewhere in the country. We just needed to arm the prosecutors and set them loose to work with investigators.

Little of what we ended up trying to do at NSD proved radical or groundbreaking—it reflected many of the tools and techniques that

---

*When I recruited Anita back to the Justice Department, she laid out the conditions that, amazingly, she'd gotten the no-nonsense Brennan to agree to at the NSC: she'd be willing to come to NSD as long as she was allowed to continue teaching her kickboxing class.

the Criminal Division had been doing for eight to ten years. Yet since NSD had been largely focused on traditional economic espionage theft and intelligence gathering—it wasn't a team heavy with computer hacking prosecutors—the new approach seemed like a big advance. It wasn't even particularly controversial: when we pitched the reorganization to Congress, we received broad bipartisan approval, even amid the partisan political wrangling that engulfed so many other issues.

Yet even as we pursued these reorganizations and tried to align ourselves to the new threat, everywhere we looked, to steal a phrase from CIA Director George Tenet talking about the terrorism threat in the summer of 2001, "the system was blinking red."

<hr />

In February 2011, the security firm McAfee released a 19-page report detailing "coordinated covert and targeted cyberattacks" against as many as a dozen multinational oil, energy, and petrochemical companies from the United States to Kazakhstan to Greece to Taiwan.[29] The attacks, nicknamed Night Dragon by McAfee, were exactly what we were seeing in other areas. The firm described "methodical and progressive intrusions into the targeted infrastructure" that relied on compromised servers in the United States and the Netherlands and a familiar set of tools—spear phishing and the exploitation of vulnerabilities inside Microsoft Windows operating systems—that helped hackers gain access to targeted computers, which were then manipulated to allow the hackers to hide their mass data exfiltrations. Using remote administration tools that allowed the hackers to install a back door and work almost as if they had been sitting at the infected computer terminals themselves, they could proceed to root around in the network directories to find useful information. The RATs were similar to commercial tools like Citrix or Microsoft Windows Terminal Services that are used by companies and network administrators to help workers access computers remotely.

Once McAfee noticed the Night Dragon attacks, they proved relatively easy to trace—the specific back door the hackers installed relied on a unique identifier to "talk" back to the command servers. The back door broadcast a "beacon" at five-second intervals telling the command server it was operational; any network administrator who knew what to look for would instantly have recognized it. The hackers also used four well-known malicious domains to route their traffic: is-a-chef.com, thruhere.net, office-on-the.net, and selfip.com. Using the unique identifiers of the attack, McAfee was able to trace Night Dragon's efforts back at least until November 2009, but they suspected the attacks might have begun as early as 2006. As security expert Dmitri Alperovitch, then at McAfee, explained, it "speaks to quite a sad state of our critical infrastructure security. These were not sophisticated attacks ... yet they were very successful in achieving their goals."[30] The thefts, completely unnoticed by the targeted companies, had yielded competitive intelligence and trade secrets likely worth millions—if not billions.

McAfee researchers traced part of the malware back to an individual who ran a web hosting service in Heze, a city of eight million in Shandong Province on China's east coast. There was plenty of circumstantial evidence, too, that the attacks emanated from China: one of the passwords used to unlock the malware was "zw.china"; the exfiltrations all came from Beijing IP addresses; the malware relied on popular Chinese-created hacking tools such as Hookmsgina, WinlogonHack, and ASPXSpy; and—perhaps most telling of all—the hackers all operated from 9 a.m. to 5 p.m. Beijing time. As McAfee concluded, "Although it is possible that all of these indicators are an elaborate redherring operation designed to pin the blame for the attacks on Chinese hackers, we believe this to be highly unlikely. Further, it is unclear who would have the motivation to go to these extraordinary lengths to place the blame for these attacks on someone else." It was a pattern we saw across numerous hacks. To China, hacking was a white-collar company job.

It wasn't long before we received yet another example of the huge damage hackers were doing: in March 2011, an employee at the computer security firm RSA downloaded a seemingly routine Excel spreadsheet "2011 Recruitment Plan," a piece of phishing malware that helped hackers undermine one of the internet's core security systems.[31] The hacking of the RSA's system was a huge problem for the technology industry—a compromise of one of the foundational parts of a security system that crossed multiple industries, a sign of how vulnerabilities in an interconnected world could undermine protections across many different parts of industry and government at once.

//////////////

Part of what made it so challenging to talk about cybersecurity both inside the government and across industries was that there wasn't a unified language; each security company and researcher had their own names for various hacker threats, and the government had a naming convention all its own. The same Chinese hacker team might be referred to as Putter Panda in one report by the security firm Crowd-Strike and MSUpdater in another report by a different security firm; the Comment Crew hacker team, as it was known by some researchers, was also dubbed Advanced Persistent Threat 1 by the security firm Mandiant and other industry researchers called it the Shanghai Group. These various names could refer to different hackers working on specific projects—or in specific units—so a hacker unit that was responsible for one attack might be next linked publicly to another attack using an entirely different name. It was as if every think tank and intelligence agency called al-Qaeda by a different name. No wonder the public had trouble keeping up.

That same summer, a team of private security researchers watched as Comment Crew hackers pillaged more than 20 commercial-focused targets—from energy giant Halliburton to the Washington law firm Wiley Rein to ITC, an Indian conglomerate. *Bloomberg News* later reported they also stole the emails of the European Union Council president, as well as rooted through the data of a Canadian magistrate overseeing the extradition of a Chinese man wanted for more than a decade.[32] "The logs also show how nimbly [the Comment Crew hackers] could respond to events, even when sensitive government networks were involved," *Bloomberg* wrote. Just days after the magistrate had freed the alleged smuggler to await a hearing, the Comment Crew hackers hopped through the network of the Immigration and Refugee Board of Canada, starting with computers in Toronto, then stealing and decrypting passwords that allowed them to move to the board's network in Vancouver, and then ultimately to the magistrate's work computer.

Just like earlier attacks, this latest wave showed special dedication—even though the head of ITC, Y. C. Deveshwar, didn't use a computer personally, the Chinese hackers targeted the computer of his personal assistant to steal sensitive documents from his office. Stymied in an attempt to open a password-protected directory, they simply installed a piece of malware to steal the password the next time the assistant used it. Elsewhere, they proved equally methodical—at a Washington nonprofit, Business Executives for National Security, they carefully turned off the antivirus program before exploring the system, and at another prodemocracy nonprofit, the International Republican Institute, they carefully consolidated copies of the senior staff's files on a single computer, chose 220 documents that appeared most relevant to China, zipped them into encrypted files, and exfiltrated them right off the network. Thanks to a mistake in their malware that an alert security researcher noticed, American security teams were able to watch the hackers' stolen files in transit as they moved all the way back to Chinese servers.[33]

The hackers used hijacked websites to help communicate with infected computers, attempting to hide their real fingerprints by commandeering the websites of a south Texas high school teacher, an Idaho drag racing track, and even Pietro's, a famous Italian restaurant in New York City. Later that year, they targeted North American energy companies by stealing a subscriber list for a nuclear industry newsletter and targeting those subscribers with spear-phishing emails, helping them penetrate a computer at the Diablo Canyon nuclear plant in California. As Shawn Henry, the FBI executive, told *Bloomberg* shortly after he left the bureau, "What the general public hears about—stolen credit card numbers, somebody hacked LinkedIn—that's the tip of the iceberg, the unclassified stuff. I've been circling the iceberg in a submarine. This is the biggest vacuuming up of US proprietary data that we've ever seen. It's a machine."

That summer turned into a busy one for revelations about China's myriad intrusions into Western systems. In August 2011, McAfee issued another public report, tracing the work of a single Chinese APT known as Shady Rat. Their researchers gained access to a specific command-and-control server used by the hackers since 2006 and pieced together that group's activities over those five years. "After painstaking analysis of the logs, even we were surprised by the enormous diversity of the victim organizations and were taken aback by the audacity of the perpetrators," McAfee reported. All told, they found 71 victim organizations spread across 14 countries—from economic targets such as the Department of Energy research laboratory and defense contractors to US real estate and accounting firms, as well as targets clearly chosen for their political interest: a major US news organization's Hong Kong bureau and the ASEAN Secretariat just before the organization's annual summit in Singapore, the United Nations, the International Olympic Committee, and the World Anti-Doping Agency, as well as companies in South Korea, Vietnam, Taiwan, and other Chinese rivals in Asia.[34]

The public exposure of Shady Rat was another example for us of the odd bifurcation of cyber headlines. Even as hacktivist groups such as Anonymous and Lulzsec grabbed headlines that year with their attacks on HBGary—a company investigating WikiLeaks—and by hacking the website of the Bay Area Rapid Transit system's police department after a controversial police shooting there, we continued to be most concerned about the foreign nation-states attacking our systems— threats that were much quieter, longer lasting, and deeply damaging to the core of our economy and national security. The headlines dominating news coverage often seemed flashy attention-grabbing surface-level stunts, even as China and Iran carefully and quietly dug far deeper.

///////////////

In late 2011, the US government took its first tentative step toward talking about the Chinese hacking threat. "Chinese actors are the world's most active and persistent perpetrators of economic espionage," the US Office of the National Counterintelligence Executive concluded in a report that fall. "Chinese attempts to collect U.S. technological and economic information will continue at a high level and will represent a growing and persistent threat to U.S. economic security."[35]

As Robert Bryant, the nation's head of counterespionage, said, "If our research and development—$400 billion a year—is pilfered, frankly, it will destroy part of our economic viability in this country."[36]

The comments didn't register widely with the public, but we knew China heard them. Nothing happened—good or bad. That, in and of itself, was a significant sign. We had named the Chinese threat, and the sky did not fall. After years of internal debate and fears about confronting China—fears that somehow by publicly discussing China's digital robbery we would lead to a dangerous diplomatic breakdown between the two countries—we did just that and life went on. I hoped it was just the start.

In the months ahead, the pace of intrusions didn't slow: NASA in February 2012 announced that Chinese hackers had successfully penetrated the network of the Jet Propulsion Laboratory and gained "full, functional control" over their computer systems such that they were even able to manipulate user accounts for mission-critical systems. That same year, we saw the People's Liberation Army release a bomb disposal robot that we could immediately tell was modeled on the plans for a robot stolen from the defense contractor QinetiQ, which had been hacked in 2007.

We could see alarm bells ringing across government—and, belatedly, government leaders began addressing the issue more seriously in public. In an essay in the *Wall Street Journal* on July 19, 2012, President Obama warned, "the cyber threat to our nation is one of the most serious economic and national security challenges we face."[37] As he said, "Foreign governments, criminal syndicates and lone individuals are probing our financial, energy and public safety systems every day. Last year, a water plant in Texas disconnected its control system from the Internet after a hacker posted pictures of the facility's internal controls. More recently, hackers penetrated the networks of companies that operate our natural-gas pipelines."

We needed to be doing more. The United States needed to be making a public case for arresting China's pillaging of our intellectual property. Watching wasn't working. We saw in industry after industry, sector after sector, the Chinese thefts caused real harm to American companies and American workers. This wasn't traditional international espionage. It was just as Justice Stephen Breyer had said years earlier in the *Grokster* case, "deliberate unlawful copying is no less an unlawful taking of property than garden-variety theft."

We certainly understood there were pros and cons to a public confrontation, and we began making the rounds of the intelligence world to make the case for public action. If we were going to be successful, we wanted to have the government's leadership on board at the start of our effort. While we often spoke of the US intelligence community as a monolith, inside it was anything but. Each agency had its own strengths, weaknesses, and internal politics—and, above all, preferred to preserve its own equities and capabilities on the global stage. Putting country above agency, the leaders of the intelligence world quickly embraced the idea—after all, they had a better view of the threat and the harm than most. At the NSA, Deputy Director Chris Inglis was blunt: "Look, it may make our jobs harder to collect [intelligence], but given the scope of the problem that we're seeing we need to do something to change the dynamic. Maybe this will help."

"That's the goal," I said.

More broadly, we began the long and slow process of outreach across the country; we knew we'd never be able to get our efforts off the ground without support from the nation's US attorneys and, from inside Main Justice, the backing of the CCIPS team. As it turned out, we found great partners in both places: Jenny Durkan, the Seattle US attorney and the chair of the attorney general's cybercrime advisory group, and John Lynch, the head of the Criminal Division at CCIPS. They recognized that the Justice Department broadly lacked the capability to tackle complex cases like this. "The experienced [cybersecurity attorneys] you [could] count on one hand," recalls Adam Hickey, who became one of the founding members of our team.

We hoped to build a larger team, modeled on the approach I had seen when I coordinated the Justice Department's CHIP network. The CHIP prosecutors, with their special training on computer crimes, cut across the various US attorney's offices, working in a peer-to-peer model, helping to provide technical expertise. We wanted to emulate that in national security cases, combining the CHIP model with another national Justice Department team known as ATAC, the Anti-Terrorism Advisory Council, prosecutors in each office specially trained in dealing with classified sources and methods who were responsible for working with the FBI's Joint Terrorism Task Force to help share information with state and local partners on counterterrorism cases. By taking the best of both the CHIP and ATAC models, we hoped we could establish a team of computer-savvy prosecutors trained in protecting and using classified sources and methods.

That vision led to what we originally called the national security cyber specialist, an acronym, NSCS, pronounced *nis-cus*. "The NSCS was supposed to be the repository for all the information we were gathering behind-the-scenes," Lisa Monaco recalls. We never meant the awkward name to be permanent, but it quickly took on a life of its own in a government system where everything seems to have its own acronym. "I remember sitting in meetings where people started to use 'NSCS' and thinking, 'Wait, we never meant for that to be the real name,'" Anita recalls. "It was just supposed to be a placeholder, but everyone adopted it before we could come up with a real name."

Lisa announced the new approach and explained the vision for the new NSCS positions at an October 2012 conference in Seattle, convened there by Jenny Durkan. She explained that we also wanted to revamp the traditional counterespionage section to focus on asymmetric threats and bring more national security–focused cyber cases, such as what we were starting to pursue against China.

John Lynch proved key to helping us focus our team, as well as helping to provide the initial training for the prosecutors we brought in. We asked US attorneys to choose who they wanted to send to the new training program, and their nominations gave us an interesting window into how they themselves viewed cybersecurity. About 40 percent picked existing terrorism and national security specialists, another 40 percent chose CHIP prosecutors—those who already specialized in computer hacking and intellectual property—and the remaining 20 percent tapped promising prosecutors entirely new to the field. At the same time, we assembled what we called the NSD's Threat Cell, a team specially focused on Chinese economic espionage, and we posted a nationwide call for prosecutors interested in tackling the threat who wanted a temporary transfer to Main Justice.

I had been carefully cultivating my own mental list of assistant US attorneys across the country who seemed like they'd be a good fit for the new job. In the Southern District of New York, I'd had my eye on Adam Hickey, who had spent years as a terrorism prosecutor. He had come to NSD in early 2012 to do a short-term rotation on cyber policy. When he made a quip about the NSCS network to his supervisor, asking whether he should attend its kick-off meeting, she replied, "Wait—you know that's going to be you, right? That's Carlin's plan for you."

The Justice Department's normal training centers wouldn't provide the level of security we needed to discuss the required classified foreign intelligence, so on November 7, 2012, we brought the prosecutors to a secure facility at Main Justice for a three-day conference and intense courses that included trainings on the Computer Fraud and Abuse Act, the Electronic Communications Privacy Act, and also what we called Internet 101, a training that explained the technical details of how the internet itself operated. Both Mueller and Attorney General Eric Holder spoke to the inaugural class.

As confident as I was that nation-state cases could be prosecuted, we needed to actually bring one as proof of concept and encourage other US attorneys to devote resources to bringing more. We didn't get off to an auspicious start. The first US attorney we took the idea to, one of the most credible voices in the department, turned us down. He asked: *When did we think we could bring a case—and were we confident we would bring a case?* I told him I had no idea how long it would take, but I did think we would be successful. He demurred. He explained his office was strapped for resources—many US attorney's offices had seen only modest budget increases since 9/11 despite a massive increase in intensive, time-consuming cases—and my idea presented another intensive, time-consuming gamble. We heard that echoed around the country. The dysfunction in Washington meant the government seemed perpetually stuck in a budget freeze, which meant US attorneys felt they couldn't spare extra resources for new projects. One US attorney told us he couldn't assign an assistant US attorney if we weren't positive we could bring a case—his resources were already stretched too thin.*

Then we found David Hickton, the US attorney in Pittsburgh. He was brusque: "Sure, screw it, I'll put people on it," he said. He wanted to stick it to China—and he was adventurous. He was happy to dive into a long-shot case.

The China case would prove ultimately to be another chapter in Pittsburgh's unique history as a center of groundbreaking cyber prosecutions, as the old steel town–turned–tech hub leveraged its unique cyber resources, like the National Cyber Forensics Training Alliance and one of the FBI's most daring cyber agents, J. Keith Mularski, the agent who went undercover early in the 2000s as the administrator of the criminal forum DarkMarket.

The Pittsburgh team worked closely with our team at Main Justice. In Washington, the prosecutors we recruited for the Threat Cell came from all over the country. Originally, there were just three: Nick Oldham, a prosecutor from Atlanta; Brian Resler, a prosecutor temporarily lent to us from Wisconsin; and Adam, from the Southern District of New York. They each brought a crucial specialty: Brian was a courtroom veteran, experienced in putting together prosecutions; Nick was one of the few assistant US attorneys in the country who had put together a complicated cyber case, leading the investigation into a piece of malware known as SpyEye that targeted the financial sector, and he spoke "tech." As Anita says, "Nick was an attorney who could actually help shape the data and make sense of the tech side of a case." Lisa had to put in a special call to

---

* The message was underscored when, just as we were getting the NSCS going, the entire federal government shut down due to a congressional budget fight. For 17 days the government was shuttered, our work paralyzed by congressional dysfunction.

the US attorney in Atlanta, Sally Yates, to get Nick transferred temporarily to DC. Adam, meanwhile, had experience in counterterrorism and understood how to apply national security policy in court. Later, Sean Newell joined them from the intelligence side of NSD.

We appointed Adam the head of what we'd called the Threat Cell; when he saw his title, officially, "Chief, Cyber Investigations Unit," he told Anita, "Great, I'm the chief of a section that doesn't exist." They were an unlikely team; Adam, a Harvard-educated veteran of what considers itself the nation's most elite US attorney's office, was always impeccably dressed in the Justice Department's unofficial uniform—dark suit, white shirt, and a blue or red tie. Nick, a graduate of Boise State, embraced the ethos of the tech community: he wore khakis and rumpled button-downs and, on a daily basis, was the only person inside Main Justice wearing bright orange tennis sneakers at work. And both Adam and Nick, hard-driving Type-A personalities, contrasted with the low-key, laid-back midwestern Resler.

The structure of the Threat Cell was unique inside the Justice Department—a team of prosecutors reporting directly to the top of the division—and its uniqueness carried its own message about the seriousness of our efforts. "Just legitimizing the team was a big step. That was seen as cool. 'Oh, good, NSD wants to play—they've built a real thing,'" Anita recalls.

We had to undertake the entire project with existing resources because we didn't have any money to launch something new. We were doing it "out of hide," as we said in government, and briefed Congress so everyone knew we were directing resources toward cyber even though it wasn't officially budgeted. We also scrounged office space for the team. The first place we found was out at the FBI's Northern Virginia Resident Agency in Manassas; Sean and Adam journeyed the hour outside Washington to survey their new digs and were led to a locked room overflowing with old computers—they had been assigned to work from a storage closet. The agent who unlocked the door turned on the lights, pushed aside a few rolling chairs, and gestured toward the piles of old servers and desktops: "This'll work, right?"

"It was such a funny mission," Anita recalls. "*Here*—we're not giving you anything, but can you make a groundbreaking international case against China, one of our most formidable global adversaries?"

The team embraced the challenge. "As a prosecutor, the Chinese threat was always the buzz among agents," Nick recalls. In talking over potential cases during his work in Atlanta, agents would run through what they'd been investigating and then, thinking there was no appetite in the Justice Department for tackling China, dismissively tell him, "This is a China case, we can't bring it to you." Now he had his chance. That opportunity—the chance to do the thing that you'd long been told not to do—helped us across the country, motivating the numerous prosecutors and agents who we leaned on to help assemble a case. "That's an energy you can capitalize on," Adam recalls. "They had the frustration of someone who had spent years watching a threat they'd been told they couldn't touch."*

We didn't have to look far to see the threats. Each morning, the Justice Department's top officials—the attorney general and the FBI director—received a binder of the day's threat matrix, outlining all the unfolding national security concerns, both on the terrorism side and on the foreign nation-state side. By that point, the staff who organized those morning briefings knew China and the cybersecurity threat particularly interested me, so I'd also receive a supplementary binder focused just on those topics. Yet until our team began work, there was no easy mechanism to share that threat intelligence with prosecutors; a process that was a daily—even hourly—routine on the counterterrorism side simply didn't exist at all in the cyber realm. "You had to create the permission structure on intelligence," Lisa recalls.

---

*In my experience, it's that energy—the sense that you're biting into something real—that fires up the career prosecutors who drive the Justice Department; all of our team could have been earning far more money in the private sector, often even working fewer hours than they toiled in the government, and yet the chance to pursue critical investigations, identify threats, and act on them to change behavior was a tremendous motivator.

Adam, the first to arrive in DC, went to visit the FBI's NCIJTF, where he received a detailed presentation from agents who showed him evidence of individual Chinese hackers they'd identified in a specific incident. At the end, the agents said the FBI was thinking of just releasing the evidence and hack attribution to the public. "The bureau was rightly very proud of making an individual attribution," Adam recalls. He suggested letting the new Threat Cell take a stab at it all: "You know, we already have a really good vehicle for making public information about an incident—it's a criminal indictment," he said. *Give us a chance to prove this new approach*, he pleaded. The bureau was skeptical. "Who knows this [information]?" he asked, still feeling his way through the new territory. As it turned out, all of the information had been gathered on the intelligence side of the house, meaning that no assistant US attorney had been told that the FBI possessed it. "There was no moment when a lawyer would have looked at this and said, 'Okay, this could be a criminal case,'" Adam recalls. He also asked where the information contained in the presentation "lived" inside the FBI. *Who had been working the cases that gathered the attributions?* As it turned out, investigators had pieces of information about the threat group in almost all of their Field Offices—43 of the nation's 56 Field Offices had been watching the same group—but three of those offices, however, held the best evidence on individual attribution. Adam went to those offices, organizing meetings with their agents and local US attorney's offices to get briefings on the evidence and pitching them on participating in the new case and contributing their evidence to the endeavor.

From there, the team began to zero in on specific units and individuals and see what looked promising for a case. There were crimes everywhere we looked—but what in that mountain of evidence was prosecutable? At their converted Manassas storage closet, Nick sketched out on a whiteboard the different pools of possible evidence, the different databases, and how they could be assembled to put together a criminal case. "It was 'Here's a bunch of evidence and here's a lot of bad guys,' go charge people," Nick says. "The first six months was just fumbling."

One of the first challenges we faced was that the government wasn't set up to combat cybersecurity at the level of specificity necessary to bring a criminal prosecution. For the purposes of an intelligence report, you could look at an IP address, see the type of behavior it was conducting, decide it looked like China, and then attribute all future activity from that same IP address as Chinese-related. The amount of hacking activity proved so voluminous analysts didn't have time to do the deep dive required to prove a fact beyond a reasonable doubt. But such conclusions fell far short of building an indictment. "That just doesn't translate into a criminal case," recalls Sean Newell, who served as the team's "intel whisperer," walking the other prosecutors through the various available pools of information and explaining the roles and capabilities of different agencies and units across the intelligence community.

"We just kept asking folks 'What do you actually have?' 'What's the chain of custody?'" Nick says. "It's not enough in a court to say 'here's the server the Chinese broke into,' you need to trace that server all the way to court. You need the company technician who says, 'Yes, I gave this image of the server to the FBI,' you need the evidence to prove that the IP actually belongs to who you think it does. Then, it's not enough to say it's a Chinese military computer, you have to link a crime to an individual. Whose fingers were actually on the keyboard?"

For Nick, the early stages of the China case gave him flashbacks to when as a young trial attorney he worked on cases against suspected terrorists at Guantánamo—the main challenge was the same: mountains of vague evidence and intelligence, little of which followed the strict guidelines necessary for trial. Reading through the intelligence reports day after day about China, he recalls, gave him the same feeling he had at Gitmo. "I don't doubt these are bad actors, but there's nothing I can say in a court of law against them," he says.

As the team got to work, they represented precisely what the NSD had been created to accomplish—lawyers and intelligence analysts working side by side with law enforcement to address critical threats. I've never been great with the inspirational speech, but as the team reminded me, I hit a new low with my first pep talk to the Threat Cell. My first question: "How long is it going to take you?"

///////////

Our first months were spent just setting up our protocols, gathering information, and learning how to convert good intelligence into clear evidence of criminal activity that could withstand the scrutiny of a trial and justify charges against individual actors. Plenty of people doubted our effort would yield results; our agents in the Pittsburgh Field Office were constantly teased by their squadmates that the result of their hard work would end up like the final scene of *Raiders of the Lost Ark*, where the Ark of the Covenant is locked away in a box and wheeled into an endless secret government warehouse to be forgotten. "That's going to be you," our agents were told. *This whole investigation is going to be boxed up and never see the light of day.*

The Threat Cell only lasted a month or so in the Manassas storage closet before we moved them into a spare room at Main Justice. As it turned out, the room was strangely fitting. The second-floor SCIF— Sensitive Compartmentalized Information Facility, a secure room specially designed to repel eavesdropping—had been where our nascent National Security Division had been first housed in the chaotic months after 9/11. Then, it had served as the focal point for America's attempt to combat a new global threat using new tools; now, it was serving the same purpose as we again confronted an all-new threat to the American way of life.

One of the biggest challenges we ran into was the simple bureaucracy: every time I met with Adam's team, I asked what they needed and how I could help. Their answer was consistent—and simple: *We need one FBI agent, the same FBI agent, to put the case together.* Whereas people in the field offices generally worked on squads for years at a time, agents at headquarters normally rotated with relative frequency— sometimes even coming to DC for just 90-day or 180-day temporary assignments—and we needed a single agent who could see the case through. We fought repeatedly as headquarters' normal processes tried to reassign our agent to other matters. Even knowing how the FBI operated from my days working there, it seemed insane to me—out of the 13,000 agents in the FBI, we just needed one of them to go up against the most populous country in the world, and it was still a fight for us. Special Agent Casey Harrington worked the phones relentlessly to cajole other agents across the country to carve out time from their other cases to run searches on their evidence. The FBI supervisor on the case, Jeffrey Tricoli, did yeoman's work navigating the bureau's internal dynamics to get us the evidence we needed, as did the agents in Pittsburgh who leaned on their colleagues in other offices to cooperate with what always seemed like "one more unreasonable request from Washington."

Even procuring basic office supplies proved challenging for the Threat Cell, which we came to call, inside the division, Cyber Island. At the start, they had only one phone, and no secure communications at all. Adam Hickey came to Anita one day asking simply for more lamps; later, as the case progressed, they couldn't get their own copy machine and asked for lock bags—the secure zippered bags used to transport classified documents—so that they could trudge across the building to make photocopies. Their effort ran on a comically shoestring budget. "Adam came to me one day asking for $300 so that they could hire an expert witness. I literally didn't know where to get the money," Anita says. "Our division had a budget of upwards of $80 million, but I didn't know where to find $300. Who can authorize it? Who gets charged for it?"

The Threat Cell pleaded with the FBI for direct access to its databases—something prosecutors effectively never have—and when that request finally was granted, it required adding new FBI computers inside Main Justice and laying new wiring to connect to the FBI's secure network. Because the databases weren't easily searchable, Nick spent months helping to realign and redesign the tools to make them useful to our investigators. "The key to any attribution is to line up a known person with a known intrusion," Adam says. "Your ability to make that claim is based on how well you can read your data." As we got deeper into the research, the evidence appeared stronger than we expected; James Comey's characterization of the Chinese as drunk burglars rampaging across the internet seemed true—online, the paths of the Chinese hackers were easier to track than we had imagined. "They were so unsophisticated—if Russian coders are college grads, the Chinese were like sixth-graders in hacking," Nick said. "They were noisy, sloppy. It was just a numbers game—if you throw 100 people at a system, sooner or later someone gets in. The evidence was stronger than you thought."

Adam, who had only ever worked cases as a line prosecutor in New York, quickly came to understand how different working at the head-quarters level was—there was much finessing and wheeling and deal-ing to get the needed cooperation. Adam did not have a poker face: he'd turn a bright pink as his frustration mounted in meetings. Nick similarly had little patience for roadblocks, and it often fell to the more laid-back Sean, a picture of calm, to smooth over Nick's requests with the bureau. Sean, in his role on the intelligence side, had worked with numerous FBI teams and assistant US attorneys across the country to help them file FISA requests, and had deep relationships to lean upon as he pleaded for help.

Across the Justice Department, we were consistent in our message: *we would put together a case.* In private meetings at the White House and with our intelligence community peers, Eric Holder began to add a new refrain to his running laundry list of what the Justice Department was aiming to accomplish. "And we're charging China with economic espionage," he says. "People [elsewhere in government] always found it interesting, but until you've got something tangible, people always find an expedition like this sort of cute—like, 'Hey, it looks great to chase China if you've got the time to do it,'" Anita recalls.

In December 2012, I gave an interview to a DC news outlet known as *Defense News*, explaining our new approach, how we'd created these new NSCS positions, and were in the process of training 100 prose-cutors to follow these crimes. I explained that with this new cadre of assistant US attorneys, we hoped to bring new cases—and potentially even name the governments sponsoring and directing the hackers. "I'll give you a prediction," I said. "Now that we are having people look at bringing one of these cases, it's there to be brought, and you'll see a case brought."

The goal, I explained, was to force our foreign adversaries to recalculate their cyber efforts—until that point, they'd faced almost no cost and so there was little reason to cease or alter their behavior. "Whether it is a state-owned enterprise or a state-supported enterprise in China—if you can figure out and prove that they've committed the crime, charging the company means they can't do business in the U.S., or in Europe," I said. "It affects their reputation and that then causes them to recalculate: 'Hey, is this worth it?' "[38]

Those statements, as seemingly benign as I thought they were, quickly got people worried that we might actually bring a criminal case. The National Security Council and the Pentagon both called us, panicking, expecting that we were just about to drop a major case and hadn't told anyone. I reassured everyone we had a long way still to go, but I remained confident that once we had the right people looking at it, a case could be made. I was equally confident that after the first case, there'd be more. But we still had big questions ahead: *Where were those people—and what was the case?* Answering those questions would take many more months, months when we began to confront a shifting cyberthreat from other nation-states and foreign adversaries as well.

CHAPTER 4

Qassam Cyber Fighters

IRAN TRIED TO attack the United States in the real world before they attacked us in cyberspace—and they started with perhaps the most unlikely target I could have imagined: Cafe Milano, a bustling, loud Italian eatery in DC's Georgetown neighborhood that serves a $43 plate of veal Milanese and was a favorite of Angelina Jolie and Vice President Biden.

My mornings at the National Security Division always began with what we called the current threat brief, the daily window into potential threats being tracked across the intelligence community, the sheer width and breadth of which would stagger the imagination of most Americans. The brief included both specific tactical terrorist plots—which we would monitor closely for days, weeks, or even months—and larger strategic challenges posed by new technologies or new geopolitical developments. In the spring of 2011, I first heard a snippet that the DEA appeared to have gotten wind of a potential assassination plot by the Iranian government, a plot that focused on the Italian restaurant.

As the plot pieces came together, it appeared Iran wanted to bomb the restaurant to kill the Saudi ambassador. The idea that Iran might try to carry out an assassination plot inside the United States seemed far-fetched. We knew the Islamic Republic regularly backed, aided, or incited violent terrorist acts overseas—particularly against Israeli targets—but the idea that they'd attack within the United States belied what analysts had long told us. The consensus view until then held that while Iran and its terrorist proxy, Hezbollah, used the United States for fundraising operations, the risk of taking action or inciting violence inside the United States was so high that there would clearly have to be an international red line crossed first—some major external shift, such as a US attack on Iran or even outright war.

America's low-grade hostility with Iran dated back decades. Most people today forget that we spent much of the 1980s engaged in a guerrilla-style war with Iran in the Persian Gulf, as Iranian dhows covertly mined the Strait of Hormuz and fast mosquito boats from the Islamic Revolutionary Guard Corps engaged in running battles with US Navy vessels. During that period, the brutal Iran–Iraq War saw mass casualties on both sides during fierce land battles and an expansive naval war that ultimately saw more than 500 ships attacked around the Gulf—the total tonnage lost or damaged was equal to roughly half what was lost in the Battle of the Atlantic during World War II. During the same period, Iranian intelligence embarked on a wide-ranging pattern of international assassinations—from 1980 to 1995, the US government tracked more than 80 Iranian-backed killings around the world, including an August 1991 incident where a hit team in France talked their way into the home of the shah's last prime minister and killed him and his secretary with a kitchen knife.[1] As US historian David Crist wrote, war and the conflict with the United States devoured Iran in the 1980s: "Iran spent its revolutionary fervor, leaving the country isolated, with a profound sense of grievance and insecurity."

By the mid-2000s, the United States and Iran had again come into an active shadow war, as the Islamic Revolutionary Guard Corps and the Ministry of Intelligence and Security supplied weapons to insurgents in Iraq and Iranian-designed roadside bombs began to exact a deadly toll on US forces. In December 2006, the United States arrested in Iraq a dozen Iranian intelligence officers, including Brigadier General Mohsen Chizari, the head of its Iraq operations.

Just months before the Cafe Milano plot surfaced, the National Security Division had helped lead an investigation into four businessmen in Singapore who had been illegally exporting thousands of radio antennas from the United States and smuggling them to Iran, where the United States had found them inside unexploded improvised explosive devices (IEDs) meant to target American troops on the battlefield.[2]* As Lisa said at the time, "This case underscores the continuing threat posed by Iranian procurement networks seeking to obtain U.S. technology through fraud and the importance of safeguarding that technology."

Yet even as we focused on Iranian activities overseas, Iran wasn't a foe we saw attempting operational attacks inside the United States until that summer of 2011, when the DEA and the FBI worked together to pursue the odd lead on Cafe Milano: a DEA informant reported he'd been asked by a onetime used car salesman and down-on-his-luck Iranian named Manssor Arbabsiar to assist on blowing up a target for the Iranian government; Arbabsiar's cousin was, evidently, a general in Iran's elite Quds Force, a special forces–style component of the Islamic Revolutionary Guard Corps, and the Quds Force wanted to hire the informant—who they believed was a link to a Mexican drug cartel—as a hitman. Iran was willing to pay as much as $1.5 million to facilitate the assassination of the Saudi ambassador in Washington; if that plot went well, there'd be others to pursue: attacking the Israeli embassy in Washington, as well as perhaps Saudi targets in South America.

There were initial doubts across Washington that the plot was real; it seemed too unbelievable that Iran really recruited a Texas used car salesman to carry out such a Jason Bourne–style plot. Yet those doubts dissipated as a $100,000 down payment arrived in a Manhattan bank account. That kind of cash meant serious action. This was the real deal.

The plot was unprecedented. Washington had only seen two assassinations since the 1881 shooting of President Garfield at a DC train station: the 1973 murder of Israeli military attaché Yosef Alon—the first

---

*Ultimately, we arrested all four in Singapore, with the help of local authorities there, but a fifth target of the investigation, an Iranian named Hossein Larijani, remains at large.

assassination of a foreign diplomat inside the United States—and in 1976, a car bombing near Dupont Circle that killed Orlando Letelier, the former ambassador from Chile's Marxist President Salvador Allende and critic of the country's new dictator, Alberto Pinochet.

Then, 35 years later, came Arbabsiar, who had long lived in Corpus Christi and was known by locals there for his drinking and carousing with women. Local bartenders knew him by the nickname "Jack," for his preferred order of Jack Daniels. Even as high-level meetings in Washington debated how to respond to the new threat, Arbabsiar met repeatedly with the informant over the summer in Mexico as the plot came into focus. The informant warned about the target restaurant's popularity and that there would likely be innocent bystanders as casualties. "They want that guy done, if the hundred go with him, fuck 'em," Arbabsiar said. It didn't even matter, he said, if US senators who frequented Cafe Milano happened to be killed, too: "No big deal."[3]

In August, Arbabsiar traveled back to Iran, where he met with a Quds Force leader, Gholam Shakuri, and another senior Quds Force officer to review the plan; they approved and told him to move forward. We never fully knew how far up the ranks of Iran's government the plot went—the Quds Force and Islamic Revolutionary Guard Corps both operated with a level of independence unthinkable to Western governments and militaries. Yet none of us doubted Iran—or at least some faction of the Iranian government—sponsored the plot. By killing the Saudi ambassador, Iran would have achieved a "two-for," embarrassing the United States and proving Iran's ability to carry out covert action within US borders, while at the same time striking back at the Islamic Republic's biggest regional rival. Saudi Arabia and Iran, separated by only those few miles of the Persian Gulf, had been locked in a long shadow war of their own driven by centuries-old Islamic divisions. Iran is the world's biggest funder of Shia organizations; Saudi Arabia is the largest funder of Sunni organizations.

In September 2011, the plot seemed ready to go. Arbabsiar called the informant from Iran and asked if the "building is getting painted?"

The informant replied briskly, "We're still doing that." The plot was a go, exacerbating what was an already tense time inside government, as the ten-year anniversary of 9/11 neared and we worried about a possible anniversary-inspired attack by al-Qaeda. The DEA and the informant came up with a scheme to get Arbabsiar back into the United States—the informant told the Iranian-American that the cartel, which he thought was the brutal Zetas, required holding him as collateral in Mexico while the assassination was carried out to guarantee their payment. When Arbabsiar flew to Mexico, he was turned away at the border and sent back to Europe on a flight through New York's JFK airport. When he landed on his layover, he was arrested by the FBI.

The FBI interrogated him, with a new emphasis on intelligence gathering first, using a specially trained team of interrogators both to maximize the gathering process of classified intelligence and to preserve evidence and testimony for a public criminal prosecution; Arbabsiar largely cooperated, even successfully identifying the senior Quds Force leader he met with. The FBI arranged a lineup of seven photos that included a non–publicly available photo of the senior Iranian official, which Arbabsiar quickly fingered. Then he placed a telephone call to Gholam Shakuri, his main Iranian contact, using the code word they'd previously agreed upon. Arbabsiar asked, "I wanted to tell you the Chevrolet is ready—it's ready to be done. I should continue, right?"

"Yes, yes, yes," Shakuri said. "Just do it quickly, it's late, just buy it for me and bring it already." That conversation had a dramatic impact inside the US government; officials across the administration were chilled by listening to a Quds Force leader casually authorizing and pushing for a bombing in our capital, at a restaurant, nonetheless, where many officials regularly ate.

From the government's perspective, the plot gave rise to a real fear: we had only stumbled across it because the man behind it had contacted a DEA informant—was this part of a larger operation or were there other plots unfolding that we didn't know about? What else was Iran trying to pull off? As columnist David Ignatius wrote in the

Washington Post after the plot became public, "If the Quds Force will talk to a loser like Arbabsiar, who else might they have on the line?"[4] It was a question that kept us nervous for months.*

///////////////

Intelligence analysts generally consider two main factors in their work: *intent*, whether an entity plans to carry out an operation, and *capability*, whether it can conceivably pull it off. As strange and seemingly incompetent as the attempt on the Saudi ambassador's life was—as lacking in capability as it was—what troubled us is how the plot showcased Iran's intent. Ultimately, a nation-state can almost always achieve capability, given time, focus, and resources. Intent, meanwhile, is a political question: *Is someone willing to cross a red line?* The Iranian plot answered that definitively for us.

That answer on intent dramatically shifted the Obama administration's approach to confronting Iran. Even as US intelligence agencies believed Iran remained far from developing a nuclear weapon, we knew we could no longer question their intent to do so.

The Arbabsiar case shaped future actions we'd take against Iran and other countries in cyberspace. It demonstrated to me, for instance, the effectiveness of the criminal justice system as a tool against nation-state actors—particularly when deployed in conjunction with a big diplomatic push. Criminal indictments effectively made secret information public, removing accusations from the shadows.

The Arbabsiar case also underscored that we had to respond— and respond strongly—to activities in cyberspace when nation-states crossed red lines and we had to do so in multilateral ways, instead of unilaterally. A multilateral approach was used in the years ahead as the United States ratcheted up sanctions and isolated Iran from the world in response to its terrorist backing and its nuclear program. Nation-states, after all, were capable of extraordinarily provocative behavior and had

---

*By February, in fact, three teams of Iranian agents were believed to have carried out attacks on Israeli diplomats in other overseas capitals: Thailand's Bangkok, India's New Delhi, and Georgia's Tbilisi.

no problem targeting and killing innocent bystanders. The Arbabsiar experience made me especially wary as I would listen to other cyber experts expound confidently that we didn't have to worry about other countries attacking our critical infrastructure unless we were at war. I just didn't (and don't) believe that was the case. Arbabsiar showed that we didn't always correctly judge what an adversary might do—and when they might seek to cross a red line.

///////////////

In some ways, cyberattacks were perfect for countries such as Iran that posed an asymmetric threat and had a long history of pursuing low-grade, provocative but easily deniable international attacks that stopped short of actual warfare. Iran could never seek to challenge the United States in a direct military confrontation, but in cyberspace it could prey carefully and strategically on weak targets, with a level of deniability, and largely without fear the attacks would escalate unintentionally into an open shooting war. Since the 2000s, Iran has had a stronger technology scene than one might assume, even though public internet access remained tightly monitored, and by 2007, the government was clearly moving into state-sponsored cyber activity.[5]

At the start, the Iranian government directed its cyber activity toward internal targets—dissidents, human rights activists, and the pro-democracy movement. Beginning in 2009, an online group called the Iranian Cyber Army regularly attacked and defaced anti-regime websites, both political opponents and independent media sites. The Green Movement, a prodemocracy push that followed the Iranian disputed presidential elections in 2009, became a particular focus of Iranian intelligence efforts. "The Green Movement demonstrated to the Islamic Republic that the internet could be used as an instrument of mass mobilization and posed an effective challenge to the regime's longheld information monopoly," researchers Collin Anderson and Karim Sadjadpour concluded. "The tactics, tools, and threat actors that arose during this domestic challenge to regime stability would foreshadow the cyber posture of Iran toward a wider set of internal and foreign threats."[6]

In the summer of 2011, even as the Arbabsiar plot was unfolding in the United States, Iran appeared to orchestrate one of the largest security breaches in the internet's history: an Iranian hacker managed to compromise the Dutch firm DigiNotar, one of the largely anonymous but critical behind-the-scenes operators of key internet infrastructure. DigiNotar was what is known as a certificate authority, or CA, that issued the security certificates used online to prove to your browser, for instance, that Bank of America's website is actually the Bank of America website and not a good-looking copy built by a Russian cyber criminal. While there are numerous CAs around the world, DigiNotar was one of an elite few known as so-called root CAs, whose security certificates were automatically trusted by browsers.[7] The certificates allow a web user to encrypt their communication with a trusted website, ensuring that no one can eavesdrop on passwords, banking details, or emails as they transit from a user's browser to the company's web server; normally, this entire process is all but invisible, as users only really notice when they see the green lock on a web browser that provides comfort that the website is secure.[8]

DigiNotar normally required two employees to issue a certificate together, and the certificates could only come from a specific computer inside a secure room accessed only by a biometric handprint reader. Yet through exploiting a weakness inside a software program that DigiNotar hadn't updated and patched, an Iranian hacker or hackers defeated all of the physical and virtual protections DigiNotar had in place. Over the course of the summer of 2011, the hackers issued themselves more than 500 security certificates that allowed them to mimic the websites of everything from Gmail and AOL to cia.gov and mossad.gov.il. Hundreds of thousands of Iranians who accessed Gmail and other sites that summer might have had their communications intercepted.[9]* The scale of the DigiNotar breach only became clear when users began to complain on Gmail forums about problems logging in to the site; as the scandal of the breach spread, DigiNotar collapsed

---

*It was at least the second time Iran had tried to compromise a certificate authority; the methods of the attack were consistent with an attack earlier in 2011 on another CA, Comodo.

as a firm in little more than a week. The Dutch government seized control of it and summoned the security firm Fox-IT to investigate. It concluded, "The list of domains and the fact that 99% of the users are in Iran suggest that the objective of the hackers is to intercept private communications in Iran."[10] As Hans Hoogstraaten, who led the Fox-IT investigation, reflected later, "What really shocked me was when I realized the impact it had for the people of Iran. In those days... people got killed for having a different opinion. The realization that the... security of a small company in Holland [may have] played a part in the killing or torture of people really shocked me."[11]

As the threat from the democracy movement receded, Iran applied the lessons it learned from internal cyber activities toward external adversaries, embarking on campaigns that featured both traditional nation-state espionage and industrial sabotage.

⁓⁓⁓⁓⁓

When we did private sector outreach in the late 2000s, we told companies it was only a matter of time before we saw destructive cyber-attacks aimed at the United States. Yet while companies often had a clear understanding of the threats—from a regulatory, brand, or business perspective—arising from a theft of "personally identifiable information" or the loss of intellectual property and trade secrets, the threat of a destructive attack seemed more abstract. Finally, on the morning of August 15, 2012, we had an example we could point to.[12]

At 11:08 a.m. that Wednesday morning, the few employees at work at the oil company Saudi Aramco, an energy powerhouse owned by the Saudi government that is four times the size of Exxon Mobil, noticed their computer screens start to flicker. Then the screens fell dark.

The attackers timed their assault perfectly, targeting one of Islam's holiest days of the year—Laylat al-Qadr, the Night of Power, in Ramadan, which marks when the first verses of the Koran were revealed to Muhammad. About 55,000 of the company's employees had taken a vacation day, leaving the offices running on a skeleton staff. "It was a great time to attack infrastructure," explained Chris Kubecka, whose security firm helped respond to the incident. "You figure half of your

IT staff is gone, half of your regular staff is gone. If you have an incident, you're going to have to call all over the place to grab people off of vacation."

The malware, known as Shamoon or W.32Distrack, proved vicious and unforgiving; researchers later determined it penetrated the system through a simple spear-phishing email. When activated, Shamoon corrupted files on infected computers and wiped clean the machines' master boot records, rendering the computers effectively expensive desktop bricks. Infected computers displayed only a haunting image of a burning American flag. The malware also used a specific company server to collect the IP addresses of infected computers, which each reported back its infection to the command server—allowing the hackers behind the attack to post the addresses of thousands of broken computers as evidence of their success.

The malware ravaged Saudi Aramco, destroying 35,000 workstations, about three-quarters of the company's computers, and sent the company back to the 1970s. Aramco promptly disconnected its network from the wider internet—IT staff literally ripped cables out of the backs of Aramco servers in data centers—and set about diagnosing what had happened.

Within three hours, a Saudi tech blog posted a vague report about the attack: "I received certain information from a private source who preferred not to be named that Aramco was exposed to a major breach in its network and the theft and loss of a lot of data about the company and the staff."[13] News of the attack spread to *Reuters* seven hours later, but even then it appeared to be just a minor incident—only in the following days did security companies begin to point out the odd scale of the Shamoon attack. "Threats with such destructive payloads are unusual," Symantec reported the following day, in one of the first public warnings about the incident.[14] Although inside the US government we were tracking the case closely and quickly realized its import and the scale of the damage, it would take until the end of August for word to leak publicly about the incident's full scope.

The computer systems that ran the oil production equipment never ceased operating—they were kept on a separate network—and so the oil continued to flow, a blessing for both the global economy and Aramco. Nevertheless, the attack led to months of disruption—employees reconstructed the company's operations using 20th-century technology—typewriters, fax machines, and even hard-copy paper forms. Their voice-over-IP phone system fell silent, and paperwork was passed around through hard copies and interoffice mail.

Late in the month, Shamoon also targeted the Qatari gas company RasGas, and even into September, tanker trucks lined up for miles in Saudi Arabia, all waiting fruitlessly to be filled with oil. Finally, the company gave oil away for free inside Saudi Arabia in order to ensure that the country's economy continued functioning—it simply didn't have the systems to keep track of who was buying or selling what. Getting the company back to normal required a Herculean effort: company representatives flew to Asia to purchase every computer hard drive currently in production, ultimately buying more than 50,000 new computers and paying a healthy premium to skip the global line with computer manufacturers. Their race to replace their computer systems drove up the worldwide prices for computer hard drives for nearly six months. "Never underestimate how dependent you are on your information technology and systems," Aramco's CEO, Khalid A. Al-Falih, warned an industry audience months later.[15] It took more than five months before the company was ready to reconnect to the internet.*

///////////////

During one of my normal morning threat briefings with Robert Mueller and the attorney general, we discussed the attack, outlined its effects, and heard that the likely suspect was Saudi Arabia's major rival, Iran. Iran, among other things, had been angry about the country's

---

* The incident underscored how critical resilience planning was for cyber incidents; there can be massive downstream effects from a cyberattack—outages can disrupt supply chains, upend associated industries, scramble logistics, and paralyze partners far removed from the attack itself. Companies needed to have an internal plan for resurrecting their operations manually if the digital systems were interrupted—a lesson that we'd see again all too soon with the hacking of Sony in 2014.

decision to boost oil production earlier in the year. The attack appeared to rely upon malware that mimicked part of the Flame malware that had targeted Iran earlier in the year and disrupted its oil production. A group calling themselves the Cutting Sword of Justice claimed responsibility for the Shamoon attack, but we doubted they were the real attackers; we were accustomed to seeing nation-states launch cyberattacks under false, made-up names in an attempt to provide plausible deniability.

In many ways, we had been waiting for an attack like the Aramco attack—it was only a matter of time before we saw a destructive cyberattack on critical infrastructure. Ever since Russia's attacks on Estonia and Georgia, we'd seen steadily escalating attacks around the world. Nevertheless, the attack's scale proved worrisome: it had been a surprise and successful destructive attack against a core state asset—the most valuable company in the world, fully owned by the Saudi government, an asset central not just to the global economy but also to the functioning and financing of the entire Saudi regime. It was only a matter of time before similar attacks began to hit the United States—and few companies had the manpower and deep pockets to undertake the recovery efforts that Aramco did. In fact, an attack of that scale would have bankrupted almost any other company in the world—particularly if a future attack was able to actually affect production networks. Moreover, had the attack disrupted the flow of oil in the Middle East, the entire globe might have felt the economic ramifications. The question in our minds was clear: *Would we be prepared when the first attack hit the United States?*

Unfortunately, cyberthreats remained far under the political radar. In fact, just days before the Shamoon attack, Congress's first major effort to pass legislation on cybersecurity failed. The bill—introduced by Senators Joe Lieberman and Susan Collins and aimed at improving information sharing and strengthening efforts to protect critical infrastructure—failed 52 to 46. "How can the Senate ignore these repeated warnings from the experts of how at risk our national security, our economic prosperity, and indeed our American way of life it is?"

Collins said.[16] To those of us living with cyberthreats day to day, the inaction was incredible.

That fall, we saw Iran turn its online attention to us.

////////////////

On Tuesday, September 18, 2012, a moderate-sized DDoS attack hit Bank of America, slowing some of its websites to a crawl. That same day, a group calling itself the Cyber Fighters of Izz Ad-Din Al Qassam posted a message online declaring the DDoS attacks punishment for an anti-Muslim video on YouTube titled *Innocence of Muslims*. "All the Muslim youths who are active in the Cyber world will attack to American and Zionist Web bases as much as needed such that they say that they are sorry about that insult," the Qassam Cyber Fighters wrote.[17]

The following day, beginning at 9:21 a.m., shortly before the stock markets opened, customers received an error message when they tried to access their accounts at JPMorgan Chase and the New York Stock Exchange's Euronext, as those faced an overload of nefarious traffic. The waves of traffic, for a while, seemed a mere nuisance—they didn't affect operations or the stock market, just customers trying to access their accounts electronically. The attacks paused briefly that fall—stopping in October for the Muslim holiday of Eid—but then a second wave hit in December and continued without interruption through the end of January, always hitting banks in the middle of the US workday—maximizing their disruption for customers. Other financial institutions found themselves targets: US Bank, Wells Fargo, PNC Bank, BB&T, HSBC, Capital One, Key Bank, and others, nearly four dozen in all.[18]

We knew almost immediately that despite the public statements, the attacks weren't coming from some hackers aggrieved about a low-budget YouTube movie. Just as with Shamoon, this was another false flag to distract from the most likely suspect: Iran. Senator Joe Lieberman, the chair of the Senate Homeland Security Committee, announced that he blamed an elite unit of Iran's Islamic

Revolutionary Guard Corps. "I don't believe these were just hackers who were skilled enough to cause disruption of the Web sites," Lieberman told C-SPAN in late September 2012. "I think this was done by Iran and the Quds Force, which has its own developing cyber-attack capability."[19]*

Across government, the dire warnings increased. That October, even as the DDoS attacks continued, Leon Panetta gave the first major address on cybersecurity ever by a defense secretary and warned of a cyberstrike "as destructive as the terrorist attack of 9/11," an attack he called "a cyber Pearl Harbor."[20] He said that in terms of cyber we were in a "pre-9/11 moment." As he explained, "Before September 11, 2001, the warning signs were there. We weren't organized. We weren't ready and we suffered terribly for that lack of attention. We cannot let that happen again."

///////////////////

At the end of January, the Qassam Cyber Fighters announced their attacks would stop because YouTube had removed one of the copies of *Innocence of Muslims.* But then, in February and early March, the group issued new statements demanding additional online copies be taken down. On March 5, 2013, they announced a new third wave of attacks through what had become their normal communication channel, a page on the website Pastebin, a tool normally used by computer programmers to temporarily store text and code.

The scale of the attacks surprised us. Akamai, an internet company that helps other websites manage spikes in their traffic and had been working to help defend some of the bank targets, noted that the DDoS attacks had been hitting with up to 65 gigabits of traffic per second—many orders of magnitude larger than a routine attack.[21] The traffic was persistent, well organized, and—perhaps strangest of all—relatively uniform and unvarying. Usually, a DDoS attack will come

---

*Iran quickly denied any involvement: "Unlike the United States, which has per reports in the media given itself the license to engage in illegal cyber-warfare against Iran, Iran respects the international law and refrains from targeting other nations' economic or financial institutions," one of Iran's UN officials wrote the *New York Times* in an email.

in disorganized waves as an attacker's different tools harness hijacked machines differently. These attacks came instead like a constant, onrushing flood. "This isn't consistent with what hacktivists are capable of," an Akamai engineer explained to the media at the time. Over time, we saw even larger numbers: 100, even 140, gigabits per second—more than ten times what was normally needed to knock a site offline. A normal midsized business might only have website capacity to support a single gigabit or two of traffic.

The traffic itself seemed suspicious, too. In a typical DDoS attack, hackers hijack a collection of unrelated infected computers—known as zombie machines—and direct them all to flood a target website with fake traffic. But in the financial DDoS attacks, we noticed entire data centers had been hijacked, the first time we'd seen hackers turn to cloud computing in the same way major companies did.

The hackers relied on a well-known DDoS toolkit, known as ItsOKNoProblemBro, that evaded normal malware detectors.[22] While most large enterprises like banks have special filters that can help block nefarious traffic and defend against a denial-of-service attack, ItsOK-NoProblemBro helped disguise much of the fake traffic as legitimate, overloading the filters. The attackers finely tuned their assault; as one security firm noted, the botnet's control server commanded the hijacked sites "to work in 'shifts,' maximizing its efficiency and ordering it to renew the attack just as the target would start to recover."[23] ItsOKNoProblemBro also allowed hackers to launch multiple different attacks simultaneously, attacking both the underlying internet infrastructure—the network servers that actually house a website—and the content management systems that load and power a website.[24] That combination allowed them to use a smaller number of infected machines to deploy a more punishing attack. As the New York Times wrote, the technique provided nearly unprecedented power, "transforming the online equivalent of a few yapping Chihuahuas into a pack of fire-breathing Godzillas."[25]

In their statements to the media, the Qassam Cyber Fighters referred to their attack as Operation Ababil, referencing a Koran passage in which flocks of swallows defended Mecca and defeated an invading elephant army by dropping clay tablets on the beasts from the sky. Watching the DDoS attacks continue, I couldn't help but think there was some truth in the metaphor: somewhere out there, a network of hijacked computers was crippling the most powerful banks in the world.

Everything about the attack screamed nation-state to us.[26] The hackers were apparently only interested in disruption—there were no demands for extortion money, no attempts to breach individual accounts and steal electronic sums. The fact that the attacks continued unabated pointed to a well-funded and patient organization, too—for example, a foreign adversary. Criminal gangs and hacktivists rarely have the time and money to devote to long-running passion projects aimed simply at annoying a target. By January, in fact, the DDoS attacks became the longest recorded attacks in the history of the internet. As Arbor Networks, one of the security firms brought in to defend Wall Street from the attacks, reported, "They were very much premeditated, focused, advertised before the fact, and executed to the letter."[27] You didn't often see that combination from regular hackers—who almost by definition proved disorganized, distractible, and stealthy by choice.

As the DDoS attacks unfolded, we pushed our division to act faster. We weren't used to the operational tempo in cyber cases that we routinely had in unfolding counterterrorism cases. And I wanted the same granular level of detail related to cybersecurity that I'd come to expect in an ongoing counterterrorism investigation. I found obscure security blogs online that often had better information about the latest wave of DDoS attacks than I was getting sitting atop the National Security Division. Adam Hickey got tired of me calling him to complain about why I was reading about new DDoS attacks in the newspapers or on blogs rather than in intelligence reports. Adam pressed investigative agents to pass details up the chain faster; throughout the fall and winter, as the attacks continued, he'd message me during the day: "We're under attack." Sean Newell, detailed to our team from the Office of Intelligence, ended up with a crash course on DDoS techniques so that he could explain the threat accurately in briefings.

The FBI is often the agency informing the White House about unfolding terror plots—and I wanted us to be in a position to help inform cyber decisions at the national level, too. "What we could add in counterterrorism was often the most accurate set of facts, in a relatively flat organization, directly from those on the ground," Adam recalls. We needed to be part of the conversation in cyber cases, too—and this case seemed like a perfect one for our newly formed Threat Cell to partner with a US attorney's office to pursue criminally.

//////////////////

The nature of the unfolding attacks also shifted the government's thinking about our role vis-à-vis aiding the private sector. Although initially frustrated by our response, I was not surprised. We were still early in the administration's ongoing debates over how to approach cyber cases—many of the questions about our cyber transformation were still under active debate. Our default position in government was still to keep what we knew secret. The DDoS case came amid years of entrenched reluctance to publicly discuss cyber cases and threats.

The government proved slow to take action and slow to help the victims. We monitored the attacks without passing our information and analysis to the targeted banks. Whereas in cases of Chinese espionage we often uncovered historical data that had little immediate relevance, here the government knew things that could have helped the private sector stop an attack in real time. "We know this set of IP addresses is troubling—we have an obligation to share that and to help the victim," Adam says.

We met with some of the banks' security officials—including some former officials I knew from FBI—who expressed their frustration at being caught in the middle of the attacks and yet not knowing what the government knew. Their complaints were valid, but we didn't have good vehicles, mechanisms, or relationships to convey information back to the private sector—either about what we were seeing across the spectrum or about what we knew about the defensive measures Wall Street firms could take to mitigate the attacks. "You could see the entire federal government change," Adam says. "Skulls got cracked." At the same time, the lack of preparation by the financial sector surprised us inside government; the DDoS attacks were sophisticated, but expected—a routine online threat. A large tech company would have likely easily weathered them, having contingency plans in place to increase bandwidth to keep websites running. When we wanted to do more to help, there was a serious argument inside government from those who said, *Hey, this is the financial sector. They can pay to resist this—and they should.* The firms that had been targeted should have taken the necessary defensive steps so that their outward-facing computer servers couldn't be easily knocked offline. Those critics worried about creating an expectation that the government would step in during future DDoS attacks. They argued it couldn't be the government's responsibility to essentially get businesses to put locks on their doors.

In some ways, the DDoS attacks did us a favor: it forced a conversation inside the government about who was in charge of responding to attacks, and what the nature of the response should be. It also marked a lasting change in the private sector's awareness, helping to educate industry leaders about what we'd been seeing for years but hadn't been able to talk about publicly because of the sensitivity of the classified intelligence. Hackers were inside our critical infrastructure and had achieved the ability to cause immediate property damage and potential loss of life.

The attackers had carefully chosen their target, targeting a publicly visible soft spot in our financial system, one that wasn't as well defended as the systems that actually govern the way a transaction occurs or is recorded. The targets were consistent with Iran's geopolitical viewpoint and its political themes: banks represented the heart of the Great Satan's financial system, and attacking them inflicted harm on the US economy just as the sanctions we backed inflicted harm on theirs. But it was a low-threshold attack—by only attacking the outward-facing systems, which was a nuisance but didn't threaten the integrity of our financial system or our economy, Iran didn't approach a clear red line for the United States, even though the attack did cause real economic harm, inconveniencing hundreds of thousands of customers and costing tens of millions of dollars in remediation and repairs.

Then came an even stranger attack.

The Bowman dam was a tiny, 20-foot-tall dam that held no strategic importance, except ensuring that Rye's Blind Brook didn't flood basements in the small New York town. "It's ridiculous how little that dam is, how insignificant in the grand scheme of things," the mayor of Rye Brook, Paul Rosenberg, said later. "We're not talking about something vital to the infrastructure of the country."[28] To be frank, we were never even sure that the Iranians meant to attack it. There was another Bowman dam and we always wondered whether they meant to hit it instead: the 245-foot-tall Arthur R. Bowman dam on the Crooked River in Oregon, which held back the 3,500-acre Prineville Reservoir.

Yet, for reasons that to this day remain a mystery, Hamid Firoozi—network engineer for an Iranian company named ITSecTeam who had helped attack the financial system—penetrated the New York Bowman dam's so-called supervisory control and data acquisition (SCADA) system, the computers that help run the dam, over the course of the summer of 2013. Firoozi repeatedly obtained information about the dam's operation—including the water levels, water temperature, and the status of the sluice gate, which controlled the water flow. Under normal circumstances, he could have operated and manipulated that sluice gate—potentially flooding those local basements—but luckily, the sluice gate at that moment happened to be disconnected for maintenance. Resecuring the dam ultimately cost more than $30,000.

We'd gotten lucky that the dam was down for repairs, but I joked at the time that I didn't think we should rely on America's crumbling infrastructure to protect us from foreign cyberattacks. The hacking of the Bowman dam demonstrated what our foreign adversaries were doing—or trying to do—with different critical infrastructure facilities around the country. We'd seen similar behavior from China, Russia, and Iran elsewhere—and North Korea certainly aspired to such attacks. It worried me that if North Korea ever achieved the type of access that Iran had at the Bowman dam, they might pull the virtual trigger.

Ultimately, we zeroed in on seven Iranians who had carried out the financial sector DDoS attacks and the intrusion at the Bowman dam:

Hamid Firoozi, Ahmad Fathi, Amin Shokohi, Sadegh Ahmadzadegan (known by his online handle "Nitr0jen26"), Omid Ghaffarinia (known as PLuS), Sina Keissar, and Nader Saedi (known as Turk Server). Collectively, they worked at two Iranian security companies, ITSecTeam and Mersad Company.

We saw their fingerprints in the attacks: Firoozi, a network manager at ITSec, had worked to procure, lease, and set up the computer servers used in the DDoS attacks. Fathi, Shokohi, and others helped assemble the botnet, known as Brobot, that powered the attack; they exploited known vulnerabilities in outdated popular content management systems such as WordPress and Joomla to line up computers.[29] Saedi touted his own expertise in DDoS attacks, and had written the computer scripts that Mersad used to locate vulnerable servers and assembled its botnet for the attacks. For his part, Keissar helped do the preliminary testing on the botnet.

While the painstaking indictment—overseen by the Counterintelligence and Export Control Section in our office and prosecutor Tim Howard in the Southern District of New York—did not explicitly say the Iranian government or military had directed the attacks, it did make clear that ITSec and Mersad did regular work with the Iranian government, including the Islamic Revolutionary Guard Corps, and even as Shokohi worked on the financial system DDoS attack, he "received credit for his computer intrusion work from the Iranian Government towards completion of his mandatory military service," according to our indictment. Mersad had been founded in early 2011 by members of two Iranian hacker groups, Sun Army and the notorious Ashiyane Digital Security Team, which was famous for attacking Western websites as a political protest. Originally founded in the early 2000s by Behrouz Kamalian, the Ashiyane Digital Security Team had been a thorn in the West's side for years—defacing thousands of websites, from local UK government to Israeli and Danish websites, as part of a protest following a cartoon about the Prophet Muhammad.[30] Even in the midst of the financial DDoS attacks, in October 2011, Kamalian had been sanctioned by the European Union for the hacker group's role in aiding a crackdown on protesters in Iran two years earlier.[31]

A few days before we finally announced the indictments in the case of the Bowman dam and the financial sector DDoS attack, I went over to the FBI's Cyber Division and hosted a video conference call with its assistant director, James Trainor, to tell the bank victims we'd identified the attackers and were going to be able to bring charges, as well as to share some of what we learned from the case. On the day we announced the indictments, we didn't have any of the six in custody, but as FBI Director James Comey said to reporters in unveiling the charges, "Never say never." As he said, "The world is small and our memories are long."

////////////////

It wasn't only nuisance attacks or critical infrastructure penetration that we were seeing from the Iranians—we also saw espionage-related hacking similar to what the Chinese did. We'd been looking for the right one, with the right evidence, when a Burlington, Vermont, defense contractor called its local FBI office.

The small tech firm, Arrow Tech, only employed about ten engineers and it primarily manufactured software to calculate aerodynamics and design projectiles such as GPS-guided artillery shells. Arrow Tech's software was normally protected by a special hardware key, known as a dongle, that permitted the software to run on a given machine. Given its sensitive military nature, the technology was protected by the government's export controls, ensuring that it couldn't be shipped internationally without special permission.

One morning in October 2012, the network administrator at Arrow Tech noticed that something strange was taking place on their network and called the FBI. Burlington is overseen by the FBI's Albany Field Office, and a few days later a cyber agent made the three-hour drive up along Lake Champlain to check out the tip. It didn't take long for the agent to realize he was dealing with the real thing. The software was a potential boon to a variety of Iranian defense projects. Within hours, the FBI and Arrow Tech were tracking every keystroke the hackers made inside their system. "We were very impressed with what [the FBI] got done in just a few hours," Arrow Tech's president, Charles Hillman, said later.[32]

The case made its way to our nascent NSD Threat Cell, where Sean Newell began working on it alongside his China casework. What the FBI was able to unravel was a group of three Iranians—Mohammed Reza Rezakhah, 39, Mohammed Saeed Ajily, 35, and Nima Golestaneh, 30—who worked diligently to steal protected software like Arrow Tech's and then sell it for use by the Iranian military and government through a network of Iranian shell companies such as the Andisheh Vesal Middle East Company in Tehran.[33] Beginning at least in 2007, Golestaneh established overseas servers, in places like Canada and the Netherlands, to help them crack into protected networks; then, Ajily, who oversaw the scheme, would have Rezakhah work to break the software and allow it to be resold without the standard intellectual property protections like the dongle.[34] In 2012, the group successfully broke into Arrow Tech's network, stole its protected software, and then began offering it for sale in Iran to entities such as Tehran University, Sharif Technical University, and Shiraz Electro Optic Industry, a missile company owned by the Iranian military. Their scheme as mercenary hackers had been so successful that they'd received certificates of appreciation from the Iranian military. "They are essentially nonsanctioned espionage groups," Brian Wallace, a security expert at Cylance, explained as the case was made public. "The government doesn't create them, they don't own them. They operate and get almost all of their income from the government."[35]

As the case unfolded, the FBI figured out that Nima Golestaneh, a student at an Iranian university, was heading to Turkey for vacation and we raced to ready the paperwork to arrest him overseas; in November 2013, Turkish police arrested him as he toured Istanbul's main Sultanahmet district. He spent 16 months in prison there awaiting extradition to the United States in February 2015.[36] He pleaded guilty that December in a Burlington courtroom, a long way from his home in Iran. It marked an important milestone for us—one of the first cases where we possessed sufficient evidence to bring an indictable criminal case. As I said in announcing the guilty plea, "With continued partnerships like these, cyber crimes will not go unanswered. At the National Security Division, we will continue to follow the facts and evidence wherever they lead to ensure there are no safe havens for hackers."[37]

The case underscored that economic theft and espionage wasn't just a China story. This wasn't just a bilateral disagreement with another foreign adversary—this was an across-the-board cyber story. Different nation-states were all engaged in similar behavior and we, the US government, needed to have a unified and consistent response that was "state agnostic," but instead focused on punishing and prosecuting specific behaviors regardless of who was on the other side of the keyboard. We wanted to establish that prosecutions were normal. We were going to prosecute people we caught stealing or attacking American interests regardless of who they were, regardless of whether they were an individual, a criminal group, or a nation-state. Similarly, if you did a destructive attack against the United States, we wanted to establish no doubt that the United States would track you down and take retaliatory action. Our view was that we were enforcing clear, established laws and international norms of behavior if we caught someone violating those, we were going to move when we were ready, just as we would against a terrorist or ordinary criminal.

That view, though, was not universally held—in fact, we met with repeated opposition at the White House and State Department. It became a running joke in the Situation Room: when we would announce we were close to bringing a new case, it would be met with almost audible groans from the diplomatic sides of the table among those who would be forced to defend and explain our action to their counterparts.

Whereas my former colleague Lisa Monaco and representatives from the Department of Commerce understood how vital these prosecutions were in sending a message to our adversaries, National Security Advisor Susan Rice, Secretary of State John Kerry, and officials at the National Economic Council often believed that the prosecutions brought too many complications to sensitive bilateral relationships. We often faced questions like: Why would we bring this case now, when we're trying to work out with China a global climate change agreement or negotiate a nuclear deal with Iran or something else that was entirely unrelated to the nation-state's bad cyber behavior? In the

17-level game of geopolitics, cybersecurity too often seemed to take a backseat. Ultimately, we never settled the debate—it came up time and again.

⁓⁓⁓⁓⁓

The first destructive cyberattack to hit the US mainland targeted a place almost as unexpected as a fancy Georgetown Italian restaurant: the Sands Casino company, a name for decades all but synonymous with gambling and glitz, but hardly at the top of the list of the nation's critical infrastructure.

The original Sands Hotel and Casino in Las Vegas had once been home to Frank Sinatra's Rat Pack, and after Sheldon Adelson bought the original property in 1988—razing it to build the luxurious Venetian resort and casino—he transformed it into a global gambling empire, stretching from Macao to Singapore to the Las Vegas Strip. The effort made Adelson fabulously wealthy, turning him into a powerhouse in both American business and politics; by the 2010s, he was the 11th-wealthiest person in the country and the top contributor to political action committees during the 2012 election, handing out more than $50 million to conservative causes. Adelson, an outspoken voice on Israeli issues, was close friends with Israeli leader Benjamin Netanyahu, and during an October 2013 panel at Yeshiva University he argued that the United States needed to take a stronger stand against Iran's nascent nuclear weapons program—including a military strike designed to demonstrate to Iran that the United States meant business. As he told the audience, "You pick up your cell phone and you call somewhere in Nebraska and you say 'OK, let it go' and so there's an atomic weapon goes over, ballistic missiles in the middle of the desert that doesn't hurt a soul, maybe a couple of rattlesnakes and scorpions or whatever."

At the time, the comment passed largely unnoticed; Israeli outlets covered his remarks and an Adelson spokesperson quickly backed down, explaining the gambling magnate had been "using hyperbole to make a point." Iran didn't see it that way; in early November, Iran's Supreme Leader Ayatollah Ali Khamenei responded, saying Adelson "should receive a slap in the mouth," and that America, if it was serious about peace with Iran, "should slap these prating people in the mouth and crush their mouths."[38]

Soon after, Iranian hackers began digging around, probing the Sands Casino's digital infrastructure. In January, they launched three separate brute-force attacks on the company's Bethlehem casino—running automated programs that tried thousands of possible passwords in an attempt to log in to the computer network. The Sands Casino security staff noticed, but such attempts were common, and they moved to provide additional security on the targeted accounts—requiring what is known as two-factor authentication so that cracking a password alone wouldn't have been enough. At the time, though, the Sands Casino staff didn't realize how badly outgunned they were against the resources of a persistent and patient foreign adversary. The company, like the vast majority of companies around the globe at that point, did not have adequate resources to fight the cyberthreat. As late as 2012, just five computer security engineers protected the network's 25,000 computers—an impossible task.[39]

The Iranian hackers kept at it—trying new avenues and new attack vectors—and by February 1, they were inside the Sands Casino system, exploiting a weakness in the company's development server that it used for testing. Then, once inside the system, they kept probing for even more access. They installed a free, easily downloadable hacking tool known as Mimikatz to record users' passwords inside the networks, following a common path for hackers—who first target a network weak point and exploit it to gain further access to more high-value targets, leapfrogging step by step inside the system until they access a company's crown jewels.

Mimikatz had been created in 2011 by a security engineer named Benjamin Delpy, who wrote the program partly as a lark to help teach himself the programming language C. It demonstrated part of what makes cyberdefense so challenging—the same tools can be used both for "white hat" hackers testing security infrastructure and probing for possible vulnerabilities, and for "black hat" hackers seeking to do damage. Mimikatz—available to all with nothing more than a Google search—was simultaneously a standard tool for security researchers and also a powerful tool for hackers.[40] Installed inside the Sands network in Pennsylvania, Mimikatz had the infinite patience of a machine, collecting passwords employees used on the system. Mimikatz was representative of what we often saw nation-states use: on lower-value targets, particularly in the private sector, they preferred patience and old-school tools—they surely possessed more sophisticated tools and zero-day vulnerabilities, but they didn't want to waste them or tip their hand to sophisticated tradecraft when simple ones would accomplish the job. Finally, the Iranians got what they needed: a senior Sands engineer visited the Bethlehem casino and used his password on their local network, a password that also granted the hackers access to the more valuable, wider corporate network in Las Vegas.[41]

There, inside the broader system, the hackers installed a relatively simple—but deadly—piece of malware. Investigators later determined it was just about 150 lines of code, written in the programming language Visual Basic. The malware, when activated, wiped hard drives clean, restarted them, and also wrote over the existing files with random gibberish, making it next to impossible to recover the lost files. The Iranian hackers set loose their destructive malware ten days later, at the beginning of a new workweek—marking the first time that an American company faced a destructive attack at the hands of a nation-state.

Employees of Adelson's company, the Las Vegas Sands Corporation, noticed their email seize up on the morning of Monday, February 10, 2014. From there, the attack rippled through the company. The following day, shortly after noon, people who logged on to the website of the world's largest gambling company found the Sands site replaced with a world map marked with flames showing the locations of its American casinos. Under the taunting heading "a bit of many," the hackers included a scrolling list of employees' names, titles, and personal details such as Social Security numbers that they'd stolen, as well as a photo of Adelson and Netanyahu standing together. "Damn A, don't let your tongue cut your throat. Encouraging the use of weapons of mass destruction, under any conditions, is a crime," a message in green type read. The message was signed by a group calling itself the "Anti WMD team." The local Las Vegas newspaper likened the attack to "scenes out of the 1983 movie *WarGames*."[42]

The attack spread panic through the company. Inside the casinos, staff raced to understand what was happening; as they realized the scale of the attack, engineers ran through the casinos, disconnecting computers from the network without permission—ripping the cords out of servers and the machines that helped run the multimillion-dollar games on the casino floor. For the most part, they were too late. Nearly everything electronic in the casino had been destroyed. According to an account later published in *Bloomberg Businessweek*, Sands President Michael Leven personally made the decision "to sever the company entirely from the internet."[43] Luckily, the hackers hadn't penetrated the system that runs the hotel operations—guests were still able to access their hotel rooms, and, amazingly, most casino-goers were able to go right on playing their favorite slot machine.

The websites were shuttered for nearly a week, but the company kept up a strong public face.[44] "Company-operated websites have been hacked, as have some office productivity systems in the U.S.," Sands spokesman Ron Reese told the local Bethlehem newspaper in a statement. "The company is working closely with the appropriate law enforcement agencies to determine who initiated the hacking activity."[45] That public confidence evidently angered the Iranians, who of course knew better than anyone just how extensive their internal attack had been. On YouTube, they posted an 11-minute video, mocking the company and documenting their internal damage and the thousands of files they evidently purloined, all set to the haunting, dramatic cantata "O Fortuna" from Carl Orff's *Carmina Burana*.[46] A text box on the screen mocked: "Do you really think that only your mail server has been taken down?!! Like hell it has!!" The link to the YouTube video, purportedly posted by someone named Zhao Anderson, was emailed to news outlets who had covered the initial attack.[47] When the Sands staff saw the video, they knew the hackers were right: until then, they hadn't even known those files had been stolen. The breach had been even worse than they had imagined.[48]

Leven later said it might cost as much as $40 million for the company to rebuild and resurrect its files and servers. Weeks after the attack, the Sands Casino filed a notice with the Securities and Exchange Commission that "legally protected data" had been stolen, and the company said it believed the hackers had gained access to sensitive personal data for a group of customers or employees totaling in the "mid five-figure range."[49] Beyond the physical damage into the computers, the attack injected lasting psychological damage to the casino's workforce. "It's freaking me out," said Joshua Cesanek, an employee of the Bethlehem casino. "I can monitor my bank account and credit cards, but how do I monitor my Social Security number? Am I going to have to worry about this for years?"[50] Much like the Saudi Aramco attack, the Sands Casino attack passed without widespread public notice. Even though a heist from a Las Vegas casino of $40 million would have generated months of news leading headlines, a similarly damaging cyberattack barely attracted notice outside of the locations where the employees were affected.

Iran was suspect #1 from the start, and we pushed our team to figure out whether this was a case we could pursue publicly. We wanted to make clear to the public just how provocative Iran's attacks were across the United States. We heard early on about the attack, and thought, *This is it! We've been talking about Saudi Aramco and warning that it would come to us*, but just like so many other instances, it turned out we had to stay mostly silent on the Sands Casino attack—both because of the sensitive sources and methods involved in our knowledge of the attack and because of the victim's overall reluctance to publicize the attack.

The company perceived—accurately—that it had been targeted precisely because of its public statements, and thus it had no wish to bring any further attention or publicity to its woes. Despite some local press coverage, there was almost no mainstream or national attention. The forced silence was immensely frustrating—it was a missed opportunity to highlight the attack to get the private sector to pay attention or to help encourage them to defend their systems. Finally, Director of National Intelligence James Clapper announced that Iran was responsible for the attack, but even after he talked about it publicly, we tried to limit our discussion, doing our best not to revictimize the victim. Clapper highlighted the incident as a turning point for America, saying, "for the first time, [we saw] destructive cyberattacks carried out on U.S. soil by nation-state entities, marked first by the Iranian attack against the Las Vegas Sands Casino Corporation."[51]

The Sands Casino attack challenged us inside government to rethink our handling of destructive attacks. Much like the financial sector DDoS attacks—which targeted consumer-facing digital infrastructure, rather than threatening the integrity of the financial sector itself—the Sands Casino attack hit an unexpected target. We'd never considered casinos as critical infrastructure before. What do you do and how do you treat an attack when it's gaming, not the electrical grid? How do you respond in kind? What does a national security response look like when the target's a casino? For the private sector, the Sands Casino attack made one lesson clear: *we're all vulnerable to an attack, so keep your head down and stay off an attacker's radar.*

With hindsight, we looked at the problem wrong. It wasn't a critical-infrastructure problem. It was a free-expression problem. Because of what someone said, a hacker had targeted that individual's business in an attempt to silence him. By not taking public action to defend an American businessman who was exercising his First Amendment right to freedom of speech and expression, the US government failed to address something that we paid for down the line: we couldn't work to safeguard just our infrastructure. We had to protect our values as well.

CHAPTER 5

APT1

As 2013 STARTED, we were increasingly confident we could bring a prosecutable case against China. Our ragtag Threat Cell was making progress, gathering evidence and sifting through classified intelligence to assemble something that increasingly resembled a "normal" criminal case. Lisa Monaco, Adam Hickey, and I went to the White House then Homeland Security Advisor John Brennan to advise him we were moving forward.* Lisa showed Brennan a photo of a Chinese PLA hacker named Wang Dong, also known as Jack Wong, who went online by the name UglyGorilla. Brennan studied the photo and understood the message: there was no doubt that we were targeting officially sanctioned Chinese behavior. "We've got the goods," Lisa said.

Later, Lisa cornered White House Deputy National Security Advisor Denis McDonough to make sure he understood the case NSD was putting together. "I want to bring the Arbabsiar of cyber economic espionage cases," she said, referring to the Iran assassination plot we'd used to send a message that we would respond forcefully to attacks. Denis got the reference immediately: the United States needed to send a

---

* It wasn't a "permission" meeting, just an advisory one—the Justice Department's tradition carefully protects its ability to make independent decisions on prosecutions—and White House Counsel Kathy Ruemmler sat in to help ensure everyone stayed on their own side of the line. NSD often did similar awareness briefings on major counterterrorism cases, to ensure the White House wasn't surprised by news of arrests or plots, and we wanted to establish a similar rhythm on these new types of cases.

similar signal to China. This was a foreign nation-state whose government had violated international norms—they deserved to be publicly named and punished. These were all actors who had been clearly directed by their own governments to cross a red line.

I knew we needed to be pushing harder and faster on cybersecurity inside government. At Main Justice, I saw the daily intel reports about the massive pillaging taking place across the country. As I walked back from the FBI threat briefings in the morning, I kept turning over in my mind the rising cyberthreats. For nearly a decade, I'd attended the threat briefings; when I started, they were almost entirely focused on terrorism, but as the years progressed, we saw more and more cyberthreats popping up on the agenda. The Shamoon attack made clear that it was only a matter of time before our foreign adversaries began to assault our digital society, and we were living day by day through the DDoS attacks on the financial sector by Iran. We weren't exactly losing this shadowy Code War, but we certainly weren't winning.

We never believed that we could prosecute our way toward a safe and secure internet—any more than hundreds of years of prosecution have halted crime in the real world. We knew we needed to bring all the tools of government to bear on the problem. To that end, we had been working with the White House national security advisor, Tom Donilon, to elevate the strategic importance of cybersecurity and intellectual property theft on the geopolitical agenda. We needed to escalate the message that economic cybertheft was not acceptable, using both private conversations and public actions, until China's behavior changed.

In early February 2013—even as both the *Wall Street Journal* and the *New York Times* publicly announced that their systems had been attacked by Chinese hackers—the government took another step toward confronting China: a new "National Intelligence Estimate," a document that represents the consensus of the country's various intelligence agencies, named China as pursuing what the *Washington Post* summarized as "a massive, sustained cyber-espionage campaign that is threatening the country's economic competitiveness," explaining that China was "the country most aggressively seeking to penetrate the computer systems of American businesses and institutions to gain access to data that could be used for economic gain."[1]

As banal as they sometimes seem to the general public, events like the presidential State of the Union address are enormously helpful in driving change and action inside the federal government. An approaching State of the Union address tends to break bureaucratic logjams and free up long-standing debates as the White House assembles its annual agenda. Such was the case with President Obama's Executive Order 13636 in February 2013, which established new cybersecurity protections for the nation's critical infrastructure and allowed for better information sharing with the private sector.[2] The executive order had been more than a year in the making, as the White House's cybersecurity coordinator Michael Daniel had carefully collected viewpoints from across the government and the private sector, but little of it was all that different from the approach the Bush administration and Director of National Intelligence Mike McConnell had pursued back in 2008 and 2009—the four-year delay indicative of how long it had taken cybersecurity to regain traction inside the government.

That night, in his annual State of the Union address, President Obama trumpeted the new protections and said, "Now, we know hackers steal people's identities and infiltrate private emails. We know foreign countries and companies swipe our corporate secrets. Now our enemies are also seeking the ability to sabotage our power grid, our financial institutions, our air traffic control systems. We cannot look back years from now and wonder why we did nothing in the face of real threats to our security and our economy."[3]

///////////////

That same month the efforts to highlight and identify China's state-sponsored hacking efforts received a big boost from the private sector: the cybersecurity firm Mandiant released a 75-page report describing years of efforts by an online foe it called "APT1." The group had been known over the years by various online nicknames—such

as the Comment Crew or the Comment Group—as different pub-
lications or researchers identified it differently, but Mandiant had
settled on "Advanced Persistent Threat 1," a nod to its prominence
and ubiquity online. The moniker "Advanced Persistent Threat" had
been popularized in 2006 by Air Force Colonel Greg Rattray as
a pseudonym to talk about nation-state adversaries in unclassified
settings. To those who monitored online attacks, an APT designa-
tion indicated specific attributes: it characterized a well-resourced,
organized, and mission-focused online actor with sophisticated technical abilities that included the use of custom exploits and zero-day
vulnerabilities.

Since APTs were usually working toward a specific goal, their behavior in a compromised network often followed a predictable pattern.
After an initial compromise—such as a run-of-the-mill spear-phishing
attack—they didn't rush through a system. Instead, they planted remote access tools, creating back doors that ensured their ongoing access
even if the initial compromise was uncovered; then they often worked
through multiple layers of a network, escalating their own user privi-
leges through additional account compromises or vulnerabilities until
they achieved administrator- or root-level access that gave them the
run of the network. Along the way, they carefully mapped the network,
downloading file lists, directory structures, and server details to understand thoroughly what information was available. APTs were patient,
directed threats to online networks—often spending weeks, months,
or even years exploring and learning penetrated systems, exfiltrating
only selected data that fulfilled whatever goal had led the team to its
target. Sometimes they returned to the compromised network months
or even years later to see what new information was available.

Anyone who spent time monitoring computer systems came to
know APTs, teams of hackers who behaved in similar ways, targeting
similar systems. It was usually pretty easy to identify them: their hacking usually occurred during regular business hours in their home countries, and many teams and individual hackers had online patterns and
user tics that were as unique as any set of fingerprints.

Mandiant had been working independently on their report on APT1, and one of the FBI agents working with our Threat Cell received a hard copy just before Mandiant released it. Sean Newell met the agent in the parking lot of a hockey rink to pick it up. The Threat Cell carefully parsed the document and ensured that any overlapping evidence it was going to make public had already been preserved—nearly all of the evidence was historical, so there wasn't much fear that the Chinese could delete anything material when the news became public. Once they were confident the report didn't compromise the case in any way, members of our Threat Cell were ecstatic at the idea of the report. "We wanted this information shouted from the rooftops," Hickey recalls.

The Mandiant report, trumpeted and amplified by the *New York Times*, had grown out of the *Times* itself being hacked by the Chinese. The paper had enlisted Mandiant to help clean up and study the attack on its computers; as it turned out, more than 60 *Times* employees had been spied upon the Chinese had sought information on the newspaper's coverage of the Chinese government and particularly a series on the massive, illegal wealth amassed by relatives of the prime minister, Wen Jiabao.

Mandiant's report came as a public bombshell—it went far beyond what the US government had publicly identified and outlined a pattern of behavior that shocked the general public. Kevin Mandia—the founder of the security firm and a pioneer in cybersecurity who had, years before, helped train me in my first computer hacking class—understood our approach and supported the effort to "name and shame" China through every available avenue. The more voices condemning China's economic espionage, the better—and the information Mandiant made public helped ease internal government fears about exposing sensitive sources and methods. As Adam Hickey says, "It took the private sector to call out a nation-state's illegal behavior to help make the government comfortable to do so." Mandiant carefully identified the hackers behind APT1, pointing the finger at the Second Bureau of the PLA's General Staff Department's Third Department, known as Unit 61398, located on

Datong Road in Gaoqiaozhen, on the east bank of the Huangpu River across from the main part of Shanghai, in Pudong, the well-known financial district.

Unit 61398—just one of perhaps two dozen distinct Chinese hacking teams—was based in a 12-story compound, built in 2007, that encompassed 130,000 square feet; as the cyber unit expanded China Telecom installed special fiber-optic communications in the building. The compound included nearby logistics support, a clinic, and even a kindergarten, all signs that it supported a large, privileged workforce. "We estimate that Unit 61398 is staffed by hundreds, and perhaps thousands of people based on the size of Unit 61398's physical infrastructure," Mandiant wrote. "Unit 61398 requires its personnel to be trained in computer security and computer network operations and also requires its personnel to be proficient in the English language." The report walked in exhaustive detail through the online bread crumbs they'd assembled: a graduate student affiliated with Unit 61398, Li Bingbing, who published a paper about embedding covert communications in a Microsoft Word document; a Shanghai businessman, Wang Weizhong, who discussed his training as an English linguist from Unit 61398; academic papers by veterans of 61398 that related their skills with operating systems, digital signal processing, and network security.

APT1 conducted economic espionage at an industrial-scale level, carrying out attacks against dozens of targets simultaneously. Mandiant reported that it had identified at least 141 organizations across 20 industry sectors that had all been penetrated by APT1; collectively, those organizations had seen hundreds of terabytes of data stolen. Mandiant had been able to determine that APT1 had, in one penetration, exfiltrated more than 6.5 terabytes of data—the equivalent of more than 3 billion printed pages, a pile of paper roughly 190 miles tall. Of the penetrations Mandiant had been able to track, the elite Chinese team generally had access to an organization's system for 356 days—nearly a year—but sometimes they stayed much longer. One victim had unknowingly hosted the Chinese for 1,764 days, nearly five years.

Mandiant laid out a complex global technical infrastructure that supported APT1's online endeavors. The Chinese unit had established nearly 1,000 command-and-control servers around the world, in a total of 13 countries, including 109 servers inside the United States. They used hundreds of domain names to conduct their attacks, often relying on names that mimicked legitimate websites: CNNdaily.com, myyahoonews .com, reutersnewsonline.com, applesoftware.com, microsoft-update -info.com. They even mimicked sites run by the very companies that protected against attacks like them, such as symanteconline .net, which to a casual observer might appear to be sent from the security company Symantec.

None of these endeavors came cheap: in addition to the hackers themselves, the infrastructure would have required a "sizable IT staff," including teams dedicated to finances, logistics, and technical support. To bolster their credibility and to aid other systems administrators the world over in identifying further APT1 targets, Mandiant released a list of 3,000 attributes that indicated Unit 61398, including specific domain names, IP addresses, encryption certificates, and variants of malware they used. The list included nearly four dozen different types of back doors that would allow Unit 61398 to maintain long-term access to a compromised network.

In demonstrating how APT1 worked, Mandiant even released information about a spear-phishing attack that the unit had launched against the security company itself: an email to company executives that purported to be from Mandiant founder Kevin Mandia. Coming from kevin.mandia@rocketmail.com, a popular free email service, with the subject line "Internal Discussion on the Press Release," the message read, "Hello, Shall we schedule a time to meet next week? We need to finalize the press release. Details click here." If anyone had clicked on the link, it would have downloaded a file, *Internal_Discussion_Press_ Release_In_Next_Week8.zip*, that contained a unique custom back door used by Unit 61398 known as WEBC2-TABLE. That particular type of exploit, one of APT1's most prevalent attacks, retrieved a webpage that contained special code hidden inside the HTML programming language that all websites are built upon. The nefarious commands were hidden inside an HTML comment tag, a special aside that programmers can use to document or explain what they are doing in building a website. Such comments are not displayed to a regular web browser, but are visible if someone chooses to read the site's underlying source code. This habit of APT1 of embedding nefarious activity in such a mundane place was what led some researchers to name the group the Comment Crew. Once those hidden commands granted APT1 access to the targeted system, the hackers could then download and execute additional malware, opening pathways for future attacks.*

One lucky break for researchers was that China's own internet monitoring—the so-called Great Firewall of China—made it difficult to access popular Western websites like Facebook or Twitter from mainland China. Instead, Unit 61398 personnel often accessed social media sites directly from the foreign internet sites they controlled as part of their work, thereby allowing researchers to link their "work personas" to their offline identities. Researchers determined one hacker, known as DOTA, who had a Shanghai-registered cell phone, appeared to be a Harry Potter fan, since he often answered online security questions with variations of "Harry" and "Poter." Mandiant also identified a hacker known as SuperHard, one of APT1's most capable coders, who apparently was born in 1982 and whose real-life name was likely Mei Qiang.

Mandiant publicly outed perhaps the most infamous member of APT1, UglyGorilla, or Wang Dong, a hacker researchers were able to trace back nearly a decade. In January 2004, UglyGorilla had asked in an online question-and-answer session with Zhang Zhaozhong, one of the fathers of China's information warfare doctrine, about his own country's cyber resources. He'd asked, "Professor Zhang, I read your book *Network Warfare* and was deeply impressed by the views and arguments in the book. It is said that the U.S. military has set up a

---

* Similar spear-phishing attempts in the past had focused on a plethora of geopolitical and military themes, from files labeled *Oil-Field-Services-Analysis-And-Outlook.zip* to *The_Latest_Syria_Security_Assessment_Report.zip* to *MARKET-COMMENT-Europe -Ends-Sharply-Lower-On-Data-Yields-Jump.zip*. Even savvy users weren't immune. Mandiant saw one instance where a spear-phishing target replied to a suspicious email saying, "I'm not sure if this is legit, so I didn't open it." Within twenty minutes, someone at Unit 61398 wrote back encouragingly, "It's legit."

dedicated network force referred to as a 'cyber army.' Does China have a similar force? Does China have cyber troops?"

As best as threat researchers could tell, UglyGorilla had soon joined that very same "cyber army," becoming part of Unit 61398's hacker corps. The first online trace of his military hacking appeared in October 2004, when he registered a domain, hugesoft.org, that in the years ahead became one of APT1's best-known websites. In 2007, UglyGorilla authored one of the unit's primary hacking exploits, proudly signing it personally in imperfect English: "No Doubt to Hack You, Writed by UglyGorilla." By tracing his other online activities, researchers were able to find a developer website where UglyGorilla had included both his English nickname (Jack Wang) and his real name: Wang Dong.[4]

The Mandiant report surprised precisely no one who had been paying attention in government. As House Intelligence Chairman Mike Rogers said, the report is "completely consistent with the type of activity the Intelligence Committee has been seeing for some time."[5]*

We also knew by that point, though, that APT1 was just one of numerous forces China was deploying against the world economy. Altogether, we calculated that the PLA Third Department had a dozen operational bureaus, three research institutes, four operations centers, and sixteen technical reconnaissance units in military regions with operational forces.[6] When Mandiant issued its APT1 report, it was tracking what it believed were more than 20 distinct Chinese "APTs."

The month after the Mandiant report, in March 2013, White House National Security Advisor Tom Donilon used a speech at the Asia Society in New York to highlight the challenge of Chinese economic espionage; he said such activity posed "a growing challenge to our economic relationship with China" and represented a "key point of concern and

---

* In a similar example of using the government's "all tools" approach to apply every possible carrot and stick, Congressman Rogers himself had issued a similar report, from Capitol Hill, examining the links between the Chinese government and the telecommunication manufacturers Huawei Technologies and ZTE Corporation, claiming they represented a "national security threat" to the United States. As a White House official said when the report was released, "We have a process that is not aimed at one specific company but using all the assets and parts of U.S. government aimed at protecting our telecommunications and critical infrastructure."

discussion with China at all levels of our governments." The comments, the first made publicly by a White House official focused on China's cyber activities, represented a watershed. He called for China to "take serious steps to investigate and put a stop to these activities."[7]

Then, that May, the Pentagon in its annual report to Congress also accused China of widespread cyberespionage against the United States. The language was subtle—and bureaucratic—but for those who were paying attention, it was a remarkable step. "In 2012, numerous computer systems around the world, including those owned by the U.S. government, continued to be targeted for intrusions, some of which appear to be attributable directly to the Chinese government and military," the Pentagon wrote on page 36 of its 90-page report. "China is using its computer network exploitation (CNE) capability to support intelligence collection against the U.S. diplomatic, economic, and defense industrial base sectors that support U.S. National defense programs."[8]

As bland as that statement might appear, it was the first time the US government had publicly accused China of state-sponsored, coordinated attacks aimed at advancing economic goals.[9] Moreover, the Pentagon concluded that China's efforts also appeared aimed at "building a picture of U.S. network defense networks, logistics, and related military capabilities that could be exploited during a crisis."

China, though, continued to deny any such activities. "I don't think anybody has so far presented any hard evidence, evidence that could stand up in court, to prove that there is really somebody in China, Chinese nationals, that are doing these things," China's ambassador to the US, Cui Tiankai, told *Foreign Affairs*.[10] That final sentence seemed to come across to our prosecutors like a dare: our goal was to offer precisely that hard evidence and proof of China's behavior.

—————

As President Obama's second term began in 2013, there were numerous personnel changes across the upper ranks of government. Lisa Monaco was tapped to become the White House homeland security advisor, the president's top advisor on counterterrorism, counterintelligence, and other domestic threats. When she moved to the White House, that made me, her principal deputy, the acting assistant attorney general for national security.

When Eric Holder talked with me about the position, though, he emphasized that I shouldn't look at myself as a temporary "acting" chief, even though I was a career Justice Department employee. NSD, he said, was too important a job. "Do it like it's yours," he told me. Too quickly, I was faced with little choice. I learned almost immediately just how much there was to balance in the job—each day numerous threats competed for attention. Since NSD sat at the intersection of day-to-day law enforcement and intelligence gathering while also simultaneously monitoring national threats as they evolved, we needed to be able to map out where the country should be heading strategically in the long term, regardless of what might be happening tactically day to day.

That unique mix of responsibilities—and its inherent challenge— were underscored just a few weeks after I took over as the acting head of the division when we confronted the Boston Marathon bombing. At the FBI's command center, I watched as our lawyers worked side by side with FBI agents responding to an ongoing terrorist attack, processing and analyzing real-time video and intelligence feeds. The FBI deputy director, Sean Joyce, was a native Bostonian himself, and you could hear his Boston accent over the tumult of the command post as he directed the teams up in Massachusetts. It was a tense and terrible week as the FBI raced to respond to a fast, unfolding crisis, culminating in the Watertown shoot-out and the dramatic citywide lockdown before both of the Tsarnaev brothers were stopped. Throughout the aftermath of the attack, the national security team worked smoothly together, with none of the infighting or distrust evident in some past incidents. At one point, Joyce came over to Mueller and me as we stood together in the command post and gestured to the team of investigators and lawyers working before us: "Can you believe how far we've come?" Standing there, I knew that we needed to get to the same point on cyber issues; if instead of a terrorist bombing, we'd faced a serious cyberattack on our nation's critical infrastructure, we were nowhere near as nimble or fast as we needed to be in our ability to respond.

Weeks later, we faced another crisis inside government: the leaks of Edward Snowden. On June 5, the *Guardian* newspaper published a scoop about a secret government program that required Verizon to turn over to the FBI "telephony metadata"—for example, the billing details of telephone calls made and received within the United States. That report was the first of a trove of classified files leaked by a onetime NSA employee and contractor who had illegally downloaded thousands of files on Western surveillance programs from his workplace and then fled to China-controlled Hong Kong, where he handed over the files to journalists that included Glenn Greenwald, Laura Poitras, the *New York Times*, the *Washington Post*, and *Der Spiegel*. When his location in Hong Kong became public, Snowden fled to Russia, where he sought temporary asylum from Vladimir Putin.

The subsequent weeks of public revelations about secret programs and Western surveillance operations caused an international uproar. The Snowden revelations shifted the global dialogue; this world of nation-state cyber activities that had long been some of the most closely held secrets of not just our government but of countries around the world was splashed across the front pages of newspapers on every continent. Critical sources and methods and technical techniques, developed over years in secret at a cumulative cost of billions of dollars, were publicized almost daily.

Initially, our team feared the Snowden revelations would derail all of our work to bring public cases against China and other foreign adversaries. Yet as the dust began to settle, the opposite became clear. Even as prosecutors investigated the criminal leaks and intelligence agencies struggled with the loss of critical insight into what our adversaries were doing online to harm American interests, the revelations also removed some of the government's reluctance to prosecute cybersecurity cases publicly. After so much nervousness behind closed doors about publicizing sources and methods that might cause our adversaries to shift their tactics, our adversaries, after Snowden, already knew from reading the news stories how we had been watching them. "This wasn't in the shadows anymore," Adam recalls. "We felt there was an obligation to make public what we knew about China's behavior. It was already the world we were living in."

Similarly, the Snowden revelations made clear how little the average American understood about cyberthreats. The fact that journalists convinced themselves and much of America—even much of the world—that the top cyberthreat in America was the United States running presidentially authorized covert intelligence operations and court-ordered surveillance programs that were conducted with oversight from inspectors general underscored how little people understood the cyberthreat from countries such as China, Russia, Iran, and North Korea, let alone the massive financial frauds we were seeing criminals undertake. Court-ordered, lawful surveillance should have been the least of worries for average users and companies around the world, when compared with the threats from nation-states, criminals, and terrorists.

Those of us inside the government had taken for granted that the American people—and especially the US Congress—understood the basics of surveillance law, that all of our programs were subject to myriad checks and balances, including court approval, internal auditing, and congressional oversight. It confounded us to watch the reaction to Snowden, as we saw what at the start was a perfectly valid debate about where policy lines should be drawn spiral into a condemnation that the NSA and US intelligence led an out-of-control dystopian surveillance state, that the people who administered these programs were doing something wrong and illegal, and that somehow the court-authorized activities of the United States could be conflated with the behavior of autocratic regimes that didn't even pretend to share our values.

From our vantage point, working in the center of this world, our country's surveillance programs were among the most tightly regulated corners of the American government—in fact, from years of experience working with international partners, it was clear the United States was the most tightly regulated *in the world*. Each morning at NSD began with reviewing and signing applications for search warrants before they went to the Foreign Intelligence Surveillance Court, the body whose operations and orders were at the center of the Snowden revelations. The FISA warrants we sought from that court represented the only legal way for the United States to gather intelligence information domestically, and obtaining them was an extensive process—the warrant applications stretched to dozens, sometimes hundreds, of pages, far more elaborate than a normal warrant used for criminal cases. There was even a stage, known as the Woods procedure, where every single fact in the warrant application was independently reviewed and double-checked.

We were in disbelief that in the midst of confronting this unprecedented plague of cyberthefts by China, massive financial frauds, and worldwide aggression emanating from Russia, somehow the United States was losing a public relations battle about democratic values with Snowden, who was sheltered first by China and then by Vladimir Putin's Russia. "These countries don't even pretend to embrace democratic values," we thought. We needed to be making the case that the real danger lay overseas; we needed to make public what we knew about the devastation being inflicted on American companies and American jobs by those same countries who were sheltering Snowden and professed their mock horror at US cyber capabilities.*

Even as we worked to defend ourselves against the outraged American public, our other adversaries continued their cyberattacks. In June 2013, Justice's Criminal Division filed charges against a Chinese energy firm, Sinovel Wind Group, alleging it stole trade secrets from a Massachusetts company known as AMSC (previously American

---

*I got a keen sense of the conflicting expectations from the American public and journalists about our national security and the still-controversial but age-old balancing act between security and liberty. At the Aspen Security Forum that summer after the Boston Marathon attacks and the Snowden revelations, I was cross-examined by a prominent reporter both about the unfolding Snowden scandal and the government's collection of anonymized telephone records—and then he quickly switched gears to criticize the technology used to track the suspects in the Boston Marathon bombing: *How can it be in this day and age that the US government doesn't have a facial recognition database of people's faces that they could run the marathon bombers' photos against to identify them?*

Superconductor Corporation), in what proved to be the beginning of a massive case. The Sinovel case was charged simply as straight-up corporate espionage; the two companies, Sinovel and AMSC, had partnered on large wind turbine projects in China, with AMSC providing the software to control the turbines and wind farms manufactured and built by Sinovel. AMSC knew many American companies struggled against the theft of trade secrets, so they'd gone to great lengths to lock down their software and ensure it remained accessible only to a small number of their own employees.

Then, in March 2011, with Sinovel owing more than $100 million in back payments and under contract for another $700 million in work with AMSC, the Chinese firm canceled everything. Three months later, AMSC figured out why: the Chinese firm had stolen the control software and installed it on the turbines. To accomplish the theft, Sinovel targeted an Austrian employee of AMSC and offered him untold riches if he would leak them the software. "They offered him women. They offered him an apartment. They offered him money. They offered him a new life," the head of the company, Daniel McGahn, later told *60 Minutes*. The Chinese firm offered a $1.7 million contract for the theft of the trade secrets; the employee was all too happy to oblige, writing in one text message to Sinovel, "I will send the full code of course." As the engineer wrote in an email McGahn later recovered, "All girls need money. I need girls. Sinovel needs me." The loss of business and unpaid bills devastated AMSC; it had to lay off more than 600 of its 900 workers.[11]

The Justice Department indicted Sinovel and also three related employees, including its deputy director of research and development. The criminal charges arose, ironically, from four wind turbines that Sinovel sold back to Massachusetts, where AMSC was based, that contained the stolen software. One of the turbine projects had even been underwritten by state government bonds issued as part of the postrecession federal stimulus program; US and Massachusetts taxpayers were unwittingly helping to subsidize the theft of a Massachusetts company's own intellectual property. "The allegations in this indictment describe a well-planned attack on an American business by international defendants—nothing short of attempted corporate homicide," the US attorney who led the case, John Vaudreuil, said.[12]

McGahn ultimately filed suit against the Chinese firm, suing for $1.2 billion, only to discover that Chinese hackers then targeted his company to learn its litigation strategy. The security firm brought in to respond to the hack, CrowdStrike, said they traced the hack to Unit 61398. As CrowdStrike's George Kurtz later said, "Whenever there's a big lawsuit we'll see the Chinese government actually break into that company, break into the legal department and figure out what's going on behind the scenes so they can better deal with that lawsuit."[13]

///////////////

Soon after the Sinovel indictment, we struck another blow against Chinese economic espionage in one of the oddest cases we'd ever worked. One of the attorneys in NSD, Richard Scott, helped coordinate the indictment and trial of Walter Lian-Heen Liew (also known as Liu Yuanxuan), his company, USA Performance Technology Inc., and another individual, Robert Maegerle, for stealing from the industrial giant DuPont what we called its "chloride-route titanium dioxide production technology." In layman's terms, Liew—a 56-year-old California man who had worked for Hewlett-Packard and then opened his own technology consulting firm—stole the recipe for the color white, which he then turned around and sold for large sums of money to state-owned Chinese companies.

In 1991, Liew had been invited to a Beijing banquet, where government officials told him they appreciated that he was a "patriotic overseas Chinese," and began the process of recruiting him to steal for them. As the federal prosecutor, Pete Axelrod, explained in court, "[A high-level government official] provided Mr. Liew with directives. And those directives, through Chinese agencies, included key task projects for the benefit of the Chinese government. Chief or key among those was the development of chloride-route TiO_2 technology. And with Mr. Luo's directives to Mr. Liew, so began a 20-year course of conduct of lying, cheating, and stealing."

Turning rocks into the specific white paint color that DuPont man-ufactures, known as "titanium white," is a massive $2.6 billion business on its own. There aren't many companies in the world that can do it, and China wanted a piece of the business itself—so it set out to steal it. As I later told *Bloomberg*, "This is theft. And this—stealing the color white—is a very good example of the problem. It's not a national secu-rity secret. It's about stealing something you can make a buck off of. It's part of a strategy to profit off what American ingenuity creates." Liew worked to befriend and exploit a DuPont engineer, eventually paying him $15,000 for blueprints of the production process, and also hired another DuPont engineer, Robert Maegerle, as a "consultant."

After years of work, Liew in 2004 sent a letter to the head of the Chi-nese Pangang Group, announcing his success at obtaining DuPont's proprietary information. He wrote, "After many years of follow-up research and application, my company has possession and mastery of the complete DuPont way of titanium white by chlorination."[14] Over the next five years, Liew received more than $28 million in contracts from the Chinese company as the company sought to build a planned 100,000-ton titanium dioxide factory in Chongqing. Finally, tips in 2010 provided to DuPont pointed them toward Liew's scheme—they filed their own lawsuit and, in July 2011, the FBI had raided the homes of Liew and Maegerle.

In early 2014, Liew, his company, and Maegerle were all found guilty at trial of economic espionage and a host of other charges—marking the first conviction by a federal jury under the Economic Es-pionage Act of 1996, one of the new tools we were trying to bring to bear on China. Liew was sentenced to 15 years in prison and ordered to forfeit the $28 million he'd earned from the Chinese. According to *Bloomberg*, the plot was unfortunately successful: while the Chongqing plant was never finished, a smaller manufacturing plant in Jinzhou "is operational and is widely believed to use DuPont processes."[15]

We saw similar cases in nearly every industrial sector. David Yen Lee, a chemist with Valspar, downloaded 160 secret formulas for paints and coatings, and intended to take them overseas to Nippon Paint in Shanghai—a theft that was valued at as much as $20 million, about an eighth of Valspar's entire profits that year. Hong Meng tried to steal information from his employer, DuPont, about LEDs and take it to Peking University, where he'd accepted a teaching position. And Xiang Dong Yu, an employee of the Ford Motor Company, stole 4,000 Ford documents as part of his efforts to secure a job with a Chinese automotive company.[16] Each of them was arrested and ultimately pleaded guilty.

Then there was the case of Avago Technologies, which specialized in a technology known as bulk acoustic wave (BAW) filters. The California company was an international leader, with facilities in Colorado and Singapore, in manufacturing a specific type of BAW filter known as FBAR, film bulk acoustic resonators, which are tiny acoustic resonators that are hermetically sealed inside a wafer-thin silicon package and are critical to helping mobile phones and similar wireless devices filter out electrical interference.* The market was huge; Avago has sold more than 12 billion of the high-tech filters, helping to make it possible for cell phones to get stronger and smaller at the same time as they more finely tuned out interference even as the world's airwaves became increasingly crowded with wireless devices. FBARs represented a tremendous technical accomplishment, an accomplishment that owed much to Dr. Rich Ruby, who had earned a PhD in engineering physics from UC-Berkeley and had devoted nearly all of his career to perfecting FBAR filters.

In the northern Chinese city of Tianjin during a 2011 visit to an old Avago colleague named Wei Pang, Ruby noticed something odd: his old colleague's new lab in Tianjin appeared to be using Avago's own technology to make the same FBAR. When he confronted Wei Pang and the university's assistant dean, they denied any link to Avago's work.

They were lying.

In fact, as the FBI uncovered, Wei Pang had worked closely with as many as five others for years to steal Avago's proprietary technology

---

*A modern iPhone 6, for instance, has more than a dozen FBAR filters, each containing seven or eight acoustic resonators—a total of more than 100 per phone.

and Ruby's lifework. The groundwork for the plot had been laid almost a decade earlier, when Wei Pang, Hao Zhang, and Huisui Zhang had all come to the United States in the early 2000s to attend graduate school at the University of Southern California (USC). That in and of itself was hardly uncommon: American colleges and universities have thrived in recent decades because of the flood of foreign students arriving on campus. From 1995 to 2015, the population of foreign university and college students nearly doubled, rising from 452,000 to 975,000. Many of them stayed in the United States after school, making important and valuable contributions to our own education system, technological research, and economy; the number of foreign-born scientists and engineers rose from 360,000 to 517,000 in the decade between 2003 and 2013.[17] As Daniel Golden wrote in his book *Spy Schools*, which traces foreign espionage in higher education, "Academic research offers a valuable, vulnerable, and low-risk target....Despite pursuing groundbreaking technologies for the Pentagon and the intelligence community, university laboratories are less protected than their corporate counterparts."[18]

Particularly for Chinese families, an American education remains a key sign of social standing and a tool for future prosperity. It's a path that could begin early: the population of Chinese high school students in American private schools soared from 65 in 2005 to 7,000 in 2010.[19] Roughly a third of the foreign college student population in the United States comes from China, as do about 15 percent of the foreign-born scientists and engineers in the country. Certainly, the overwhelming majority pose no national security threat to the United States, but that doesn't stop the Ministry of State Security from trying to recruit and identify potential spies. Since 2000, at least 30 Chinese-born or -raised graduates of American colleges and universities have been charged with economic espionage.[20]

After earning their degrees at USC in 2006, all three men went to work for various high-tech manufacturers. Pang joined Avago in Fort Collins, Colorado; Hao Zhang joined Skyworks Solutions in Massachusetts; and Huisui Zhang stayed in California, joining Micrel Semiconductor. By October of that year, they were clearly plotting to steal their employers' trade secrets. They carefully covered their tracks—warning each other not to use their company computers to check their personal emails—and were clear-eyed about their activities. At one point, they joked about naming their new company "ClifBaw," short for "China lift[s] BAW technology." "Haha," Pang wrote. Wei Pang emailed his colleagues, "My work is to make every possible effort to find out about the process's every possible detail and copy directly to China." They were, as one wrote in another email, "moving Avago to China," albeit without Avago's knowledge or permission.

Their plan was to redirect the technology to Tianjin University, where they hoped to land jobs and help manufacture the FBAR filters. Tianjin University was part of a Chinese program known as PRC 985 Project that devoted government funds to building world-class educational institutions. In turn, under the PRC 985 Project, China's top universities had an explicit duty to advance the Chinese economy. Since its first "study abroad policy" in 1978, the Chinese government has launched numerous initiatives aimed at expanding opportunities overseas and then encouraging those educated at foreign universities to return, preferably with skills and technology that would help China thrive. "The Chinese government has been the most assertive government in the world in introducing policies targeted at triggering a reverse brain drain," concluded David Zweig, a professor at the Hong Kong University of Science and Technology, and Huiyao Wang, director general of the Center for China and Globalization in Beijing.[21] It worked: over 100,000 students returned in 2009 alone.[22]

To woo back talent, the Chinese government established more than 150 tech incubators across the country and, through programs like Hundred Talents (for recruiting new PhDs and postdocs) and Thousand Talents (for recruiting established professors), promised returning researchers access to the country's best perks—housing, schools for their children, and even jobs for their spouses. The Chinese government used all of those potential levers in encouraging Pang and his colleagues to return.

In January 2008, Wei Pang traveled to China to present at an FBAR symposium and met with a senior academic from the Tianjin

University's College of Precision Instrument and Opt-Electronic Engineering, an official who also had close ties to the Chinese Communist Party. In the months ahead, he emailed the Chinese official—known as "J.Y."—draft patent applications from Avago, and then, in June, returned to China to meet with Tianjin's dean and vice president. In September, the dean and vice president traveled together to California to meet in secret at a San Jose residence and finalize plans for the new endeavor.

One week later, the official word came from Tianjin: *the plan was a go.* The university would give Pang's team what prosecutors later said was "full support by actively obtaining the funding, equipment, and space required to conduct the work." It would be a uniquely profitable venture, they explained, since by stealing the plans they'd "save" the money a normal company spent doing research and development. "We save that money a lot," Wei Pang wrote in an email. "No filter (FBAR or SAW) company can compete with us." The university asked Pang to list his needs—equipment requirements, development plans, staffing, and so forth, and to carefully note in his list which parts of the scheme needed to remain confidential.

By May 2009, they had everything they needed to open a new FBAR fabrication facility. To disguise the province of their theft, Hao Zhang—who had no connection to Avago—began filing more than a half-dozen patent applications relying on the stolen technology. They began working to enlist Chinese partners in their work, which didn't always go smoothly. "The material which you sent [one company] last time shows very clearly the word AVAGO," one of the conspirators emailed Pang and Zhang in August 2011. "[I] suggest the necessary revisions be made just to avoid any unnecessary problems for us later."

That fall, though, Avago became aware of the stolen technology when they first saw the patent applications—and Ruby confirmed the suspicions during his visit. It took years for the FBI to piece together the case, but FBI agents were waiting when Hao Zhang—who until that point thought he'd gotten away with his ambitious theft—arrived in Los Angeles to speak at a conference.[23] Agents boarded his plane as soon as it landed, and, three days later, the Justice Department released the previously sealed 32-count indictment that charged six individuals—Wei Pang, Hao Zhang, and Huisui Zhang, as well as another Tianjin professor, another corporate official, and a Tianjin graduate student who worked at Avago—with economic espionage and theft of trade secrets.

These cases were exactly what Lee Rawls had advocated for years earlier: we needed to confront China—and soon. It wasn't going to get easier as their economy strengthened, and the theft of intellectual property like FBAR filters did irreversible damage to the economy of the United States—and, in turn, to our own national security.

///////////////

AMSC's willingness to come forward and be part of a public court proceeding in the case against Sinovel was a welcome—and all-too-rare—step. One of the major evidentiary challenges our team faced was finding victims who would cooperate; many victims either didn't want the public attention or placed too much value on the chance to do business in China. One of the cybersecurity firms we approached for technical help turned us down, too, out of fear that helping us would compromise its growing China portfolio. Many victims were simply fearful about the unknown; no one knew how the Chinese government would react to such an unprecedented case. Staying silent had definable risks; coming forward, though, opened a host of unknown risks. Companies were understandably nervous about their personnel overseas; if they allowed themselves to be publicly outed as a victim, as part of the government's push against Chinese economic espionage, what would happen to their staff in China or employees who traveled to China for work?

Putting together cases against state actors such as China required extra-close cooperation with the victims. It wasn't sufficient to just have the bits and bytes of where a hacker went inside a system, we needed to sit with the victim and understand why the hackers attacked when they did and what the significance of the theft was to the business. Without that crucial explanation—both from the victims we named and from victims we never named—we found it would be impossible to put together the heart of a criminal case. These cases weren't like a traditional bank theft or the robbery of a jewelry store, for instance, where the motive and financial gain were self-evident. Without the company explaining the importance of their loss to us, we couldn't explain the motive in an indictment. For economic espionage, it wasn't enough for us just to show who took it—which element of the PLA stole—we had to show why they would've targeted specific information and who would have benefited in China in order to demonstrate that the motive was to help a competitor of the victim.

The Pittsburgh US attorney, David Hickton, used his own political capital and local influence to encourage victims such as US Steel to come forward and participate. We likely couldn't have made this first case work in almost any other jurisdiction, but Hickton's deep Pittsburgh roots and his own work in the private sector before becoming US attorney paid dividends. Hickton had literally grown up with one of the victim's CEOs—they had attended elementary through high school together.

Yet it wasn't until FBI Agent John Hauser contacted a renewable energy company in Hillsboro, Oregon, that we knew we would have the case we needed. SolarWorld, a company of about 1,100 employees, had been an unwilling leader in fighting China, protesting to the Department of Commerce and the International Trade Commission in 2011 and 2012 what it saw as illegal "price dumping" by Chinese companies. SolarWorld had argued that Chinese firms sold solar panels in the United States for below-market rates because they'd benefited from illegal government subsidies.

In announcing the company's petition in October 2011, its president, Gordon Brinser, explained, "Artificially low-priced solar products from China are crippling the domestic industry." Chinese sales had been soaring—up more than 300 percent from 2008 to 2011, and totaling more than $1.6 billion through the first eight months of 2011—but none of that growth was the result of normal market forces. China had no material, labor, or production advantage other than massive state backing, and the result was products flooding into the United

States at prices below what domestic manufacturers could provide. The result, Brinser said, came at a clear cost to American workers: in the months before SolarWorld's complaint, seven US solar employers had shut down or downsized. As he said, "China's systematic campaign to dismantle the U.S. industry has cost thousands of jobs in Arizona, California, Maryland, Massachusetts, New York and Pennsylvania."[24]

That litigation—which resulted in the Chinese solar manufacturers facing duties on their imports—had evidently made SolarWorld a target for military hackers. As FBI Agent Hauser and SolarWorld officials reconstructed—and our charging documents later made public— Chinese hackers penetrated the company's network using a spear-phishing attack just weeks after the Department of Commerce made a preliminary determination that China had been illegally dumping solar panels in the United States. From May 3, 2012, until at least September 26, 2012, the hackers made at least a dozen intrusions into the SolarWorld network to steal files and emails from senior executives. SolarWorld had been unaware of the intrusions until the FBI contacted them.[25]

The SolarWorld team was able to walk us through specifically what was stolen—and even more importantly, why the files would have mattered to a competitor. The Chinese hackers stole, for instance, the CFO's cash-flow spreadsheets, which would have helped a competitor identify how long the company would weather a financial shock, as well as the documents detailing specific production costs that would help a competitor calculate precisely how to underprice its own solar products. They also took, as our indictment later explained, "detailed manufacturing metrics, technological innovations, and production line information that would enable a Chinese competitor to mimic SolarWorld's proprietary production capabilities without the need to invest time or money in research and development." And, to add insult to injury, just as we had seen in the wind turbine case in Massachusetts, the hackers stole privileged attorney-client files outlining the strategy for the company's litigation against China.

SolarWorld represented an important milestone to me: the moment when I knew we could bring a publicly convincing case. When I looked over the new evidence collected from SolarWorld, I found one fact particularly telling: we were able to see that the hackers had been targeting SolarWorld during the Beijing workday. There was no doubt about it—they were hacking American companies as their day job.

As it turned out, the two most prominent victims in the eventual indictment, SolarWorld and the Pittsburgh-based US Steel, not only went to great lengths to cooperate with the investigation but also noisily advocated publicly for a more aggressive response to China. It was no coincidence that the three sectors represented in the government's major actions against China—solar, steel, and wind—also happened to be the sectors getting crushed by their own products, stolen and exploited by Chinese manufacturers. Even while too many victims still felt cowed by China, and were tempted to stay silent because of the short-term business opportunities the Chinese market presented, those three sectors understood it was a fool's bargain.

The universe of possible suspects and cases had been broad at the start, but to put together a case, the prosecutors and FBI needed to be able to demonstrate certain specific actions. We needed identifiable suspects who had perpetrated specific intrusions that were demonstrably aimed at economic purposes—and we needed to be able to identify clear links between the various suspects in order to charge that it was a conspiracy. "China was very busy. There was a lot of thought about who would be the target," Adam recalls. "Our hook was a conspiracy—there had to be an agreement together, a connection among the players."

As Nick says, "It was a puzzle—we were constantly moving pieces until we could line up a person. There was an inevitability that we'd find enough. You're tying together so many pieces of circumstantial evidence, piecing it together into something substantive."

Gradually, as we pieced together the case and the best evidence we could gather, we arrived at five identifiable suspects: Wang Dong—the hacker known as UglyGorilla who we'd been watching for a while and who had been made public in Mandiant's report—as well as Sun Kailiang, Wen Xinyu, Huang Zhenyu, and Gu Chunhui, all officers in the PLA's elite hacking group, known as Unit 61398. As the case unfolded, it became deeply personal for our Threat Cell. The members came to know the personal habits of each of their targets—what they liked and what they didn't like—reviewed a multitude of photos of the hackers, and even learned about their families. The small team thought a lot about the five Chinese military officers on the other side of the planet, pawns in a battle between the two nations. "We had long conversations—'How would you feel if Nick Oldham got indicted for doing his job?'" Nick recalls. "China's got a different moral set, obviously, but these guys were doing what their government told them to do."

By the fall of 2013, the team had zeroed in on their case. After six months as the "acting," I was nominated in September 2013 to formally take over the role of assistant attorney general for national security; I spent much of my time on Capitol Hill during the confirmation process explaining our approach on China and cyberthreats to senators, and was gratified to find that many who didn't agree on much—including Ted Cruz, Sheldon Whitehouse, Mike Lee, and Jeff Sessions—all strongly backed our approach.*

A critical stage of any case is the drafting of the so-called "pros memo," the prosecution memo from the investigators recommending that the US attorney's office move forward with formal charges. The first draft of the pros memo in this case, when it came over from Pittsburgh, was just a couple pages; Nick looked it over and realized just how much more work there would be to bring the case to a conclusion. This was a historic case; it couldn't just be *pro forma*. To figure out the right approach, Adam ended up going back to the pros memo that had been assembled for the 9/11 terrorist attacks, a document that filled a three-inch binder. "I learned how to do a pros memo for an impossible case by looking at an impossible case," he recalled. The final draft of the pros memo stretched to some 300 pages, outlining in great detail the evidence against the five members of the PLA.

---

* After the case was publicly announced, we got a note from Senator Whitehouse to our team: "Nice job! I knew you'd get 'em."

Nick and another Threat Cell prosecutor, Brian Resler, decamped for weeks—and later, months—at a time to Pittsburgh to help piece the case together, working alongside Pittsburgh Assistant US Attorney James Kitchen, the lead local prosecutor on the case. They worked long days alongside the FBI team, walking through what evidence existed.* One night, after a long day working through technical details, they ended up at a quiet bar in downtown Pittsburgh—only to find the bar overrun with a swarm of runners from a local running-and-drinking club known as the Hash House Harriers, their evening instantly transformed by boisterous drinkers who had just completed the night's running course. Anonymous in the sea of loud athletes, away from their families, exhausted from weeks of work on what we all hoped would be a historic indictment against America's main superpower rival, the two prosecutors turned to one another. "This is our life," Nick said. "No one has any idea what we're doing right now."

I encouraged the team to make sure that the indictment framed the case correctly; this wasn't about computer hacking writ large, this was theft. It was about staking a claim that government-backed hacking for economic purposes was wrong, a violation of an international norm that governments shouldn't interfere in the private sector. "We've carved out areas where we [could] charge without hypocrisy," Adam says. The shaping of that indictment has paid dividends in cases since—this wasn't about espionage, this was about trying to gain an unfair and unearned economic advantage. The first sentence of the eventual indictment left no doubt of the case's import: "Members of the People's Liberation Army (PLA), the military of the People's Republic of China, conspired together and with each other to hack into the computer of commercial entities in the Western District of Pennsylvania

---

* The investigation confronted a cultural divide within the FBI; many of the cyber agents who had long focused on computer crime had experience only on the intelligence side, the "bits and bytes" of the technical analysis. They had little experience away from their computers, interviewing witnesses, compiling evidence for prosecution, and they had never received any actual courtroom or investigative experience. Nick was intensely hands-on and found himself actually coaching one agent on-site about how to conduct a victim interview; the agent had worked cyber cases for years without ever speaking to a real-life victim.

and elsewhere in the United States, to maintain unauthorized access to those computers, and to steal information from those entities that would be useful to their competitors in China, including state-owned enterprises."[26] We then went into great detail, offering just the kind of hard evidence and proof that China had long insisted didn't exist about their hacking activities; Mandiant had previously listed the street address where the hackers worked—208 Datong Road, Pudong District, Shanghai, China—and we not only did that, but were able to put individual fingers on the keyboards.

Even as I awaited Senate confirmation, the outline of the case was briefed to the attorney general, and it began to move forward inside government. We faced a final major internal hurdle, what's known as the National Security Council's Deputies Committee. The Deputies Committee, the DC for short, represents where the heavy lifting and nuts and bolts of policymaking play out. It's a system that was designed in the wake of the coup d'état against Panamanian dictator Manuel Noriega in 1989, when George H. W. Bush's national security advisor, Brent Scowcroft, grew frustrated that there was nobody working on implementing the decisions made in the Situation Room and decreed that the DC would be "responsible for day to day crisis management."[27] In the years since that time, it grew into what Robert Gates has called "the engine of the policy process." It was at the Deputies Committee level where we met in the months leading up to the China indictment to talk through what we called "use approval," securing the permission from other intelligence agencies to discuss some of the classified intelligence we had gathered to inform our case. I was pleasantly surprised: after I explained the case and talked through the strategy at the White House, those around the table nodded their assent. We were going to be able to use everything we needed.

There were concerns at every stage of the approval process before we could take action. In the final steps of the investigation, prosecutors and agents feared White House National Security Advisor Susan Rice might put the kibosh on the whole thing. She worried a criminal prosecution was too blunt a tool; she saw that indicting Chinese military officials could be extraordinarily provocative, but she wondered if it would really change any behavior. We believed that all of the strategies thus far hadn't changed anything—and we couldn't keep up the status quo.

Lisa Monaco, at the White House, and I, at the Justice Department, thought that in a large, complicated, sprawling relationship such as the one between the United States and China—one that spanned trade, climate change, defense, human rights, North Korea, the South China Sea, allies and adversaries around the world, and so many more issues—there would always be one reason or another to claim that "now's not the right time" to charge China with hacking US companies. We believed strongly just the opposite: we should carve out criminal activities from the larger relationship—that anytime an adversary violated a norm we wanted to defend, we should charge that case publicly. We should arrest or "name and shame" outside of any other geopolitical consideration.

It was a message others outside of the FBI were pushing, too. The chair of the House Intelligence Committee, Michigan Congressman Mike Rogers, said cybersecurity should dominate the nation's agenda with China: "The first three issues with China should be economic espionage, economic espionage, and economic espionage."[28]

Finally, by the spring of May 2014, we got the green light. All of a sudden, it was time for the press conference to announce the charges. Attorney General Eric Holder, FBI Director James Comey, and I all took the stage, along with David Hickton, who came down from Pittsburgh.

Adam Hickey and Sean Newell walked into the press conference and were shocked to see giant poster-sized wanted posters of the Chinese hackers on easels at the front of the room. At the last minute, the FBI had mocked up the posters showing the PLA hackers in uniform. Such red-bannered FBI wanted posters were common in cases where there was a realistic sense that public awareness might help capture a suspect, but in this case we knew precisely where these suspects were. It was a diplomatic question if we'd ever see them in a courtroom—and we knew those chances were effectively zero. To Adam and Sean, the posters seemed at first like flashy overkill; they'd hoped the indictment would speak for itself. Yet they realized in the months ahead just how wrong they'd been. "I underestimated the value—a wanted poster turns out to be a powerful way of saying this person's actions are morally wrong and condemned by society," Adam says. The Chinese wanted posters turned out to be a much-requested souvenir by visiting foreign law enforcement and intelligence agencies, many of whom were struggling to confront their own Chinese hacking incidents, and they became prized office art in FBI cubicles and intelligence offices across the country—the Chinese hackers rendered in the same iconic style that once graced warnings about John Dillinger and Bonnie and Clyde.

In my remarks, I nodded to Justice Breyer's comments in the *Grokster* case, which had long since become a mantra of mine: "Cyber theft is real theft, and we will hold state sponsored cyber thieves accountable as we would any other transnational criminal organization that steals our goods and breaks our laws."

"This 21st century burglary has to stop," Hickton said. "This prosecution vindicates hard working men and women in Western Pennsylvania and around the world who play by the rules and deserve a fair shot and a level playing field."[29]*

Speaking a month after the PLA indictment, President Obama used a joint appearance with Australia's prime minister to highlight the same point: "Obviously, both the United States and Australia have enormous trade relationships with China, and we both agree that it's important to continue to see China prosper and rise. But what's also important is

---

* It was a week when it felt like we were actually maybe, just maybe, making a tiny dent in cybercrime—proving that the US government would push boundaries outward to enforce decent behavior online. The same day we announced the Chinese charges, the Justice Department announced the largest cyber law enforcement operation effort, a global effort targeting the creator and users of a piece of malware known as Blackshades, a remote access tool that sold for $40 and allowed criminals to steal passwords and banking credentials. All told, more than 90 arrests were made across 18 other countries; domestically, the FBI served more than 100 search warrants. The Swedish creator of the tool had been caught in Moldova—the first criminal ever to be extradited to the United States from that country—and eventually pleaded guilty in New York City; he was sentenced to almost five years in prison.

that as China emerges as this great world power that it also is helping to reinforce and abide by basic international law and norms."[30]

We knew, though, that a single indictment didn't mean much in the grand scheme of geopolitics; we needed to be able to sustain the pressure and push China publicly. The week before the announcement of the China case, Adam and I had gone to Pittsburgh to brief the victims on the pending indictment. It was a profound experience—the first time the victim CEOs and corporate leaders knew who else was part of the case. Looking around the room in the FBI building in downtown Pittsburgh, they realized most of them knew one another—they'd been victimized together without ever knowing. You could almost feel a palpable sense of relief in the room as they realized that they weren't alone and that there wasn't anything to be ashamed about in being targeted by China; it had been an equal opportunity attack. We showed each victim the exact language we were going to use in the indictment.

At the airport on the way back to DC, I told Adam, "The next case we need a body."

He smiled. "Actually, I've got a case I want to talk to you about," he said.

///////////////

Announcing the indictment was a proud day—the result of the team's immense efforts over many years to reshape the balance with China in cyberspace. The announcement fired up our team and boosted morale across the NSD, and it particularly encouraged the new NSCS prosecutors we were empowering across the country. It showed them that if they poured their hearts into a case, we would indict it and make it public. Yet all of us understood that prosecution was simply one tool, albeit a particularly powerful tool, to make information public. We weren't satisfied splashing some photos up at a press conference. "Naming and shaming" only went so far. Just weeks after our press conference, the security firm CrowdStrike published another report, similar to Mandiant's about APT1, documenting the hacking efforts of another Chinese unit, known as Putter Panda, or Unit 61486 of the Chinese PLA, and their attempts to infiltrate and steal from US, European, and Japanese organizations. "If you look at all the groups that we track in China, the indictments are just the very tip of the iceberg," CrowdStrike cofounder George Kurtz told the *New York Times*.[31] We agreed. If our efforts were to change behavior, we also needed some people in handcuffs.

As Adam indicated at the airport, we didn't need to wait too long for an arrest. In fact, just two days after the PLA indictment, FBI agents in California learned that two Chinese hackers traded a file outlining their multiyear attack against one of America's largest aviation companies.

The file contained a handy summary, in the hacker's own words, of their plot—everything the FBI needed to arrest the man guiding the hackers. Canada, which had been routinely victimized by Chinese hackers, too, was happy to cooperate.[32]* They—and we—finally had a chance to help even the score.

//////////////

On June 28, 2014—just one month after the PLA indictment—Canadian police arrested a Chinese businessman named Su Bin, a 50-year-old multimillionaire living in Vancouver who had helped steal billions in US defense technology, at the request of the US Justice Department, which charged him with guiding a six-year-long effort to steal design secrets from Boeing. He had spent years carefully stealing the schematics and plans for the C-17 military transport plane, a $218 million–per–unit craft that had been the third-most expensive military plane ever developed by the US Air Force when it was built, costing more than $3 billion to originally create in the 1980s and 1990s.

In the years since, the C-17 had become a mainstay of the Air Force's ability to deliver troops, vehicles, and supplies to the front lines of wars

---

* Even as we asked for their help, they were in the midst of uncovering and responding to a massive attack by "state-sponsored" Chinese hackers who had penetrated the network of their National Research Council, which leads the country's research-and-development efforts. The council was responsible for such cutting-edge work as the development of canola, the crop first bred in Manitoba that had grown into a multibillion-dollar export to countries like China. Ultimately, China's deep penetration of Canada's research networks cost hundreds of millions of dollars, in terms of both lost research and IT costs to replace hundreds of compromised laptops and servers. For a while, the Canadian government recommended that researchers across the country communicate only by fax or postal mail.

from Kosovo to Afghanistan to Iraq, as well as deliver humanitarian supplies to disaster victims the world over—it was even the plane routinely used to transport the president's armored limousines around the globe. Thanks to Su Bin, the Chinese were able to develop, build, and deploy their own copy, in barely a third of the time it had taken the United States to design, test, and build the original C-17.

Su, who in the West went by the first name Stephen, owned a Chinese aviation technology firm named Lode-Tech and had been living comfortably in a house worth $2 million; in 2012, he'd been profiled by the *Wall Street Journal* as part of a story about wealthy Chinese decamping for the West. In the article, he said he was the son of an army officer and had made millions as an aerospace entrepreneur. He told the *Journal* that he found the rules of the West less restrictive—and it was easier to spend his money in the West. "Regulations [in China] mean that businessmen have to do a lot of illegal things," Su said at the time. As it turned out, he committed his biggest crime after he moved.

In British Columbia, he ran the local office for Lode-Tech. The legitimate firm had a deep network of industry contacts that Su Bin helped mine—it even shared space one year with Boeing at a Chinese aviation expo—and he directed his hacker colleagues toward targeting particularly interesting engineers and corporate personnel. As they uncovered Su Bin's economic espionage, investigators realized the irony of Lode-Tech's mission statement—in big letters on its website, the aerospace firm advertised, "We will track the world's aviation advanced technology."

Their work began as early as 2009, and for years, Su Bin used both his work email and his personal email to correspond with two Chinese military hackers back in China. After being pointed in the right direction by Su, the hackers used relatively basic techniques—standard phishing emails—to attempt to penetrate email accounts and, from there, access restricted corporate networks. "Su Bin was what we'd call in the traditional espionage world a 'spotter,' someone who would tee up targets for a nation-state," explains Luke Dembosky, who was our deputy assistant attorney general at the time.

As our charging documents later made clear, the Chinese hackers relied on Su to tell them what was important. Since the Chinese hackers didn't speak English, once they got inside a network, they sent Su lists of the files they'd uncovered, and he carefully pored over them, highlighting the most valuable ones that they should exfiltrate in yellow and guiding them through what they were uncovering. It wasn't a minor effort: some of the file directories ran to thousands of pages; in one 6,000-page directory, Su meticulously highlighted the 22 items that seemed likely to be useful to them—files with names such as *C17Hangar Requirements 112399.pdf* and *Critical Safety Item(CSI) Report_Sep2006.pdf*. In another 137-page directory, he picked out the 17 most promising file folders—hitting on one that FBI agents later calculated had more than 2,000 documents related to the C-17. While Boeing's complicated computer networks initially slowed and stymied them, they felt their way through, relying on what they called "painstaking labor and slow groping." All told, over months, the hackers pillaged Boeing's innermost secrets. In that June 2014 report, which they titled "C-17 Project Reconnaissance Summary," Su and his two Chinese partners claimed that they had stolen 630,000 files related to the C-17, totaling about 65 gigabytes of data. As Su and his team wrote, "We safely, smoothly accomplished the entrusted mission in one year, making important contributions to our national defense scientific research development and receiving unanimous favorable comments." It was, according to their own reports, the first time that Chinese engineers had gotten their hands on C-17 plans.

Boeing wasn't the only target—and the C-17 wasn't the only victim. They pillaged more than 220 megabytes of data related to the F-22 Raptor as well, plus files related to the F-35, including its flight test protocols, that Su carefully translated into Chinese. The thefts were critical to helping the Chinese understand—and copy—America's most advanced fighter plane, an $11 billion development project that had tried to deliver a stealth plane capable of dominating the skies of the 21st century.

The effort that Su Bin led was just one part of a massive, years-long pillaging of American defense secrets. According to the *Washington*

Post, Chinese hackers stole designs for "the advanced Patriot missile system, known as PAC-3; an Army system for shooting down ballistic missiles, known as the Terminal High Altitude Area Defense, or THAAD; and the Navy's Aegis ballistic-missile defense system," as well as details of "vital combat aircraft and ships, including the F/A-18 fighter jet, the V-22 Osprey, the Black Hawk helicopter and the Navy's new Littoral Combat Ship, which is designed to patrol waters close to shore."[33] Mark Stokes, who led a think tank in Washington focused on Chinese security issues, called the thefts "staggering," saying, "These are all very critical weapons systems, critical to our national security. When I hear this in totality, it's breathtaking."

Over time, Su and his coconspirators developed a sophisticated international network for hacking, including their own servers in the United States, Singapore, and Korea. They carefully disguised the stolen files before stealing them, to circumvent the internal intrusion alarms at Boeing and other defense contractors, and then taking them on a circuitous route to get the files to China. Su's team always transited the stolen files through three foreign countries—places such as France and Japan—and ensured that at least one of the three transit countries did not have friendly relations with America, to obfuscate the files' ultimate destination. Ultimately, the files were deposited on computers located in Hong Kong, Macao, or nearby areas. "In order to avoid diplomatic and legal complications, surveillance work and intelligence collection are done outside," they reported.

There, Chinese intelligence officers picked up the files and transferred them back to mainland China in person—ensuring that there was never a traceable path for the files going from the United States to China. Yet, as the FBI investigation found, there was no doubt that the ultimate customer was the Chinese military—and that Su Bin's partners were military themselves. In fact, while the two hackers have not been charged publicly, we know who they are; according to publicly released Canadian court records, the FBI found in an intercepted email that one of the hackers had attached his military ID card, which included his photo, name, rank, unit, and date of birth. Similarly, a photo the FBI traced to the other hacker, with the subject line "boss," showed him with, presumably, his commanding officer, both of them in full Chinese military uniforms.[34]

All told, the hacking operation used more than $1 million—about 6.8 million Chinese RMB—to run their team, but it was a pittance compared to the decades of engineering knowledge, military technology, and construction details that Su and his team were able to steal from Boeing and the US Air Force. Even as Su complained in emails about how onerous the process was to get reimbursed for his expenses, the hacking effort returned thousands of times its cost.

The ultimate cost of Su Bin's theft may ultimately lie ahead: their work, particularly in terms of the thefts from the F-22 and F-35 projects, will almost certainly cost the lives of US pilots if the planes are ever used in combat against China or its allies in the future.

China was none too happy about our arrest—or the fact that we'd taken such a valuable intelligence asset off the field. The Su Bin case, all but unnoticed by the public, had a large impact on Chinese thinking. In the space of barely a month, the United States had taken overt steps against two major Chinese economic espionage operations. They knew about the case right from the moment of his arrest—and quickly sent a not-so-subtle message to Canada to stall his extradition to the United States.

Just weeks after Su Bin's arrest in Canada, China retaliated—luring two Canadian expats in its city of Dandong to a dinner where they were snatched by agents of the Ministry of State Security. Kevin and Julia Garratt—Christian aid workers who had lived unassumingly in China for decades—had long run Peter's Coffee House in the industrial city of 2.5 million along the North Korean border. Held incommunicado, the couple were separated and interrogated. As Kevin later told Canadian media, "I'm wondering—what are you talking about? Investigate for what? What's going on here? Explain yourself. And finally they said, 'Well you're accused of being a spy and we want to investigate.'"[35]

The Chinese government reported almost a mirror image of Su Bin's charges: the Ministry of State Security told the media that the Garratts were being investigated for stealing intelligence "about Chinese military targets and important national defense research projects, and engaging in activities threatening to Chinese national security."[36] They were held for 19 months in harsh conditions; afterward, Kevin could precisely recall the outline of the cell he shared with as many as 14 prisoners: "The room was 12 paces by five." As James Zimmerman, the family's lawyer, said, "The Chinese made it clear that the Garratt case was designed to pressure Canada to block Su Bin's extradition to the U.S."[37]

Then, in November 2014, even as Su Bin and the Garratts sat in jail, the Chinese more publicly touted their success. Their own knock-off military cargo plane, the Xian Y-20—code-named Kunpeng after a mythical ancient Chinese bird capable of flying long distances—was parked at the Zhuhai Air Show across the tarmac from a US C-17, the first time the Chinese plane had met its American doppelganger in real life.

Ultimately, both Garratts were released and Su Bin waived his extradition to the United States. "Getting him was not easy," recalls Luke Dembosky, who helped coordinate the case in our office. "Even with a friendly neighbor like Canada, you can see how long and tedious the process can be for international cases—and with cyber, almost every case is an international case. It's a gap that cyber-actors have long exploited."

FBI agents picked up Su Bin at the airport in Canada to bring him to the United States to face charges. Ever the aviation buff, he ended up talking with the agents about planes on the flight to California. One agent asked him what his favorite plane was. "Not the C-17," he replied, deadpan.

In March 2016, Su Bin pleaded guilty in US court in Los Angeles, and was sentenced to 46 months in prison, as well as a fine of $10,000. "There are some who say, 'You'll never catch anyone,'" I told the *Washington Post* that day. "Well, we have caught someone."[38]

CHAPTER 6

Slavik

DURING MY TIME at the Justice Department, we became quite used to seeing a Russian or Eastern European nexus on major cybercrime and online financial frauds. In fact, one of the first multimillion-dollar online thefts—the theft in the 1990s of $12 million from Citibank—had been carried out by a Russian hacker, Vladimir Levin. The Secret Service, with their particular responsibility for financial crime, had developed an early and strong expertise in computer crime, pursuing the carder forums, such as CarderPlanet.Ru, where thieves traded stolen credit cards en masse. That early era of cybercrime had largely escaped the notice of the FBI, which was primarily focused on counterterrorism in the years after 9/11, and we were still playing catch-up in the late 2000s. Unfortunately, the knowledge on our side was still too often splintered. Even as we saw Russian intelligence and Russian criminals begin to pair up online, we weren't as "blended" in government as the threat was.

Russia and Eastern Europe have long been home to some of the best hackers in the world. Cybercrime is at least a billion-dollar annual business in more than one Eastern European country—it certainly is in Russia. The strong talent pool stems, in part, from the Soviet Union's emphasis on science and technology education as well as two other important factors. First, the Russian predilection to hacking reflects how few legitimate economic opportunities there are for talented Russian engineers. Sergei Pokrovsky, the editor of a Russian hacker magazine, *Khaker,* was quoted in 2000 explaining that while talented computer scientists in the West were receiving lavish salaries amid the first dot-com boom, a Russian engineer might expect to earn only about $300 a month working for Russian companies.[1] It wasn't hard for even an unambitious but talented hacker to beat that in fraud. In 2007, the German magazine *Der Spiegel* profiled an 18-year-old Russian hacker who offered his "high-quality" DDoS service online for just $150; his competitor, known as DrDDoS, meanwhile offered a precise "35 percent discount" for customers who placed two orders to target other websites.[2] In fact, by around 2010, industry analysis showed that Russia accounted for roughly a third of the global cyber-crime revenue, somewhere between $2.5 and $3.7 billion annually— far more than the 1 percent of the global IT market that belonged to Russia.[3]

Russia's centrality to hacking also demonstrated how the state lagged on enforcing cybercrime laws. It wasn't quite as simple, though, as saying that Russian law enforcement wasn't good at catching hackers. We had seen over the last 20 years, and particularly over the last decade, that Russian law enforcement actively looked the other way from known Russian hackers—at least as long as their targets were outside of Russia. Often, hackers seemed to work with the express permission and protection of law enforcement and intelligence—operating with what was known in Russia as a *krysha,* a roof, slang for paid protection offered by a patron like the mafia or a corrupt government official.[4] "Although most hackers started on their own, as they got bigger they developed a need for protection by old-school mobsters, who were better connected politically," wrote Joseph Menn in his book on cybercrime, *Fatal System Error.*[5]

Whereas countries such as China and Iran might have blurred the lines in hacking by using government or military personnel to hack private sector targets, Russia often relied on the reverse: using individual criminals or organized crime groups to advance its state goals with the help of intelligence or military guidance. It wasn't exactly a new strategy: *Cuckoo's Egg,* the 1980s book that originally captured Bob

Mueller's attention at the Justice Department and led to the launch of its first Computer Crime Unit, recounted the story of how the KGB had recruited an East German hacker, Markus Hess, to target defense companies and laboratories in the United States in the age of dial-up modems. In fact, sometimes it seemed like the Russian Federal Security Service (FSB) only pursued hackers inside Russia as part of a recruiting effort. "There are organized groups of hackers tied to the FSB," Oleg Gordievsky, who once headed the KGB *rezidentura* in London, said at a 1998 cybercrime conference. "One man I know, who was caught committing a cybercrime, was given the choice of either prison or cooperation with the FSB and he went along."[6] It was a pattern we saw continue in the years to come.

The US government had long struggled in asking the FSB for help arresting wanted hackers and was wary of cooperation even more broadly on technical fronts. Prosecutors and investigators had successfully identified the authors of viruses like SoBig and Bagle and told Russian law enforcement the names of the leaders of a hacking group known as the HangUp Team—all fruitlessly.[7] Whatever limited cooperation existed between the two countries generally focused on areas of universal concern, such as child pornography and terrorism. Then the Snowden scandal, with Putin welcoming and exploiting the onetime NSA employee, ended any remaining hope of cooperation between the two countries.

On cybercrime, the only real success we had was when we spotted Russian hackers elsewhere on vacation and asked for international aid to bring them into custody—or when we lured them outside of Russia. In the early 2000s, one Russian hacker, Alexey Ivanov, was caught when he came to Seattle for what he thought was a job interview—only to be surprised that his "interviewers" were the FBI.[8] Later, Roman Valerevich Seleznev, wanted by the Secret Service for his role in the famous black-market trading site CarderPlanet.Ru, was caught in the Maldives—and the Russian government promptly protested that he'd been kidnapped. One hacker was dining with his girlfriend in Prague's Old Town when he was scooped up, two hackers were caught at beach resorts in Thailand, and two others were caught while vacationing in Spain.[9]

It hardly ever seemed like enough.

⁓⁓⁓⁓⁓⁓⁓⁓

We watched warily as the threat expanded, as Russian hackers—a blend of criminals and government-backed groups—launched offensive cyberattacks against Estonia in 2007 and then again against the republic of Georgia in 2008 as part of wider geopolitical crises in those countries.

My first major exposure to Russian national security cases, though, came in the real world: in a 2010 operation code-named GHOST STORIES, FBI counterintelligence agents zeroed in on ten Russian "illegals" living scattered across the United States, so-called deep cover operatives of the Russian Foreign Intelligence Service and the Main Intelligence Directorate living ordinary lives.* The Russian government had invested years of effort and untold sums in letting their agents establish identities in the United States, and it was only through some great shoe-leather work—and a special source inside Russia—that the United States managed to unravel the operation.

The case provided me with an early instance of the Justice Department being the skunk at the diplomatic garden party—the same challenge we would later face with China, Iran, and other geopolitically sensitive cases we wanted to pursue. The FBI wanted to arrest the "illegals," but the case arose just as President Obama's administration was pursuing what it called the "reset" with Russia, an attempt to establish friendlier terms with President Dmitry Medvedev. As then Defense Secretary Robert Gates recounted in his memoir, both Mueller and CIA Director Leon Panetta wanted to move forward with the case. The takedown threatened a diplomatic row. "The president seemed as angry at Mueller for wanting to arrest the illegals and at Panetta for wanting to exfiltrate the source from Moscow as he was at the Russians," Gates wrote. He quoted President Obama as saying: "Just as

---

* This case inspired the FX TV show *The Americans*.

we're getting on track with the Russians, this? This is a throwback to the Cold War. This is right out of John le Carré. We put [the nuclear weapons treaty], Iran, the whole relationship with Russia at risk for this kind of thing?"[10]

Ultimately, we did arrest them all—and in just days the government arranged a Cold War–style spy swap for four people held in Russian prisons for espionage.

///////////

The first Russia-focused national security cybercrisis erupted when Russia came after the Nasdaq stock exchange. The FBI first saw reports of malware inside the stock exchange in October 2010, kicking off a five-month investigation that escalated quickly as investigators realized that they weren't dealing necessarily with an attempt at financial fraud but perhaps with a nation-state laying the groundwork for an attack. Investigators at the FBI and DHS's National Cybersecurity and Communications Integration Center worked with the NSA to study the malware. The Secret Service initially wanted jurisdiction on the case, but as the national security ramifications became clear, it became an FBI investigation. Government officials worked on-site at Nasdaq's headquarters in the old US Steel building at One Liberty Plaza in New York, as well as its main data center across the river in a Verizon building in Carteret, New Jersey—the Verizon facility is packed with other trading firms who want to be as close to the Nasdaq as they can be to trade as quickly as possible. The officials were terrified by what they initially found: sophisticated malware that utilized two separate zero-day vulnerabilities, tools for hackers so valuable that they were often only the purview of deep-pocketed nation-states. According to *Bloomberg*, the foundation of the malware was all too familiar—a "digital bomb" placed carefully to explode later. As *Bloomberg* wrote, "The NSA had seen a version before, designed and built by the Federal Security Service of the Russian Federation (FSB), that country's main spy agency. And it was more than spyware: Although the tool could be used to steal data, it also had a function designed to create widespread disruption within a computer network."[11]

Yet as investigators dug deeper, they grew puzzled: after considering multiple motives and examining troves of evidence, they saw that the hackers had concentrated on the 13 Nasdaq servers that held the software that ran the stock exchange itself. It appeared that the penetration of Nasdaq had been an effort to help boost Russian President Dmitry Medvedev's efforts to grow Russia's domestic financial markets. As *Bloomberg* reported, "By mid-2011, investigators began to conclude that the Russians weren't trying to sabotage Nasdaq. They wanted to clone it, either to incorporate its technology directly into their exchange or as a model to learn from. And they dispatched an elite team of cyberspies to get it." What had first appeared to be a national security crisis was likely run-of-the-mill intellectual property theft, another attempt for a foreign country to profit off American ingenuity.[12]

The Nasdaq case highlighted the complicated nexus of Russian financial crime and Russian state goals. It was a pattern we continued to see in the years ahead. Two major cases in 2014 particularly demonstrated to us how Russia was beginning to blend the world of the criminal and intelligence collection. The first case actually began years earlier, underscoring how long it took to solve some of these cyber cases and just how much effort it took to untangle the identities of some hackers online. In the spring of 2009, Special Agent James Craig, a rookie in the FBI's Omaha, Nebraska, Field Office, began looking into a strange pair of electronic thefts. A square-jawed former marine, Craig had been an agent for just six months, but his superiors tapped him for the case anyway, because of his background: for years, he'd been an IT guy for the FBI.[13]

The leading victim in the case was a subsidiary of the payments-processing giant First Data, which had lost $450,000 that May. That was quickly followed by a $100,000 theft from a client of the First National Bank of Omaha. What was odd, Craig noticed, was the thefts seemed to have been executed from the victims' own IP addresses, using their own logins and passwords. Examining their computers, he saw that they were infected with the same malware: something called the Zeus Trojan horse.

In online security circles, Zeus was notorious. Having first appeared in 2006, the malware had a reputation among both criminals and security experts as a masterpiece—smooth, effective, versatile. Its author was a phantom. He was only known online, where he went by the handle Slavik, or lucky12345, or a half-dozen other names.

Zeus infected computers through fairly typical means: fake IRS emails, say, or illegitimate UPS shipping notices that tricked recipients into downloading a file. But once it was on your computer, Zeus let hackers play God: they could hijack websites and use a keystroke logger to record usernames, passwords, and PINs. Hackers could even modify login forms to request further valuable security information: a mother's maiden name, a Social Security number. The ruse is known as a "man in the browser" attack. While you sit at your computer logging in to seemingly secure websites, the malware modifies pages before they load, siphoning away your credentials and your account balance. Only when you log in from a different computer do you even realize the money is gone.

By the time Craig started his investigation, Zeus had become the digital underground's malware of choice—the Microsoft Office of online fraud. Slavik was something rare in the malware world: a genuine professional. He regularly updated the Zeus code, beta testing new features. His product was endlessly adaptable, with variants optimized for different kinds of attacks and targets. A computer infected with Zeus could even be folded into a botnet, a network of infected computers that can be harnessed together to run spam servers or DDoS attacks, or send out additional deceptive emails to spread the malware further.

Sometime shortly before Craig picked up his case in 2009, Slavik began to change tack. He started cultivating an inner circle of online criminals, providing a select group with a variant of his malware, called Jabber Zeus. It came equipped with a plug-in for the instant-messaging program Jabber, which allowed the group to communicate and coordinate attacks—as in the two Omaha thefts. Rather than rely on broad infection campaigns, they began to specifically target corporate accountants and people with access to financial systems.

As Slavik turned increasingly to organized crime, he dramatically narrowed his retail malware business. In 2010 he announced his "retirement" online and then released what security researchers came to call Zeus 2.1, an advanced version of his malware protected by an encryption key—effectively tying each copy to a specific user—with a price tag upward of $10,000 per copy. From that point on, Slavik only dealt with an elite, ambitious group of criminals.

"We had no idea how big this case was," Craig says. "The amount of activity from these guys was phenomenal." Other institutions began to come forward with losses and accounts of fraud. Lots of them. Craig realized that, from his desk in suburban Omaha, he was chasing a well-organized international criminal network. "The victims started falling out of the sky," Craig says. It dwarfed any other cybercrime the FBI had tackled before.

Craig's first break in the case came in September 2009. With the help of some industry experts, he identified a New York–based server that seemed to play some sort of role in the Zeus network. He obtained a search warrant, and an FBI forensics team copied the server's data onto a hard drive, then overnighted it to Nebraska. When an engineer in Omaha examined the results, he sat in awe: looking over at Craig, the engineer said, "You have their Jabber server." The server for the chat system contained tens of thousands of lines of instant messages in Russian and Ukrainian.

This was the gang's whole digital operation—a roadmap to the entire case. The cybersecurity firm Mandiant dispatched an engineer to Omaha for months just to help untangle the Jabber Zeus code, while the FBI began cycling in agents from other regions on 30- or 90-day assignments. Linguists across the country pitched in to decipher the logs. "The slang was a challenge," Craig says.

The messages contained references to hundreds of victims, their stolen credentials scattered in English throughout the files. Craig and other agents started cold-calling institutions, telling them they had been hit by cyberfraud. He found that several businesses had terminated employees they suspected of the thefts—not realizing that the individuals' computers had been infected by malware and their logins stolen.

The case also expanded beyond the virtual world. One day in 2009, three young women from Kazakhstan walked into the New York FBI Field Office with a strange story. The women had come to the United States to look for work and found themselves participating in a curious scheme: a man would drive them to a local bank and tell them to go inside and open a new account. They were to explain to the teller that they were students visiting for the summer. A few days later, the man had them return to the bank and withdraw all of the money in the account; they kept a small cut and passed the rest on to him. Agents pieced together that the women were "money mules": their job was to cash out the funds that Slavik and his comrades had siphoned from legitimate accounts.

By the summer of 2010, New York investigators had put banks across the region on alert for suspicious cash-outs and told them to summon FBI agents as they occurred. The alert turned up dozens of mules withdrawing tens of thousands of dollars. It was another clear example of why cyber cases couldn't just be technical investigations— we needed to blend the bits and bytes of digital forensics with the real-world investigative skills that agents typically use, because at the end of the day someone got the stolen money and was spending it somewhere. You needed to be able to trace every thread of an unfolding case, in the real world and online.

Most of the mules were students or newly arrived immigrants in Brighton Beach. One woman explained that she'd become a mule after a job at a grocery store fell through, telling an agent: "I could strip, or I could do this." Another man explained that he'd be picked up at 9 a.m., do cash-out runs until 3 p.m., and then spend the rest of the day at the beach. Most cash-outs ran around $9,000, just enough to stay under federal reporting limits. The mule received 5 to 10 percent of the total, with another cut going to the recruiter. The rest of the money was sent overseas.

The United States, moreover, was just one market in what investigators soon realized was a multinational reign of fraud. Relying upon our network of international partners and the FBI legal attachés stationed overseas—agents known as "legats"—officials traced similar mule routes in Romania, the Czech Republic, the United Kingdom, Ukraine, and Russia. All told, investigators could attribute around $70 million to $80 million in thefts to the group—but they suspected the total was far more than that.

Banks howled at the FBI to shut the fraud down and stanch the losses—and rightly so. With losses that large, we heard complaints from both the companies and the FBI and Justice Department. Over the summer, New York agents began to close in on the top recruiters and the scheme's masterminds in the United States. Two Moldovans were arrested at a Milwaukee hotel at 11 p.m. following a tip; one suspect in Boston tried to flee a raid on his girlfriend's apartment and had to be rescued from the fire escape.

Meanwhile, Craig's case in Omaha advanced against the broader Jabber Zeus gang. The FBI and the Justice Department had zeroed in on an area in eastern Ukraine around the city of Donetsk, where several of the Jabber Zeus leaders seemed to live. Alexey Bron, known online as thehead, specialized in moving the gang's money around the world. Ivan Viktorvich Klepikov, who went by the name of petr0vich, ran the group's IT management, web hosting, and domain names. And Vyacheslav Igorevich Penchukov, a well-known local DJ who went by the nickname tank, managed the whole scheme, putting him second in command to Slavik. "The amount of organization these kids—they're in their twenties—were able to pull together would've impressed any Fortune 100 company," Craig says. The gang poured their huge profits into expensive cars (Penchukov had a penchant for high-end BMWs and Porsches, while Klepikov preferred Subaru WRX sports sedans), and the chat logs were filled with discussions of fancy vacations across Turkey, Crimea, and the United Arab Emirates.

In the fall of 2010, the FBI readied to take down the network. As officials in Washington called a high-profile press conference, Craig found himself on a rickety multihour train ride across Ukraine to Donetsk, where he met up with agents from the country's security service to raid tank's and petr0vich's homes. Standing in petr0vich's living room, a Ukrainian agent told Craig to flash his FBI badge. "Show him it's not just us," he urged. Craig was stunned by the scene: the hacker, wearing a purple velvet smoking jacket, seemed unperturbed as agents searched his messy apartment in a Soviet-style concrete building; his wife held their baby in the kitchen, laughing with investigators. "This is the gang I've been chasing?" Craig thought. The raids lasted well into the night, and Craig didn't return to his hotel until 3 a.m. He took nearly 20 terabytes of seized data back to Omaha.

With 150 arrests around the world—stretching across four nations—investigators managed to disrupt the network. But crucial players slipped away. One top mule recruiter in the United States fled, staying a step ahead of investigators in Las Vegas and Los Angeles before finally escaping the country inside a shipping container. More important, Slavik, the mastermind himself, remained almost a complete cipher. Investigators assumed he was based in Russia. And once, in an online chat, they saw him reference that he was married. Other than that, they had nothing. The formal indictment referred to the creator of the Zeus malware using his online pseudonym. Craig didn't even know what his prime suspect looked like. "We have thousands of photos from tank, petr0vich—not once did we see Slavik's mug," Craig says. Soon even the criminal's online traces vanished. Slavik, whoever he was, went dark. And after seven years of chasing Jabber Zeus, James Craig moved on to other cases.

///////////////

About a year after the FBI shut down the Jabber Zeus ring, the small community of online cybersecurity researchers who watch for malware and botnets began to notice a new variant of Zeus emerge. The malware's source code had been leaked online in 2011—perhaps purposefully, perhaps not—effectively turning Zeus into an open-source project and setting off an explosion of new variants. But the version that caught the eyes of researchers was different: more powerful and more sophisticated, particularly in its approach to assembling botnets.

Until then, most botnets used a hub-and-spoke system—a hacker programmed a single command server to distribute orders directly to infected machines, zombie computers. The undead army could then be directed to send out spam emails, distribute malware, or target websites for denial-of-service attacks. That hub-and-spoke design, though, made botnets relatively easy for law enforcement or security researchers to dismantle. If you could knock the command server offline, seize it, or disrupt a hacker's ability to communicate with it, you could usually break the botnet.

This new Zeus variant, however, relied on both traditional command servers and peer-to-peer communication between zombie machines, making it extremely difficult to knock down. Infected machines kept a constantly updated list of other infected machines. If one device sensed that its connection with the command server had been interrupted, it relied on the peer-to-peer network to find a new command server.

The network, in effect, was designed from the start to be takedown-proof; as soon as one command server was knocked offline, the botnet owner could just set up a new server somewhere else and redirect the peer-to-peer network to it. The new version became known as Game-Over Zeus, after one of its file names, *gameover2.php*. The name also lent itself naturally to gallows humor: once this thing infected your computer, went a joke among security experts, it was game over for your bank accounts.

As far as anyone could tell, GameOver Zeus was controlled by a very elite group of hackers—and the group's leader was Slavik. He had reemerged, more powerful than ever. Slavik's new crime ring came to be called the Business Club. A September 2011 internal announcement to the group—introducing members to a new suite of online tools for organizing money transfers and mules—concluded with a warm welcome to Slavik's select recipients: "We wish you all successful and productive work."

Like the Jabber Zeus network, the Business Club's prime directive was knocking over banks, which it did with even more ruthless inventiveness than its predecessor. The scheme was multipronged. First, the GameOver Zeus malware stole a user's banking credentials, intercepting them as soon as someone with an infected computer logged in to an online account. Then the Business Club drained the bank account, transferring its funds into other accounts they controlled overseas. With the theft complete, the group used its powerful botnet to hit the targeted financial institutions with a denial-of-service attack to distract bank employees and prevent customers from realizing their accounts had been emptied until after the money had cleared. On November 6, 2012, the FBI watched as the Business Club stole $6.9 million in a single transaction, then hit the bank with a multiday denial-of-service attack.

Unlike the earlier Jabber Zeus gang, the Business Club focused on larger, six- and seven-figure bank thefts—a scale that made bank withdrawals in Brooklyn obsolete. Instead, they used the globe's interconnected banking system against itself, hiding their massive thefts inside the trillions of dollars of legitimate commerce that slosh around the world each day. Investigators specifically identified two areas in far eastern China, close to the Russian city of Vladivostok, from which mules funneled huge amounts of stolen money into Business Club accounts. The strategy, investigators realized, represented an evolutionary leap in organized crime: bank robbers no longer had to have a footprint inside the United States. Now they could do everything remotely, never touching a US jurisdiction. "That's all it takes to operate with impunity," says Leo Taddeo, a former top FBI official.

Banks weren't the gang's only targets. They also raided the accounts of nonfinancial businesses large and small, nonprofits, and even individuals. In October 2013, Slavik's group began deploying malware known as CryptoLocker, a form of ransomware that encrypted the files on an infected machine and forced its owner to pay a small fee, say $300 to $500, to unlock the files. It quickly became a favorite tool of the cybercrime ring, in part because it helped transform deadweight into profit. The trouble with building a massive botnet focused on high-level financial fraud, it turns out, is that most zombie computers don't connect to fat corporate accounts; Slavik and his associates found themselves with tens of thousands of mostly idle zombie machines. Though ransomware didn't yield huge amounts, it afforded the criminals a way to monetize those otherwise worthless infected computers—and the dollar amounts involved were generally low enough that victims either didn't complain to the police or law enforcement wouldn't do anything about it.

The concept of ransomware had been around since the 1990s, but CryptoLocker took it mainstream. Typically arriving on a victim's machine under the cover of an unassuming email attachment, the Business Club's ransomware used strong encryption and forced victims to pay using Bitcoin. It was embarrassing and inconvenient, but many relented. The Swansea, Massachusetts, police department grumpily ponied up $750 to get back one of its computers in November 2013; the virus "is so complicated and successful that you have to buy these Bitcoins, which we had never heard of," Swansea Police Lieutenant Gregory Ryan told his local newspaper.

The following month, Dell's security firm SecureWorks estimated that as many as 250,000 machines worldwide had been infected with CryptoLocker that year. One researcher traced 771 ransoms that netted Slavik's crew a total of $1.1 million. "He was one of the first to realize how desperate people would be to regain access to their files," Brett Stone-Gross, a researcher with SecureWorks at the time, says of Slavik. "He didn't charge an exorbitant amount, but he made a lot of money and created a new type of online crime."

As the Business Club continued to gain strength, its operators kept adding revenue streams—renting out their network to other criminals to deliver malware and spam or to carry out projects like click fraud, ordering zombie machines to generate revenue by clicking on ads on fake websites. These attempts to monetize existing botnets vexed investigators; we even sometimes saw a criminal network used for intelligence purposes, since the criminals were willing to rent to anyone who needed the massive computing power of a large botnet to distribute their own malware, conduct financial fraud, or launch DDoS attacks.

It made it enormously hard for us to uncover the motive of certain botnets—who was the real owner and what was the real purpose of the malicious network?

With each passing week, the cost to banks, businesses, and individuals from GameOver grew. For businesses, the thefts could easily wipe out a year's profits, or worse. Domestically, victims ranged from a regional bank in north Florida to a Native American tribe in Washington state. As it haunted large swathes of the private sector, GameOver absorbed more and more of the efforts of the private cybersecurity industry. The sums involved were staggering. "I don't think anyone has a grasp of the full extent—one $5 million theft overshadows hundreds of smaller thefts," explains Michael Sandee, a security expert at the Dutch firm Fox-IT. "When a bank gets attacked en masse—100 transactions a week—you stop caring about the specific malware and the individual attacks; you just need to stop the bleeding."

Many tried. From 2011 through 2013, cybersecurity researchers and various firms mounted three attempts to take down GameOver Zeus. Three European security researchers teamed up to make a first assault in the spring of 2012. Slavik easily repelled their attack. Then, in March 2012, Microsoft's Digital Crimes Unit took civil legal action against the network, relying upon US marshals to raid data centers in Illinois and Pennsylvania that housed Zeus command-and-control servers and aiming legal action against 39 individuals thought to be associated with the Zeus networks. (Slavik was first on the list.) But Microsoft's plan failed to put a dent in GameOver. Instead it merely clued Slavik in to what investigators knew about his network and allowed him to refine his tactics.

Botnet fighters are a small, proud group of engineers and security researchers—self-proclaimed "internet janitors" who work to keep online networks running smoothly. Within that group, Tillmann Werner—a tall, lanky German researcher with the security firm CrowdStrike—stood out for his flair and enthusiasm for the work. In February 2013 he seized control of the Kelihos botnet, an infamous malware network built on Viagra spam, live onstage during a presentation at the cybersecurity industry's biggest conference. But Kelihos, he knew, was no GameOver Zeus. Werner had been watching GameOver since its inception, marveling at its strength and resilience.

In 2012 Werner had linked up with Brett Stone-Gross—who was just a few months out of graduate school and was based in California—plus a few other researchers to map out an effort to attack GameOver. Working across two continents largely in their spare time, the men plotted their attack via online chat. They carefully studied the previous European effort, identifying where it had failed, and spent a year preparing their offensive.

In January 2013, they were ready: they stocked up on pizza, assuming they were in for a long siege against Slavik's network. (When you go against a botnet, Werner says, "you have one shot. It either goes right or wrong.") Their plan was to reroute GameOver's peer-to-peer network, centralize it, and then redirect the traffic to a new server under their control—a process known as "sinkholing." In doing so, they hoped to sever the botnet's communication link to Slavik. And at first, everything went well. Slavik showed no signs of fighting back, and Werner and Stone-Gross watched as more and more infected computers connected to their sinkhole by the hour.

At the peak of their attack, the researchers controlled 99 percent of Slavik's network—but they'd overlooked a critical source of resilience in GameOver's structure: a small subset of infected computers were still secretly communicating with Slavik's command servers. "We missed that there's a second layer of control," Stone-Gross says. By the second week, Slavik was able to push a software update to his whole network and reassert his authority. The researchers watched with dawning horror as a new version of GameOver Zeus propagated across the internet and Slavik's peer-to-peer network began to reassemble. "We immediately saw what happened—we'd completely neglected this other channel of communication," Werner says.

The researchers' ploy—nine months in the making—had failed. Slavik had won. In a trollish online chat with a Polish security team, he crowed about how all the efforts to seize his network had come to naught. "I don't think he thought it was possible to take down his botnet," Werner says. Dejected, the two researchers were eager to try again. But they needed help—they turned to Pittsburgh, the same cyber squad that had long helped lead the FBI's steps into cybercrime.

By 2014, the FBI agents in Keith Mularski's Pittsburgh squad—he the agent who had gone undercover online in the early 2000s to help take down the criminal forum DarkMarket—were working three of the biggest cyber cases in the country. Two agents, Elliott Peterson and Steven J. Lampo, were chasing the hackers behind GameOver Zeus, even as their deskmates simultaneously investigated the case that ultimately indicted the five Chinese PLA hackers who had penetrated computer systems at Westinghouse, US Steel, and other companies to benefit Chinese industry, and other squadmates pursued the Darkode cybercrime forum.

The FBI's GameOver case had been under way for about a year by the time Werner and Stone-Gross offered to join forces with the Pittsburgh squad to take down Slavik's botnet. Both sides realized that in order to tackle the botnet, they needed to work on three simultaneous fronts. First, they had to figure out attribution—determine once and for all who was running GameOver and build up a criminal prosecution; even after millions of dollars in thefts, neither the FBI nor the security industry had so much as a single Business Club member's name. Second, they needed to take down the digital infrastructure of GameOver itself; that's where Werner and Stone-Gross came in. And third, they needed to disable the botnet's physical infrastructure by assembling court orders and enlisting the help of other governments to seize its servers across the globe. Once all that was done, they needed partners in the private sector to be ready with software updates and security patches to help recover infected computers the moment the good guys had control of the botnet. Absent any one of those moves, the next effort to take down GameOver Zeus was likely to fail just as the previous ones had.

With that, Mularski's squad began to stitch together an international partnership unlike anything the US government had ever undertaken, enlisting the UK's National Crime Agency, officials in Switzerland, the Netherlands, Ukraine, Luxembourg, and a dozen other countries, as well as industry experts at Microsoft, CrowdStrike, McAfee, Dell's SecureWorks, and other companies. The operation required mixing the squad's cutting-edge creativity with complex legal choreography. "You've got to take all that brilliance and fit it all into legal channels," recalls Luke Dembosky, one of the prosecutors on the case.

To help nail down Slavik's identity and get intelligence on the Business Club, the FBI teamed up with Fox-IT, a Dutch outfit renowned for its expertise in cyberforensics. The Dutch researchers got to work tracing old usernames and email addresses associated with Slavik's ring to piece together an understanding of how the group operated.

The Business Club, it turned out, was a loose confederation of about 50 criminals, who each paid an initiation fee to access Game-Over's advanced control panels. The network was run through two password-protected British websites, Visitcoastweekend.com and Work.businessclub.so, which contained careful records, FAQs, and a "ticket" system for resolving technical issues. When investigators got legal permission to penetrate the Business Club server, they found a highly detailed ledger tracking the group's various ongoing frauds. "Everything radiated professionalism," Fox-IT's Michael Sandee explains. When it came to pinpointing the precise timing of transactions between financial institutions, he says, "they probably knew better than the banks."

One day after months of following leads, the investigators at Fox-IT got a tip from a source about an email address they might want to look into. It was one of many similar tips they'd chased down. "We had a lot of bread crumbs," Mularski says. But this one led to something vital. The team traced the email address to a British server Slavik used to run the Business Club. More investigative work and more court orders eventually led authorities to Russian social media sites where the email address could be connected to a real name: Evgeniy Mikhailovich Bogachev. At first it proved meaningless to the group. It took weeks' more effort to realize the name actually belonged to the phantom who had invented Zeus and created the Business Club.

Slavik, it turned out, was a 30-year-old who lived an upper-middle-class existence in Anapa, a Russian resort city on the Black Sea. Online photos showed that he enjoyed boating with his wife. The couple had a young daughter. One photo showed Bogachev posing in leopard-print pajamas and dark sunglasses, holding a large cat. The investigative team realized that he had written the first draft of Zeus when he was just 22 years old.

But that wasn't the most astounding revelation that the Dutch investigators turned up. As they continued their analysis, they noticed that someone at the helm of GameOver had been regularly searching tens of thousands of the botnet's infected computers in certain countries for things like email addresses belonging to Georgian intelligence officers or leaders of elite Turkish police units, or documents that bore markings designating classified Ukrainian secrets. Whoever it was was also searching for classified material linked to the Syrian conflict and Russian arms deals. At some point, a lightbulb went on. "These are espionage commands," Sandee says.

GameOver wasn't merely a sophisticated piece of criminal malware; it was a sophisticated intelligence-gathering tool. And as best as the investigators could determine, Bogachev was the only member of the Business Club who knew about this particular feature of the botnet. He appeared to be running a covert spying operation right under the noses of the world's most prolific bank robbers. The FBI and Fox-IT team couldn't find specific evidence of a link between Bogachev and the Russian state, but some entity seemed to be feeding Slavik specific terms to search for in his vast network of zombie computers. Bogachev, it appeared, was a Russian intelligence asset.

In March 2014, investigators could even watch as an international crisis played out live inside the snow globe of Bogachev's criminal botnet. Weeks after the Sochi Olympics, Russian forces seized the Ukrainian region of Crimea and began efforts to destabilize the country's eastern border. Right in step with the Russian campaign, Bogachev redirected a section of his botnet to search for politically sensitive information on infected Ukrainian computers—trawling for intelligence that might help the Russians anticipate their adversary's next moves.

The team was able to construct a tentative theory and history of Bogachev's spycraft. The apparent state connection helped explain why Bogachev had been able to operate a major criminal enterprise with such impunity, but it also shed new light on some of the milestones in the life of Zeus. The system that Slavik used to make his intelligence queries dated back approximately to the moment in 2010 when he faked his retirement and made access to his malware far more exclusive. Perhaps Slavik had appeared on the radar of the Russian security services at some point that year, and in exchange for a license to commit fraud without prosecution—outside Russia, of course—the state made certain demands. To carry them out with maximum efficacy and secrecy, Slavik asserted tighter control over his criminal network.

The discovery of Bogachev's likely intelligence ties introduced some trickiness to the operation to take down GameOver—especially when it came to the prospect of enlisting Russian cooperation. Over a span of months, the team painstakingly went to internet service providers to ask permission to seize GameOver's existing proxy servers, ensuring that at the right moment, they could flip those servers and disable Slavik's control. Meanwhile, the Department of Homeland Security, Carnegie Mellon, and a number of antivirus companies readied themselves to help customers regain access to their infected computers. Weekly conference calls spanned continents as officials coordinated action in Britain, the United States, and elsewhere.

Figuring out how—or even whether—to dismantle a botnet remains a difficult question for government and industry; seizing a command-and-control server is necessary, but it's insufficient. You also need to disinfect the zombie computers themselves, otherwise you're leaving a cyber weapon of mass destruction lying around the internet, ready for someone to stumble upon. Yet, since botnets are driven by malware installed on tens of thousands, or even hundreds of thousands, of individual computers, there are complicated legal questions about a company's or government's authority to reach out and disinfect zombie computers.[14] Theoretically, even determining what version of malware an individual computer is running—a critical step to deactivating it—requires a search warrant; how do you write a search warrant, at scale, for hundreds of thousands of computers that cross all of the 94 judicial districts in the United States, let alone the numerous international boundaries any digital network now encompasses? For Game-Over Zeus, investigators relied on both criminal procedure and civil injunctions, but they also required the help of private companies and the Department of Homeland Security, and they needed private industry to remediate individual computers and assist in the so-called digital hygiene of cleaning up infections. Particularly given the Russian government's involvement in GameOver Zeus, we didn't want to leave the botnet floundering around the internet for someone else to assume control.*

By late spring 2014, as pro-Russian forces fought in Ukraine proper, American-led forces got ready to move in on GameOver. They'd been plotting to take down the network for more than a year, carefully reverse-engineering the malware, covertly reading the criminal gang's chat logs to understand the group's psychology, and tracing the physical infrastructure of servers that allowed the network to propagate around the globe. "By this point, these researchers knew the malware better than the author," says Elliott Peterson, one of the lead FBI agents on the case. As Mularski recalls, the team checked off all the crucial boxes: "Criminally, we can do it. Civilly, we can do it. Technically, we can do it."

Prosecutor Ethan Arenson had helped to arrange an unprecedented set of legal authorities to make every piece fit. Working with a cast of dozens, communicating with more than 70 internet service providers and a dozen other law enforcement agencies from Canada to the United Kingdom to Japan to Italy, the team readied an attack to

---

*The case exposed holes in the government's authorities that led to an amendment to Rule 41 of the Federal Rules of Criminal Procedure—the rule that guides searches and seizures. Among other tweaks, the new amendment allowed judges to issue search warrants for investigators to hack computers outside their district. This new rule was used for the first time in 2017 by some of the FBI team that took down GameOver Zeus to attack the long-standing Kelihos botnet, giving the FBI a special 30-day warrant to help disinfect computers and "poison" the botnet.

commence on Friday, May 30. Luke Dembosky, one of the prosecutors on the case who had just wrapped up two years working in Moscow as the Justice Department's attaché in the embassy before returning to help coordinate the case, recalls being amazed at the network Mularski had built after a decade of cybercrime efforts. "I thought I had a lot of contacts around the world; Keith had many more," he recalls. "We'd be sitting there trying to figure out how to knit together this complicated international team. 'Who knows someone who can unplug this piece of hardware in this remote corner of the world?' Keith seemed to know everyone."

After careful planning, the attack finally began.* Canadian and Ukrainian authorities shut down GameOver's two command servers, knocking each offline in turn. Werner and Stone-Gross began redirecting the zombie computers into a carefully built sinkhole that would absorb the nefarious traffic, blocking the Business Club's access to its own systems. For hours, the attack went nowhere; the researchers struggled to figure out where the bugs lay in their code.

By 1 p.m., their sinkhole had drawn in only about a hundred infected computers, an infinitesimal percentage of the botnet that had grown to as many as half a million machines. A line of officials stood behind Werner and Stone-Gross in a conference room, literally watching over their shoulders as the two engineers debugged their code. "Not to put any pressure on you," Mularski urged at one point, "but it'd be great if you could get it running."

Finally, by evening Pittsburgh time, the traffic to their sinkhole began to climb. On the other side of the world, Bogachev came online. The attack had interrupted his weekend. Perhaps he didn't think much of it at first, given that he had easily weathered other attempts to seize control of his botnet. "Right away, he's kicking the tires. He doesn't know what we've done," Peterson recalls. That night, yet again, Bogachev readied for battle—wrestling for control of his network, testing it, redirecting traffic to new servers, and deciphering the Pittsburgh

---

* The takedown had actually been briefly delayed because of the announcement of the PLA case on May 19, 2014. There were so many cybercrime cases by 2014 it was sometimes difficult to schedule them all.

team's method of attack. "It was cyber-hand-to-hand combat," recalls Pittsburgh US Attorney David Hickton. "It was amazing to watch."

The team was able to monitor Bogachev's communication channels without his knowledge and knock out his Turkish proxy server. Then they watched as he tried to come back online using the anonymizing service Tor, desperate to get some visibility into his losses. Finally, after hours of losing battles, Slavik went silent. The attack, it appeared, was more than he had bargained for. The Pittsburgh team powered on through the night. "He must've realized it was law enforcement. It wasn't just the normal researcher attack," Stone-Gross says.

By Sunday night, nearly 60 hours in, the Pittsburgh team knew they'd won. "It was surreal to watch unfold in real time," Dembosky recalls. On Monday, June 2, the FBI and Justice Department announced the takedown and unsealed a 14-count indictment against Bogachev.

Amazingly, years later, the success has largely stuck: to date, the botnet has never reassembled, though about 5,000 computers worldwide remain infected with Zeus malware—the industry partners are still maintaining the server sinkhole that's swallowing up the traffic from those infected computers—and for nearly a year afterward, so-called account-takeover fraud all but disappeared in the United States. Researchers and investigators had long assumed that dozens of gangs must have been responsible for the criminal onslaught that the industry endured from 2012 to 2014. But nearly all of the thefts came from just a small group of highly skilled criminals—the so-called Business Club. "You come into this and hear they're everywhere," Peterson says, "and actually it's a very tiny network, and they're much easier to disrupt than you think."

That truism—that the population of high-level hackers was actually quite small—was also underscored by one of the other Russia-linked cases unfolding at that time.

///////////////

GameOver, after all, was hardly the only case that was worrying us in terms of Russia's ongoing attacks against US companies. Just months after the takedown of the GameOver Zeus botnet, Russian hackers broke into the main user database of internet giant Yahoo; it was one of the largest hacks ever perpetrated—while our case would focus on only one intrusion that we said involved at least 500 million accounts, the company has publicly said that the breaches compromised effectively all of its 3 billion users. From our perspective, it was a uniquely insulting crime on the international stage: a theft carried out with the express cooperation in Russia of intelligence officers whose job it was to help fight cybercrime.

In December 2014, sophisticated Russian hackers compromised Yahoo's main user database, where it stored the hundreds of millions of accounts, including not just the user's main name and account, but also backup email accounts and phone numbers, password challenge questions, and even the cryptographic codes needed for user authentication. The hacker also penetrated Yahoo's account management tool, which allowed it to manage users' accounts and track details like password changes. The combination of the two meant that the hackers effectively gained access to all of Yahoo's most critical crown jewels, the personal details of everyone on one of the world's largest online providers—a group totaling more users than the population of even the world's largest country. Amazingly, the hack continued undetected for nearly two more years, through at least November 2016.[15]

When the hack was finally caught and reported and the FBI case unfolded, investigators zeroed in on four specific suspects: two FSB officers, Dmitry Aleksandrovich Dokuchaev and Igor Anatolyevich Sushchin, and two criminal hackers, Karim Baratov and Alexsey Belan. Each of the four proved interesting in his own way: Dokuchaev was an officer with the FSB's Second Division, the Center for Information Security, known as Center 18. It was the equivalent of the FBI's Cyber Division, the unit tasked with *fighting* cybercrime. Dokuchaev had a unique background for an intelligence officer: He had spent a decade as a Russian hacker, stealing credit cards and purchasing technology such as "skimmers" and encoders that helped thieves mimic real credit cards with physical plastic. He had gone online under the name Forb and even under his own name to help edit a Russian magazine called *Khaker,* where he oversaw a section titled "Breaking In."[16] According to accounts in Russian newspapers, he joined the FSB to avoid being prosecuted in Russia for credit card fraud.[17] He had continued his magazine work even after joining the FSB, where he oversaw the prosecution of hackers accused of attacking Aeroflot's payment system.[18]

Meanwhile, his FSB supervisor, Sushchin, worked undercover as an employee and the head of information security at a Russian financial firm—the equivalent of an NSA hacker serving as the head of technology security of a Wall Street firm while on the government payroll. Baratov, a Kazakh-born Canadian national, lived in Ontario and his social media accounts documented his taste for flashy cars, especially his beloved Mercedes and Aston Martin.[19]

Belan, though, was the most interesting of the group: he was hardly a new name for investigators. The shaggy-haired Latvian, still in his 20s, went online by the name M4G and had actually been indicted three times by the United States even before the Yahoo hack. Like Bogachev, Belan had been a longtime fixture online—he'd appeared in online forums as early as 2006, when he would have still been a teenager, and had hacked multiple Eastern European sites, including an online game, lordmancer.ru, but had graduated quickly to larger and more lucrative targets.[20] "He's definitely on the radar of the most sophisticated hackers we've seen," said Vitali Kremez, a security researcher with the company Flashpoint.[21]

The US attorney in Nevada indicted Belan in 2012 for hacking into the online shoe retailer Zappos; then, the following year, he was indicted again for hacking into two large online document storage sites, Evernote and Scribd. He specialized in exploiting weaknesses in sites run on the popular content management system WordPress, which powers many small and large websites. He also targeted peripheral systems, like company intranets, development servers, or servers in branch offices that were secured less thoroughly than main systems; he even once was able to find a vulnerable server by using information posted on a company engineer's LinkedIn profile, hacking into the engineer's server on his home iMac in Santa Clara, California. "Many of the large breaches publicized during 2012 and 2013 are attributed to him, and news of others didn't make it into the public domain," wrote

Chris McNab, a cybersecurity researcher who helped respond to one of Belan's hacks.[22]

After those indictments, the United States issued a rare "Red Notice," through Interpol, asking for other countries to arrest him if they found him on their soil. Soon after, we discovered that he was on vacation in Greece, and authorities there arrested him—but he posted bail, which we believed he shouldn't have been able to receive, and then promptly fled back to Russia. He hadn't been seen outside Russia since; as his lawyer told the *New York Times*, "For the last couple of years he cannot be reached."[23] It appeared that he came back online quickly, continuing his decade-long thefts and frauds online.

We always wondered if it was precisely the Greek arrest and Interpol Red Notice that made the FSB pay attention to recruiting him in the first place. Was Russia using America's list of the world's most wanted criminal hackers as a shopping list for future recruits?

As investigators traced how the three coconspirators had utilized the Yahoo database, it was a breathtaking tour of the vulnerability of individuals online, as well as a case study in how criminals and intelligence agencies in Russia were beginning to work side by side, each to advance its own goals.

Using the credentials stolen from the user database and the account management tool, the conspirators were able to "mint" authentication "cookies" that made it appear they were authorized to log in to protected accounts. The Yahoo conspirators used the stolen information to spy on precisely those you would expect an intelligence service to be interested in: Russian journalists and government officials in both the United States and Russia, as well as employees of a prominent Russian cybersecurity firm and the employees of other tech companies that the hackers hoped to target. Their US targets included cybersecurity, diplomatic, and military leaders and even White House personnel—but also some surprises, such as a Nevada gaming official. They spied on critics of the Russian government, both inside Russia and in neighboring European countries, as well as journalists at outlets such as *Kommersant*, and even people involved in Russia's bid to join the World Trade Organization. But they didn't stop at only traditional intelligence targets. They also spied on financial firms in Russia, Switzerland, and the United States, as well as a French transportation company and a US airline. They used the account information to tailor more effective spear-phishing emails in the hope of compromising even more user accounts; at one point, while targeting the board member of a Russian financial firm, they also went after the accounts of his wife and his secretary and sent him a spear-phishing email that appeared to be from the Russian Federal Tax Service.

The power of the Yahoo hack wasn't just its email service: over the years, many other applications and sites, from the photo-sharing site Flickr to fantasy sports leagues, had been integrated into Yahoo, giving a hacker with a Yahoo password wide access to a user's digital life. Moreover, despite years of cautions to do otherwise, most internet users make the same totally human mistake—rather than using individual high-security passwords for each site, they just reuse one or two passwords, often based on the password for their main email account. A Yahoo password, in that sense, might very well be able to access unrelated banking sites, credit cards, phone companies, or almost anything else that exists online.

The FSB officers regularly tasked Baratov to use the stolen Yahoo information to crack more than 80 accounts at other email providers and websites, specifically telling him to target individuals like an assistant to the deputy chairman of the Russian Federation, the executives of a Russian cybersecurity firm, the Gmail accounts of European corporate executives, and a staffer at the Ministry of Sports of a Russian republic. They even had Baratov spy on fellow Russian investigators, asking him to target an officer at the Russian Ministry of Internal Affairs who worked in its Bureau of Special Technical Projects, known as Department K, which investigated cybercrime and child pornography cases. Each time he was successful, the FSB paid him a bounty, generally about $100. Baratov, who later pleaded guilty and was sentenced to five years in prison, said in his plea he ultimately accessed about 11,000 accounts in his hacker-for-hire business.

The unique partnership between the criminals and the FSB was beneficial all around. Belan's FSB partners helped him cover his tracks online, providing information on their own cybersecurity investigations and their techniques for tracking hackers. That information helped Belan run his own online financial fraud business, even as the FSB used his information for its own intelligence purposes. Just as Bogachev had been stealing millions in GameOver Zeus while helping spy on Ukraine, Belan used his access to Yahoo to manipulate its search results for popular erectile-dysfunction drugs—directing unwitting users to an online pharmacy that paid Belan for the referral traffic—and pillaged user accounts for credit cards that he could steal, searching user accounts for terms like "amex," "mastercard," and "visa." He also searched accounts for the email address one US retailer used to dispatch online gift cards. Then, to fuel a spam email empire, he built a special tool that faked authentication credentials faster than any human could do so—minting tens of thousands of such credentials a day that ultimately allowed him access to some 30 million accounts. He then stole the address books and contacts of those accounts to help build a massive database of users far beyond Yahoo that he could sell to potential spammers.

The case allowed the Justice Department to make public how much of a business cybercrime had become—and how increasingly gray the world online was becoming, with foreign adversaries happy to let criminals pursue their fraud unimpeded as long as they helped aid the intelligence agencies with their spying.

But even as the Yahoo hack was starting in December 2014, we were scrambling to respond to perhaps the strangest cyber incident the United States had yet seen.

CHAPTER 7

The Guardians of Peace

I ONLY ONCE watched a movie in the FBI's command center. The FBI's Strategic Information and Operations Center (SIOC) was normally the scene of tight, well-regimented briefings, with PowerPoints and secure video teleconferences. Yet that November morning in 2014, our normal morning briefing crew—including FBI Director Comey and Attorney General Holder—gathered to view the most important movie in the US government: a vulgar screwball comedy starring Seth Rogen, made by Sony Pictures Entertainment. We all watched with puzzlement; how had this movie spawned the highest-profile cyberattack yet to hit the United States? The screening seemed quite surreal— Comey cracked a joke about the movie. None of us were big fans; one person blamed North Korea for forcing the government leadership to watch it. Without a doubt, I was in the middle of the strangest 28 days of my career.

I've sat through a lot of difficult discussions in the FBI command center and in the Situation Room, but little had prepared me for the screening of the movie and the subsequent conversations. Later, I found myself briefing the administration about the unfolding crisis at the Situation Room table. I knew we had to take this attack seriously; it was, at its core, an attack on American values, but as I looked around the room and the assembled leaders of the nation's intelligence agencies and the military, none of us really knew the answer to the question tugging at all of us: How far could we go to respond when a movie company had been attacked because of a Seth Rogen comedy?

The Sony case caught us in another gray zone—a new attack by a foreign nation against a private company. It was in some ways similar to what we'd seen so far in cyberspace—our major foreign adversaries, China, Russia, North Korea, and Iran, all viewed their cyber programs as vital to advancing their own domestic political objectives. Whereas China and Russia had multiple areas where they could push the United States, smaller and weaker adversaries such as Iran and North Korea needed the asymmetric advantages of the cyberworld. Online, they could be far more successful than they could be with traditional military or economic weapons. That online power became all too clear when North Korean hackers targeted Sony Pictures for its soon-to-be-released satirical movie *The Interview*, a comedy about efforts to kill North Korea's leader. By the time it was over, the unprecedented attack on American free speech and free expression by a foreign power illustrated the need for new government authorities and the defensive challenges the cyber realm posed to private industry.

The hack of Sony—largely remembered today as a punch line—improved the government's cyber response capabilities dramatically, perhaps more than any other event in the last decade. It was a crisis unlike any other we had experienced, but thanks in part to the lessons we'd learned in government from the Chinese PLA case and the Iranian investigations, we had a sense of how to tackle it—and, in a record 28 days, had figured out who did it and made that information public. The case accelerated the change already under way across government: by the time the dust settled, we had instituted new procedures for handling such incidents, we had launched a new classified cyber center, and the White House had issued a new executive order. And, although we didn't know it at the time, it was an event that others were watching closely around the world: more than any other cyber incident, it presaged the attacks by Russia against the presidential election just two years later.

The incident started on Friday, November 21, 2014, when top executives at Sony Pictures, including its two cochairs, Amy Pascal and Michael Lynton, received an odd, threatening email: "We've got great damage by Sony Pictures. The compensation for it, monetary compensation we want. Pay the damage, or Sony Pictures will be bombarded as a whole. You know us very well. We never wait long. You'd better behave wisely." The email appeared to be from a group calling themselves "God'sApstls," a name that didn't register with anyone. In fact, even the email itself didn't register with the studio executives: Pascal's went to her spam, and Lynton never opened it.[1]

The following Monday, as the workday began in Thanksgiving week, attackers struck. Lynton received a telephone call from his CFO while he was driving his Volkswagen to work warning that there appeared to be a security breach; then, quickly, he received a follow-up call—the company needed to take its network offline. Something terrible had happened. "We didn't understand the extent of the damage, what had been stolen, any of it," Lynton recalled.[2]

Across the company, users found their computers frozen—and a screen declaring "Hacked by #GOP." An image of a ghastly red skeleton reached toward the user beneath text that read, "We've already warned you, and this is just a beginning. We continue till our request be met. We've obtained all your internal data including your secrets and top secrets. If you don't obey us, we'll release data shown below to the world." The screen then contained five links to purportedly stolen data files, as well as a warning that the company had until 11 p.m. GMT that very evening to "determine what will you do," but the graphic didn't make clear what it was demanding, how much—or what—ransom was being demanded, or why the company was being targeted. Not all of the links functioned, making it difficult to determine what was happening, but those who did root through the 217-megabyte zipped file found a collection of oddities: copies of passports of actors from Sony movies, password-protected spreadsheets, Outlook mailboxes, film budgets, and what appeared to be pirated copies of movies from other studios.[3]

Beyond the frozen computers, several Twitter accounts used to promote movies were compromised. They too posted "Hacked by #GOP" images featuring freaky skeletons, along with the message "You, the criminals including Michael Lynton will surely go to hell. Nobody can help you."[4] Pascal had seen the warning herself at her computer as she prepared to start her holiday-shortened workweek on the third floor of Sony's executive offices in Culver City, a storied movie lot that stretched back to the glory days of Metro-Goldwyn-Mayer in the 1930s.

At 10:50 a.m. Pacific Time—just four hours before the ransom demand's zero hour—the Hollywood news site Deadline.com reported the first word of the unfolding attack: "Things have come to a standstill at Sony today, after the computers in New York and around the world were infiltrated by a hacker."[5] The company scrambled to figure out what was going on—reduced to paper communications, signs were posted across the studio lot and staff raced Paul Revere–style office to office telling employees to turn off their computers and disconnect any phones or tablets from the company's Wi-Fi. The company set up a command center on the soundstage where *Singin' in the Rain* had been filmed, and called the cybersecurity firm FireEye, who dispatched a dozen crisis responders to California. At the start, there was confusion, but not panic. "A one-day problem," one executive called it, and a spokesperson told the press the company was investigating "an IT matter."[6]

Yet the problem stretched on. "It was a very chaotic, tumultuous period," Lynton recalled. "They destroyed two-thirds of the servers, most of our computers, they'd obviously stolen a huge amount of data, and you have tremendous unrest among the employee population concerned about what's going on."[7] The company's computers had, it turned out, been nuked—not just frozen, but wiped clean, turned into expensive bricks sitting across 3,000 desks. On Tuesday, four unreleased Sony movies were posted to the web by the Guardians of Peace, but it was still unclear what the "GOP" hackers wanted or why they were attacking Sony. Thanksgiving came and went, and Sony remained frozen.

Finally, early Saturday morning, November 29, a tech reporter named Kevin Roose received another strange email: "Hi, I am the boss of G.O.P. A few days ago, we told you the fact that we had released Sony Pictures films including *Annie, Fury* and *Still Alice* to the web. Those can be easily obtained through internet search. For this time, we are about to release Sony Pictures data to the web. The volume of the data is under 100 Terabytes." He was puzzled by the email, but followed the link to the website Pastebin, which allows users to easily share information online. He found a carefully organized trove of Sony's most closely held corporate secrets. Roose zeroed in on a spreadsheet showing salaries of 6,000 employees. Floored by what he found, Roose used it to write a story on December 1, titled "Hacked Documents Reveal a Hollywood Studio's Stunning Gender and Race Gap," that ran atop a smiling photo of Pascal and Lynton. It was, looking back now and knowing what a landmark moment the hack of Sony Pictures turned out to be, an oddly normal news story—similar to many stories of what was becoming an all-too-familiar genre as corporate and government secrets were leaked by disgruntled insiders, whistle-blowers, or hackers the world over. Written quickly, with minimal research and with no response from an attempt to ask Sony for comment, the nine-paragraph story alluded only in passing to the hack's unknown origins, referencing briefly that Sony was "reportedly investigating whether North Korea could be involved," in part because of the controversial movie, *The Interview*, about North Korea that Sony soon planned to release.[8]

Kim Zetter at *Wired* magazine, one of the industry's most knowledgeable security writers and the author of a book about the Stuxnet Worm, all but dismissed the North Korea theory—the attack was just too bizarre, too showy, and too unprofessional: "If that sounds outlandish, that's because it likely is. The focus on North Korea is weak and easily undercut by the facts."[9] The "likely culprits," she wrote, "are hacktivists—or disgruntled insiders." Inside government, though, we knew quickly that the theory was not just possible—it remained probable. In fact, unbeknownst to the press or the public at that time, North

Korea had already pulled off a similar attack against a British media company earlier that year.

Inside Sony, none of the executives were smiling. The day after Roose's initial story, personal details of some 3,800 employees began to leak out onto the web—some of what would ultimately end up being nearly 40 million files—including not just identity information such as Social Security numbers, but also, in some cases, performance reviews and reasons for the termination of former employees. Employees who in the first week saw the hack as an inconvenience and impediment to productivity realized in the second week that their lives and careers were being fundamentally altered. The *New York Times* pointed out that the opening salvos from the hackers had smartly targeted "two things the secretive movie industry is extremely sensitive about—the piracy of films and details about executive compensation."[10] And as the crisis entered its second week, it was clear that the hackers were only getting started. This was no garden-variety data breach; there was a clear message and a motive behind the targeted attack. "This was like a home invasion where after taking the family jewels the hackers set the house ablaze," one security executive said.

A new email threat arrived from the Guardians of Peace—telling all employees that they should speak out against Sony "if you don't want to suffer damage. If you don't, not only you but your family will be in danger." What had started as an IT inconvenience was quickly turning into a potentially existential threat to the company and America's values of free speech and free expression. There was a deep irony that America's free press was being exploited to do the bidding of one of the world's most repressive and anti–free press countries. The *Washington Post* reported, "If nothing else, perhaps *The Interview* will benefit from the swirl of attention brought on by the incident when it hits the box office on Christmas Day."[11] The password to open many of the purloined files wasn't subtle: "DieSPE123." *Die Sony Pictures Entertainment.* As Lynton said in an employee town hall meeting, they were in uncharted territory: "There is no playbook for us to turn to."[12] Sony was ultimately a Japanese company and it had employees around the world, including in South Korea—were they all safe?

The people at Sony Pictures were scared—the FBI deployed agents to help reassure them. They were understandably nervous—they had stumbled into an international incident. To me, that was an important part of the attack's impact: a hacker had made US workers, working in the United States, afraid to show up and do their jobs. "The North Koreans had a psychological angle to their attack as well," recalls Luke Dembosky, who was part of our team on the case. "They used their communications to instill fear in people. They performed a mini-psyops operation as part of this."

///////////////

On December 8, after weeks of puzzling silence about what the hackers actually wanted, a demand finally arrived: "Stop immediately showing the movie of terrorism which can break the regional peace and cause the War! You, SONY & FBI, cannot find us."

We all knew what the "movie of terrorism" meant: *The Interview*, a movie by actor Seth Rogen and his producing partner, Evan Goldberg, about a fictional plot by the CIA to assassinate the leader of North Korea using hapless TV journalists who had obtained an interview with the reclusive dictator. Rogen and Goldberg had worked together earlier on *Da Ali G Show*, whose star Sacha Baron Cohen had become famous as Borat, the fictional bumbling journalist from Kazakhstan. The experience had planted the seed of cultural comedy as a way to examine repressive, backward regimes—an interest that eventually led them to create *The Interview*, a movie originally titled "Kill Kim Jong Un."

Controversy had swirled around the film since June, when Sony released the first trailer. Sony's chief executive in Tokyo objected privately—fearing the movie would inflame tensions with North Korea—and those fears quickly became reality. On June 25, North Korea's state news agency said the movie was "terrorism" and that releasing the film would be "intolerable." It said that there would be "merciless" retaliation if the movie moved forward; the following day, the country lobbed three short-range missiles into the Sea of Japan.[13] Seth Rogen took the news lightly—joking on Twitter, "People don't usually wanna kill me for one of my movies until after they've paid 12 bucks for it. Hiyooooo!!!"

The early controversy worried the studio behind the scenes: they spent the summer quietly checking with think tanks and US government officials about how afraid they should be, and they also hired a strategic consulting firm, McLarty Associates, to advise them on North Korea's behavior. McLarty said that the danger was real—and most likely it would come virtually. "A physical strike in the U.S. would be beyond North Korea's capabilities," McLarty's Rich Klein recalled advising them. "But we firmly believed that the North Koreans could try to stop the movie through a cyber-attack."[14]

North Korea has been a general threat to US interests dating back to long before I was alive; in the decades since the stalemated war in the 1950s, the Korean peninsula had turned into perhaps the most heavily fortified and defended border in the world, protected by tens of thousands of American troops. Yet for most of the six decades since the war, the weak and isolated North Korea had not projected its force much further than the waters around the peninsula.

While North Korea in the early years after the war possessed the upper hand, over time South Korea's growing economic stability and technological advances flipped the balance of power. North Korea's authoritarian dictatorship became increasingly isolated globally as it pursued a nuclear weapons program that it hoped would help secure its independence. Its onetime hope for what it referred to as "quick war, quick end" against South Korea became increasingly unrealistic, and so it began to turn to other less-than-war means to advance its goals.

For decades, North Korea had engaged in provocative low-level military operations and offensive stabs at the south, other Asian neighbors, and the United States—operations that allowed it to demonstrate its capabilities and project military might while remaining far below the geopolitical threshold for war—even though some such operations, from terrorist bombings to brief artillery bombardments to the sinking of naval vessels, were quite deadly. In recent years, cyber activity had grown into a particularly valuable tool for North Korea because it generally carried a low risk of escalation and online financial fraud helped prop up the cash-starved state. As the military imbalance grew, North Korea realized it wasn't going to win with tanks and artillery; instead, as one team of researchers explained, it "began to invest in asymmetric military capabilities, like special forces, investment in ballistic missile technologies, nuclear development, and, most recently, cyber capabilities."[15] Just a year before the Sony attack, Kim Jong-un himself had said, "Cyber warfare, along with nuclear weapons and missiles, is an all-purpose sword that guarantees our military's capability to strike relentlessly."[16]

For most of my tenure in government, though, we weren't primarily concerned about North Korea's cyber activities—we mostly worried about its nuclear program. It was a major threat in what we called the "counterproliferation" space—a country actively trying to illegally acquire technologies that would help its nascent nuclear weapons program. We had a major initiative to try to prevent the export of so-called dual-use goods and other technologies that were banned because of the international sanctions that North Korea faced for its reckless geopolitical behavior.

We were constantly trying to police North Korea's hunt for key technologies, working with other countries around the world to limit North Korea's ability to acquire tools that could help them build nuclear weapons or boost their military. One of the biggest counterproliferation cases we worked was the years-long pursuit of a merchant named Hsien Tai Tsai, or Alex Tsai, and his Taiwanese companies, Trans Merits and Global Interface. It was a multigenerational family scheme, which also included his wife and his son, Gary Tsai, that saw them attempt to export key dual-use technologies from the United States to Taiwan, falsely declaring that the final user would be Trans Merits when they really intended to move the technology on to North Korea. Alex Tsai had been involved in such export schemes since the 1990s and had been indicted in Taiwan in 2008 for "illegally forging invoices and shipping restricted materials to North Korea." He had then also been targeted by US sanctions in January 2009, when he was working as a procurement agent for the Korea Mining Development Trading Corporation, an innocuous-sounding company that is actually one of North Korea's main military technology importers.

Red flags kept popping up indicating that the Tsais were still in the illegal export business; in Illinois, his son, Gary, had set up a US company, Factory Direct Machine Tools, but continued to hand out business cards listing Trans Merits, and relied on a Trans Merits email account for some of his work. The FBI's investigation turned up a variety of illegally exported technologies that Alex Tsai had helped facilitate, including machine tools, LED road lights, and oil pumps.[17] We were able to arrest Alex Tsai while he was on vacation with his wife in Estonia, and we scooped up Gary at his home in Glenview, Illinois.[18] While they ended up pleading guilty in federal court in Chicago, the case also pointed to a number of important holes in the ways that the United States tried to combat such illegal trading: Gary appeared easily able to evade the eye of banks, even though he had the same last name as someone under sanctions.[19]

///////////////////

By and large, North Korea appeared as a cyberthreat late in the game—both because they were slower to develop the capability and because we, as an intelligence community, were still maturing our understanding of who did what online. Much of North Korea's cyber infrastructure funneled through China, so it was sometimes hard—especially in the earlier days of the Obama administration—to untangle what was what. In fact, in 2013, South Korea initially blamed China for a cyberattack that it later realized had been North Korean in origin.

We ran a sophisticated system for producing intelligence reports on counterterrorism and even on counterproliferation, but nothing near the same level of sophistication when it came to cybersecurity. Too many agencies still shared information poorly, making it difficult to develop a full picture of what the US government itself knew.

The US government certainly knew North Korea posed a threat online: it was one of the four main nation-states named as the world's top cyberthreats. North Korea appeared regularly in our morning intelligence briefings, particularly in the context of its attempts to use cyber means to steal valuable technologies and circumvent sanctions. We'd even seen North Korea attempt destructive attacks overseas.

Much like Iran, North Korea found cyber operations—an umbrella that included its own unique mix of criminality, intelligence gathering, data theft, and offensive operations—particularly useful as an asymmetric response and counter against the vast military superiority of its southern neighbor, South Korea, and the United States. North Korea is effectively the most militarized state in the world; in the years after the Korean War, it had dedicated itself to the goal of reuniting the peninsula and turned the demilitarized zone between it and South Korea into a fortified region unlike any other border in history, with massed artillery and troops ready for defense or offense.

One of the aspects of cyber that made it uniquely attractive to North Korea was it actually helped exploit North Korea's retarded economic development—whereas any Western government or company by the 2000s was deeply wired, with daily operations and communications intensely reliant on computers, North Korea's infrastructure, all but frozen in time in the 1950s, possessed very little in terms of technical vulnerability. Its web presence measured effectively zero; the total number of government and foreign-based websites numbered in the dozens and the first reliable broadband internet connection for the entire country had only been installed in 2010; as late as the early 2000s, anyone in North Korea who wanted to send an email message to the outside world had to use one of just two gateways, one in Pyongyang and one in the border city of Shenyang, where the emails were collected and sent via China once an hour; and an email cost about $1.50.[20] In 2014, the country primarily relied on just a single block of IP addresses, 1,024 of them, or roughly what a midsized company might utilize for a single office building; it was fewer IPs than an average New York City block possessed.[21] (It also used 256 Chinese web addresses.)[22] In 2012, the cofounder of the Pyongyang University of Science and Technology explained that the entire university shared a single IP address—a third or a fifth of what a single American college dorm usually possessed.[23] "Students can't spend a long time for the internet. They only use it for their study," Park Chan-mo told *Reuters* at the time. The gateway to the world that made the internet so valuable to the rest of the 21st century was considered a dangerous, destabilizing force by Kim Jong-un's government. Instead, the North Korean regime primarily invested in its own internal intranet, known as Kwangmyong, which remained unconnected to the broader global internet.

That blankness is part of what makes North Korea a uniquely hard country for anyone—including the US government—to understand. It is isolated to a degree unlike any other government or country on earth; we know more about certain primitive civilizations from millennia ago than we do about the day-to-day operations of the so-called Hermit Kingdom. Its web presence is effectively zero, its decision making uniquely opaque. "North Korea is considered one of the hardest intelligence targets in the world," Center for Strategic and International Studies researchers concluded, after examining North Korea's cyberstrategy.[24]

The FBI had begun paying attention to North Korea's interest in computers in the 1990s, when counterintelligence agents in New York noticed that some of the country's diplomats at the United Nations were enrolling in computer science classes.[25] Much like China's digital awakening in the wake of the overwhelming American military might in Kosovo in 1999 and the invasion of Iraq, North Korea's interest in digital warfare as a way to level the playing field accelerated after leader Kim Jong-il watched how easily the United States defeated the tanks and artillery of Iraq in 2003.

North Korea's cyber operations are primarily run by its main intelligence and covert operations arm, the Reconnaissance General Bureau (RGB), and what was known originally as Bureau 121. The more traditional military cyber operations are under the General Staff Department of the Korean People's Army (KPA).[26] North Korea had combined many of its cyber units around 2009 and 2010, joining with different units from the Korean Worker's Party and the Ministry of People's Armed Forces into the newly formed RGB, which served as the rough equivalent of a combined CIA, NSA, and US Special Operations Command, SOCOM.[27]*

In 2009 around the time of the consolidation of cyber units in RGB, North Korea began to appear regularly to be behind DDoS attacks on United States and South Korean websites—including attacks in July 2009 that targeted two dozen websites from the White House to the South Korean Ministry of Defense. The attacks were unsophisticated, garden-variety denial-of-service attacks, but they continued regularly in the following years. In 2012, the top US general on the peninsula, General James D. Thurman, warned Congress about North Korea's "growing cyberwarfare capability," saying the country "employs sophisticated computer hackers trained to launch cyberinfiltration and cyberattacks" against adversaries like South Korea or the United States. As he said, "Such attacks are ideal for North Korea, providing the regime a means to attack [South Korean] and U.S. interests without attribution, and have been increasingly employed against a variety of targets including military, governmental, educational and commercial institutions."[28]

Many—but perhaps not all—of the country's elite cyberwarriors were part of Bureau 121, which, according to public estimates, had grown from only a few hundred to a few thousand personnel by the time of the Sony hack.[29] (Other estimates had the number much lower: one defector was quoted as saying he believed North Korea only had a few dozen top-flight hackers.)[30] Many of the well-trained hackers lived in relative privilege in the capital, Pyongyang, getting access to

---

*In fact, just 10 days before the Sony attack, the US director of national intelligence, James Clapper, had actually traveled to North Korea, at the direction of President Obama, in a successful attempt to free two Americans held hostage by the regime; Clapper had met with the head of RGB, General Kim Yong-chol, his rough equivalent, during an "extraordinarily tense and unpleasant" 12-course banquet. It was the highest-level US delegation to enter North Korea in more than a dozen years. According to South Korea's media, Kim Yong-chol personally okayed the Sony attack—not altogether surprising, since such a high-profile attack would have certainly gone through high-level approvals—which got our attention: he almost certainly entertained Clapper with seafood, kimchi, and beer even as he knew his warriors were preparing an unprecedented attack on the United States.

the government's better schools, housing, and medical care. They were recruited early; according to what a defector who taught computer science said to Al Jazeera in 2011, elementary school students who showed a proficiency in science and math were brought to Pyongyang to attend one of two top schools, known as Keumseong 1 and 2 High-Middle Schools. "There is a pyramid-like prodigy recruiting system, where smart kids from all over the country—students who are good at math, coding and possess top analytical skills—are picked up to be grouped at Keumseong," he said. "When they graduate [from Keumseong], they are sent to attend North Korea's top technology institutes and universities, such as the Kim Il-sung University, Kim Chaek University of Technology, and various others in Pyongyang or Hamheung [a city near the country's eastern coast]."[31]

One of North Korea's few publicly known cyberwarriors, Jo Myung-lae, had graduated from the prestigious Miriam College, the country's top military technology school—a combination of West Point and Carnegie Mellon—and helped develop a piece of malware known as Win32/JML in the late 1990s that specifically targeted Windows systems only in South Korea.[32]

North Korea's cyber teams worked closely with other US adversaries; would-be hackers also often spent at least a year working in China or Russia, learning advanced skills.[33] According to a 2009 US Army paper published by Major Steve Sin, North Korea based at least one team of its hackers in a four-star luxury hotel in China's city of Shenyang, about a three-hour drive north of its border. The North Korean government partially owned the Chilbosan Hotel with the Chinese government. "The residences are communal, but by North Korean standards, are a great place to live," the defector told Al Jazeera in 2011. "If they save up enough of the stipends they receive abroad, they can live very well when they return to the North."

China, though, wasn't North Korea's only cyber partner: the isolated regime had evidently been learning from other US adversaries, too, adopting the tactics of Iran's Saudi Aramco attack from the summer of 2012 the following spring as US and South Korean military units gathered for high-profile annual exercises in March 2013. The similar tactics were unlikely to be a coincidence, given the close cooperation of the two rogue governments on other issues such as nuclear technology. "We have to assume they are getting help from the Iranians," said the former head of Britain's GCHQ, Robert Hannigan.[34]

At 2 p.m. in the afternoon of March 20, 2013, three banks and two media companies in South Korea found their computers erased by a so-called logic bomb, a piece of malware, a file named *AgentBase.exe*, that "exploded" at a preset time, wiping clean the infected computers' hard drive and then rebooting the computers.[35] When the device restarted, there was nothing left to see: users just got a heart-stopping message: "Boot device not found. Please install an operating system on your hard disk."[36]

Employees at South Korea's two main TV stations, the Korean Broadcasting System and the MBC, both reported the loss of many computers, as did employees at three large banks: Shinhan, NongHyup, and Jeju. Another cable channel, YTN, and another bank, Woori, reported lesser, unsuccessful attacks.[37] Customers across South Korea were frozen out of ATMs for hours as the banks struggled to reset their networks and allow access to cash again. All told, as many as 32,000 computers were lost to the attack across the affected organizations— a stunning, destructive swipe at high-profile targets.[38] It was another warning sign of just how destructive even a "low-profile" cyberattack could be—as companies continually shifted their value into the intellectual property and work product contained on their computer servers, it was clear that a piece of malware could wipe out weeks, months, or even years of collective effort.

The malware, which came to be known as Jokra Trojan, appeared to have been delivered the day before in a suspicious phishing email. The suspicious email had been the product of a shadowy online group dubbed DarkSeoul, which was always believed to be either North Korean hackers or North Korean hackers who were aided by sympathetic Chinese hackers.[39] Jokra Trojan also appeared to be a warning shot from the north: just days before the attack, the North Korean state news agency had warned the West that the country would "never remain a passive onlooker to the enemies' cyberattacks that have reached a very grave phase as part of their moves to stifle it." It left unsaid what cyber-attacks North Korea had evidently faced. Later that spring, several top websites—including the website of the South Korean president—were hit by DDoS attacks on the June anniversary of the start of the Korean War.[40]

In the summer of 2013, South Korean think tanks and other advocates of Korean reunification were also targeted by espionage malware that opened back doors in a user's system and attempted to steal user credentials. The attack came to be known as kimsuky, after the name one of the attackers used to register a Hotmail email account, and the malware was specially built to defeat the popular security software made by a South Korean company known as AhnLab. "It is not accidental that the malware author has singled out AhnLab's security product," researchers at Kaspersky security explained. "These attackers don't even bother evading foreign vendors' products, because their targets are solely South Korean."[41] The attacks appeared to emanate from IP addresses in the two Chinese provinces that border North Korea and were routed through a command-and-control server in Bulgaria.[42]

By the following summer, North Korea's cyber activities were showing special creativity: they infected nearly 20,000 South Korean cell phones with malware hidden inside free mobile games that allowed them to eavesdrop or activate video from the user's phone.[43] Games had long been part of their modus operandi. For years, North Korea had paid for its cyber activities in part by using automated tools to rack up points in the South Korean role-playing game *Lineage*, which they turned around and sold to other users.

That same summer of 2014, just months before the attack on Sony, North Korea had first tried to apply cyber pressure against someone embarrassing its leader. The North Korean government had vigorously complained to the UK government in August 2014—just weeks after the first trailer for *The Interview* had been released—because the UK TV broadcaster Channel Four had announced plans for a drama set in North Korea. The 10-episode show, *Opposite Number*, was to be written by Matt Charman, a rising screenwriter celebrated for his Tom Hanks drama *Bridge of Spies*. As the show's creators explained its plot, "On a covert mission in North Korea, the world's most secretive nation, a British nuclear scientist is taken prisoner, triggering an international crisis which itself must be kept secret. Realizing their man could be forced to help North Korea finally weaponize its nuclear technology, the British Prime Minister and the U.S. President, two leaders of very different political stripes, must work together and mobilize every level of their governments to pull the world back from the brink." Charman saw the show as a chance to "blow the lid off our understanding of who we think the North Korean people are and what their government truly wants."[44]

That was precisely what North Korea was afraid of—its government called the British series a "scandalous farce," but when their protests failed to halt production, hackers attacked Channel Four. The attack was discovered before any damage could be done, and Channel Four tentatively proceeded, but the Sony attack further chilled the broadcaster's ambitions. The series was dropped in the wake of the Sony attack after no other investors stepped forward to bankroll the series' development.[45]

As the attack on Sony unfolded, it was clear that North Korea had learned the lesson of those earlier 2013 attacks against the South Korean banks—and that perhaps Channel Four's quick action had prevented a previous catastrophic attack. A successful cyberattack could disrupt and paralyze a company from afar without ever firing any missiles, bombs, or artillery shells that might risk a dangerous military escalation.

////////////////

Sony, through its general counsel in New York, Nicole Seligman, had reached out to the FBI almost immediately, exactly as it should have. "She knew who to call," Lynton said. "That to me was one of the bigger lessons. When these things happen, you can't just pick up the phone and call the local police department." Nicole had worked in government herself and knew, when her company's reputation was on the line, the name of the right person to call inside government. Within hours, a 20-person FBI team was dispatched to Sony's office, arriving quietly to help the company's response. They remained on-site for more than two months.[46]

The Sony breach showed up in one of my morning threat briefings. I pulled our team into my office and asked how we could help respond. *Was this an incident where we could try to make a case?* As it happened, just weeks before the Sony hack, we had reorganized the office to install a new deputy assistant attorney general whose job was to focus on protecting "national assets," for example, the country's critical infrastructure.[47] The new role was responsible for overseeing the response to a cyber incident, serving as a point of contact for victim companies, and ensuring that we were bringing together all the intelligence and law enforcement resources we could. The new post and the division reorganization, announced in October 2014, seemed a long time coming. We had had to brief Capitol Hill on the proposed changes and get their blessing, and there had been tension inside the Justice Department itself that we were trying to steal more of cybersecurity away from other divisions; in the end, there was plenty of cybercrime to go around. As I told *Reuters* about the reorganization, "We need to develop the capability and bandwidth to deal with what we can see as an evolving threat."[48]

We selected Luke Dembosky, the experienced computer crimes prosecutor from Pittsburgh, to take over the new post. Luke had worked some of the biggest cybercrime cases of recent years, including the GameOver Zeus botnet case, and he'd helped coordinate the takedown of the crime forum Silk Road. Luke had also served as the Justice Department's attaché to the Moscow embassy, so he was intimately familiar with the challenges of cybercrime prosecutions; he'd spent two years negotiating with Putin's government an unprecedented accord aimed to de-escalate cyber tensions, establishing the cyber equivalent of the Moscow–Washington "hotline" used in nuclear emergencies. When the Sony hack happened, he was still so new to NSD that he'd only hung a single picture on his office wall. As he joked to me later, "The national asset program started off with a swift kick in the national assets."

Although an entertainment company that was about to release a buddy comedy movie wasn't exactly the "national assets" we had anticipated Luke would protect, we recognized almost immediately what the Sony Pictures case represented: a destructive foreign nation-state attack on a high-profile company inside the United States. This was, in many ways, what we had been building toward with our staffing and in our exercises, and what we had been predicting would inevitably arrive on our shores. We explained in crisis meetings and in calls to my counterparts at other intelligence agencies that, as unlikely a target as Sony was, we needed to treat the attack as a national security threat and move quickly both to help the victim get back up and running—that help is its own form of deterrence, underscoring to an attacker that they can't knock a company offline—and to figure out who did it in such a way that we could make that information public and impose a public consequence. The second goal was in my head from day one—it was crucially important that our reaction didn't just stay bottled up in the intel circles. To achieve it, we needed two things: clear agreement on who did the attack and a list of clear response options. The attack wasn't necessarily an act of war—and our response shouldn't treat it as such—but in the Code War, which is governed less by long-standing treaties and international law and more by norms created and refined in real time, we needed strong action.

<hr/>

As we raced to respond to the escalating and broadening attack on Sony, we realized the immaturity of the tools on which we relied in the cyber realm. Ever since she had arrived at the White House as homeland security advisor, Lisa had been working to codify the so-called bubble chart, delineating which agencies handled what in cyber. She had also at the National Security Council helped create a so-called Cyber Response Group, modeled on the NSC's Counterterrorism Security Group (CSG), a long-running, highly refined operational group used to respond to terrorism incidents. The CSG coordinated the government's reaction hour to hour and even, at times, minute to minute as an attack or would-be attack unfolded. But there had never been a similar body for cyber incidents. When the NSC weighed in on cyber, it generally was only in the slow-moving policy realm, helping to coordinate conversations across multiple agencies over months and even years. She recognized that we needed to have something similar, geared toward operational information, in cybersecurity. The Sony attack, as it turned out, would be the first time the CRG was put to the test.

In cybersecurity we also lacked another tool that we used regularly in counterterrorism—a "community-wide assessment" that pulled together evidence and analysis from across different agencies, both law enforcement and intelligence. In the years since 9/11, the government had actually built the National Counterterrorism Center (NCTC) for precisely that role—to speed information sharing and ensure cross-agency analysis of threats and unfolding incidents. NCTC was a massive complex in Northern Virginia with a central command post that resembled the set from the TV show 24, with FBI agents down one side, CIA officers and analysts down the other, as well as seats for dozens of other agencies. In counterterrorism you sometimes had competing groups claiming credit for the same attack—and the actual perpetrator might not claim credit at all. NCTC's collective assessments were key to establishing a common understanding of the facts of a situation, thus allowing government decision makers to state publicly that such-and-such group conducted such-and-such attack. Given the life-or-death decisions that arose from terrorist attacks—do we launch a military strike in response? do we launch a rescue mission to free hostages?—it was critical that the policymakers around the table had clear information about who believed what.

None of that process existed in cybersecurity—which caused some bumps in the road in the original NSC meetings about the Sony attack because agencies offered slightly different assessments. Attribution in cyber has been a combination of technical analysis and what we called "all-source" intelligence, that is, all the noncyber streams of information that the government was collecting through open-source reporting (what a foreign country might be saying publicly) as well as through more covert means such as human sources (human intelligence or HUMINT) and intercepted communications (signals intelligence or SIGINT). The process actually was quite similar to how an investigator and prosecutor build a normal criminal case, but we hadn't always applied that "all-source" method well to cybersecurity; particularly in the early days, some FBI cyber experts could be too technically focused, ignoring the broader portrait that needed to be created.

Frustrated by the conflicting theories, Lisa Monaco at the White House asked Michael Daniel, the cybersecurity coordinator at the NSC, for an official assessment she could present to the president. "I had gotten used to that after a terrorist attack, the next morning in my [threat briefing] binder, there would be a document laying out the assessment of who was responsible," she says. She wanted the same thing for cyberattacks.

Daniel cautioned that there was no mechanism for producing the assessment Lisa wanted, but he said he'd ask the National Intelligence Council, a coordinating body, for help. They responded that they could produce such an assessment within 45 days. "I lost my mind," Lisa recalls. There was no way we could wait 45 days; Lisa, instead, asked the FBI to coordinate with other intelligence agencies on an assessment that could be presented to the president in his daily brief. That, though, didn't happen overnight—it took about a week for the assessment to be ready.*

Lisa was pushing hard for faster action. It helped that many of the people at the table had already been through some of this with the Chinese PLA case—we had overcome much of the initial reluctance with that first-of-its-kind case and had a playbook and even some institutional "muscle memory," as Lisa called it, of the steps that needed to be taken to make information public. The challenge, though, was that the PLA case had taken a long time—years, in fact—to work through institutional objections and refine evidence for public display. We didn't have that kind of time in the Sony case. While not every other agency

---

*Later, Lisa used the Sony attack to work the internal levers at the White House to get language into the 2015 State of the Union address calling to formalize this process. That effort resulted in February 2015 in the announcement of the cyber equivalent of NCTC, a body known as the Cyber Threat Intelligence Integration Center (CTIIC). "That presidential language meant we would have to deliver on it, and the interagency would have to put their turf wars aside," Lisa recalls. "It made my job leading the discussions and development of CTIIC slightly easier."

agreed, we at the FBI and the Justice Department pushed for fast, public action.

We realized we needed to get in a pretty quick cadence—I was in regular contact with the FBI deputy director, Mark F. Giuliano, and the NSA's deputy director, Richard Ledgett. All three of us agreed that the United States needed to be much more aggressive. The attack on Sony was the first of its kind, but we knew there would be more. And we needed to be ready faster the next time. "We need to develop the same muscle memory in the government response to cyberthreats as we have for terrorist incidents," Lisa said later in a speech at the Wilson Center two months after the Sony attack.[49]

As agencies across the government examined their respective evidence and the attack unfolded, it didn't take the FBI and the broader intelligence community long to zero in on the perpetrator. As the evidence accumulated, the list of suspects began and ended with North Korea. Because of the Channel Four incident earlier that summer—an incident that was not publicly known at the time but was familiar to us in the intelligence community—we were already aware North Korea appeared to be actively defending its leader's public image online. Each additional piece of evidence only reinforced that hypothesis, from the technical methods the attackers used to the "staging" of the attacks to the absence of anyone else with a convincing motive to hurt Sony.

First, there were the hackers' own statements and actions. To help analyze those, the FBI enlisted a unit that had never been deployed on cyber cases before: the elite Behavioral Analysis Unit at Quantico, best known as the "profilers" behind tracking serial killers and pop culture references like *The Silence of the Lambs*. The FBI's National Center for the Analysis of Violent Crime contains several Behavioral Analysis Units that assist law enforcement with criminal investigative analysis for a wide range of offenses—from counterterrorism to bombings to white-collar crime. In 2012, the FBI had created the Cyber Behavioral Analysis Center (CBAC), which expanded the work to include cyberthreats. By analyzing the behavioral patterns of malicious cyber actors—from the kind of malware they use to the way they communicate with victims to the way that hackers "stage" a scene—the CBAC profilers use the traditional skills of law enforcement to help attribute malicious activity online.

It was a familiar concept to those of us who had investigated street crimes: any evidence left behind that wasn't critical to the execution of the crime represented a message that the criminal wanted to send to the viewer of the crime scene. The behavioral analysts knew that when they found extra information like this, those clues could be helpful in attributing the activity. For instance, in addition to the data-deletion malware, the Sony hackers left a "splash screen" on infected Sony computers with the name Guardians of Peace and various logos. The analysts went over the images and the lines of the malware's source code to figure out what messages were hidden inside. As Comey explained later, "We compared it to other attacks that we know the North Koreans have done and they say, 'Easy for us. It's the same actors.'"[50]

The second category of evidence was related to the technical fingerprints of the hackers—the malware deployed against Sony appeared to have been built in the Korean language and it notably overlapped technically with the March 2013 attack we'd seen against South Korea's banking and journalism targets. "The tools in the Sony attacks bore striking similarities," Comey said later.[51] As government and private sector engineers dissected the malware, they found that it was a wiper, designed to carefully target Sony's networks and then systematically delete everything it found. The malware files, which US-CERT said were generally labeled *usbdrv3_32bit.sys* and *usbdrv3_64bit.sys*, talked back to command-and-control servers located in Italy, Thailand, and Poland. The malware showed how carefully the hackers had mapped Sony's network before the attack launched: the tool made sure that it was on one of about 50 specific Sony systems, located in either the United States and Britain, before activating, and then relied on compromised user accounts to access the system.[52] As one security expert told *Wired*, the malware "contains a user name and password and a list of internal systems and it connects to each of them and wipes the hard drives [and deletes the master boot record]."[53] By "phoning home" to the command-and-control servers, the malware was able to help the attackers carefully compile a list of the servers and computers they destroyed, each indicated by an IP address.

Third, the intelligence community carefully "scrubbed" other potential motives and possible offenders, taking each piece of evidence and analyzing alternatives other than North Korea. The tactic, known as a "red team analysis," was common in military and intelligence cases, but it was relatively rare to see it deployed in a criminal case. As Comey recalled, "We brought in a red team from all across the intelligence community and said, 'Let's hack at this. What else could be explaining this? What other explanations might there be? What might we be missing? What competing hypothesis might there be? Evaluate possible alternatives. What might we be missing?' And we end up in the same place."

Fourth, and most convincingly, there was the additional digital evidence. For most of their operations, the Guardians of Peace dispatched their threats and statements hidden behind proxy servers that disguised where they were based. "But several times they got sloppy," Comey said later. "Several times, either because they forgot or because they had a technical problem, they connected directly and we could see them. And we could see that the IP addresses that were being used to post and to send the emails were coming from IPs that were exclusively used by the North Koreans."

By the time all the evidence was assembled, there was no doubt the attack stemmed from North Korea. "There is not much in this life that I have high confidence about. I have very high confidence about this attribution, as does the entire intelligence community," James Comey said weeks later, in his only public comments on the attack.

That particular phrase, "high confidence," may have seemed to those outside government to be simply reassuring, but Comey meant for it to be understood as a technical definition that was used by the intelligence community—a term that meant even more than the public realized. The "confidence" level of the government's attribution of the attack to North Korea had been precisely what had been driving Lisa

Monaco crazy inside the White House Situation Room: *What exactly did the intelligence community believe?*

The labeling of the relative "confidence" of analytic estimates had become a major focus of the intelligence world in the previous decade; since intelligence analysis is part art, part science, there was always some measure of uncertainty in the conclusions presented to decision makers. Since the 1960s, the US intelligence community had struggled with how to express their analytic uncertainty in preparing reports for decision makers like the president.[54] There had been a long-running debate between the "poets," who emphasized the art in analysis, and the "mathematicians," who desired precision and probability.[55] The debate reached new urgency and importance in the years following the Iraq War, as the CIA struggled to understand the catastrophic misdiagnosis that Saddam Hussein's regime had been actively developing weapons of mass destruction.

Ever since, the intelligence community had begun to put great emphasis on presenting the "confidence" of its assessments—attempting to capture the relative uncertainty of one conclusion versus another—when it made a report. As onetime CIA Acting Director Michael Morell explained, "It turns out that the real mistake in the Iraq war was not the judgment that they came to, but the fact that if they had really thought about it, the analysts would have only said that they only had low confidence in that judgment that Saddam had weapons of mass destruction. That would have been a completely different message, right?"[56]

As Morell said, "The lesson learned from Iraq was to really focus on your level of confidence in the judgment you're making. 'Not only do I think it's going to rain tomorrow, but I have high confidence in that,' or 'It's going to rain tomorrow but you guys have to know that I only have low confidence in that.'"

Today, when the intelligence community makes an assessment, it adds one of three caveats to a conclusion explaining how much analysts trust their own decisions. A "low confidence" assessment means that "the information's credibility and/or plausibility is questionable, or that the information is too fragmented or poorly corroborated to make solid an-alytic inferences, or that we have significant concerns or problems with the sources." A "moderate confidence" reflects that "the information is credibly sourced and plausible but not of sufficient quality or corrobo-rated sufficiently to warrant a higher level of confidence." Finally, a "high confidence" indicates that the analysts' "judgments are based on high-quality information, and/or that the nature of the issue makes it possible to render a solid judgment."[57]

It wasn't initially clear whether the government should react or not. Normally, in NSC meetings, we went around the table and each person or agency using their expertise went through a list explaining, "OK, under my legal authorities, here are the things that I think we could do in response." Depending on the topic, the Justice Department might list prosecutorial actions, the military might explain "kinetic" options for a response, the State Department might explain possible diplomatic options, and the Treasury Department might talk about possible sanctions. It was clear as the NSC meeting on the Sony hack proceeded that we just didn't have that many ready-to-apply options in the cyber realm, nor the pace to do so quickly, as we did with terror-ism. These facts weren't exactly news to me—we'd already spotted the response gap and it was partly why we were already doing our division reorganization—but it did catch other agencies off guard. We talked about a wide set of options—some of which remain classified today—but we were also shocked at how few tools the United States truly pos-sessed under these circumstances.

The response scenarios also presented a clash of two worlds; there was a lot of frustration as decision makers asked, *If we were going to try to disrupt the attack, what would that look like?* The response back from those more technically minded around the table sounded like gobble-dygook, as they listed various IP addresses, tools, and what sounded like a choose-your-own-adventure cyber story—*this tool could work like this, that tool could work like this or that.* The policy people instantly lost the conversation's thread. They were used to concrete options they understood—*bomb this target, sanction this company, charge that person.* Cyber offered none of that certainty and, for a policy person who didn't know their bits from their bytes, none of the options translated into English.

Some government leaders wondered if we could simply block North Korea's attack on Sony; Lisa Monaco and Rick Ledgett, the deputy director of the NSA, both knew that was impossible. Ledgett demurred, and then Lisa, picking up the still-sore feelings in government about the Snowden leaks, joked, "Unlike what everyone thinks, the government is not actually sitting atop the whole internet."

///////////////

The same day, December 8, that the hackers made their demand clear—linking the attack definitively to North Korea and *The Interview*—they made the corporate hack personal: the Guardians of Peace dropped more than 5,000 of Amy Pascal's Outlook emails online, exposing her life's most intimate details. In addition to everything positive or negative Pascal had ever said privately about friends, colleagues, actors, and other Hollywood players, the Guardians of Peace leak included her life's mundane secrets. The website Gawker pawed through the exposed emails to compile a list of all of Amy Pascal's Amazon purchases. It was every employee's worst nightmare. The media hemmed and hawed about whether to report on the salacious details, and many did.

The leaked emails and the escalating attacks left Sony isolated. Hollywood—and corporate America writ large—wasn't sure how to respond. George Clooney tried to circulate a petition supporting Sony, saying that the movie industry wouldn't be cowed by the attack. But the truth was, Hollywood was cowed. Whereas the financial industry had banded together in the face of the Iranian DDoS attacks, Hollywood splintered.

Clooney's petition of solidarity met nothing but crickets—no other studio head, agents, or industry executives publicly rose to stand with Sony.[58] Clooney, with his Hollywood agent Bryan Lourd, wrote, "This is not just an attack on Sony. It involves every studio, every network, every business and every individual in this country.... We know that to give in to these criminals now will open the door for any group that would threaten freedom of expression, privacy and personal liberty." But no one would stand with Sony, Pascal, or Lynton. Clooney said it was a reflection of how afraid the other studios and executives were that they might be next.

Separately, Aaron Sorkin, the writer behind *The West Wing* and *The Social Network*, rose to Sony's defense, writing a December 14 op-ed for the *New York Times* arguing that the media was doing the hackers' work for them, punishing and undermining Sony and its executives through its race to publish the most embarrassing documents the press could find. These were not typical whistle-blower leaks, Sorkin said, as there was no sign—or even hint—in Sony's leaked documents of criminality, wrongdoing, or claims that publishing the leaks was anything more than tawdry gossip. Instead, the hackers had managed to weaponize embarrassment. As the piece, titled "The Sony Hack and the Yellow Press," said, "The Guardians just had to lob the ball; they knew our media would crash the boards and slam it in."[59] Reading his op-ed, we agreed with almost every word. We couldn't believe how Sony had been left to dangle on its own. We were making the same arguments inside briefing rooms up and down Pennsylvania Avenue: America needed to come together to defend its values.

Most inside the Situation Room agreed, including President Obama. He was very conscious that others were watching our response; North Korea was a uniquely difficult actor on the world stage to deter or influence, but we knew other countries were carefully monitoring the situation, too. North Korea couldn't be allowed to be seen to succeed.

Yet the Sony incident was about to get even stranger—and more serious.

❦

On December 16, the Sony incident began to take on a new dimension—one more like terrorism than a cyberattack by a nation-state. Sony, which had been proceeding with plans to release *The Interview*, received another email. The Guardians of Peace announced, "Warning /

We will clearly show it to you at the very time and places *The Interview* be shown, including the premiere, how bitter fate those who seek fun in terror should be doomed to. / Soon all the world will see what an awful movie Sony Pictures Entertainment has made. / The world will be full of fear. / Remember the 11th of September 2001. / We recommend you to keep yourself distant from the places at that time. (If your house is nearby, you'd better leave.) / Whatever comes in the coming days is called by the greed of Sony Pictures Entertainment. / All the world will denounce the SONY."[60]

The warning sent fear cascading across the industry. Interviewers canceled publicity events booked for the cast and directors. Movie theaters across the country backed out of showing the comedy—starting with the theater in New York meant to host the premiere. The nation's five largest theater chains all announced they wouldn't air the film—it was, for them, strictly a business decision. The holiday movie season remains one of the most important times of the year; the chains feared families would avoid seeing even noncontroversial films if they thought terrorists might attack the local cineplex.

Even as the intelligence community and the Department of Homeland Security believed there was no "credible" plot to attack moviegoers, it took just a day before Sony realized it had lost the battle. On December 17, Sony announced, "In light of the decision by the majority of our exhibitors not to show the film *The Interview,* we have decided not to move forward with the planned December 25 theatrical release."[61]

The studio, though, tried to stand its ground: "Sony Pictures has been the victim of an unprecedented criminal assault against our employees, our customers, and our business. Those who attacked us stole our intellectual property, private emails, and sensitive and proprietary material, and sought to destroy our spirit and our morale—all apparently to thwart the release of a movie they did not like. We are deeply saddened at this brazen effort to suppress the distribution of a movie, and in the process do damage to our company, our employees, and the American public. We stand by our filmmakers and their right to free expression and are extremely disappointed by this outcome."[62]

Without firing a single shot, a foreign country had singled out a major motion picture that they found objectionable and had derailed its release inside the United States.

Even as so much of Hollywood had refused to stand with Sony, the company was broadly denounced after it pulled the movie. Hollywood stars like Judd Apatow and Jimmy Kimmel blasted Sony and North Korea; Kimmel wrote on Twitter, "An un-American act of cowardice that validates terrorist actions and sets a terrifying precedent." Actor Rob Lowe said, "Wow. Everyone caved. The hackers won. An utter and complete victory for them. Wow."[63] But in the moment Sony felt it had little alternative—the criticism that Sony had "chickened out" was at a certain level a misunderstanding of how the movie industry works. They needed a distributor to get the movie to the public—and none of the traditional ones were willing to shoulder that risk.

Though no one knew it publicly at the time, Sony's Michael Lynton began trying an alternative way to still get the movie out, and we quickly began our own series of telephone calls to encourage some alternative distribution. With help and support behind the scenes from the FBI and the White House, Sony ultimately changed tack, announcing that it would release *The Interview* on Christmas Eve, as originally scheduled, through 330 independent movie theaters as well as unprecedented new online channels—including Google, YouTube, and a custom website, seetheinterview.com.

The transformation of the cyber incident to a potential counterterrorism issue helped drive a new sense of urgency inside government, instantly clarifying our internal ambiguity: *Was this a national security issue?* We knew now that we had to make a public response. The threat also helped clarify another long-running internal government cyber debate: *How much help do you give a victim?* Providing aid raised a complicated moral-hazard question—if you think you're going to be compensated and made whole every time a thief breaks into your car, what's the incentive to lock your doors? We always tried to balance the need to step in and aid a victim after an attack with encouraging companies to do their own smart defensive work.

I didn't want to get bogged down in the philosophy—we didn't have time. The attack was still unfolding day by day, and we needed to plot a response. For those of us pushing action, we were helped because the White House wanted everything wrapped up by December 19: the president was leaving for Hawaii for his annual Christmas vacation, and he traditionally held a rare, expansive press conference before departing. If he was going to address the Sony hack and condemn the attacks, we needed to be ready with the attribution. Luckily, thanks to the PLA case, we'd already worked through many of the thorny questions about how to make public what the government knew about a particular hack—and, reassuringly, the sky hadn't fallen when we'd released details before. Absent the PLA case, we never would have been able to meet such a tight deadline for intelligence.

///////////////////

On December 19, the FBI announced in a nine-paragraph statement that North Korea was responsible for the Sony hack. "As a result of our investigation, and in close collaboration with other U.S. government departments and agencies, the FBI now has enough information to conclude that the North Korean government is responsible for these actions," it said.[64] While we supported going public, I originally resisted using the FBI as the vehicle to make that attribution; I thought it should come from the Office of the Director of National Intelligence, reflecting the consensus of the country's intelligence professionals. Inside the FBI, too, there had been some reluctance about such a public statement; it was highly unusual and a big decision for the FBI to go public without a criminal charge and indictment, one they were confident they could back up in a court of law. Many bureau leaders—trained in the criminal burden of proof of "beyond a reasonable doubt"—felt uncomfortable with the lower burdens acceptable in the intelligence world. Yet Mark Giuliano, the FBI's deputy director, felt strongly it should be the bureau telling the world: Americans were used to the FBI as the voice in a crisis. In hindsight, he was right.

Later that same day, Barack Obama, speaking at his traditional year-end press conference, spoke at length about the hack, Sony's response, and the studio's decision to pull the film. He tried to draw a firm line against North Korea's assault on American values. "Sony is a corporation. It suffered significant damage. There were threats against its employees. I am sympathetic to the concerns that they faced. Having said all that, yes, I think they made a mistake," he said.[65] "We cannot have a society in which some dictator someplace can start imposing censorship here in the United States. Because if somebody is able to intimidate folks out of releasing a satirical movie, imagine what they start doing when they see a documentary that they don't like, or news reports that they don't like. Or even worse, imagine if producers and distributors and others start engaging in self-censorship because they don't want to offend the sensibilities of somebody whose sensibilities probably need to be offended."

Cyberassaults, Obama said, were going to continue—and to be increasingly the norm. The government needed to get better at working with the private sector, to get better at hardening sites, and so on. As Obama said, when it came to cybersecurity, "We're not even close to where we need to be."

In comments to CNN later that week, President Obama stopped short of calling the attack an "act of war." Instead, he said, "I think it was an act of cybervandalism that was very costly, very expensive.... We take it very seriously and we will respond proportionally."[66] Obama's attempt to define what North Korea had done made clear how much everyone involved in cybersecurity continued to struggle to delineate how virtual attacks translated into the traditional world of geopolitics. In part, we had made the situation more confusing behind the scenes: lawyers had cautioned that the president calling it an "act of war" would likely trigger certain provisions in Sony's insurance policies, meaning that there were significant financial implications for even casually using the phrase.

General Michael Hayden, the former head of the CIA and the NSA, recalls how frustrated he was by the president's comments that day—he says he heard Barack Obama's reference to "cybervandalism" and angrily got out of his chair at home. *This was a foreign nation-state's attack on a US company on US soil.* "It's not cybervandalism, it's cyber-...." Hayden started to exclaim. He recalls that he wasn't able to finish the sentence. *Was it war? Was it a crime?* Years later, he says, he was still not able to finish that sentence to his satisfaction—a testament to how limited our traditional vocabulary is as we find ourselves in this Code War. I'm not sure I have a better end to his sentence either; we called it a "national security event," but that was an equally imperfect phrase. The Code War challenged many of our traditional definitions of conflict.

Regardless of the nomenclature, though, Sony saw an immediate benefit to the public declaration of North Korea's involvement; it shifted the public questions and narrative about the attack from mocking Sony to—rightfully—focusing on how the government planned to respond to a nation-state attack. It became another example to us of how important it was for government to take these attacks out of the shadows and to directly—and quickly—confront foreign adversaries when they sought to harm us. The public appreciated it, and the targets appreciated it.

/////////////

In its limited release, *The Interview* grossed $6.1 million theatrically and about $40 million digitally—it was viewed more than 2 million times in the first few days of release and became the best-selling digital movie ever, but it was hard to view the movie as a triumph. The movie was a loss even before Sony calculated in the additional $40 million it spent in response to the attack.[67] However, the company bounced back strong: Sony's stock price was actually up two months after the attack.

North Korea's hacking efforts, meanwhile, continued apace: even while we were consumed by the attacks on Sony, that December hackers also launched a phishing attack and stole documents from Korea Hydro and Nuclear Power Co Ltd, the company responsible for South Korea's 23 nuclear reactors. Stolen files were also posted online. "The malicious codes used for the nuclear operator hacking were the same in composition and working methods as the so-called 'kimsuky' that North Korean hackers use," Seoul's central prosecutor said.[68]

At his year-end press conference, President Obama had promised, "They caused a lot of damage [in the Sony attack], and we will respond. We will respond proportionally, and we'll respond in a place and time and manner that we choose. It's not something that I will announce here today at a press conference." He explained that behind the scenes, we had been working up a "range of options," but was purposely vague about what those might be. Just days later, it appeared to the public that the United States was hitting back: North Korea's small portal to the wider internet came under a sustained assault from a denial-of-service attack. "For the past 24 hours North Korea's connectivity to the outside world has been progressively getting degraded to the point now that they are totally offline," Doug Madory, the director of internet analysis at Dyn Research, told *Reuters* on December 22.[69]

US officials played coy for a few days; the State Department's spokeswoman, Marie Harf, said, "We aren't going to discuss publicly operational details about the possible response options," and added that as the United States implemented its response to North Korea, "some will be seen, some may not be seen." But we knew inside government it wasn't us. Hacker vigilantes online had come together to launch their own attack against North Korea—itself a new wrinkle in the evolving world of cyberdoctrines, as we watched a non-nation-state actor retaliate against a nation-state for its attack on an unrelated private sector company.[70]

The government's main formal and public response came on January 2, when we levied economic sanctions against the RGB, as well as two North Korean companies—the Korea Tangun Trading Corporation and the Korea Mining Development Trading Corporation—that helped facilitate its illegal weapons program.[71] The sanctions also named 10 of the country's leaders, including Kim Yong-chol, the head of the RGB.[72]

In working through the process for those sanctions, government leaders realized that on one level, we were lucky we'd been attacked by North Korea. Under President George W. Bush's Executive Order

13382, which is used to sanction those who proliferate weapons of mass destruction and their supporters, we could take action against the regime—but if it had been another country, one not involved in WMD proliferation, we might have been out of luck. Unlike terrorist or nuclear proliferators, there was no executive order covering cyber activity. That gap had been evident to some of us who worked on the issue regularly, and we'd been trying to push forward changes, only to see the changes gnawed to death at low levels of government. As Lisa says, "Sony made clear we needed to yank all that stuff up and put it into high gear."

It was all part of coming up with workable "cyber deterrence," which was increasingly a topic of concern inside government. As Director of National Intelligence James Clapper put it, "Cyber is a powerful new realm for [North Korea], where they believe they can exert maximum influence at minimum cost, and this recent episode with Sony has shown that they can get recognition for their cyber capabilities."

Days after the sanctions were announced, NSA Director Mike Rogers spoke at a conference about how much work was needed in cybersecurity. As he said, "We've got to get to an idea of deterrence, because when I look around the world right now, my conclusion is that nation-states, groups and individuals seem to have come in large measure to the conclusion that there is little price to pay when engaging in these behaviors that are leading to among the greatest transfers of intellectual property and knowledge we have ever seen, the outright destructive activity we've seen in the Sony issue, for example. Those are all bad trends for us."[73]

The Sony hack accelerated the push to tackle cybersecurity both inside government and inside the private sector—exposing the potential damage, both physical and reputational, of a sophisticated attack. Yet even as the government began to implement some of the lessons it learned in responding to North Korea's attack, an even bigger attack was unfolding right under our noses.

CHAPTER 8

Black Vine

THE SONY HACK launched months of fevered efforts to implement lessons across government, including the creation of the Cyber Threat Intelligence Integration Center to ensure that the White House could get quick assessments of future attacks. In the private sector, companies took the threat seriously, too. We hosted a meeting of the general counsels of the top entertainment companies to talk about how they could work together on cybersecurity and in responding to a future attack. "I think the Sony hack and response did more to raise national security cyber awareness than any other single event," I observed in an interview later. "The lessons learned from Sony have changed board practices across the country as companies examine whether they are ready to respond in a world where every company in every sector is vulnerable in a way they have not been before."[1]

On April 1, 2015, President Obama signed a landmark step forward in the nation's cyber realm, outlining sanctions the country could impose against nations engaged in nefarious cyber activities—a move meant to ensure that if the next cyberattack came from a country other than North Korea, we could respond quickly.[2] Blandly known as Executive Order 13694, "Blocking the Property of Certain Persons Engaging in Significant Malicious Cyber-Enabled Activities," the order authorized the use of sanctions against individuals and entities that the United States determined were "responsible for or complicit in malicious cyber-enabled activities that are reasonably likely to result in, or have materially contributed to, a significant threat to the national security, foreign policy, economic health, or financial stability of the United States."[3]

In layman's terms, it meant we could start punishing China, Iran, and Russia for their activity in cyberspace.[4] We had been building up numerous cases where such sanctions could be applied, and we immediately began to push for the new powers to be used. It took more than a year and a half, though, before the government first utilized the powers—long enough that doubters began to refer to it as the "April Fool's order."*

China particularly began to understand that its behavior had to change. We saw an almost immediate shift in its online activity after we brought the PLA case. With its hacking made public, China cut back on its economic-focused espionage. "Since mid-2014, we have seen a notable decline in China-based groups' overall intrusion activity against entities in the U.S. and 25 other countries. We suspect that this shift in operations reflects the influence of ongoing military reforms, widespread exposure of Chinese cyber operations, and actions taken by the U.S. government," the cybersecurity firm FireEye concluded in one report.[5]

In December 2014, even as inside government we were struggling to respond to the Sony attack, China's head internet official, Lu Wei, had come to the United States. During his visit, he had received a personal tour from Mark Zuckerberg of Facebook's headquarters and had met with Jeff Bezos and Tim Cook—meetings that publicly had them all smiling, given the business opportunity Lu, the gatekeeper to the Chinese internet, offered. But he also had tense meetings in Washington with officials from the National Security Council.[6] In a public address at George Washington University, Lu offered that he felt China and the United States had become "one community of common interest" when it came to internet policy and that they should follow "common rules."

---

*Unfortunately, as it would turn out, the executive order had a hole in it. It was aimed at protecting attacks against critical infrastructure—and, just as we'd never considered a movie company critical infrastructure before, the first time Obama's executive order was used, it had to be amended to include a new area of attack: our country's elections.

Lu Wei was both the Chinese internet's main champion and its main censor. During a 2015 Lunar New Year festival, he had helped orchestrate a bizarre celebration of the "Cyberspace Spirit," where his employees at the Cyberspace Administration of China sang about the internet as "a beam of incorruptible sunlight, touching our hearts. Uniting the powers of life from all creation," and proclaimed that China was an "internet power—tell the world that the Chinese dream is uplifting China."[7]

Yet even as Lu Wei toured the United States, China was engaged in its most critical theft yet.[8]*

////////////////

In a sign of where the cybersecurity debate was heading, President Obama journeyed to the Federal Trade Commission, a couple of doors down Pennsylvania Avenue from Main Justice, to preview his cyber agenda in January 2015 and talk about an increasingly central issue: protecting the identities and privacy of the American people. By 2015, almost every month seemed to bring some data breach of once-unthinkable size. Americans became used to getting new credit cards in the mail after one retailer or another had seen their system compromised. Social Security numbers, which had never been intended to be a public identifier, had become the default for too many companies to identify individuals in arm's-length transactions, such as applying for a credit card over the phone.

"If we're going to be connected, then we need to be protected," Obama told the gathered FTC employees. He called for the passage of the Consumer Privacy Bill of Rights, as well as a single, national standard on when to tell Americans that their personal data had been stolen. Versions of that legislation had been a long-standing push inside government; I'd worked on similar efforts in the Bush administration, too. As President Obama said, "Under the new standard that we're proposing, companies would have to notify consumers of a breach within 30 days. In addition, we're proposing to close loopholes in the law

---

* Lu Wei was expelled from the Communist Party and charged with corruption in 2018.

so we can go after more criminals who steal and sell the identities of Americans—even when they do it overseas."

By that point, identity theft had risen to the top of the list of the consumer complaints fielded by the FTC—including 332,000 in 2014 alone, representing almost one in seven complaints from American consumers.[9] It was part of a major shift in crime overall; as the nonprofit Police Executive Research Forum later explained, the old measures of "crime" weren't necessarily capturing the reality of the 21st century. While street crimes and violent crimes were hitting generation lows— my hometown of New York City had seen an almost 90 percent reduction in crime since the days of my childhood—those measurements, such as stolen automobiles, burglaries, and muggings, failed to capture an increasingly frustrating epidemic of small-dollar online crimes.

The age of epic database breaches arrived in 2007, when TJ Maxx reported more than 94 million accounts had been stolen by hackers.[10] The hack occurred during my early stint working on the Justice Department's computer hacking program, and served as a wake-up call to everyone in the field about the dangers of generating massive databases as part of normal business practices. It took the retailer months to unravel the theft; eventually they realized that it had been ongoing from July 2005 to January 2007.[11] The breach involved about 65 million Visa cards and 29 million Mastercards; Visa alone reported over $80 million in fraud losses.

The TJ Maxx case marked an important turning point for the government: whereas in early credit card breaches, the Justice Department had supported keeping the business's identity private, to protect against its customers losing faith after a breach, in this case the Justice Department argued that TJ Maxx's name should be public.* The government had determined that the very public sunshine of an embarrassing breach might help encourage companies to invest up front in better security. "Most people want to know when their credit or debit card numbers may have been put at risk, not simply if, and after, they have clearly been stolen," the Justice Department argued. "Knowing

---

* Many states had similarly passed data breach notification requirements.

that card holders will be concerned whenever their credit or debit card information is put at risk, if they know of it, provides an incentive to companies to invest in the protections their customers would want. Transparency makes the market work in this area."[12] The TJ Maxx case was a tough call; I was never sure which incentive worked better—did our response to it encourage or discourage other companies to come forward?

Nevertheless, the tidal wave of massive breaches had arrived; each passing year brought even more. Over the holiday season in 2013, Target saw more than 100 million credit cards stolen—a breach that cost its CIO and CEO their jobs.[13] The following year Home Depot saw 56 million accounts compromised.

Even as many companies built massive databases on customers and potential customers, too many companies still didn't realize how exposed that data truly was. The warning letters companies sent to customers after a breach became a routine part of American life. As Steven Chabinsky joked, "Speaking to some people who get these notices in the mail saying, 'We've suffered a data breach; your personal, identifiable information is available to who knows whom, and we'll pay for credit monitoring,' what's happening is there's really diminishing cost to the companies to send out those letters because the recipient already got the credit monitoring three letters ago from someone else."[14]

I spent countless hours talking to private companies about strengthening their internal security—meeting with CEOs, CIOs, and general counsels about locking away their customer databases, about only retaining the minimal necessary amount of data, and so forth. When speaking to the private sector, I had my patter down and the presentations were all but rote to me. Then we received a reminder of why it's always good to be humble: as it turned out, the government itself hadn't thought smartly enough about its own data. We were about to confront two of the lessons I repeated ad nauseam to the private sector: first, while it was critical that organizations partook of the basic "blocking and tackling" of cybersecurity, there was no internet connected system that was secure from a dedicated, persistent adversary, and, second, if you accepted that, then you needed to be practiced in incident response—ready for the day when your system was inevitably breached.

///////////////

The Chinese, as it turned out, were thinking creatively about how digitization of our daily lives transformed the internet into a rich trove for traditional espionage, too. On January 26, 2015, a systems administrator for the health care company Anthem noticed that his computer account had repeatedly queried an internal database—except he knew that he'd never done so. *Someone was inside the system.* Alarms went off and Anthem promptly called the FBI for help. The potential exposure was monumental: Anthem was hardly a household name in the United States, but it had grown since the 1940s from a small Indiana mutual company to the second-largest health insurer in the United States, the backbone of well-known insurance products such as Blue Cross Blue Shield.

The company—like so many others in the previous decade—had already struggled with data breaches: in 2009 and 2010, a routine upgrade of the web portal that the company used to let customers track their applications for health coverage left the data of more than 200,000 customers freely exposed online. As it turned out, the web URLs generated by the portal could be easily changed to bring up the applications of other customers. At the time, the company had explained the security hole as stemming from a third-party vendor and said that the customers' confidential information had primarily been accessed only by attorneys seeking to launch a class action lawsuit against the company.[15] Despite the uniquely sensitive information health and medical companies possessed on their customers—and even as more and more health care companies became targets—the industry sector struggled to adapt to the new digital environment. It was endemic of many sectors we saw that had been pushed to convert to digital; technology was outside the sectors' core competencies and the government had not yet made clear the risks.[16] Customers, though, clearly understood the stakes: "There's not one place that has more information on you than your health insurer," one customer said. "It's the absolutely most personal level of information all the way down to Social Security numbers. That would be about the last place I would want someone to gain access."

The breach discovered in January 2015 proved to be unprecedented. Even though the Anthem breach didn't involve any medical data itself, it included nearly all other personal details of 78 million people: names, emails, addresses, Social Security numbers, birthdays, even employment information and household income data. At the time, the Anthem news stunned the industry. "This is one of the worst breaches I have ever seen," Paul Stephens, a privacy rights advocate told the *New York Times*. "These [hackers] knew what they were doing and recognized there was a treasure trove here."[17]

The attack on Anthem exploited a relatively basic security hole: Anthem did not encrypt its customer database. This lack of encryption was common. Many companies built extensive firewalls and network protections, but left their own data unencrypted once someone was inside the system. It was the equivalent of a bank locking the front door but leaving the vault inside unlocked. Security in the physical world reflected a layered approach, and yet in the digital world companies often only erected an outer wall. While the government required companies to encrypt data while it was "in transit" to protect against interception or eavesdropping, federal data laws and guidelines, under the Health Insurance Portability and Accountability Act (HIPAA), didn't at that time require companies to encrypt "data at rest." The guidelines only said it was advisable if a health insurer believed it was "reasonable and appropriate," but left that interpretation up to the company—and many companies avoided encryption because of the complexity it added for daily users.[18] At the Justice Department, we had long encouraged companies to encrypt sensitive data. Such protections could make a big difference: in the JPMorgan Chase breach in 2014, the 83 million people whose records had been compromised only had nonfinancial information stolen, basics such as names and addresses, which in and of themselves aren't all that useful to a hacker. The bank had done a good job protecting its innermost secrets, storing them separately, to foil just that kind of attack.

Anthem later settled a class action lawsuit with affected customers; the company agreed to pay just $115 million, about $1.43 per affected customer. The company was careful to state in announcing the settlement, "Anthem does not admit any wrongdoing or acknowledge that any individuals were harmed as a result of the cyber attack."* But those monitoring the "dark web" where hackers trade stolen information noticed something strange about the Anthem theft: the data, once taken, never appeared online. Even to this day, security experts note that the data has never popped up for sale on hacker forums, nor have there been identity fraud cases linked to the theft, nor any of the other common signs that a breach represented the work of a criminal organization. Quite the opposite: someone stole one of the wealthiest troves of data ever and, apparently, never tried to use it publicly. That was notable because health records were normally considered quite profitable for hackers: a full health record could fetch $40 or $50 on a hacking forum—meaning the value of the Anthem database, sold piecemeal, was over $3 billion.[19] That was an enormous amount of ill-gotten money for a hacker to sit on—unless they weren't criminals and they were after something they considered even more valuable.

Indeed, private sector research traced the hack and data breach back to a group known publicly by a variety of monikers—Black Vine, Deep Panda, or Group 13—which, as the FBI said euphemistically, "emanated from infrastructure located within China." As the FBI explained, while "stolen [personally identifiable information] has been used in other instances to target or otherwise facilitate various malicious activities such as financial fraud...the FBI is not aware of such activity by this group." Naming the perpetrator of an attack matters a

---

* The settlement underscored how imperfect lawsuits are as a vehicle for encouraging best practices in cybersecurity; companies need to be encouraged to invest in the cybersecurity practices necessary to protect their data, yet when a data breach happens, it's enormously hard for an individual victim to show the "damage" necessary to establish the standing required for a meaningful lawsuit.

great deal to a victim, particularly when communicating with affected customers or employees: if a nation-state is stealing your data for espionage purposes, credit monitoring is a general waste of time. Identification also affects the public narrative for blame around an attack: if you're attacked by a dedicated, sophisticated nation-state, there can be a different level of corporate culpability than if you're breached by a run-of-the-mill cybergang.

The Anthem hack fit a troubling emerging pattern. For years, a team of sophisticated hackers had vacuumed up personal data—data that disappeared into a black hole. As *Bloomberg* reported, another major US health insurer had been breached recently by Chinese hackers— hackers had studiously worked their way into the system, first by compromising a translation website that the insurer relied on to deal with foreign clients, then by working to insert malware directly into the main network.[20] Once inside, they'd gone after a specific target, useful for intelligence purposes: they were interested primarily in the employees of a defense contractor that worked on advanced weaponry systems, just the type of information a nation-state would be interested in if it was trying to identify possible spies to recruit. In writing about the Anthem attack, *Bloomberg* said, "The attack appears to follow a pattern of thefts of medical data by foreigners seeking a pathway into the personal lives and computers of a select group—defense contractors, government workers and others."[21]

Such thefts prompted a wider rethinking about the importance of bulk data; for years, we warned about "critical infrastructure" as things and systems—electrical grids, air traffic control networks, hydroelectric dams—but we were seeing adversaries think creatively about wider areas that should have concerned us more—democratic values, in the case of the Sony attack, and the weaponization of stolen data and communications in attacks such as the one on Anthem. At what point does run-of-the-mill data become "critical infrastructure"? Could someone assemble enough data to damage an economic sector or undermine a wider commercial ecosystem?

The national security threat from the theft of bulk information encouraged the government to think more critically about corporate data troves. An obscure government panel, the Committee on Foreign Investment in the United States (CFIUS), had long had oversight over corporate mergers and acquisitions by foreign companies or governments that might impact the national security of the United States. CFIUS dated back to the Ford administration and brought together 16 government agencies, including the National Security Division on the part of the Justice Department, to review investment cases that might affect the country's security. Up until events like the Anthem breach, CFIUS had only paid attention to "obvious" secrets: ensuring that a foreign takeover or merger with an American company wouldn't unduly compromise either our defense industrial base, our manufacturing capabilities, or the supply chains of critical government systems. In the Obama administration, for instance, it had forced a Chinese company to divest itself of four small wind farms that were too close to a Navy training range out of concern that the Chinese could use the wind turbines as an intelligence-gathering platform to spy on the Navy's development of unmanned aerial systems.[22] In the wake of breaches like that, though, we pushed for CFIUS to take a broader view of national security risks and to consider the importance of bulk data in its reviews, to consider both the sensitivity of troves of personally identifiable information and the potential of large databases as the building blocks for technologies like artificial intelligence and machine learning. As part of protecting against the next generation of technological threats to America, we needed to recognize that secrets could be mined from large data collections that weren't immediately obvious.

That possibility proved particularly true as we soon confronted another trove of data even more central to the country's infrastructure than a health care insurer: the government's own.

///////////////

The Office of Personnel Management (OPM) is the federal government's human resources back office, an agency of 5,000 employees responsible for everything from administering benefits to processing time-off and vacation requests to deciding if a winter snowstorm warrants closing federal agencies in Washington, DC. The office does incredibly important work—decisions that affect over a million families around the country—but it's hardly glamorous. OPM conducted much of its work as if it was the 1950s.

Across the government, the federal bureaucracy struggled for years to adapt to computerization. I knew firsthand from my days at the FBI how complicated these transitions could be; Robert Mueller had inherited an antiquated computer system when he took over in 2001—so bad, in fact, that it didn't have a way to attach files to emails and, after 9/11, the bureau had to FedEx copies of the hijackers' photos to the Field Offices—and struggled for years to build a better system. The first overhaul failed, costing hundreds of millions of dollars.

OPM was in even worse shape. In 2014, the *Washington Post* ran a feature story about an old limestone mine outside Pittsburgh where 600 OPM employees worked underground amid 28,000 file cabinets, processing the retirement paperwork of 100,000 retirees each year entirely by hand.[23] The system had run the same way since 1977—even though $100 million had been spent since 1981 trying to update it.*

On April 15, 2015, an IT contractor for OPM named Brendan Saulsbury was examining the encrypted traffic passing through the agency's servers when he noticed something strange: the network was pinging a site called opmsecurity.org, which, despite its name, was definitely not an official government website. Saulsbury had become an expert on OPM's system in his time working on its security—and had even played a key role in responding to a breach the year before—and the system's antiquated and unsafe nature terrified him. As he said later, OPM's network was "very insecure, insecurely architected," and riddled with "lots of legacy infrastructure" that made it difficult to secure.[24] The agency's inspector general and the US Computer Emergency Response Team (US-CERT), the government's computer crisis response team, had made numerous recommendations to improve the system, but little

---

* As it turned out, OPM's data—and all of the government's data—might have been safer in hard-copy form, buried in an old limestone mine.

had been done and OPM still badly lagged among government agencies in its cybersecurity spending.

With colleagues, Saulsbury used a malware detection tool, CylanceV, to trace the ping through the network, uncovering that it came from a file, *mcutil.dll*, that appeared at first glance to be part of the standard suite used by McAfee's security systems. Except OPM didn't use McAfee's software. "I was 100 percent certain that this is malware," Saulsbury said later.[25] OPM raised an alarm at 6:53 p.m. that night, telling US-CERT that it had identified four pieces of malicious malware on its network.[26]

One of the pieces of malware was a file known as a Windows Credentials Editor (WCE), a hacking tool whose mere presence represented a particularly bad sign. While many computer systems the world over have the presence of malware, most exist somewhat benignly—the equivalent of normal germs or bacteria that exist on many surfaces—and don't necessarily reflect that a system was specifically targeted by a hacker. As one Cylance employee explained later, a WCE, though, meant something more nefarious: "That's usually a sign of an overt act, so something that somebody with ill intent actually was trying to achieve versus just the presence of a malicious file, which may or may not have been used. A WCE 64 doesn't just appear."[27]

When investigators took a closer look at opmsecurity.org, their hearts sank: the domain had been registered to Steve Rogers, the alter ego of Marvel Comics superhero Captain America. They also found a second spoofed domain, opm-learning.org, that the malware was communicating with—and it was registered to Tony Stark, the alter ego of the superhero Iron Man.

Those fictitious registries represented another bad sign: the tongue-in-cheek calling card of the Black Vine hacker group was registering domain names under the aliases of Avenger superheroes. The Black Vine team often used a distinct set of intrusion tools, which US officials designated by the code name COLD CUTS. As the Defense Cyber Crime Center explained in an unclassified report, "'COLD CUTS' registers domain names that are very similar to legitimate domain names of organizations they intend to or have targeted.... These domains are referred to as 'doppelganger' domains. Through in-depth analysis of domain registrant data, [we have] identified approximately 70 doppelganger domain names likely indicative of a potential target for COLD CUTS operations."[28] For instance, one of the Anthem hack domains had drawn upon the company's previous name, Wellpoint, registering Wellpoint .com, which at a quick glance looked the same.[29]

Whoever was behind the COLD CUTS tradecraft was a true fan of Marvel Comics: we saw domains registered in another attack registered to Natasha Romanoff, the *nom de plume* for the heroine Black Widow, as well as John Nelson, the Oscar-nominated visual effects guru for the movie *Iron Man*. In a hack directed at United Airlines, one of the domains (united-airlines.net) was registered to James Rhodes, a friend of Tony Stark in the *Iron Man* movies.[30] There was even a domain registered simply to Dubai Tycoon, a brief role in the *Iron Man* movie that had been played by Wu-Tang Clan rapper Ghostface Killah.

Government investigators became even more worried when they saw the day the opmsecurity.org domain had been originally registered: April 25, 2014. OPM had been aware of a penetration in the spring of 2014, but it had conducted a special operation that it thought had cleansed the system of outsiders. This was evidence that someone might have been inside the government's personnel records for a year.

On Friday, April 17, the cybersecurity company Cylance arrived at OPM and installed its malware detection system on the network. The team worked through the weekend to sort out the threat and begin to assess the damage, creating an impromptu command post to fight the breach in a basement storage room. "They were under severe attack," the company's founder, Stuart McClure, recalled. Another Cylance employee, Chris Coulter, recalled that when they activated the malware detection system, "to put it bluntly, [the security system] lit up like a Christmas tree." The OPM situation was dire—they quickly found evidence the hackers had been in and been successful, locating an encrypted and compressed stash of files that had evidently been collected and then exfiltrated from the OPM network. Coulter emailed McClure on Sunday morning: "They are fucked."[31] (Hackers often will encrypt and compress stolen files before exfiltrating them from a system, both to make them easier to move and to help defeat network monitoring tools that search for specific types of traffic. The encryption and compression also make it enormously difficult after the fact to reconstruct what was accessed and stolen, and to judge the full scope of the theft.)

‍‍*‍*

All told, OPM discovered more than 2,000 pieces of malware operating on its network, effectively one piece of malware for every five devices OPM possessed; only about ten were the advanced malware from Black Vine, known as PlugX—an advanced remote access tool (RAT) that allowed a hacker to enter the system.[32] The variant of PlugX the hackers had installed allowed them to record keystrokes, modify or copy files, take screenshots or video of users, and do basic network administrative tasks like logging off users or restarting machines; in short, it gave the attackers "complete control over the [infected] system."[33]

The systems where PlugX did exist, though, were more than sufficient to provide access to the entire OPM network. As the investigation by OPM, other federal agencies, and the CERT crisis team discovered, the Black Vine hackers had carefully worked their way up through the system over the course of a year.

Black Vine was a well-known advanced persistent threat, a group the security industry had been watching at least since 2012. In addition to its predilection for the Avengers, it was well-known for "watering-hole" attacks, in which the hacker takes control of a legitimate website that a target is likely to use, such as their bank or favorite online retail site or the homepage of a business partner.* The attacker will infect that third-party website with malware that, whenever the target visits, exposes the target's own home network or computer.

In the years since Black Vine appeared on the security industry's radar as an organized threat group, researchers had traced its work across the internet. It consistently aimed for targeted espionage operations, not fraud or financial theft. In one report, Symantec declared,

---

* The name of the attack comes from the analogy of a predator waiting at a watering hole in the desert, knowing the prey will show up sooner or later.

"Black Vine appears to have access to a wide variety of resources to let it conduct multiple simultaneous attacks over a sustained period of time. These resources include the development of custom malware, access to zero-day exploits, and attacker-owned infrastructure." At least portions of its online infrastructure were traced back to a Chinese cybersecurity company known as Topsec, which originally started as a research institute and later grew into one of the country's most prominent security firms—even hosting an annual hacking competition known as the Topsec Cup. The firm received half of its start-up funding from the PLA itself.[34]

Figuring out how Black Vine had gotten into the OPM system was one of the first priorities for investigators. That summer, as the totality of the Anthem and OPM hacks became clear, the security industry raised the alarm. "The rules of the game have greatly changed, and all organizations in today's market need to stop and reassess the standards at which they operate and the systems they once thought were sufficient," said Carl Herberger, who had also been on the front lines of Iran's DDoS attacks and was vice president of security solutions at Radware, a cybersecurity firm.

As investigators later determined, a cascading series of failures at almost every level eventually allowed the theft of some of the government's most valuable data. The biggest problem with the OPM attack was that it was actually the second attack on OPM.

On March 20, 2014, DHS's US-CERT had alerted OPM to an intrusion within its network—the government's intrusion-detection system had actually noticed data being exfiltrated from OPM's servers. Within five days, OPM verified the malicious activity. The hacker was clearly looking for files on background checks, logging on to the system after 10 p.m. when most staff would have gone home. While the OPM team was never able to determine how the adversary breached the system in the first place, Brendan Saulsbury—who discovered the second hack—was able to reverse-engineer the hackers' systems to watch in real time the commands coming from the "actual attacker sitting at the keyboard." For weeks, they watched the adversary root through the system, but the hacker never successfully acquired the background check files. By May, OPM officials got nervous: they saw the attacker install on each of the computers of multiple database administrators a "keylogger"—a piece of malware that would record every keystroke on those computers and, had OPM not been watching carefully, all but ensured that the attackers would have access to the innermost agency secrets.[35]

Finally, convinced they'd gathered enough intelligence and understood the attackers' modus operandi, footholds, and infrastructure well enough, OPM moved to undo all their adversary's access and infrastructure in one fell swoop—an operation they dubbed BIG BANG.[36] The BIG BANG was carefully choreographed, including the changing of administrator passwords, the creation of new accounts for previously compromised accounts, resetting passwords across the agency, and taking entire penetrated systems offline.[37] Afterward, OPM and DHS conducted intensive checks for weeks and saw nothing suspicious. OPM's system administrators thought there was a 95 percent chance they'd removed the hackers' access to the network.[38] On June 22, 2014, DHS certified: "No new systems communication with known C2 servers; no new attacker activity observed."

At the time, OPM touted its handling of that incident and reassured Congress that no personally identifiable information had been stolen. In fact, agency officials noted that OPM was effectively too obscure to bother being the target of a determined adversary; it didn't have any national security secrets. "OPM should have raised the alarm and recognized this initial attack as a serious and potentially devastating precursor given how close the early attackers got to the background investigation systems and the related data," Congress later concluded.[39]

As we later learned, the attacker had already established a new foothold, unknown to OPM, even before the BIG BANG, dropping in new malware on May 7, 2014. It went entirely undetected until the following April. In the second attack, the US-CERT team dispatched to the agency determined the Black Vine hackers had used a very common approach to access OPM, penetrating the system by using the credentials of a government contractor, a company known as a Keypoint Government Solutions, which helped OPM perform the basic background checks that many federal employees undergo.[40]

From there, Black Vine continued to root around, compromising other accounts, gaining increasingly powerful credentials, until they were able to access the entire system. Once inside, they gained too much access too easily; the government did a poor job of segregating data and segmenting networks to limit hackers who breached one area from getting access to wider resources.* Moreover, OPM had not implemented safeguards, such as two-factor authentication, that would have made it nearly impossible for the systems to be compromised just with a username and password. While two-factor authentication was an industry best practice, many organizations resisted the complexity it added to daily use—even as Congress later berated OPM for not having two-factor authentication, Capitol Hill was operating without it as well.

Since much of the attack on OPM had been done with genuine user credentials, it was particularly difficult to sort out what traffic was authentic and what was malicious. Investigators spent a month interviewing OPM employees in groups of six, just to determine who might have legitimately been using their account at what time—with much legwork, they were able to spot some account usage when employees were out on vacation or otherwise not using the system, helping investigators piece together how the hackers explored the system and what they took.[41]

Later analysis showed the first major data exfiltration took place over Fourth of July weekend in 2014, meaning that OPM was aware of the first breach for more than three months before the first major data theft. Had OPM used that window to act more quickly or aggressively—for instance, forcing users to implement two-factor authentication—Black Vine might very well have been stymied before it ever, as Congress said, "had the chance to commit the most significant digital violation

---

*Data segregation and segmented networks also make it easier to understand what an adversary wants to target.

of national security to date."[42] Additionally, even though it was clear that OPM had been targeted by a "sophisticated, persistent actor" in 2014, OPM hadn't installed preventive cyberthreat tracking software until after the second breach was discovered in April 2015. That monitoring software—an investment that would have helped provide a multilayered defense, assuming that the network's outer walls were likely to be breached but helping to catch and limit such exposures inside the system—would have easily detected the PlugX malware calling out to spoofed domains like opmsecurity.org.

Over time, OPM ultimately determined that the Black Vine hackers successfully exfiltrated three separate data sets—all with devastating long-term effects for the US government. The hackers had stolen the personnel files of millions of federal employees—everything from basic details such as names and addresses to details such as the service of veterans, health insurance information, and pay records.

From an intelligence and counterintelligence perspective, though, two other categories of information were even more valuable: the hackers took 5.6 million fingerprints of US government personnel, a powerful tool to identify intelligence officers and potential spies for decades to come as they traveled around the world. Black Vine also took answers to the SF-86 form, the 127-page form filled out by personnel in sensitive positions in order to receive security clearances. The completed forms were a treasure trove for a foreign power: addresses, careers, business endeavors, and family members, as well as past relationships, illicit drug use, alcohol use, criminal records, financial status, mental health issues, travel histories, and every foreign official a person had met with. They were roadmaps of personal weaknesses and foibles useful for recruitment of intelligence assets—and also powerful tools for a foreign power to map family members, friends, and even overseas contacts and foreign relationships that might prove useful for recruitment or surveillance. After the breach, one former NSA official said, "This is crown jewels material...a gold mine for a foreign intelligence service."[43] As Director of National Intelligence James Clapper wrote later, "We all but knew from the start that Chinese intelligence was responsible for the theft, and the counterintelligence implications were staggering, not just from what they had, but from what they didn't have. OPM didn't conduct security clearances for all the Intelligence Community elements, and whoever had the wherewithal to penetrate its systems would certainly know which agencies and departments OPM conducted investigations for and which they didn't. They could therefore also start making assumptions about cover for cleared people whose files they didn't have."[44]

To Clapper, the OPM hack indicated where cyberattacks were going. As he saw it, there were three distinct ways hackers could affect information: First, they could undermine *confidentiality*, taking private information and making it public; second, they could alter its *availability*, as a DDoS attack does, by blocking people from accessing needed information like bank accounts. OPM heralded a new, third fear: That hackers could start altering the *integrity of* data. "An offensive cyber organization with the skills, technology, and persistence of the Chinese could change our data itself, without doing anything as noticeable as exfiltrating it or blocking our access to it," he wrote later. "I urged people to imagine the chaos that could have resulted if the Chinese had actually changed people's security-clearance background investigation results."[45]

The OPM thefts came in distinct time periods, showing the patience and persistence of the attackers. In July and August 2014, Black Vine took the background check files for security clearances; then, in December, Black Vine stole the personnel records; finally, in late March 2015, in the third mass exfiltration, they took all of the fingerprint data.[46] Three weeks later, OPM recognized it had been breached.

Speaking later at an event in Washington, James Clapper remarked, "You have to kind of salute the Chinese for what they did." Then he added, "You know, if we had the opportunity to do that, I don't think we'd hesitate for a minute."[47] His comments reflected one of the central tensions of this battle to shape the norms of international online conduct: one reason we hoped to punish China for its economic espionage was to draw the line between state-sponsored espionage done for commercial benefit, which is not done or defended by the majority of nations, and the other types of traditional espionage that are recognized under international law and are a routine part of the geo-political landscape.

//////////////

The OPM hack shocked the government apparatus—it presented, after all, an event that every federal employee felt personally. As FBI Director James Comey stated later, "It's a treasure trove of information about everybody who has worked for, tried to work for, or works for the United States government." When we gathered at the NSD's SCIF, at the White House for a National Security Council meeting, or anywhere else among others with security clearances, we all knew China now possessed intimate details of our own lives—details we by and large didn't even share with our colleagues. In meetings in years to come, it became a dark joke: sometimes when we were struggling with personnel challenges, you would hear someone say, "We should just outsource that question to China—they already have the data."

The breach demonstrated we weren't all that much better prepared than the private sector companies we were constantly berating and cajoling to respond and take data breaches more seriously. For one thing, we weren't thinking about cybersecurity correctly. We needed as a government to map out and inventory what we valued and where that information lived, and then to determine how to secure it. Those processes routinely happened with defense and intelligence agencies, but had evidently never occurred in the government writ large—an oversight that left incredibly valuable information lying around with little attention. In hindsight, OPM—like many private sector companies we saw—approached their network security and the penetration of their system with the wrong mindset. They handled it as an IT problem, not as a national security problem. The case underscored one of our constant refrains: cybersecurity can't just be an IT problem—it needs to be central to those involved in the core of a business's functions. And to top it off, we then discovered we were similarly unprepared for the incident on the management side of the government.

When discussing how to respond to the breach, we knew the Office of Management and Budget had issued a directive on data breaches, but no one really knew what it said. *How should we decide to notify victims? What should we tell them?* I witnessed the enormous confusion about the time frame within which we had to report the breach and notify potential victims—all questions we'd been telling the private sector to sort out for years—and I asked my team to grab from our policy staff a copy of the proposed Consumer Privacy Bill of Rights legislation the administration was actively pushing on Capitol Hill: *How many of these guidelines was the US government following itself?*

The answer, unfortunately, was shockingly few. It turned out that we hadn't wrestled with the hard questions inside the government. Particularly for departments and agencies that hadn't been involved in the day-to-day rise of cyberthreats, there was little recognition of what we'd been pushing the private sector toward for years: a data breach is inevitable if you have a network-connected system; thus you need both layers of defense and a sophisticated response plan, geared toward resiliency and incident response. Once you move from the mindset of "not if but when," your organization's focus needed to include a plan for "right of boom," what happens after a breach. Whereas we regularly hosted table-top exercises to respond to incidents such as hurricanes and terror attacks, we had never practiced with federal agencies the incident response to a data breach—what to do the day after. It was a mistake we rectified going forward.

While we'd often heard complaints from the private sector that the government wasn't sharing enough information with them, the OPM breach made clear that the reverse was true, too—the government didn't have a defined system by which to use information from the private sector to defend itself. In the fall of 2014, a group of security firms had issued a report collectively examining Chinese intelligence espionage—using an industry moniker for the APT, known as the Axiom Threat Actor Group—that specifically mentioned how it appeared the hackers were targeting government personnel files. Even more concerning, the security firm ThreatConnect had actually published in February 2015, in its analysis of the Anthem hack, that the domain name opm-learning.org had been registered to the suspicious Tony Stark, but there's no record anyone in government saw that report and communicated the suspicious domain to OPM itself. As Threat-Connect said at the time, "The fact [that] this domain was registered after the breach occurred suggests that OPM could be an ongoing direct target of Chinese state-sponsored cyber espionage activity."[48]

When we tried to get high-level attention to the problem after the hack, the initial efforts continued to flounder: multiple times, Denis McDonough and Lisa Monaco tried to convene Cabinet leaders to discuss data security at the National Security Council, but each time, most Cabinet secretaries sent their CIOs rather than coming themselves. At the first meeting, I showed up in the attorney general's place, along with the Justice Department's CIO. Lisa grew increasingly frustrated as the departments brushed off the gatherings as an IT question. Finally, a clear order had to go out from the White House: *you, the cabinet secretary, will show up personally—and you will pay attention.* We had a consistent mantra: data security isn't just an IT issue. The heads of the organization needed to help determine what was worth protecting; they were the ones, after all, who knew what mattered most to the enterprise, not the IT staff. Similarly, the heads of the organization needed to be able to understand the recommendations and be conversant with the IT security side; if, in an incident, they didn't understand what the IT security staff was saying, that was an indication that they were unprepared for the attack in the first place. The White House message was clear: *you, as the Cabinet secretary, are the official that needs to know and choose what matters most to your department, where your department keeps that information, and how it's secured.* That message was reinforced when the White House added IT security to every Cabinet secretary's quarterly management meeting with the president.

That message hit home when, in one of the first pieces of mail my then three-year-old daughter ever received, she got a letter from the US government apologizing that her Social Security number and personal details had been stolen as part of the OPM hack. She was too young to have ever had a chance to use or establish her identity online—and already it was stolen. Rob Joyce, a career NSA official who would go on to lead the Trump administration's cyber efforts at the White House, joked to me and others that he'd had his Social Security number stolen in at least six data breaches. With so many breaches and an active trading market on dark web crime forums for stolen identities, we as a society clearly needed a better way to identify people online and secure arm's-length transactions.

More broadly, understanding how vulnerable our data is—and how we need to begin rethinking the procedures and protections behind our lives as they move online—will be key to securing cyberspace in the future. This is especially true as we shift more of our mechanical lives into the cloud—with driverless cars, medical devices, and home appliances moving online. The threat is quickly increasing. According to the Identity Theft Resource Center, an average of three major data breaches—of a US company or a government agency—occurred each day in 2016, a 40 percent increase over the year before.

In the summer of 2015, the US government hosted a 90-day "cyber sprint" to push agencies and departments to boost their security profile. With the clock ticking down on the administration—all of us who lived through the Bush-to-Obama transition that knocked cybersecurity far back down the agenda were sensitive to how much could be lost or slowed as presidents changed—there was a great emphasis on what we could do to quickly harden the government. At the conclusion of the cyber sprint, the good news was that 15 of 29 agencies met basic cybersecurity standards, up from just four when the OPM hack was discovered. The bad news was that still barely half had done the basic "blocking and tackling" to secure their systems. All of which wouldn't keep a determined adversary out—but it was a help.

/////////////

As the dust settled from the initial response—caring for the needs of our system and for the victims—our conversation shifted to what to do about China's successful attack. What was the appropriate response? The PLA indictment in 2014 was never supposed to be stand-alone; we had intended it as one step in a campaign telling China, consistently, that we would keep taking action until their cyber behavior changed and we stopped seeing the theft of economic data to aid economic competitors. The OPM breach, though, appeared to represent a more traditional case of nation-state espionage, and we were well practiced as a government in the available tools for a response—from formal diplomatic protests, known as *démarches*, to expelling suspected spies to, when possible, criminal espionage charges. The OPM breach also presented an opportunity to use President Obama's new executive order, allowing the United States to issue sanctions on countries or entities that engaged in malicious cyber activity.

A year removed from the PLA case, we knew that despite the heartfelt warnings from certain government circles that the sky would fall if we indicted Chinese military officials, China hadn't blown up the entire superpower relationship. In fact, the case had proved helpful to precisely our original goal—shaping China's behavior online and encouraging a clear set of norms. I had imagined that it would take much more than a single criminal case, but in fact China had responded quickly. As we'd always imagined, China saw its economic espionage—like all espionage—as a cost-benefit analysis. And with our indictment, we'd changed one side of that equation.

Over the course of 2015, the Chinese government began to further reevaluate that equation as the US government kept up diplomatic pressure. Through meetings and exchanges of groups such as the bilateral US-China Joint Economic Committee, government leaders such as National Security Advisor Susan Rice and Deputy Secretary of State Tony Blinken kept repeating that China's cyber behavior had to change. President Xi was scheduled that fall to have his first state visit with President Obama in Washington, and cybersecurity would surely be on the agenda. Obama had pressed the issue in their first meeting in 2013, at Sunnylands in California, but it hadn't gone far—China had continued to deny that they'd been engaged in state-sponsored hacking.

In August 2015, the *Washington Post* ran an article warning that the US government was preparing to use the sanctions allowed by the April 1 executive order to target China for its hacking. As Ellen Nakashima reported, "The U.S. government has not yet decided whether to issue these sanctions, but a final call is expected soon—perhaps even within the next two weeks."[49] By September, the cyber issue had risen to the top of the geopolitical agenda. Early that month, while speaking to a group of business leaders, President Obama said, "We are preparing a number of measures that will indicate to the Chinese that this is not just a matter of us being mildly upset, but is something that will put significant strains on the bilateral relationship if not resolved. We are prepared to take some countervailing actions in order to get their attention."[50]

The warnings, both public and private, got through to the Chinese. Just days before Xi's visit was set to begin, they dispatched a large delegation of high-level emissaries to Washington. "The Chinese saw they had a big potential embarrassment brewing ahead of Xi's first state visit," Luke Dembosky recalls. "They had to let the air out of the balloon on cyber."

The conversations, which included DHS Secretary Jeh Johnson and White House cybersecurity coordinator Michael Daniel, began with a firm message: *Don't even bother denying this is your typical behavior. Let's move past that.* But the conversations didn't go very far. It was days of tense, stilted conversations, with little progress. Finally, on Friday night, the night before the Chinese delegation was set to return home, the Chinese called the White House for a final set of negotiations. "I was all set to go home and got a call at 6:30: 'Can you be at the White House at 8?'" Luke Dembosky recalls.

In the end, the small group met at a hotel in DC's Woodley Park because it was too late to arrange access to the White House; aides from the White House, the Justice Department, DHS, and the State Department, among others, talked through the night with the much larger Chinese delegation, all aware that the Chinese had a deadline to make their 7:30 a.m. flight home. "It was one of the most constructive dialogues I've ever been part of. For a brief moment, the stars were aligned. They were highly motivated to do the right thing," Luke recalls. By morning, they'd worked out an agreement for the two presidents to sign later in Washington.

Over the course of September, China also—for the first time—arrested a series of hackers domestically.[51] We debated whether the move was an actual crackdown or just geopolitical face-saving. President Xi told the *Wall Street Journal* in an interview at the start of his visit, "China takes cybersecurity very seriously. China is also a victim of hacking. The Chinese government does not engage in theft of commercial secrets in any form, nor does it encourage or support Chinese companies to engage in such practices in any way. Cyber theft of commercial secrets and hacking attacks against government networks are both illegal; such acts are criminal offenses and should be punished according to law and relevant international conventions. China and the United States share common concerns on cybersecurity. We are ready to strengthen cooperation with the U.S. side on this issue."[52] The timing of his remarks was a bit odd: the next morning was when OPM, which was still struggling to wrap its arms around its data breach, announced that more than 5 million fingerprint records had also been stolen in the attack.

Finally, we got to the big event. On September 25, 2015, the two leaders, US President Barack Obama and Chinese President Xi Jinping met privately, continuing a conversation that had started the night before during dinner at the presidential guest house, Blair House, across from the White House. As Obama recapped the meeting to the press, he said he had "raised once again our very serious concerns about growing cyber-threats to American companies and American citizens. I indicated that it has to stop. The United States government does not engage in cyber economic espionage for commercial gain." Then, the president made an announcement in the Rose Garden that we never thought we'd hear: "Today, I can announce that our two countries have reached a common understanding on the way forward. We've agreed that neither the U.S. nor the Chinese government will conduct or knowingly support cyber-enabled theft of intellectual property, including trade secrets or other confidential business information for commercial advantage. In addition, we'll work together, and with other nations, to promote international rules of the road for appropriate conduct in cyberspace." It was an agreement codified in writing, as the official White House fact sheet on the visit proclaimed, "Both sides are committed to making common effort to further identify and promote appropriate norms of state behavior in cyberspace within the international community."[53] That breakthrough was later endorsed by the G-20.[54]

By no means did that end Chinese hacking—over the months ahead, we continued to see Chinese attacks on defense companies, as well as an attack against four firms that worked on semiconductors—but we did see the behavior of the Chinese change. I had been cynical about the agreement, but I was wrong. China, at least in a narrowly defined box, had agreed to a new cyber norm. Consistent with their agreement, they largely ceased state-sponsored hacking that targeted a private US company for the direct economic benefit of a Chinese competitor. It was a narrow definition, to be sure—the exact contour of the agreement may have been narrowly defined—but they were indeed following a new norm, and it was finally, after many years, an example of true progress.

By 2018, though, the norm had broken down. China's economic espionage was on the rise again. In March of that year, FBI director Christopher Wray stated in public what people in cybersecurity circles had been seeing for a while: China was back to its old tricks. It was once again infiltrating US computer systems and stealing information at a massive scale. "There's no country that's even close," Wray told NBC News. And by 2019, China and the United States would once again be locked in a showdown over intellectual property, economic espionage, hacking, and the national security implications of next-generation technology by Chinese companies like Huawei.

As China grew more aggressive, the Justice Department responded with an organized initiative, announced by Attorney General Jeff Sessions, and a series of new indictments targeting Chinese hackers—including a May 2019 indictment charging Fujie Wang with the theft of millions of health records from the insurance company Anthem.

"In 2015, China committed publicly that it would not target American companies for economic gain. Obviously, that commitment has not been kept," Sessions said. As he put it, "the problem has been growing rapidly, and along with China's other unfair trade practices, it poses a real and illegal threat to our nation's economic prosperity and competitiveness."

CHAPTER 9

Fake News

EVEN AS WE scrambled inside the government to respond to the Office of Personnel Management data breach in the spring of 2015, we were living through that terrible, scary spring as ISIL's homegrown, internet-driven recruiting was at its peak—every week brought us new cases and worrisome leads. A new attack always seemed to be around the corner. In the beginning Silicon Valley was reluctant to see terrorists on social media as a problem—let alone as their problem to solve. Twitter, in particular, seemed to shirk any responsibility for how ISIL recruiters and propagandists were using its platform on a daily basis; it certainly didn't want to be on the spot to stop them.

ISIL's online Twitter megaphone swamped the company's capacity to react—the very informality and ease of launching a new account that made Twitter successful allowed terrorists to exploit the system. Even though Twitter moved to suspend prominent ISIL-associated accounts, the sheer volume of such accounts left hundreds—even thousands—untouched. And anyone who was suspended could easily launch a new one. "American ISIS sympathizers are particularly active on Twitter, where they spasmodically create accounts that often get suspended in a never-ending cat-and-mouse game," researchers Seamus Hughes and Lorenzo Vidino wrote after studying ISIL's use of social media. "These suspensions have become a badge of honor and a means by which an aspirant can bolster his or her legitimacy. In most suspension cases, a new (and often more than one) account with a variation of the previous username is created within hours."[1] There was even a clear pattern those with suspended accounts followed in starting new accounts: users would first tweet a screenshot of Twitter's announcement of the suspension of their previous account, thereby establishing that they were the same person and owned the previous account.

Hughes and Vidino were able to trace three distinct types of ISIL sympathizers online. First were the "nodes," the primary drivers of online engagement who were prominent voices and provided new material to ISIL's online followers. Second were the "amplifiers," sometimes real, sometimes automated bots, who primarily retweeted and spread material online. Third were the "shout-outs," which the researchers realized were "a unique innovation and vital to the survival of the ISIL online scene. They primarily introduce new, pro-ISIS accounts to the community and promote newly created accounts of previously suspended users, allowing them to quickly regain their pre-suspension status." The "shout-outs" provided "little substantive content," but often had the largest online followings because they represented something like an online directory for other accounts, playing "a pivotal role in the resilience of ISIS's Twitter community."[2] It was clear that Silicon Valley was not applying its best thinking to fighting extremism if terrorists were able with such ease to bypass suspensions.

Encouraging free speech online represented a legitimately challenging area for the US government; we simultaneously wanted to protect Americans while supporting free speech around the world. Tools that we could use to catch criminals under the American system could also be used by governments overseas who didn't share our values to catch people they defined as "criminals," such as human rights activists, journalists, and political opponents. The State Department had even helped fund the development of online anonymity tools that made it easier for activists overseas to speak out without risk of retribution, even though those same tools could be adopted by child predators and terrorists to obscure their communications. If we as a government stood online for free speech, we had to stand for all free speech.

Yet we knew we needed to enlist the tech companies as stronger partners in the fight against extremism. In January 2016, White House and intelligence officials went to Silicon Valley to push for more action.[3] Then, in February, Secretary of State John Kerry traveled to Los Angeles to talk with the entertainment industry. Our efforts helped to a certain extent: Twitter agreed that month to shut down 125,000 ISIL-linked accounts.[4]

In the spirit of being creative, we held a meeting in late February 2016 at the Justice Department that I cochaired with the head of the National Counterterrorism Center, Nick Rasmussen, bringing together people from tech companies such as Apple, Twitter, Snapchat, and Facebook; Madison Avenue advertisers and PR firms such as Edelman; nonprofit groups; and even some reporters, as well as entertainment and Hollywood executives. Nick thanked the group for their more aggressive efforts to combat ISIL: "We've seen more aggressive takedowns across social media platforms, which is a really good thing."[5] Then Nick and I, along with other government leaders, such as the US chief technology officer, Megan Smith, and representatives from the National Security Council, tried to explain what we were seeing in terms of the threat: *this is how terrorists are exploiting social media services; this is the type of advertising that they're doing.* We felt there must be some way we could use the collective talent gathered in the room to help keep our young kids from being exploited and turned into human IEDs by foreign terrorists overseas. We showed one video that depicted a terrorist handing out cotton candy to kids in the Middle East—an example of the benign, warm and fuzzy image that ISIL wanted to convey about what life was like in the territories they controlled in the Middle East.

Over the course of the five-hour meeting, we explained that if the target audience was disaffected youth, we knew the US government would be the world's worst messenger—we needed the help of smart minds from outside the government to countermessage in this area. Someone nicknamed the meeting the "Madison Valleywood" summit, more proof that government is no good at branding. If we were going to address the problem, we needed to work together in some combination of the group we assembled. While the US government might not have been the world's best at messaging, the West, collectively, certainly was the world's slickest advertiser.

The conversation was fascinating; I heard all sorts of concepts that were new to me, including information about the specific microtargeting of demographics. One participant, who worked on designing recruiting campaigns for the Marines, talked about how they used similar themes as the terror groups used to target a very similar demographic—for instance, emphasizing to young men the importance of belonging. The Hollywood and Madison Avenue participants helped walk us through why the terrorists' material was so compelling—analyzing the craft involved, the soft lenses, the camera angles, even the consistent branding for the Islamic State of Iraq and the Levant down in the corner of the videos, just like a cable channel would do.

The technology companies continued to struggle with the legitimately challenging questions about how to equally apply initiatives across the many jurisdictions and nations where they worked; for instance, Google and Facebook expressed concern about what the repercussions could be if they tweaked their algorithms to hide content from ISIL and what requests they would then field from less democratic countries eager to stifle other speech.[6]

///////////////

Part of what made ISIL complicated to combat online was that we were at that time doing battle online with multiple sides of the Syrian conflict. As 2016 began, we finally began to close in on a group of online backers of the Syrian dictator who had bedeviled US websites for years.

The Syrian conflict at that point was years old. A group of pro-regime hackers had dubbed themselves the Syrian Electronic Army (SEA) and moved aggressively to contest cyberspace, refusing to cede it to the prodemocracy activists. Initially, much of the SEA's efforts was little more than attempts to create the appearance of a groundswell of support for the embattled dictator, Bashar al-Assad. At the start, their favorite medium appeared to be Facebook—on their own Facebook page, the SEA posted a guide on how to flood other Facebook pages with pro-Syria comments. Initially, the efforts did appear to be from real Syrians. As researchers Max Fisher and Jared Keller noted, "A random selection of the group's Facebook activists appeared to all have real accounts, and hundreds of pro-regime comments showed enough variation that they are unlikely to have been manufactured en masse."[7]

In May 2011, hackers flooded a White House Facebook page with pro-Syria messages such as, "We love Bashar Alassad so, leave us alone Obama!" Similar efforts unfolded on Facebook pages for ABC News, the US Department of Treasury, and even Oprah.[8] They also launched denial-of-service attacks against media outlets that posted news reports that were critical of the Syrian government. Al-Assad himself praised the group in June 2011, saying, "the electronic army...has been a real army in virtual reality."[9] What exactly the group's ties were to the Syrian government was publicly unclear: while they denied being government forces, if you dug into their details, the group's website, syrian-es.com, had been registered by the Syrian Computer Society, a group that Bashar al-Assad had led.

Regardless of its ties, though, the group was unabashedly pro-Assad: when the *Atlantic* posted a story about an activist tortured by the regime, the SEA asked its supporters to flood the magazine's site with critics, explaining, "It is our duty to explain to them the truth of these peaceful protests."[10] One of their favorite tactics was to post, simply, that even as news reports documented the country's descent into chaos and civil war, everything was absolutely fine: "I live in Syria, stop lying, nothing is happening in Syria."[11]

The SEA's efforts didn't go unchallenged: by the summer and fall of 2011, they were engaging in regular skirmishes with the hacker collective Anonymous, which attacked and defaced regime websites. Anonymous had harassed each government in turn across the Arab Spring, at one point attempting to fax copies of embarrassing WikiLeaks documents into Egyptian schools so that students could spread the word in the streets.[12]

On August 7, 2011, Anonymous hacked the Syrian defense ministry, posting a message for the Syrian Army and people: "To the Syrian people: The world stands with you against the brutal regime of Bashar al-Assad. Know that time and history are on your side—tyrants use violence because they have nothing else, and the more violent they are, the more fragile they become. We salute your determination to be non-violent in the face of the regime's brutality, and admire your willingness to pursue justice, not mere revenge. All tyrants will fall, and thanks to your bravery Bashar al-Assad is next."[13]

SEA moved from Facebook "astro-turfing," with its coordinated messages purporting to represent indigenous grassroots support, to low-level, unsophisticated internet vandalism. An SEA hacker broke into Harvard's website in September 2011 and defaced its homepage, posting a photo of Bashar al-Assad and a message, "Syrian Electronic Army Were Here." The next month, they broke into a *Washington Post* server and posted on live.washingtonpost.com a blog saying, "Hacked by Syrian Electronic Army," authored by someone named Th3 Pr0. Beginning that fall, they also tried repeatedly to spear-phish White House staff, using LinkedIn requests and emails such as whitehouse _online@hotmail.com. The next year, they raised the stakes: in August 2012, they accessed the Twitter feed and website of *Reuters*, posting false tweets and a fake interview with the head of a Syrian rebel group stating that he was pulling his forces back from Aleppo after losing to the Syrian Army.[14] It was a warning of what was to come: news websites became one of SEA's favorite targets, as all sides of the Syrian conflict fought the propaganda war online.

The initial compromise of *Reuters'* Twitter appeared relatively straightforward—the password had been cracked. In some ways, large corporate websites and social media accounts—whether they're companies or media organizations—are uniquely vulnerable because they often eschew the two-factor authentication that's available for regular users: it's seen as too complicated to rely on two-factor authentication given the number of people sharing a single social media account or login, often working in different offices, remotely, or even in different time zones.

Yet as news organizations strengthened their security in the wake of that attack, the SEA hackers got more creative, approaching new attack vectors that continued to surprise media companies. SEA also expanded their targets, going after employees of Human Rights Watch (HRW), a watchdog nongovernmental organization that had been critical of Syria's behavior in the civil war, sending out an email that purported to be a press release from the Qatari government with a link that installed malware; successful in stealing passwords and usernames from employees who clicked on the malicious link, the hackers then posted attacks on HRW's work on its own website. "All Your reports are FALSE!!" SEA posted online. "Stop lying!!!"[15] While the attack appeared at first glance to be nuisance vandalism, the attack could have had a chilling effect on HRW's ability to document the abuses of the Syrian regime: since so many of its reports—including a report it had issued just days before the attack, documenting the regime's use of cluster bombs against civilians—were based on hard investigative reporting and relied on anonymous sources who were still in the conflict zone, the SEA's demonstrated ability to access HRW's platforms was meant to send a clear warning: *we can figure out who you are.*[16] SEA wasn't just looking to change the narrative online around the Syrian civil war—they wanted to silence voices of opposition and make people think twice before reporting on Syria.

We made some early attempts to shut down the SEA's online infrastructure—the Department of Treasury used its trade sanction powers to seize seven hundred domain names registered to the Syrian efforts, many by the Syrian Computer Society—but the effort only caused a ripple.[17] In April 2013, SEA went after National Public Radio, successfully duping employees to click on a suspicious email and, once they got in, defacing the NPR website. Similar attacks that spring and summer hit CNN, E! Online, the *Daily Dot*, the *New York Post*, and even the satirical news site The Onion.

The Onion attack was a good illustration of SEA's persistence and sophistication: a wide phishing attack against employees from an email address purporting to be someone from the UN Human Rights Commission included a link that looked like a *Washington Post* article (the

link actually went to an SEA-controlled site: http://hackedwordpress
site.com/theonion.php). At least one employee clicked on it, and was
asked to enter his or her Google password. Then, once the hackers had
access to that employee's Gmail account, they re-sent the same message
from that "trusted" person, which encouraged even more employees to
click on the link and collect even more user credentials. Then, when
The Onion's staff realized the compromise and asked employees to all
change their passwords, the SEA hackers sent yet another email that
purported to include a link to a password-reset page—thereby trick-
ing two more employees. The Onion, once they discovered the attack,
began to post mocking articles, such as "Syrian Electronic Army Has
a Little Fun Before Inevitable Upcoming Deaths at Hands of Rebels,"
which only angered the hackers and led them to post Onion employees'
emails on the SEA Twitter account.

Until that point, though, the attacks had remained relatively
harmless—annoying but effectively just the equivalent of unsightly,
easily repaired graffiti. The Onion obviously had been able to literally
laugh it off.

On April 23, 2013, something different arrived: a spear-phishing
email sent to employees of the Associated Press allowed SEA hackers
to access the wire service's Twitter feed. It was, the AP said, "an im-
pressively disguised phishing email," pointing to news stories that appeared to be on the websites of *Reuters* or the *Washington Post*.[18] The
AP's information security team quickly sent out a warning to its staffers just 17 minutes after the phishing attempt at 12:12 p.m., but at least
one person had apparently already clicked on it.

At 1:07 p.m. Eastern Time, @AP tweeted out to its two million
followers: "Breaking: Two Explosions in the White House and Barack
Obama Is Injured." The stunning report caused the stock market to
tumble; in just one minute, the Dow Jones Industrial Average fell
by 1 percent—erasing $136 billion in market value.[19] It took only a
few minutes for the AP to correct the report, explaining it had been
hacked, and the stock market recovered quickly. The hack prompted
NPR reporter Andy Carvin, who had made a specialty of covering the
Arab Spring online through social media, to ask, "When do vandals

graduate to cyber terrorists?"[20] Even though the stock market recovered, the fake tweet remains the largest financial loss attributed to cyberattacks thus far.

By the summer of 2013, SEA was getting even more creative—targeting the IT infrastructure that supported news websites and at one point targeting an Australian company that ran domain names. When they obtained system administrators' credentials, the hackers promptly redirected websites such as the *New York Times* and *Huffington Post*, among others, to other SEA websites.[21] Later, it did the same thing to Vice's website, redirecting visitors of the news and culture site to a website controlled by SEA. In another attack, the hackers targeted the US Marines' recruiting site, defacing it and encouraging Marines to "refuse your orders."

At the National Security Division, the case was an early example to us—and a clearly demonstrable one—of the damage that could come from what we later defined as "fake news," the weaponizing of manipulated information online to spark specific reactions and emotions. Yet even as SEA toyed with some of the highest-profile news organizations in the world—and even as its pranks graduated to market-moving events—no one online had any idea who SEA really was.

Ultimately, with court approval for various search warrants, we were able to trace an email address associated with an SEA hacker known as ThePro to a specific mobile telephone number.[22] The account holder had emailed a copy of his personal identification documents—which made clear it was Ahmad Umar Agha, aged 22—and had even set up a LinkedIn account under the name theprosea as part of a specific spear-phishing campaign, using the same IP address as the Gmail address. We also pieced together the identity of another leading SEA hacker, Firas Dardar, aged 27, who went online by the name The Shadow.

Similar evidence piled up in the other SEA hacking and spear-phishing efforts; we saw the same IPs and the same email addresses again and again. We could even see from their search histories that they had looked for and read news articles about their own hacking attacks.

The case also led us in some new directions, less public than the high-profile attacks on social media accounts: as it turned out, the purportedly ideological Syrian Electronic Army—fighting supposedly to defend Bashar al-Assad's regime—had also been using its hacking activities to line its own pockets.

We uncovered how another Syrian, Peter Romar, a 36-year-old who lived in Germany, had contacted Th3 Pr0 and volunteered his help on Facebook, indicating his expertise as a hacker and asking for assistance in carrying out attacks against Saudi Arabia, Qatar, and Turkey. Dardar and Romar had then worked together to execute an extortion scheme to help funnel money toward themselves, victimizing at least 14 companies internationally and demanding more than $500,000 from the victims to leave their systems alone.

We ultimately charged them for an attack against one of their first victims, an extortion attempt against a Chinese gaming company with US-based servers. Dardar had broken into the company's systems in the summer of 2013 and had then emailed the company demanding to be paid "or / I will did [sic] something you do not like." The company had paid him $500, but he had persisted, pointing out "other vulnerabilities" and demanding additional payments; the company kept paying him.

Finally, in November of 2013, they had tried to cut him off—and he had freaked out, demanding €50,000, an amount he eventually dropped to €15,000. A similar scheme against a British company netted them about €16,000. In another scheme, he had redirected a victim company's website to his own domain, which bore a message explaining the site had been "HACKED." The hijacked website read, "I told you [expletive] don't [expletive] with me go now and cry like a little bitch you and your [expletive] CEO all your data downloaded and one of has been sold." Ultimately, the company had agreed to pay €5,000, and the SEA hackers had attempted to launder the victim company's blackmail money through Romar in Germany, since the United States and other Western countries had made it so difficult to access the global banking system because of sanctions in Syria. We saw them pull the same type of scheme, with mixed success, on other companies, too. The case was an example of the danger of these blended threats that we saw all too frequently: mainstream, upstanding companies—companies who would never consider paying ransom to a terrorist group if they knew it was a terrorist group—agreeing to pay shadowy figures online to make what appeared to be minor nuisances go away. Even major companies whose general counsels or compliance officers would never approve doing business with an organization that was under Treasury sanctions or with a criminal on a Most Wanted list saw their IT departments pay a few hundred to make a hacker leave them alone. The payments underscored a lesson for us: cybersecurity is a universal challenge, not just an IT challenge.

As we readied the SEA indictment, there were dozens of pages of examples linking up attacks to the individuals we suspected. There was no doubt in our minds that we'd run down the guys who had been toying with Western news organizations: we even included the rare step of posting photos of Agha, Dardar, and Romar right in the criminal complaints; Agha, ThePro, hardly looked like a hard-core terrorist: gangly, with wire-rimmed glasses and floppy hair, he looked like a college computer science student. By September 2015, we had the charges ready under seal.

On Tuesday, March 22, 2016—the same week that we announced the guilty plea of Chinese spy Su Bin and the charges against the Iranian hackers behind the financial system DDoS attack—the Justice Department unsealed charges against Agha, Dardar, and Romar, and the FBI added Agha and Dardar to its "Cyber's Most Wanted" list. The charges ranged widely, indicative of the different tactics, vandalism, and attacks the SEA had executed over more than two years—including "criminal conspiracy relating to engaging in a hoax regarding a terrorist attack; attempting to cause mutiny of the U.S. armed forces; illicit possession of authentication features; access device fraud; unauthorized access to, and damage of, computers; and unlawful access to stored communications."[23] We also indicted Dardar and Romar for money laundering, wire fraud, and other charges related to their extortion scheme.

In May, Romar was put on a plane from Germany by authorities there and was successfully extradited to Dulles Airport to face criminal charges here. By September, Romar pleaded guilty in the Eastern District of Virginia.[24] By then, though—September 2016—we were increasingly concerned about two new threats, one from one of America's oldest adversaries and another new one, the likes of which we'd never seen before.

///////////////////

September and October 2016 were my final months working for the US government, and they were not quiet. By the fall, as the presidential campaign unfolded, it was quite clear Russia was running an extensive intelligence operation targeting the election—aiming a full range of cyber tools against our democratic process. After we learned that they had targeted entities such as the Democratic National Committee and the email of Clinton Campaign Chair John Podesta, we waited anxiously to see if and how they would weaponize that stolen information. Then we began to get reports that Russian operatives had penetrated state-level voting systems.[25]

Together, the Russia election attacks represented, in many aspects, the culmination of ten years of threats that we'd watched develop: simultaneous attacks on critical infrastructure and American values, weaponized stolen information, and subversive social media campaigns targeting the homeland. And, just as we had been surprised by the original targets of many of this first generation of cyberattacks—a movie studio, the consumer-facing websites of the financial industry, a casino, the government's personnel records—Russia's first major cyberattack on the United States hit a target that was critical to the United States but was not technically designated as "critical infrastructure." They targeted our confidence in our own democratic process, attempting to sow discord online and lead Americans to question the legitimacy of their own elections.

It was not exactly a surprise, though, that Russia attacked us. Vladimir Putin had taken an increasingly aggressive stance since his return to power. On a broad range of issues, from the Brexit vote to the rise of nationalist parties in Europe to Russia's attack on the 2016 election, Putin guided Russia's interference with a singular strategy: undermine Western democracies and weaken multilateral alliances that Russia sees as opposing its future, from NATO to the European Union, not to mention the international institutions—like the internet itself—that he believed threatened Russian interests. After decades of the Cold War, Russia had experience in attempts to exploit the seams and systemic weaknesses in Western democracies. As Robert Hannigan, former head of the British intelligence agency GCHQ, says, "The Russians have always used the openness of democracy against us."[26]

Putin's efforts included an unprecedented harassment campaign against US diplomats. State Department diplomat Victoria Nuland had seen her telephone calls intercepted and leaked online, and US Ambassador to Russia Michael McFaul, who had arrived in Moscow the same year Putin returned to power, had been harassed by government-paid protesters. The US Agency for International Development was thrown out of the country entirely. As McFaul wrote later, "Harassment was not limited to my immediate security team and me. Anyone who worked at the embassy could become a target. They slashed the tires of one of my junior staffers. They broke into the homes of embassy employees, oftentimes just rearranging the furniture or turning on all the lights to let people know that they were vulnerable."[27]

Tensions rose steadily after the Sochi Olympics in 2014 and Russia's subsequent invasion of Crimea and destabilizing attacks in eastern Ukraine, including the shoot-down of Malaysian Airlines Flight 17, which killed all 283 passengers and 15 crew. Russia's response to such events was always the same: they outright denied any involvement, no matter how overwhelming the evidence of their culpability, and instead flooded the field with false statements and conspiracy theories.

Online, Russia's behavior worsened too in the years since Game-Over Zeus and the Yahoo hack and grew more provocative; Russia's shadow war against Ukraine had seen wide-ranging, damaging cyberattacks on Ukraine's infrastructure.

While there's still much that we cannot discuss about how those final months of 2016 unfolded with regard to Russia's attacks on the election, it's safe to say that I believed in a response consistent with the playbook we'd been developing over the last decade: *These attacks shouldn't take place in the shadows. We should be public about the attribution of the attacks and use the various levers of government, including diplomatic condemnation and other tools, such as sanctions, to respond—just as we had when we'd been targeted by China, Iran, and North Korea.*

Inside government, we had watched with growing alarm as the campaign unfolded and warnings arose about Russia's multifaceted attack on our election. As Special Counsel Robert Mueller later reconstructed in his charges against 12 Russian military intelligence officers, government hackers targeted the Democratic Party and Clinton campaign officials, as well as state and local voting infrastructure across the country. As Lisa Monaco recalls, the questions and concerns swirling in the administration revolved around real concern about what the government didn't know. "We realized that we were playing a different game, that we had thought that we were dealing with the normal sort of espionage routine that was associated with presidential elections," White House Cyber Coordinator Michael Daniel later told *60 Minutes*.[28] "It was always our working assumption that we did not detect all of the potential Russian activity that was going on." Most of the reports of state-level targeting appeared to be routine scanning and probing, but what hadn't been caught? Were we seeing the full picture—or just looking through a soda straw? Had the Russians succeeded in getting inside voting databases somewhere the US government hadn't spotted? Had they altered voting machines we didn't know about? Had they changed voter registrations somewhere that wouldn't be visible until election day? "You're always worried about escalation, but this felt different because there was a specific day we had to get through," Lisa recalls. "We were worried about whether this election would actually come off."

As Mueller would later conclude in his final report as special counsel, "the Russian government interfered in the 2016 presidential election in sweeping and systematic fashion." In fact, Mueller revealed that Lisa's fears were evidently right—and the attack was even worse than originally understood. After Mueller wrote the FBI believed the GRU gained access to the network of at least one Florida county government, the state's governor Ron DeSantis said publicly, "Two Florida counties experienced intrusion in the supervisor of election networks," adding, "It did not affect any voting."

As Vice President Biden recalled, the whole issue was "tricky as hell. It's easy now to say, well, maybe we should have said more." At the time, though, all of government was uncertain. As Biden said, "The president and I would sit there, literally, after the [President's Daily Brief], and everybody's walked out of the room, and say: 'What the hell are we going to do?' 'Now, Mr. President, you go out and you unilaterally say this is what's happening, you're going to be accused of—in this environment—of trying to tip the election. And unless you can give harder data than we have now, you're going to be in a terrible position and it's going to play into the delegitimizing of our electoral process.'"[29]

By 2016 we had directly and publicly confronted the other three major foreign adversaries we had faced—China, Iran, and North Korea—yet we hadn't taken any public action against Russia. (The Yahoo indictment wasn't made public until the spring of 2017.) This presented an important opportunity to make public Russia's nefarious activity online and to deploy the tools we'd developed in the other cases, from criminal prosecutions to trade sanctions. We wanted to act quickly.

Lisa believed we should follow our developing playbook: gather evidence of who did it, make it public, and determine an appropriate deterrant response. Many others across government were wary of taking any public steps before the election, though President Obama raised the issue privately with Vladimir Putin and CIA Director John Brennan complained privately to his counterpart at Russia's FSB.

Confronting Russia publicly presented legitimate risks: for one thing, confrontation might have encouraged them to take even more provocative action, perhaps attempting to disrupt the voting process itself. For another, if their goal was to divide America and lead Americans to question the legitimacy of their elections, then being public about Russia's efforts might actually help accomplish that goal. To that end, the best route the administration saw going forward was to make whatever action it took bipartisan—to enlist Republican leaders on

Capitol Hill as part of any condemnation and response. However, Senate Majority Leader Mitch McConnell shot down such attempts.

Lisa Monaco recounted to me the pivotal meeting on September 8, 2016. Although she was an Obama appointee at the White House, she was a career Justice Department prosecutor, one of the most apolitical, nonpartisan officials I've ever run across, and her area, coordinating homeland security efforts, was about as nonpartisan as you could get. As she recounted, Lisa had journeyed that day to Capitol Hill with Comey and Secretary of Homeland Security Jeh Johnson to brief the 12 top congressional party and intelligence leaders on the available evidence and Russia's unfolding attack. There still hadn't been a single public statement from the government. They carefully laid out the Russian threat and explained that they were asking for Congress's help in speaking as a bipartisan, unified voice against the attack to ensure cooperation of states on cybersecurity. DHS could help states shore up their cybersecurity, but it needed to be bipartisan, so secretaries of state didn't feel they were wading into a minefield. In the briefing, she said, McConnell torpedoed any attempt at bipartisanship. In fact, he questioned whether the evidence actually even backed up the warning that Russia was attacking the election—and accused the intelligence leaders of being partisan tools. "You intelligence people shouldn't let yourself be used," McConnell said.

The meeting degenerated quickly into a partisan scrum. The administration officials left dejected. "It was the most depressing day I had in government," Lisa recalled. She was hardly the only one: James Clapper recalled his own reaction to the dispiriting meeting: "I was disappointed but not surprised. It seemed [Speaker Paul Ryan and McConnell] had decided by then that they didn't care who their nominee was, how he got elected, or what effects having a foreign power influence our elections would have on the nation, as long as they won."[30]

"The president asked the four leaders in a bipartisan meeting in the Oval Office to join him in asking the states to work with us [on securing the election]," White House Chief of Staff Denis McDonough later recalled. "It took over three weeks to get that statement worked out. It was dramatically watered down."[31]

It wasn't until after the election that the US government took stronger action. On December 29, President Obama announced the expulsion of Russian diplomats, as well as sanctions against the Russian security and intelligence agencies and private companies that were believed to have been involved in the attacks and a handful of top Russian cyber officials. He used the sanctions mechanism that we'd put into place following the Sony attack. The administration worked to position the sanctions to condemn the full spectrum of Russia's operations online as a rogue state, pushing successfully to include people such as Evgeniy Bogachev, the criminal–turned–intelligence operative who was responsible for the GameOver Zeus botnet. The election attack—while uniquely provocative and effective—was, to those of us who had watched the previous decade unfold in cyberspace, just another chapter in a long-running story of Putin's aggression online.

The year ahead, after I left the government, underscored that Russia was a uniquely dangerous actor online. In the spring of 2017, Russia unleashed ransomware that became known as NotPetya, an attack aimed at Ukraine that spun beyond Russia's control and caused massive disruptions at companies as varied as the shipping company FedEx ($300 million in damages[32]), drugmaker Merck ($310 million in damages[33]), and the advertising firm WPP ($15 million in damages[34]). The aftermath of NotPetya required the replacement of 45,000 computers and 4,000 servers at the cargo giant Maersk alone.[35] "We saw an indiscriminate attack launched by Russia against Ukraine in the ongoing hostilities there. What they used was a cyber weapon that was launched in the dark, that hit numbers of companies, individuals, and caused damage to our economies, it stopped shipping from moving…it literally shut [companies] down," White House Cybersecurity Coordinator Rob Joyce said. "And that is unacceptable."[36]

If Russia harbored terrorists whose attack caused FedEx $300 million in damages, or if the Russian government attacked a FedEx transit hub, our retaliation would be swift and decisive. It must be the same in cyberspace. Russia's behavior is undermining consumer trust and posing a systemic risk to an increasingly wired world, particularly as we move more of our infrastructure and daily life online.

We must recognize Vladimir Putin's Russia for the rogue actor it is online, and how both the Russian government's own behavior and the freedom it provides criminals are making the world less safe. Russia is operating far outside the bounds of civilized countries online. It's a problem similar to the rogue behavior we're seeing from North Korea on nuclear issues—and we need a similar, collective global approach to punish and isolate Russia. "Russia is ripping up the rulebook by undermining democracy, wrecking livelihoods by targeting critical infrastructure and weaponizing information," British Defense Secretary Gavin Williamson said in citing Russia's role in NotPetya. "We must be primed and ready to tackle these stark and intensifying threats."[37]

Also in the spring of 2017, the FBI, working with Spanish national police, captured Russian hacker Peter Levashov—one of the most notorious spammers in the internet's history—while he was on vacation outside of Russia, after years of living safely inside Russia. There are many more hackers like Levashov to catch. If you look at today's list of Cyber's Most Wanted, you will find a who's who of Russian hackers. Among others, there's Bogachev, who in addition to the sanctions has a $3 million reward for his capture, and Alexsey Belan, the criminal indicted in three separate major cybercrimes, most recently along with another criminal and two Russian FSB intelligence officers who were involved in the theft of a billion user accounts from Yahoo. Vladimir Putin enables these online bazaars and shields their leaders from criminal prosecution—or, worse, as appears to be the case with both Belan and Bogachev, signs up criminals as intelligence assets, to help enable further thefts and espionage by the Russian government. The uncomfortable truth is that Bogachev and other Russian cyber criminals—including those who attacked our elections—lie far beyond America's reach.

It is critical for the US government to draw a firm line against Russia. We cannot allow Vladimir Putin to ruin the internet for the rest of us. If he won't take action to prevent imminent damage to online communities from people harbored inside his country, the rest of the world must act together to do so.

One of the lessons of the 2016 election seems clear: well-meaning people with good intentions reached the wrong results. With hindsight, we didn't achieve the objective of deterring Russia. Every expert believes that Russia views its attack on the 2016 election as successful.

Until we change that calculus going forward, they're going to do it again—and others are going to consider doing it too. Looking ahead, we need to make sure they are, in fact, deterred. Yet right now, America hasn't made any progress toward building a nonpartisan system that could respond to Russia—or any other foreign adversary. The United States has made no policy changes to ensure that if the exact same situation presented itself in next year's congressional midterms or in the 2020 presidential election, its leaders wouldn't face the same hard choices that Obama's White House faced last summer.

The presumption should be that we will retaliate for such attacks, regardless of who is being attacked and who is being helped, and the response options should be prescribed in advance—agreed upon by the intelligence community, the White House, and congressional leadership. An attack on any candidate or party is an attack on the whole country. This response should begin with mapping out a nonpartisan process in advance, one that relies on the career government intelligence professionals and analysts whose professional lives have been spent drawing conclusions about foreign motives—and then relies upon the tools the United States already has at its disposal to respond. Discretion should be taken out of the equation. We need something like a "Dead Man's Switch" for our election system.

A body like the National Intelligence Council (NIC), the group of career analysts who help issue consensus national intelligence assessments, could be designated in advance to analyze whether a foreign actor is seeking to interfere with an election—whether through disinformation campaigns, hacking candidates or political parties, or actual attacks on the election infrastructure. Then, on a certain date—say 100 days before a national election—that team and the intelligence community should be obligated to report to Congress whether they have witnessed any suspicious foreign interference and then issue a second report if they later do detect interference. If the NIC finds with a "high degree of confidence" that a foreign power—Russia or any other country—is trying to influence the election or undermine confidence in it, it should transmit that report to Congress as fast as possible. Even if it can't say in detail what precise impact a foreign adversary is having, in order to protect intelligence sources and methods, the American people deserve better real-time information regarding the sanctity and security of the democratic process.

This analysis and conclusion should be conducted entirely removed from political appointees, just as the Justice Department traditionally defers to career professionals and prosecutors in making sensitive decisions around political corruption cases to avoid even the appearance of a conflict of interest. Taking his inspiration from Article 5 of the NATO treaty, which sees an attack on one country as an attack on the whole alliance, Senator Lindsey Graham has called for bipartisan agreement in advance that "an attack on one party is an attack on all."

This nonpartisan report should automatically trigger a response, allowing any future president to, as James Clapper said, avoid the charge that he "put his thumb on the scale of the election."[38] Retaliation for such attacks should be prescribed in advance—a menu of options, agreed upon by the intelligence community, the White House, and congressional leadership—that would pull from the many tools used over the past decade to deter and influence foreign countries' bad behavior in cyberspace. We've spent a decade outlining and creating a playbook for responding to these attacks—including public condemnations, international sanctions, the expulsion of foreign diplomats, and even the filing of criminal charges. Plus, we can and should employ additional covert methods developed by our intelligence agencies and military.

Too much of this cyberworld remains secret, but we need to bring it out of the shadows. Just as President Obama ultimately gave a speech at the National Defense University outlining how, where, and why the United States employs armed drone strikes—years after such attacks became a common tool of US counterterrorism—we need a president or high-ranking official to give a public speech outlining how, where, and why the United States will use cyber tools offensively and defensively.

The cyber responses we've put into place over the last decade have already helped shape the behavior of adversaries like North Korea, China, and Iran—and the United States should make more use of them in the future. After all, one thing's clear: we're nowhere near the end of the Code War.

Winning the Code War

THE ASSAULT ON our democratic values by Russia was hardly the only cyberthreat we faced in my final weeks working for the government. We also saw the largest and most powerful internet attacks ever measured unfold across the world—attacks that are continuing to this day. Using malicious networks of insecure home gadgets—thermostats, DVRs, security cameras, and other so-called Internet of Things devices—three hackers assembled what's known as the Mirai botnet and used it to attack websites around the world, including the backbone infrastructure of the internet itself, such as the domain name server company Dyn, an attack that slowed nearly the entire internet on the East Coast on a Friday afternoon in October 2016. The DDoS attacks were an order of magnitude more powerful than anything yet seen—so large that there was no way for internet companies to mitigate them. "There's no bandwidth large enough," said one person who worked on the response.

This incredibly destructive force—one that disrupted the internet for tens of millions of people across the globe—appears to have grown largely out of a group of college-aged gamers seeking an advantage in their *Minecraft* video games.[1] At the time of this writing, though, the Mirai botnets they created have spiraled far beyond their creators' control and will continue to wreak havoc for years to come. That such a small group could unintentionally unleash such a destructive—and perhaps permanent—online force is a perfect illustration of how our digital world remains fragile.

We are still today in the early stages of this Code War, trying to sort the asymmetric threats and use multiple instruments of power from both the government and the private sector to build international alliances of countries and companies that share our values. The criminal tactics, such as ransomware, botnets, and DDoS attacks, that were so novel when Bogachev helped pioneer them have grown commonplace.

In May 2018, four hackers from the Boston collective known as L0pht Heavy Industries returned to Capitol Hill, to mark the 20th anniversary of their original appearance at that first congressional hearing on cybersecurity. The moment—coming as the investigation into Russia's attack on the 2016 election continued—seemed to mark perhaps the end of the beginning of the Code War. The abstract threats they'd predicted years before were now a constant, daily presence in American life. As Joe "Kingpin" Grand told the packed audience of Room 2237 in the Rayburn House Office Building, "Nearly all of what we said 20 years ago still holds true. Yes, there have been improvements, but the general class of problems are the same."

Back in 1998, during L0pht's first appearance, just as the dot-com boom was beginning to take off, they'd warned a dubious Congress that any of them could take down the internet in just half an hour. While all four looked a bit older and the world of technology had changed dramatically, in ways both imaginable and unimaginable in their original 1998 hearing, their return appearance hardly offered much more hope. Back then, "it all seemed so theoretical—that a nation-state would have a team of guys like us, and they would be attacking the United States," Chris "Weld Pond" Wysopal said. "But we all know that 20 years later this is happening constantly."

"We keep building new things on old infrastructure that never seems to get fixed," Wysopal lamented. "Back then the threat was the teenage hacker. It was like, 'Yeah, they're kind of ankle-biters'... Now it's nation-states. So every vulnerability got a lot more risky."

Users today still make all the same mistakes L0pht warned about in 1998, from choosing simple passwords to not turning on extra security features—and the security of the underlying systems is still too weak. Grand pointed to recent news reports that President Trump was using an unsecure iPhone to make telephone calls and browse Twitter. "He's basically choosing to live with the risk of having a hacked phone because he feels the convenience is more important than security," Grand said. "The fact that the president—who's possibly the most targeted person in the world—doesn't want to trade his phone, makes you really think about, 'Is anybody else going to do that, and why should they?'" Grand's comments hit squarely on one of my constant refrains when I discuss this problem: Cybersecurity isn't just a challenge for government or businesses—it's a challenge for each of us and for our society. We need to be rethinking our embrace of the internet and how both our national geopolitical strategy and our corporate strategies should adapt to these new threats.

So what comes next? It's clear that these threats aren't disappearing anytime soon—and, in fact, cybersecurity is likely to get worse in the years ahead before it gets better. How should we as a society tackle this next era of the Code War?

The dynamism of the internet is reflected in the rapidly evolving nature of these cyberthreats—their perpetrators, their motivations, and their tools. The government and our society at large will have to think creatively about how to keep ourselves safe while preserving the dynamism and openness that have made the internet such a revolutionary invention. Strengthening our defenses will include rethinking how we approach building new technologies.

Despite the unprecedented challenges ahead of us—despite all of the numerous low- and high-profile moments explained in the preceding pages—our approach as a nation and as a society remains inadequate. We continue to be moving too slowly online. We continue to lag behind the threat. We need to be thinking faster—and smarter—or we risk seeing the internet overwhelmed by nefarious attackers, and our society's and our economy's strength depleted, perhaps not just by large-scale infrastructure attacks such as on the electrical grid, but also through the everyday decisions of ordinary people to not engage, to not speak out, or to not do business because of their fears and distrust of life online.

To return to my earlier analogy about how we're living online in a straw house—that even as the wolf approaches the door, not only are we not seeking shelter in a stronger house, we're continuing to cram ever more stuff into our straw house—meeting today's threat requires both building a stronger house (defense) and chasing away the wolf (offense).

On the defense side, our society needs at every level to improve cybersecurity education, from corporate C-suites to elementary schools, just as in previous generations we as a society committed to teaching people to be responsible users of other new technologies like cars. As President Trump's first White House cybersecurity coordinator, Rob Joyce, said, "It really comes down to doing the basics. So much of this, these intrusions, can be handled by addressing the basic blocking and tackling of security."

Users need to be savvier about using websites—and be more wary about how they go about their daily lives online. Companies and organizations need to invest in training and programs like "penetration testing" that investigate the vulnerabilities in their own networks as well as demonstrate to users what not to do.* We need also to expand the use of efforts like "bug bounty" programs that encourage civic-minded "white hat" hackers to point out problems in websites, software, and hardware in exchange for rewards such as cash or public bragging rights. When the US Air Force gathered 25 "ethical hackers" in December 2017 for its Hack the Air Force effort, the first two bugs in its network were found within 30 seconds, and over the course of 9 hours the hackers uncovered 55 vulnerabilities across more than 300 military websites; in return, the Air Force paid out $26,883 in "bounties," including a $10,650 reward to a hacker who uncovered a critical

---

* Many companies today actually test their own workforce with fake phishing emails, to encourage people to be wary about suspicious links and too-good-to-be-true offers.

vulnerability in the military network.[2] It's far cheaper to address such problems before an organization is breached in the first place. "The cost-benefit of this partnership is invaluable," the Air Force's chief information security officer said.

Humans will always be the weak link in technology; normal human behavior—the entirely predictable ways that all of us are lazy, forgetful, and distractible—will always make us vulnerable to both sophisticated and unsophisticated attacks online. We need both to educate people to minimize that risk—all of us need to be smarter users of the internet—and to ensure our technologies don't rely on unrealistic expectations about users' sophistication and savviness. We're not all going to rely on unguessable 30-character, mixed-case, alphanumeric passwords, use a different one for every website, and change them all once a month, so our security protocols shouldn't assume that we do. And when it turns out that someone didn't use an unguessable password, we need systems and procedures in place to ensure organizational resilience—that a compromise of a specific user account or a specific network isn't sufficient to steal all of an organization's secrets or paralyze its work.

These changes won't be easy. Addressing things as straightforward as spear phishing to ensure people don't click on nefarious links in emails requires changes by users, companies, and the technical underpinnings of the internet. That tactic—a favorite of hackers in almost every chapter of this book, from the Russians who attacked John Podesta to the Iranians who attacked Saudi Aramco to the Chinese who stole trade secrets from Coca-Cola—will continue to be effective and prey on us for years to come because the average office worker today sends and receives more than 120 emails a day—more than 30,000 a year. We read and send much of that email while our minds are consumed with other tasks, such as commuting, walking, meetings, or conference calls. To combat phishing, users need to be more wary than they are about checking the sender of an email; companies need security systems, such as two-factor authentication, that ensure a single wrong click and a single password aren't all it takes to compromise a network; and the internet writ large needs to adopt new protocols such as Domain-based Message Authentication, Reporting & Conformance (DMARC), which makes it impossible to spoof someone else's domain and to ensure that if an email comes from FBI.gov or BankofAmerica .com, then you know it's really from that organization. All of those changes need to happen just to combat phishing, which is basically the simplest form of cyberattack.

We're still today playing a massive game of digital catch-up. We spent billions—likely even trillions—of dollars moving our society's information online without adequately pricing the risks we were injecting into our lives in terms of possible theft and daily disruptions. We can't make the same mistake with the next generation of technology and the next generation of moving our infrastructure and "things" online. The rise of machine learning, artificial intelligence, and the Internet of Things (IoT) is already injecting new risks and new threats into our lives—and, further down the road, technologies such as superpowerful quantum computers will make much of the way that we think about security today obsolete.

These new security threats are already appearing. The Mirai attacks, which linked together upward of about 2.5 million devices into a dangerous botnet, represent only a tiny fraction of the IoT devices expected to be connected to the internet in the years ahead. Every single day in 2016 there were 5.5 million such new devices connected to the internet—refrigerators, drones, robotic vacuums, light fixtures, "smart" televisions, medical devices, and so on. Almost all of them were and are insecure and vulnerable to attack. It's one thing, for instance, if a hacker's malware insists on a $300 ransom to unlock your computer; it's something else entirely if the hacker insists on a $300 payment before grandma's home dialysis machine will be turned on again.

These problems will only worsen as IoT devices flood our lives. Too often, what we consider in our lives "smart" devices are, in fact, shockingly "dumb" and insecure, with default passwords and easy-to-exploit vulnerabilities. And they're arriving in America's homes and businesses for use by people ill-equipped with the knowledge to operate them securely. In some cases, these stories appear amusing: a *New York Times* story after Christmas 2017 focused on the rising phenomenon of people using neighborhood list servs to report drones that had gone missing or crashed after their users lost control of them. One tech executive quoted in the story explained, "We're seeing a convergence of once-futuristic technology with mainstream America." Yet this same public naïveté has a dark side, too: malware accidentally installed by an inexperienced user infected two entire British hospitals, forcing them to close for three days, cancel hundreds of medical procedures, and divert incoming trauma patients to other facilities.

Looking down the road, longer-term, we cannot seek to solve the cybersecurity problem unless we recognize and confront the problem at the core of the internet: our digital lives are built upon technology that was inherently insecure by design, tools never designed with security in mind. The original designs and standards of the internet—built for ease of use, not for security—need to be updated to focus on security by design, ensuring that the devices and systems not only work as intended but also are secure from nefarious actors seeking to do harm.

If the internet is going to be the core backbone of our daily lives and our economy going forward, we need a system that is secure—characterize it as whatever analogy you want, a Cyber Moonshot or a Cyber Manhattan Project. (Indeed, under the Trump administration, there were two government-industry commissions, known as the Cyber Moonshot and the Cyberspace Solarium Commission, aimed at envisioning what solutions are needed—rapidly—to secure the internet's future.) And we need a high-level, societal commitment and research effort to innovate our way to a more secure future, one that reconsiders the digitization of our daily lives and our infrastructure and how we can separate and untangle mission-critical tasks from today's internet. This will almost certainly mean building new networks—new internets, really—that offer a high degree of security and authentication for critical tasks. Being able to play Pandora stations on your car radio shouldn't allow a hacker to access the vehicle's brakes. We must—as a government and as consumers—press Silicon Valley and the private sector to change the mindset on security, to tackle security as part of the initial design of a product, not just as an after-the-launch cleanup process, one patch or software update at a time.

Government must play a stronger—and more savvy—role in securing our lives online. We need to continue—and accelerate even—confronting cybersecurity problems publicly and be transparent about threats, so people can better judge the risks ahead. Our goal at the Justice Department over the last decade was to shift the default inside government from keeping attacks secret to making them public. Going forward, there's still much to do in this area, to make public as much as we can as quickly as we can, but that shift will help the public understand the threat better and allow companies and organizations to be more vigilant. To see how powerful the "name and shame" approach can be, look no further than Special Counsel Robert Mueller's indictments of the GRU and the Internet Research Agency for their attack on the 2016 election. Mueller's indictments did more than anything else to publicly outline and explain how Russia attacked America, giving Americans an important window into the government's intelligence and understanding of Russia's role just days before President Trump took the stage in Helsinki with Putin himself. By relentlessly following the facts, proving attribution, and then making them public, we make clear to the public just what our adversaries are doing online—and by laying out the facts, we can help the American public demand action.

Similarly, we need to continue to streamline and simplify the government's response to cyber incidents. The reporting of breaches should be mandatory to help both the government and the public understand the risks better. Government entities such as Congress and the executive branch are unfortunately not particularly effective at anticipating policy needs and adopting forward-looking strategies; instead, they respond best to outside pressures and demands. Making cyber risks more transparent will help to shape the demand for effective action both within government and in the private sector. You can't drive action unless people know what's happening (which is part of the point of writing this book). Consumers should better understand who is doing what with their data and who takes security seriously.

We should also make it simple for organizations to report breaches and attacks—there's still no one-stop "cyber 911" that a company or organization can call to report a breach or attack and ask for help. Instead, as I find when I advise clients confronting cybersecurity problems today, there's often a mix of as many as nine different government agencies people have to call and work with to respond to an attack—and some want to help, but others want to punish. This situation sets up a confusing and complicated system that hurts companies and individuals at the very moment they most need help.

We must also think creatively and innovatively about the next generation of technology; the United States has dominated the rise of the first generation of the internet, delivering manifold benefits to our society both economically and geopolitically. We cannot allow ourselves to be overtaken by China or other advancing economies; government research-and-development funding is falling precipitously, and while we have entities—such as the Committee on Foreign Investment in the United States—that help protect against foreign companies and governments buying up our leading companies and swiping our technologies, we have precious little focus on ensuring that our companies and our governments are investing sufficiently in the next generation of technological advances. Yet US security, for a country and for individuals, will be increasingly dependent on our remaining the world leader in everything from GPS technology to quantum computers to artificial intelligence. While the last two decades of Chinese technological advancement and economic growth have been powered in large part by stolen American intellectual property, China is increasingly delivering its own innovations. In January 2018, China announced that it had completed the world's first quantum-encrypted video conference, a 75-minute conversation between China and Austria that was protected by unbreakable encryption.[3] China's space program is preparing to launch a probe to the dark side of the moon, a technically difficult task never before accomplished by the US or Soviet space programs, and China's version of GPS allows its satellites to broadcast text in addition to locations, a militarily significant advance. We're starting to lose ground in this technological race today in part because of intellectual property theft, but also because of how we're not investing in the next generation of our economy and how we're actively discouraging those who want to come to the United States for education and to start businesses—a tide of talent that has been at the core of our economic success in the digital age.

These challenges—and the myriad other ways that our society and our technology need to change and adapt for a new era—may seem like insolvable problems, but they're not: just think of the amazing technological transformation that has taken place over the last decade. It is, at the time of this writing, just ten years since the iPhone was invented. We're in the middle of a societal and behavioral revolution that has played out in big ways and small: my young daughter, when she first learned to read, first tried to swipe the page on her book. That rapid pace of change that we've already lived gives me hope for the future—that in the years ahead we can accomplish another societal shift that restores security to our digital lives while preserving and expanding the freedom and openness that the internet first promised at its inception. With a strong national will, I believe we can innovate out of this problem and secure the internet, data, and our way of life for my daughter's generation.

When we first began confronting the full magnitude of cybersecurity, our focus inside government was on defense and hardening our own systems. But recent years have shown us that defense is not enough. Cybersecurity and societal security in the 21st century need to be risk-management exercises. There is no internet-connected system or device that can be secure from a hacker. We must focus on resilience and risk management, ensuring that catastrophes can be averted if a hacker is successful at accessing a system and that companies, organizations, and individuals can recover their data and their digital lives.

Rebuilding our straw house into something more resilient and more secure is only part of the solution. We need efforts, too, on the offense side. We need to chase the wolf away. We can begin with the model we started to build while I was at the National Security Division: after an attack, the government needs to commit the resources to find out who did it, why they did it, and how they did it—and then impose proportional consequences on the perpetrator. Beyond building better defenses, we need to be thinking about deterrence for the Code War, too. Unlike the Cold War, where thousands of intercontinental ballistic missiles and nuclear missiles were meant to keep us safe, deterrence in the cyber age will not be a one-size-fits-all strategy. Instead, it will be a complicated multilayered strategy that determines what each adversary hopes to gain from attacks and what each adversary values.

The Code War requires the government to keep up our all-tools approach to shaping this online environment, and discouraging and deterring threats through every means possible, whether through international sanctions, prosecutions, diplomatic protests, public shaming, or military strikes such as the one that targeted Junaid Hussain. Thankfully, the government is now more routinely deploying these tools against online perpetrators: in September 2017, the Department of Treasury sanctioned the supporters of Iran's Islamic Revolutionary Guard Corps who were responsible for those DDoS attacks on the financial sector, and in March 2018, it sanctioned the Russians who were indicted by Special Counsel Robert Mueller for their role in the Internet Research Agency's efforts against the 2016 presidential election.[4] Over the course of 2017, the Justice Department also brought new criminal charges against hackers from China, Russia, and Iran, expanding the precedents we had established over the previous decade. In March 2018, the Justice Department charged nine Iranians working for a contractor for the Islamic Revolutionary Guards Corps with a massive hacking campaign that targeted hundreds of universities and private sector companies and resulted in the theft of intellectual property totaling more than $3.4 billion. In fact, over the course of the year, nation-state indictments would become (unfortunately, perhaps) all but routine.

After North Korea launched the destructive WannaCry ransomware in 2017, the United States and its allies went public with that attribution, pointing out how the rogue nation was "increasingly using cyberattacks to fund its reckless behavior and cause disruption across the world." Then, in the fall of 2018, the Justice Department brought a public criminal complaint against North Korean hacker Park Jin Hyok for his role in WannaCry, the attack on Sony Pictures Entertainment, and a cybertheft from the central bank of Bangladesh. As my successor as assistant attorney general for national security, John Demers, said at the time, "The scale and scope of the cyber-crimes alleged by the complaint is staggering and offensive to all who respect the rule of law and the cyber norms accepted by responsible nations."

When North Korea launched the destructive WannaCry ransomware in 2017, then White House Homeland Security Advisor Tom

Bossert went public with that attribution: "North Korea has acted especially badly, largely unchecked, for more than a decade, and its malicious behavior is growing more egregious. WannaCry was indiscriminately reckless," he wrote in the *Wall Street Journal* in December 2017.[5] "It is increasingly using cyberattacks to fund its reckless behavior and cause disruption across the world."

To make the announcement about North Korea's role in WannaCry, as well as Russia's role in NotPetya, America stood with its allies: the United Kingdom, Australia, and other like-minded nations. That's critical. Just like in the Cold War, the Code War requires us to build—and to lead—an international alliance of countries and organizations that share our values. Unlike NATO, which, as its name implies (the North Atlantic Treaty Organization), is based on geography as much as it is on values, the Code War's global coalition will require allies on every continent and will require mixing lessons we've learned in public safety with lessons we've learned in public health about how to confront and defeat cross-border problems and ensure the safety of critical systems with a rational set of rules. This isn't just a government problem; it's going to require working intimately with the private sector, whose systems and employees represent on a daily basis the front lines of attacks from criminals, terrorists, and foreign adversaries.

The Iranian indictments, Russian sanctions, the Mueller indictments, and the public attributions all marked more steps forward in the work we began with charging the Chinese PLA hackers in 2014 and came as the Justice Department forcefully confronted what it called the "malign foreign influence" threat in the wake of the Russian attack on the presidential election. "Like terrorism and other national security threats, the malign foreign influence threat requires a unified, strategic approach across all government agencies," Deputy Attorney General Rod Rosenstein said in a speech in July 2018. "Other sectors of society also need to do their part. State and local governments must secure their election infrastructure. Technology companies need to prevent misuse of their platforms. Public officials, campaigns, and other potential victims need to study the threats and protect themselves and their networks. And citizens need to understand the playing field."[6]

America since its inception, since the days of George Washington, has always stood for a certain set of values. What made our international leadership so critical over the last century and through the Cold War has been the way that we used our muscle—economic and political—to benefit the world at large, from defeating fascism to rebuilding Europe with the Marshall Plan to gifting to the world technologies such as the internet, which have transformed economic opportunities in every corner of the planet. We must do the same now, helping to lead the world to a safer and more secure online experience that puts freedom of expression and freedom to conduct commerce at the center of our digital lives. We need to help lead and form coherent rules and regulations consistent with our values on how personal data can be used, stored, and controlled by users online—rules that make consumers confident without preventing the rise of opportunities such as artificial intelligence and the era of "big data." These rules need to become standard around the world. We're already seeing Orwellian advancements by China in terms of facial recognition and ubiquitous video surveillance systems, and it won't be good for the United States if the country that sets the ground rules for the next generation of technology doesn't share our values and commitment to individual freedom and expression.

Today, we need to carry those values into the internet and ensure that they're preserved for future generations. We cannot allow China and Russia—countries that don't share our democratic norms—to set the rules for this new world.

Winning the Code War first requires recognizing that the war has already begun.

John P. Carlin
Washington, DC
August 2018

Acknowledgments

This is a book about the achievements of others. Our government's dedicated public servants are a model to the world. The colleagues I was privileged to serve with at the Washington, DC, US Attorney's Office, the FBI, and Main Justice work day in and day out at the Department of Justice to protect us under the rule of law and, in doing so, protect not just our safety but our way of life. I'd like to specifically thank my colleagues at the National Security Division for their work, even knowing that public acknowledgment is not what motivates them. The mission goes on.

There are many people not named in the book because they would not want the attention or can't be named. Reconstructing the past quarter century of fighting cyber attacks underscored that there are scores—hundreds, even—of people whose names don't appear in the preceding pages but whose tireless efforts as analysts, investigators, prosecutors, computer scientists, and network engineers on behalf of the government or the broader internet community made possible any success to date. The partners we had across the intelligence, law enforcement, and military communities similarly believed that we needed to be more public and aggressive about disrupting those who sought to do harm online and included prosecution as one tool in that process, even if bringing cases could make their missions harder. I wish I could name them all. This is their story: any mistakes in the book of fact or judgment are mine.

Outside of government, I want to also express my sincere gratitude to the many private sector partners who were part of this story, from security companies to social media platforms to victim companies who trusted us to seek justice on their behalf.

I want to thank President Obama for the honor of serving as assistant attorney general of the National Security Division; Robert S. Mueller, for his leadership and for providing the opportunity to serve at the FBI and as his chief of staff—there is no greater role model; and Lisa O. Monaco for her friendship, extraordinary competence, and dedicated service to the country.

I'm especially grateful to Michael Gaynor and Vanessa Sauter for helping gather court records, indictments, and other research, and my editor Ben Adams for his vision and patience, as well as Melissa Veronesi and Melissa Raymond at PublicAffairs. In my new life outside of government, Walter Isaacson and the Aspen Institute and my new colleagues at Morrison & Foerster have welcomed me and allowed me to continue to work to improve cybersecurity.

Thank you to Garrett Graff, for your craft, your good humor, and your patience: without you, there would be no book and I know I fought every minute of the process, conflicted between a belief that the story needs to be told and a long-ingrained professional trait of saying as little as possible. Not a coauthor's dream partner.

Last and most important, my family. To my parents, for their strong belief in public service. And to my wife, Sarah, and daughter, Sylvie.

Notes

FOREWORD

1. Eduard Kovacs, "Hackers Around the World: It's No TriCk, He's Among the Best in the UK," *Softpedia*, February 18, 2012, http://news.softpedia.com/news/Hackers-Around-the-World-It-s-No-TriCk-He-s-Among-the-Best-in-the-UK-253652.shtml.

2. Ibid.

3. Hannah Furness, "Team Poison: Profile of the Hackers," *Telegraph*, April 12, 2012, www.telegraph.co.uk/technology/9200751/Team-Poison-profile-of-the-hackers.html.

4. Brendan Koerner, "Why ISIS Is Winning the Social Media War," *Wired*, April 2016, www.wired.com/2016/03/isis-winning-social-media-war-heres-beat/.

5. David Ensor, "Al Qaeda Letter Called 'Chilling,'" CNN, October 12, 2005, edition.cnn.com/2005/WORLD/meast/10/11/alqaeda.letter/.

6. Rita Katz and Michael Kern, "Terrorist 007, Exposed," *Washington Post*, March 26, 2006, www.washingtonpost.com/wp-dyn/content/article/2006/03/25/AR2006032500020.html.

7. Brian Krebs, "Terrorism's Hook into Your Inbox: U.K. Case Shows Link Between Online Fraud and Jihadist Networks," *Washington Post*, July 5, 2007, www.washingtonpost.com/wp-dyn/content/article/2007/07/05/AR2007070501153_pf.html.

8. Gordon Corera, "The World's Most Wanted Cyber-jihadist," *BBC News*, January 16, 2008, www.news.bbc.co.uk/2/hi/americas/7191248.stm.

9. Andrea Elliott, "An American Jihadist Now Has a Memoir Out," *6th Floor*, May 23, 2012, www.6thfloor.blogs.nytimes.com/2012/05/23/an-american-jihadist-now-has-a-memoir-out/.

10. William H. Webster et al., "Final Report of the William H. Webster Commission on the Federal Bureau of Investigation, Counterterrorism Intelligence, and the Events at Fort Hood, Texas, on November 5," https://archives.fbi.gov/archives

/news/pressrel/press-releases/judge-webster-delivers-webster-commission -report-on-fort-hood.

11. Scott Shane, "Inside Al Qaeda's Plot to Blow Up an American Airliner," *New York Times*, February 22, 2017, www.nytimes.com/2017/02/22/us/politics/anwar -awlaki-underwear-bomber-abdulmutallab.html?_r=0.

12. Scott Shane, "The Lessons of Anwar al-Awlaki," *New York Times Magazine*, August 27, 2015, www.nytimes.com/2015/08/30/magazine/the-lessons-of-anwar-al -awlaki.html.

13. J. M. Berger, "How ISIS Games Twitter," *Atlantic*, June 16, 2014, www .theatlantic.com/international/archive/2014/06/isis-iraq-twitter-social-media -strategy/372856/.

14. Brendan Koerner, "Why ISIS Is Winning the Social Media War," *Wired*, April 2016, www.wired.com/2016/03/isis-winning-social-media-war-heres-beat/.

15. Emerson T. Brooking and P. W. Singer, "War Goes Viral: How Social Media Is Being Weaponized Across the World," *Atlantic*, November 2016, www.theatlantic .com/magazine/archive/2016/11/war-goes-viral/501125/.

16. Charlie Winter, "Documenting the Virtual 'Caliphate'," Quilliam Foundation, October 2015, www.quilliaminternational.com/wp-content/uploads/2015/10/FINAL -documenting-the-virtual-caliphate.pdf.

17. Greg Miller and Souad Mekhennet, "Inside the Surreal World of the Islamic State's Propaganda Machine," *Washington Post*, November 20, 2015, www.washington post.com/world/national-security/inside-the-islamic-states-propaganda-machine /2015/11/20/051e997a-8ce6-11e5-acff-673ae92ddd2b_story.html?utm_term =.4c6da4dfe120.

18. Rukmini Callimachi, "Not 'Lone Wolves' After All: How ISIS Guides World's Terror Plots from Afar," *New York Times*, February 4, 2017, www.nytimes .com/2017/02/04/world/asia/isis-messaging-app-terror-plot.html?_r=0.

19. Winter, "Documenting the Virtual 'Caliphate'."

20. Koerner, "Why ISIS Is Winning the Social Media War."

21. Shane Harris, "This Is ISIS's New Favorite App for Secret Messages," *Daily Beast*, November 16, 2015, www.thedailybeast.com/this-is-isiss-new-favorite-app-for -secret-messages.

22. @MichaelSSmithII, "App Created by IS-affil Amaq Agency 'News' Org to Stream-line Access to IS Propaganda, Screenshots Courtesy @CtrlSec," Twitter, December 7, 2015, 7:21 a.m., twitter.com/MichaelSSmithII/status/673885130377703424.

23. J. M. Rieger, "FBI Chief: Terrorists Can Attack US 'in Their Pajamas in Their Basement,'" *Roll Call*, September 18, 2014, www.rollcall.com/news/-236428-1.html.

24. Del Quentin Wilber, "Here's How the FBI Tracked Down a Tech-Savvy Ter-rorist Recruiter for the Islamic State," *Los Angeles Times*, April 13, 2017, www.latimes .com/politics/la-fg-islamic-state-recruiter-20170406-story.html.

25. *US v. Ardit Ferizi, a/k/a Th3Dir3ctorY*, Criminal Complaint, US District Court for the Eastern District of Virginia, Case No. 1:15-MJ-515, 11, www.justice.gov /opa/file/784501/download.

26. Wilber, "Here's How the FBI Tracked Down."

27. Adam Goldman and Eric Schmitt, "One by One, ISIS Social Media Experts Are Killed as Result of F.B.I. Program," *New York Times*, November 24, 2016, www.nytimes .com/2016/11/24/world/middleeast/isis-recruiters-social-media.html?_r=0.

28. Intelligence and National Security Alliance, "2016 Intelligence and National Security Summit—The Homeland Enterprise View," YouTube, October 5, 2016, www .youtube.com/watch?v=J93wFxhx--A, 18:00.

29. See Alexander Meleagrou-Hitchens and Seamus Hughes, "The Threat to the United States from the Islamic State's Virtual Entrepreneurs," *CTCSentinel*, vol. 10, no. 3, March 2017, 5. Elton Simpson's discussions with Hussain were presented as evidence for the prosecution in *US v. Abdul Malik Abdul Kareem*, US District Court for the District of Arizona, Case 2:15-cr-00707-SRB, Document 441-7, 18.

30. *US v. Munir Abdulkader*, US District Court for the Southern District of Ohio, Case 1:16-cr-00019-MRB, Sentencing Memorandum, www.investigativeproject.org /documents/case_docs/3152.pdf.

31. Wilber, "Here's How the FBI Tracked Down."

32. US Department of Justice, Office of Public Affairs, "Ohio Man Sentenced to 20 Years in Prison for Plot to Attack U.S. Government Officers," November 23, 2016, www.justice.gov/opa/pr/ohio-man-sentenced-20-years-prison-plot-attack-us-govern ment-officers.

33. Michele McPhee, "Boston Jihadi Plot Gets Top ISIS Leader in Syria Killed," *Newsweek*, November 8, 2017, www.newsweek.com/boston-jihadi-plot-gets-top-isis -leader-killed-703994.

34. Garrett Graff, "The FBI's Growing Surveillance Gap," *Politico*, June 16, 2016, www .politico.com/magazine/story/2016/06/orlando-terror-fbi-surveillance-gap-213967.

35. Steve Clemons, "The Biden Doctrine," *Atlantic*, August 22, 2016, www.theatlantic .com/international/archive/2016/08/biden-doctrine/496841/.

36. Jeffrey Goldberg, "The Obama Doctrine," *Atlantic*, April 2016, www.theatlantic .com/magazine/archive/2016/04/the-obama-doctrine/471525/.

37. Goldman and Schmitt, "One by One, ISIS Social Media Experts Are Killed as Result of F.B.I. Program."

38. Alan Sipress, "An Indonesian's Prison Memoir Takes Holy War into Cyberspace," *Washington Post*, December 14, 2004, www.washingtonpost.com/wp-dyn /articles/A62095-2004Dec13.html.

39. Rachel Weiner, "Hacker Who Sent 'Kill List' of U.S. Military Personnel to ISIS: 'I Feel So Bad,'" *Washington Post*, September 23, 2016, www.washingtonpost.com /local/public-safety/hacker-who-sent-kill-list-of-us-military-personnel-to-islamic -state-i-feel-so-bad/2016/09/23/dc0ba0ea-8196-11e6-b002-307601806392_story .html.

40. "We can confirm that Junaid Hussain, an ISIS operative was killed in a U.S. military airstrike on August 24 in Raqqa, Syria," said Air Force Col. Pat Ryder, spokesman for US Central Command. See "U.S. Confirms Islamic State Computer Expert Killed in Air Strike," *Reuters*, August 28, 2015, www.reuters.com/article/us-mideast -crisis-hacker/u-s-confirms-islamic-state-computer-expert-killed-in-air-strike -idUSKCN0QX2A420150828.

INTRODUCTION

1. "Lessons from Our Cyber Past: The First Cyber Cops," Atlantic Council State Cybercraft Initiative, Washington, DC, May 16, 2012, web.archive.org/web/2012 0826235220/http://www.acus.org:80/event/lessons-our-cyber-past-first-cyber -cops/transcript.

2. Patrick Smith (ed.), *Conversations with William Gibson* (University Press of Mississippi, 2014), https://books.google.com/books?id=hAAbBwAAQBAJ&pg=PT 51&lpg=PT51&dq=william+gibson+%22cyberpunk+era%22+%22whole +earth+review%22&source=bl&ots=KQAtiyYq5k&sig=aOJsAekdx0rvUnZr9z ki6uBP6zg&hl=en&sa=X&ved=0ahUKEwiP0tXXqvfVAhVDWCYKHQwa A14Q6AEILjAB#v=onepage&q=postures&f=false.

3. "Lessons from Our Cyber Past: The First Cyber Cops."

4. "There's Nowhere to Hide from the Economics of Cybercrime," McAfee, 2018, https://www.mcafee.com/us/solutions/lp/economics-cybercrime.html.

5. "Economic Impact of Cybercrime—No Slowing Down," McAfee LLC, February 2018, www.mcafee.com/us/resources/reports/restricted/economic-impact-cyber crime.pdf.

6. US Committee on Energy and Commerce, Subcommittee on Oversight and Investigations, *Cyber Espionage and the Theft of U.S. Intellectual Property and Technology,* July 9, 2013, docs.house.gov/meetings/IF/IF02/20130709/101104/HHRG-113-IF 02-Wstate-WortzelL-20130709-U1.pdf. Text transcription of hearing.

7. Ibid.

8. See Fred Kaplan, *Dark Territory: The Secret History of Cyber War* (Simon & Schuster, 2016), 191, and Andrew Blum, *Tubes: A Journey to the Center of the Internet* (HarperCollins, 2012), 61.

9. "Gartner Says 6.4 Billion Connected 'Things' Will Be in Use in 2016, Up 30 Percent from 2015," November 10, 2015, www.gartner.com/newsroom/id/31 65317.

10. Craig Timberg, "Net of Insecurity: A Flaw in the Design," *Washington Post,* May 30, 2015, www.washingtonpost.com/sf/business/2015/05/30/net-of-insecurity -part-1//?utm_term=.0126c73b6f8.

11. David D. Clark, "The Design Philosophy of the DARPA Internet Protocols," *Computer Communication Review,* vol. 18, no. 4, August 1988, 106–114, tdc.iorc .depaul.edu/media/internet-design-philosophy.pdf.

12. Patricia Sullivan, "Computer Pioneer Bob Bemer, 84," *Washington Post,* June 25, 2004, www.washingtonpost.com/wp-dyn/articles/A4138-2004Jun24.html.

13. Rajiv Chandrasekaran, "Y2K Repair Bill: $100 Billion," *Washington Post,* November 18, 1999, www.washingtonpost.com/wp-srv/WPcap/1999-11/18/077r -111899-idx.html.

14. Timberg, "Net of Insecurity: A Flaw in the Design."

15. Steven Millward, "China Now Has 731 Million Users, 95% Access from Their Phones," *Tech in Asia,* January 22, 2017, www.techinasia.com/china-731-million -internet-users-end-2016.

16. Emma Hinchliffe, "China's Biggest E-Commerce Holiday Raked in Three Times More Than Black Friday," *Mashable*, November 12, 2017, mashable.com/2017 /11/12/singles-day-alibaba-2017/.

17. Paul Rosenzweig, "Significant Cyber Attacks on Federal Systems—2004– Present," *Lawfare*, May 7, 2012, www.lawfareblog.com/significant-cyber-attacks-federal -systems-2004-present.

18. John Brenner, *America the Vulnerable: Inside the New Threat Matrix of Digital Espionage, Crime, and Warfare* (Penguin, 2011), 73.

19. Garrett Graff, "How the FBI Took Down Russia's Spam King—and His Massive Botnet," *Wired*, April 11, 2017, www.wired.com/2017/04/fbi-took-russias -spam-king-massive-botnet/.

20. Government of Georgia, Ministry of Justice, "Cyber Espionage Against Georgian Government," http://dea.gov.ge/uploads/CERT%20DOCS/Cyber%20Espion age.pdf.

21. "Exclusive: The Aspen Institute and Morrison & Foerster's John Carlin Speaks with White House Cybersecurity Coordinator Rob Joyce from the Cambridge Cyber Summit Today," CNBC, October 4, 2017, www.cnbc.com/2017/10/04/exclusive -morrison-and-foersters-john-carlin-speaks-with-white-house-cybersecurity -coordinator-rob-joyce-from-the-cambridge-cyber-summit-today.html.

22. US Department of Defense, Office of General Counsel, "Department of Defense Law of War Manual," June 2015, www.defense.gov/Portals/1/Documents /law_war_manual15.pdf.

23. Adam Segal, *The Hacked World Order: How Nations Fight, Trade, Maneuver, and Manipulate in the Digital Age* (PublicAffairs, 2016), 37.

24. Henry Kissinger, *World Order* (Penguin, 2014), 344.

25. Bruce Schneier, "Click Here to Kill Everyone," *New York Magazine*, January 27, 2017, www.schneier.com/essays/archives/2017/01/click_here_to_kill_e.html.

CHAPTER 1

1. Matt Richtel, "The Napster Decision: The Overview; Appellate Judges Back Limitations on Copying Music," *New York Times*, February 13, 2001, www.nytimes .com/2001/02/13/business/napster-decision-overview-appellate-judges-back -limitations-copying-music.html.

2. Tess Vigeland, "The Marketplace Report: Operation Digital Gridlock," *NPR*, August 26, 2004, www.npr.org/templates/story/story.php?storyId=3872616.

3. US Department of Justice, "Prepared Statement of Attorney General John Ashcroft," August 25, 2004, www.justice.gov/archive/ag/speeches/2004/82504ag .htm.

4. "Two Convicted in Landmark Internet Piracy Trial," *Guardian*, January 18, 2005, www.theguardian.com/film/2005/jan/19/piracy.news; and William Triplett, "Feds Get Yet Another Pirate: Operation Yields Fourth P2P Conviction," *Variety*, June 9, 2005, variety.com/2005/biz/markets-festivals/feds-get-yet-another-pirate-1117924176/.

5. US Department of Justice, Criminal Division, "Final Guilty Plea in Operation Gridlock, First Federal Peer-to-Peer Copyright and Piracy Crackdown," May 31, 2005, www.justice.gov/archive/criminal/cybercrime/press-releases/2005/tannerPlea.htm.

6. Thomas Flexner James, *Washington: The Indispensable Man* (Open Road Media, 2017), xvii.

7. "Hello New York: Michael Fusco on Violent Crime in New York," *Saturday Night Live*, NBC, www.nbc.com/saturday-night-live/video/leftover-night/n10009?snl=1.

8. John Perry Barlow, "A Declaration of the Independence of Cyberspace," *Electronic Frontier Foundation*, n.d., www.eff.org/cyberspace-independence.

9. Steven Levy, *Hackers: Heroes of the Computer Revolution* (O'Reilly Media, 2010), ix.

10. Ibid., 27.

11. Ibid., 91–92.

12. Ibid., 134.

13. John Markoff, "The Odyssey of a Hacker: From Outlaw to Consultant," *New York Times*, January 29, 2001, www.nytimes.com/2001/01/29/business/the-odyssey-of-a-hacker-from-outlaw-to-consultant.html.

14. Ron Rosenbaum, "Secrets of the Little Blue Box," *Esquire*, October 2017, 119–226, www.historyofphonephreaking.org/docs/rosenbaum1971.pdf.

15. Craig Timberg, "Net of Insecurity: A Flaw in the Design," *Washington Post*, May 30, 2015, www.washingtonpost.com/sf/business/2015/05/30/net-of-insecurity-part-1//?utm_term=.0126c73b6f8.

16. Katie Hafner and Matthew Lyon, *Where Wizards Stay Up Late: The Origins of the Internet* (Simon & Schuster, 1998), 143.

17. Ibid., 182.

18. Ibid., 153.

19. Katie Hafner and John Markoff, *CYBERPUNK: Outlaws and Hackers on the Computer Frontier, Revised* (Simon & Schuster, 1995), 279.

20. Timberg, "Net of Insecurity: A Flaw in the Design."

21. Bob Metcalfe, "The Stockings Were Hung by the Chimney with Care," *IETF Tools*, tools.ietf.org/html/rfc602.

22. Hafner and Lyon, *Where Wizards Stay Up Late: The Origins of the Internet*, 190.

23. Levy, *Hackers*, 423.

24. Jimmy Maher, "Zork on the PDP-10," *Digital Antiquarian*, January 3, 2012, www.filfre.net/2012/01/zork-on-the-pdp-10/.

25. *MIT CSAIL Advanced Network Architecture Group*, mercury.lcs.mit.edu/~jnc/tech/header/mins06.txt.

26. Levy, *Hackers*, 424.

27. Hafner and Markoff, *CYBERPUNK*, 38.

28. In his memoir, "Ghost in the Wires," Mitnick denied attacking US Leasing's network, saying he'd stolen a password and given it to a friend, who was the one who actually set the printers to spew vulgarities.

29. Kevin Mitnick, *Ghost in the Wires: My Adventures as the World's Most Wanted Hacker* (Little, Brown, 2011), 14.

30. Ibid., 14, 28.

31. Vin McLellan, "Case of the Purloined Password," *New York Times*, July 26, 1981, www.nytimes.com/1981/07/26/business/case-of-the-purloined-password.html ?pagewanted=3&pagewanted=all.

32. Timberg, "Net of Insecurity: A Flaw in the Design."

33. Josh McHugh, "The N-Dimensional Superswitch," *Wired*, May 1, 2001, www .wired.com/2001/05/caspian/.

34. Levy, *Hackers*, 303.

35. Ibid., 432–433.

36. Kaplan, *Dark Territory*, 2.

37. NSDD 145: National Policy on Telecommunications and Automated Information Systems Security, September 17, 1984; National Security Decision Directives, 1/20/1981–1/20/1989; and Numbered National Security Policy Papers, 1981–1989, www.reaganlibrary.gov/sites/default/files/archives/reference/scanned-nsdds/nsdd 145.pdf.

38. Timothy Harper, "Was It a Game, or Was It Real?" *Bangor Daily News*, August 29, 1983, 20, news.google.com/newspapers?id=sxc0AAAAIBAJ&sjid=qy MIAAAAIBAJ&pg=1296,5369436&hl=en.

39. "Two Who Raided Computers Are Pleading Guilty," *New York Times*, March 17, 1984, www.nytimes.com/1984/03/17/us/two-who-raided-computers-pleading -guilty.html.

40. Christopher D. Chen, "Computer Crime and the Computer Fraud and Abuse Act of 1986, 10 Computer L.J. 71," *John Marshall Journal of Information Technology & Privacy Law*, vol. 10, no. 1, 1990, repository.jmls.edu/cgi/viewcontent.cgi?referer =https://www.google.com/&httpsredir=1&article=1414&context=jitpl.

41. "Timeline: The U.S. Government and Cybersecurity," *Washington Post*, May 16, 2003, www.washingtonpost.com/wp-dyn/articles/A50606-2002Jun26.html.

42. Nikki Finke, "A University Professor's 'Startling' Experiments Began It All," *Los Angeles Times*, January 31, 1988, articles.latimes.com/1988-01-31/news/vw-39340_1 _computer-virus; and "When Did the Term 'Computer Virus' Arise?" *Scientific American*, September 2, 1997, scientificamerican.com/article/when-did-the-term -compute/.

43. Michelle Slatalla and Joshua Quittner, *Masters of Deception: The Gang That Ruled Cyberspace* (HarperCollins, 1995), 16.

44. Ken Thompson, "Reflections on Trusting Trust," Turing Award Lecture, *Communications of the ACM*, vol. 1, no. 8, 1984, www.ece.cmu.edu/~ganger/712.fall02 /papers/p761-thompson.pdf.

45. Linda Greenhouse, "House Approves Measure to Make Computer Fraud a Federal Crime," *New York Times*, June 4, 1986, www.nytimes.com/1986/06/04/us /house-approves-measure-to-make-computer-fraud-a-federal-crime.html; Josephine Wolff, "The Hacking Law That Can't Hack It," *Slate*, September 27, 2016, www.slate .com/articles/technology/future_tense/2016/09/the_computer_fraud_and _abuse_act_turns_30_years_old.html; and Scott Mace, "Computer Bills in Works," *InfoWorld*, October 14, 1985, books.google.com/books?id=ii8EAAAAMBAJ&pg =PA10&lpg=PA10&dq=%22computer+fraud+and+abuse+act%22+Hughes& source=bl&ots=4l4VEFULtU&sig=KlZUHImVK--KDNDXA2CSmxWc4ws

&hl=en&sa=X&ved=0ahUKEwj2vtfR-YvYAhUkc98KHZW8Ax04ChDoAQg3MAM
#v=onepage&q=%22computer%20fraud%20and%20abuse%20act%22%20Hughes
&f=false.

46. Andrew S. Tanenbaum, "Attacks from Outside the Operating System," *InformIT*, March 29, 2002, www.informit.com/articles/article.aspx?p=26150&seqNum=6.

47. Hafner and Markoff, *CYBERPUNK*, 287.

48. Ibid., 253–255.

49. John Markoff, "'Virus' in Military Computers Disrupts Systems Nationwide," *New York Times*, November 4, 1988, timesmachine.nytimes.com/timesmachine/1988 /11/04/167588.html?pageNumber=1.

50. Hafner and Markoff, *CYBERPUNK*, 314–316.

51. Ibid., 319.

52. Timothy B. Lee, "How a Grad Student Trying to Build the First Botnet Brought the Internet to Its Knees," *Washington Post*, November 1, 2013, www.washingtonpost .com/news/the-switch/wp/2013/11/01/how-a-grad-student-trying-to-build-the -first-botnet-brought-the-internet-to-its-knees/?utm_term=.c8d2b0a6b8af.

53. Mark Bulik, "1988: 'The Internet' Comes Down with a Virus," *New York Times*, August 6, 2014, www.nytimes.com/times-insider/2014/08/06/1988-the-internet-comes -down-with-a-virus/.

54. "Student Guilty of 'Worm' Attack on Computer Net," *Los Angeles Times*, January 23, 1990, articles.latimes.com/1990-01-23/news/mn-622_1_federal-computer.

55. Max Knoblauch, "How One Hacker's Mistake Fashioned the Internet You Use Today," *Mashable*, November 1, 2013, mashable.com/2013/11/01/morris-worm /#AH09g.rYkqqW.

56. Gregory J. Rattray, *Strategic Warfare in Cyberspace* (MIT Press, 2001), 315.

57. Stacey L. Edgar, *Morality and Machines: Perspectives on Computer Ethics* (Jones & Bartlett, 2002), books.google.com/books?id=CWLyryduwMYC&pg=PT249&lpg =PT249&dq=%22harper%27s+magazine%22+%22is+computer+hacking+a +crime?%22&source=bl&ots=b-9ZsTBhyT&sig=p8cV5TacG5-DuXzuJbzb9 -IoFgc&hl=en&sa=X&ved=0ahUKEwjKzs—_ozZAhXOu1MKHYXfBQwQ6 AEINTAC#v=onepage&q=%22harper's%20magazine%22%20%22is%20 computer%20hacking%20a%20crime%3F%22&f=false.

58. Slatalla and Quittner, *Masters of Deception*, 100.

59. Ibid., 171.

60. Ibid., 173.

61. Ibid., 207.

62. Ibid., 223.

63. "Remembering Grateful Dead Lyricist and Internet Activist John Perry Barlow," *Fresh Air from NPR*, February 9, 2018, www.npr.org/2018/02/09/584508647 /remembering-grateful-dead-lyricist-and-internet-activist-john-perry-barlow.

64. "Cyber-Libertarian and Pioneer John Perry Barlow Dies at Age 70," *The Two-Way: Breaking News from NPR*, February 7, 2018, www.npr.org/sections/thetwo -way/2018/02/07/584124201/cyber-libertarian-and-pioneer-john-perry-barlow -dies-at-age-70.

65. Steve Schroeder, *The Lure: The True Story of How the Department of Justice Brought Down Two of the World's Most Dangerous Cyber Criminals* (Course Technology PTR, 2011), 27.

66. John Markoff, "A Most-Wanted Cyberthief Is Caught in His Own Web," *New York Times*, February 16, 1995, www.nytimes.com/1995/02/16/us/a-most-wanted -cyberthief-is-caught-in-his-own-web.html?pagewanted=all.

67. Thomas Rid, *Rise of the Machines: A Cybernetic History* (W. W. Norton, 2017), 309.

68. Kevin Poulsen, *Kingpin: How One Hacker Took Over the Billion-Dollar Cybercrime Underground* (Broadway, 2012), 39; and Richard Cole, "FBI Says Hacker Took 100,000 Credit Card Numbers," *New York Times*, May 23, 1997, politics.nytimes.com /library/cyber/week/052397hacker.html.

69. Kim Zetter and Kevin Poulsen, "Government Stops Shielding Corporate Breach 'Victims.'" *Wired*, March 30, 2010, www.wired.com/2010/03/sunshine/.

70. US Senate Select Committee on Intelligence, *Current and Projected National Security Threats to the United States*, US Government Printing Office, January 28, 1998, www.intelligence.senate.gov/hearings/current-and-projected-national-security -threats-united-states-january-28-1998. Text transcription of hearing.

71. US Senate Select Committee on Intelligence, *Open Hearing to Consider the Nominations of John P. Carlin and Francis X. Taylor*, US Government Publishing Office, February 24, 2015, www.intelligence.senate.gov/sites/default/files/hearings/CHRG -113shrg93212.pdf.

72. "Claiming the Lost Cyber Heritage," *Strategic Studies Quarterly*, Fall 2012, www .airuniversity.af.mil/Portals/10/SSQ/documents/Volume-06_Issue-3/Healey.pdf.

73. US House Committee on Government Reform, Subcommittee on National Security, Veterans Affairs, and International Relations, *NIPC's Role in the New Department of Homeland Security*, Federal Bureau of Investigation, June 11, 2002, archives .fbi.gov/archives/news/testimony/nipcs-role-in-the-new-department-of-homeland -security.

74. The account of SOLAR SUNRISE is based upon the following: Kevin Poulsen, "VIDEO: SOLAR SUNRISE, the Best FBI-Produced Flick Ever," *Wired*, September 23, 2008, www.wired.com/2008/09/video-solar-sun/; Richard Power, "Joy Riders: Mischief That Leads to Mayhem," *InformIT*, October 30, 2000, www.informit.com/articles /article.aspx?p=19603&seqNum=4; Kaplan, *Dark Territory*, 73–78; and Rid, *Rise of the Machines*, 314–316.

75. William M. Arkin, "Sunrise, Sunset," *Washington Post*, March 29, 1999, www .washingtonpost.com/wp-srv/national/dotmil/arkin032999.htm.

76. Rid, *Rise of the Machines*, 324.

77. MOONLIGHT MAZE details are pulled from Freedom of Information Act documents, as well as Rid, *Rise of the Machines*, 316–334, and Kaplan, *Dark Territory*, 78–88. FOIA documents available at http://goo.gl/9AMJJw.

78. Rid, *Rise of the Machines*, 330.

79. See declassified MOONLIGHT MAZE case files, released under the FOIA, at http://goo.gl/9AMJJw and at https://medium.com/@chris_doman/the-first

-sophistiated-cyber-attacks-how-operation-moonlight-maze-made-history-2adb12cc43f7.

80. Rid, *Rise of the Machines*, 333.

81. Martyn Thomas, "What Really Happened in Y2K?" Gresham College, www.gresham.ac.uk/lectures-and-events/what-really-happened-in-y2k.

82. "Newsweek Exclusive: 'We're in the Middle of a Cyberwar'," *PR Newswire*, Cision, September 12, 1999, www.prnewswire.com/news-releases/newsweek-exclusive-were-in-the-middle-of-a-cyberwar-74343007.html.

83. Rebecca Hersher, "Meet Mafiaboy, the 'Bratty Kid' Who Took Down the Internet," *All Things Considered from NPR*, www.npr.org/sections/alltechconsidered/2015/02/07/384567322/meet-mafiaboy-the-bratty-kid-who-took-down-the-internet.

84. Hersher, "Meet Mafiaboy."

85. Lynn Burke, "Hot on the Trail of 'Mafiaboy'," *Wired*, February 15, 2000, www.wired.com/2000/02/hot-on-the-trail-of-mafiaboy/?currentPage=all.

86. "Prison Urged for Mafiaboy," *Wired*, June 1, 2001, www.wired.com/2001/06/prison-urged-for-mafiaboy/.

87. "Lessons from Our Cyber Past: The First Cyber Cops," Atlantic Council State Cybercraft Initiative, Washington, DC, May 16, 2012, web.archive.org/web/20120826235220/http://www.acus.org:80/event/lessons-our-cyber-past-first-cyber-cops/transcript.

88. Greg Miller and Ashley Dunn, "Hacker Case Arrest Belies Real Challenge, Experts Say," *Los Angeles Times*, April 20, 2000, http://articles.latimes.com/2000/apr/20/news/mn-21583.

89. US Department of Justice, Criminal Division, "Justice Department Launches Web Site to Address Cybercrime," March 13, 2000, www.justice.gov/archive/opa/pr/2000/March/119crm.htm.

90. Kevin Poulsen, "Free Mafiaboy," *SecurityFocus*, April 24, 2000, www.securityfocus.com/news/22.

91. US Congressional Research Service, *China-U.S. Aircraft Collision Incident of April 2001: Assessments and Policy Implications*, Updated October 10, 2001, Federation of American Scientists, fas.org/sgp/crs/row/RL30946.pdf.

92. Xu Wu, *Chinese Cyber Nationalism: Evolution, Characteristics, and Implications* (Lexington, 2007), /books.google.com/books?id=8YWHshSSvfIC&pg=PA54&lpg=PA54&dq=china+cyber+EP-3+2001&source=bl&ots=mO1az6iZDA&sig=wDx32cykkP0edTp4B6QBUboxS7M&hl=en&sa=X&ved=0ahUKEwjbvY-UrYnWAhUKRyYKHVXiCOoQ6AEIYTAH#v=onepage&q=china%20cyber%20EP-3%202001&f=false, 55.

93. Craig Smith, "May 6–12; The First World Hacker War," *New York Times*, May 13, 2001, www.nytimes.com/2001/05/13/weekinreview/may-6-12-the-first-world-hacker-war.html?mcubz=1.

94. "Capability of the People's Republic of China to Conduct Cyber Warfare and Computer Network Exploitation: Prepared for the U.S.-China Economic and Security Review Commission," Northrop Grumman, October 9, 2009, nsarchive2.gwu.edu/NSAEBB/NSAEBB424/docs/Cyber-030.pdf.

95. Poulsen, *Kingpin*, 74.

96. See Misha Glenny, *DarkMarket: How Hackers Became the New Mafia* (Vintage, 2012), 41.

97. Brian Krebs, *Spam Nation: The Inside Story of Organized Cybercrime—From Global Epidemic to Your Front Door* (Sourcebooks, 2014), 17.

98. Ibid., 26.

99. Ibid., 20.

100. Joseph B. Tompkins and Linda A. Mar, "The 1984 Federal Computer Statute: A Partial Answer to a Pervasive Problem," *The John Marshall Journal of Information Technology & Privacy Law*, vol. 6, no. 3, 1986, repository.jmls.edu/cgi/view content.cgi?referer=https://www.google.com/&httpsredir=1&article=1512&context =jitpl.

101. See also US Department of Justice, Office of the United States Attorneys, "1029. Fraudulent Presentment and Related Unauthorized Credit Card Transactions Made by Access Device—18 U.S.C. § 1029(a)(7)," *Department of Justice*, n.d., www .justice.gov/usam/criminal-resource-manual-1029-fraudulent-presentment-and -related-unauthorized-credit-card.

102. Krebs, *Spam Nation*, 28.

103. Ibid., 125.

104. See Kevin Poulsen, "The Ukrainian Hacker Who Became the FBI's Best Weapon—and Worst Nightmare," *Wired*, May 2016, www.wired.com/2016/05 /maksym-igor-popov-fbi/.

105. Poulsen, "The Ukrainian Hacker."

106. Ibid.

107. Ibid.

108. Ibid.

109. Joseph Menn, *Fatal System Error: The Hunt for the Crime Lords Who Are Bringing Down the Internet* (Hachette, 2010), 105.

110. "Origin of the Term 'Spam' to Mean Net Abuse," *Brad Templeton*, www.temple tons.com/brad/spamterm.html.

111. "Who Wrote Sobig?" O'Reilly, 2004, www.oreilly.com/spamkings/Who WroteSobig.pdf.

112. "Ruslan Ibragimov / Send-Safe.com," *SpamHaus*, www.spamhaus.org/rokso /evidence/ROK2400/ruslan-ibragimov-send-safe.com/main-info; and Brian McWilliams, "Russian Denies Authoring 'SoBig' Worm," O'Reilly, November 2, 2004, archive.oreilly.com/pub/a/network/2004/11/02/sobig.html.

113. Menn, *Fatal System Error*, 109.

114. US Department of Justice, Office of the Inspector General, "Chapter Four: The Attorney General's Guidelines on FBI Undercover Operations," September 2005, oig .justice.gov/special/0509/chapter4.htm.

115. Poulsen, *Kingpin*, 190–191.

116. Eric M. Weiss, "Consultant Breached FBI's Computers," *Washington Post*, July 6, 2006, www.washingtonpost.com/wp-dyn/content/article/2006/07/05/AR 2006070501489_pf.html.

117. Timberg, "Net of Insecurity."

118. Kaplan, *Dark Territory*, 93; for more history on L0pht, see www.nytimes.com /1999/10/03/magazine/hack-counterhack.html?scp=2&sq=l0pht%20heavy &st=cse and web.archive.org/web/20000311135015/http://www.pbs.org/newshour /bb/cyberspace/jan-june98/l0pht_hackers.html.

119. Joe Grand, "Hackers Testifying at the United States Senate, May 19, 1998 (L0pht Heavy Industries)," *YouTube*, March 14, 2011, www.youtube.com /watch?v=VVJldn_MmMY.

120. Rene Millman, "New Version of L0phtcrack Makes Cracking Windows Passwords Easier Than Ever," *SC Media*, September 1, 2016, www.scmagazineuk.com /new-version-of-l0phtcrack-makes-cracking-windows-passwords-easier-than-ever /article/530687/.

121. See *US v. Joseph Colon*, Case #06-CR-63 RJ, US District Court for the District of Columbia.

122. "Acting Assistant Attorney General for National Security, John Carlin Speaking at the American Bar Association Homeland Security Law Institute," *IC on the Record*, 2014, icontherecord.tumblr.com/post/58835138436/acting-assistant-attorney -general-for-national.

123. "FBI Commemorates 100 Years of Fidelity, Bravery, and Integrity," *Federal Bureau of Investigation*, July 17, 2008, archives.fbi.gov/archives/news/speeches /fbi-commemorates-100-years-of-fidelity-bravery-and-integrity.

CHAPTER 2

1. Yudhijit Bhattacharjee, "A New Kind of Spy: How China Obtains American Technological Secrets," *New Yorker*, May 5, 2014, www.newyorker.com/magazine /2014/05/05/a-new-kind-of-spy.

2. US Department of Justice, Office of Public Affairs, "Former Boeing Engineer Convicted of Economic Espionage in Theft of Space Shuttle Secrets for China," Department of Justice, July 16, 2009, www.justice.gov/opa/pr/former-boeing-engineer -convicted-economic-espionage-theft-space-shuttle-secrets-china.

3. Joby Warrick and Carrie Johnson, "Chinese Spy 'Slept' in U.S. for 2 Decades," *Washington Post*, April 3, 2008, www.washingtonpost.com/wp-dyn/content/article /2008/04/02/AR2008040203952.html.

4. Ron Scherer, "Why Did It Take So Long to Catch Spy for China?" *Christian Science Monitor*, July 18, 2009, www.csmonitor.com/USA/Justice/2009/0718 /p05s01-usju.html.

5. US Office of the National Counterintelligence Executive, *Foreign Spies Stealing U.S. Economic Secrets in Cyberspace: Report to Congress on Foreign Economic Collection and Industrial Espionage, 2009–2011*, Office of the Director of National Intelligence, October 2011, www.dni.gov/files/documents/Newsroom/Reports%20and%20Pubs /20111103_report_fecie.pdf.

6. Nick Collins, "Sir James Dyson Attacks China over Designs 'Theft'," *Telegraph*, December 6, 2011, www.telegraph.co.uk/finance/yourbusiness/8936685/Sir-James -Dyson-attacks-China-over-designs-theft.html; and James Hurley, "Ask China to

Tackle Copycats, Dyson Tells PM," *Telegraph*, June 25, 2011, www.telegraph.co.uk /finance/8597773/Ask-China-to-tackle-copycats-Dyson-tells-PM.html.

7. Yudhijit Bhattacharjee, "How the FBI Cracked a Chinese Spy Ring," *New Yorker*, May 12, 2014, www.newyorker.com/news/news-desk/how-the-f-b-i-cracked -a-chinese-spy-ring.

8. Joshua Davis, "Hackers Take Down the Most Wired Country in Europe," *Wired*, August 21, 2007, www.wired.com/2007/08/ff-estonia/.

9. "Lessons from Our Cyber Past: The First Cyber Cops."

10. US House Judiciary Committee, Subcommittee on Courts, the Internet and Intellectual Property, The FBI's Cyber Division, July 17, 2003. Statement of Jana D. Monroe, Assistant Director, Cyber Division, FBI, archives.fbi.gov/archives/news /testimony/the-fbis-cyber-division.

11. Nate Anderson, "Pentagon Hacked, Chinese Army Suspected: Report," *Ars Technica*, September 3, 2007, arstechnica.com/information-technology/2007/09/chinese -military-accused-of-hacking-pentagon-computers/.

12. John Bloom, *Eccentric Orbits: The Iridium Story* (Atlantic Monthly Press, 2016), 117.

13. U.S.-China Economic and Security Review Commission, "Section 3: Chinese Intelligence Services and Espionage Threats to the United States," Government Publishing Office, n.d., www.uscc.gov/sites/default/files/Annual_Report/Chapters /Chapter%202%2C%20Section%203%20-%20China%27s%20Intelligence%20 Services%20and%20Espionage%20Threats%20to%20the%20United%20States.pdf, p. 294.

14. Evan Osnos, *Age of Ambition: Chasing Fortune, Truth, and Faith in the New China* (Farrar, Straus and Giroux, 2014), 13.

15. Ibid., p. 4.

16. Ibid., p. 24

17. Ibid., p. 22.

18. Anne S. Y. Cheung and Zhao Yun, "An Overview of Internet Regulation in China," University of Hong Kong, 2013, hub.hku.hk/bitstream/10722/193113/2 /Content.pdf.

19. See Amy Chang, *Warring State: China's Cybersecurity Strategy*, Center for a New American Security, December 2014, s3.amazonaws.com/files.cnas.org/documents /CNAS_WarringState_Chang_report_010615.pdf.

20. Timothy L. Thomas, *Dragon Bytes: Chinese Information-War Theory and Practice*, Foreign Military Studies Office, 2004, 5.

21. Jason R. Fritz, *China's Cyber Warfare: The Evolution of Strategic Doctrine* (Lexington Books, 2017), 9.

22. Thomas, *Dragon Bytes*, 43, 45.

23. Eric Jou, "*WoW* Hacker Group Mastermind Sentenced to Two Years in Chinese Prison," *Kotaku*, December 23, 2013, kotaku.com/wow-hacker-group-master mind-sentenced-to-two-years-in-c-1488458327.

24. "The National Security Agency: Missions, Authorities, Oversight and Partnerships," August 9, 2013, https://www.nsa.gov/news-features/press-room/statements /2013-08-09-the-nsa-story.shtml.

25. Shane Harris, @War: The Rise of the Military-Internet Complex (Mariner, 2014), 142.

26. Kaplan, Dark Territory, 173.

27. United States, The White House, "National Security Presidential Directive/NSPD-54; Homeland Security Presidential Directive/HSPD-23," Federation of American Scientists, January 8, 2008, fas.org/irp/offdocs/nspd/nspd-54.pdf.

28. Stephen B. Slick, "The 2008 Amendments to Executive Order 12333, United States Intelligence Activities," Studies in Intelligence, vol. 58, no. 2, June 2014, www.cia.gov/library/center-for-the-study-of-intelligence/csi-publications/csi-studies/studies/vol-58-no-2/pdfs/Slick-Modernizing%20the%20IC%20Charter-June2014.pdf.

29. US Department of Justice, Office of Public Affairs, "Alleged International Hacking Ring Caught in $9 Million Fraud," November 10, 2009, www.justice.gov/opa/pr/alleged-international-hacking-ring-caught-9-million-fraud.

30. John Markoff, "Before the Gunfire, Cyberattacks," New York Times, August 12, 2008, www.nytimes.com/2008/08/13/technology/13cyber.html.

31. Menn, Fatal System Error, 214.

32. Bowden, "Worm," 126.

33. Ibid., 180, 223.

34. Kaplan, Dark Territory, 182.

35. Brian Grow and Mark Hosenball, "Special Report: In Cyberspy vs. Cyberspy, China Has the Edge," Reuters, April 14, 2011, www.reuters.com/article/us-china-usa-cyberespionage/special-report-in-cyberspy-vs-cyberspy-china-has-the-edge-idUSTRE73D24220110414.

36. Fritz, China's Cyber Warfare, 48.

37. Shane Harris, "Chinese Spies May Have Tried to Impersonate Journalist Bruce Stokes," Washingtonian, February 2, 2011, www.washingtonian.com/2011/02/02/chinese-spies-may-have-tried-to-impersonate-journalist-bruce-stokes/.

38. See, for example, "Tracking GhostNet: Investigating a Cyber Espionage Network," Information Warfare Monitor, March 29, 2009, www.nartv.org/mirror/ghostnet.pdf.

39. James Glanz and John Markoff, "Vast Hacking by a China Fearful of the Web," New York Times, December 4, 2010, www.nytimes.com/2010/12/05/world/asia/05wikileaks-china.html?pagewanted=all&mcubz=1.

40. Ben Elgin, Dune Lawrence, and Michael Riley, "Coke Gets Hacked and Doesn't Tell Anyone," Bloomberg, November 2, 2012, https://www.bloomberg.com/news/articles/2012-11-04/coke-hacked-and-doesn-t-tell.

41. Dave Lee, "The Comment Group: The Hackers Hunting for Clues About You," BBC, February 12, 2013, www.bbc.com/news/business-21371608.

42. Elgin, Lawrence, and Riley, "Coke Gets Hacked and Doesn't Tell Anyone."

43. Dave Lee, "The Comment Group: The Hackers Hunting for Clues About You," BBC, February 12, 2013, www.bbc.com/news/business-21371608.

44. The Chinese military was reorganized in 2015 and 2016. For more background, see Mark A. Stokes, Jenny Lin, and L. C. Russell Hsiao, "The Chinese People's Liberation Army Signals Intelligence and Cyber Reconnaissance Infrastructure," Project

2049 Institute, November 11, 2011, https://project2049.net/documents/pla_third _department_sigint_cyber_stokes_lin_hsiao.pdf; and Mark A. Stokes, "The PLA General Staff Department Third Department Second Bureau," Project 2049 Institute, July 27, 2015, www.project2049.net/documents/Stokes_PLA_General_Staff _Department_Unit_61398.pdf.

45. See Stokes, Lin, and Hsiao, "The Chinese People's Liberation Army."

46. Mara Hvistendahl, "Hackers: The China Syndrome," *Popular Science*, April 23, 2009, www.popsci.com/scitech/article/2009-04/hackers-china-syndrome#page-3.

47. Ibid.

48. Ibid.

49. Grow and Hosenball, "Special Report: In Cyberspy vs. Cyberspy, China Has the Edge."

50. See also "Javaphile, Buddhism, and...the Public Security Bureau?" The Dark Visitor, December 3, 2007, https://web.archive.org/web/20080617093645/http:// www.thedarkvisitor.com/2007/12/javaphile-buddhism-and-the-public-security -bureau/; and "Founding of Javaphile (2000)," The Dark Visitor, November 17, 2007, https://web.archive.org/web/20071207234601/http://www.thedarkvisitor.com:80 /wordpress/?p=24.

51. "Capability of the People's Republic of China to Conduct Cyber Warfare and Computer Network Exploitation: Prepared for the U.S.-China Economic and Security Review Commission," Northrop Grumman, October 9, 2009, nsarchive2.gwu.edu /NSAEBB/NSAEBB424/docs/Cyber-030.pdf.

52. Evan Thomas, "Campaign 2008 Secrets: McCain Gambles on Palin," *Newsweek*, November 5, 2008, www.newsweek.com/campaign-2008-secrets-mccain-gambles -palin-85079.

53. Michael Isikoff, "Chinese Hacked Obama, McCain Campaigns, Took Internal Documents, Officials Say," NBC News, June 10, 2013, www.nbcnews.com /id/52133016/t/chinese-hacked-obama-mccain-campaigns-took-internal-documents -officials-say/#.WncNzeg-cy4.

CHAPTER 3

1. US Department of Labor, Bureau of Labor Statistics, *The Employment Situation: February 2009*, Bureau of Labor Statistics, March 6, 2009, www.bls.gov/news.release/ archives/empsit_03062009.pdf.

2. "Barack Obama's Inaugural Address," *New York Times*, January 20, 2009, www .nytimes.com/2009/01/20/us/politics/20text-obama.html.

3. "Transcripts—The National Security Division at 10," *Center for Strategic and International Studies*, www.csis.org/transcripts-national-security-division-10.

4. "President Obama Delivers Remarks on Cyber Security Strategy," *Washington Post*, May 29, 2009, www.washingtonpost.com/wp-dyn/content/article/2009/05/29 /AR2009052901260.html.

5. Kaplan, *Dark Territory*, 40–45.

6. *Critical Foundations: Protecting America's Infrastructure*, US President's Commission on Critical Infrastructure Protection, October 1997, www.hsdl.org/?abstract &did=986.

7. "DOJ Issues White Paper on Cybersecurity Information Sharing Under the SCA," Alston & Bird, n.d., www.alstonprivacy.com/doj-issues-white-paper-on-cyber security-information-sharing-under-the-sca/.

8. *Tracking GhostNet: Investigating a Cyber Espionage Network*, Information Warfare Monitor, March 29, 2009, www.nartv.org/mirror/ghostnet.pdf.

9. U.S.-China Economic and Security Review Commission, "Section 3: Chinese Intelligence Services and Espionage Threats to the United States," 297.

10. Scott Pelley, "FBI Director on Threat of ISIS, Cybercrime," *60 Minutes*, CBS News, October 5, 2014, www.cbsnews.com/news/fbi-director-james-comey-on-threat -of-isis-cybercrime/.

11. Shane Harris, "Exclusive: Inside the FBI's Fight Against Chinese Cyber-Espionage," *Foreign Policy*, May 27, 2014, foreignpolicy.com/2014/05/27/exclusive -inside-the-fbis-fight-against-chinese-cyber-espionage/.

12. Michael Joseph Gross, "Enter the Cyber-Dragon," *Vanity Fair*, August 2, 2011, www.vanityfair.com/news/2011/09/chinese-hacking-201109?printable=true.

13. Brian Grow and Mark Hosenball, "Special Report: In Cyberspy vs. Cyberspy, China Has the Edge," *Reuters*, April 14, 2011, www.reuters.com/article/us-china -usa-cyberespionage/special-report-in-cyberspy-vs-cyberspy-china-has-the-edge -idUSTRE73D24220110414.

14. Ariana Eunjung Cha and Ellen Nakashima, "Google China Cyberattack Part of Vast Espionage Campaign, Experts Say," *Washington Post*, January 14, 2010, www .washingtonpost.com/wp-dyn/content/article/2010/01/13/AR2010011300359.html.

15. Taylor Buley and Andy Greenberg, "Google China Hackers' Unexpected Backdoor," *Forbes*, January 14, 2010, www.forbes.com/2010/01/14/google-china -mcafee-technology-cio-network-hackers.html.

16. Kim Zetter, "Google Hack Attack Was Ultra Sophisticated, New Details Show," *Wired*, January 14, 2010, www.wired.com/2010/01/operation-aurora/.

17. Ellen Nakashima, "Chinese Hackers Who Breached Google Gained Access to Sensitive Data, U.S. Officials Say," *Washington Post*, May 20, 2013, www.washington post.com/world/national-security/chinese-hackers-who-breached-google-gained -access-to-sensitive-data-us-officials-say/2013/05/20/51330428-be34-11e2-89c9 -3be8095fe767_story.html.

18. John Markoff and David Barboza, "2 China Schools Said to Be Tied to Online Attacks," *New York Times*, February 18, 2010, www.nytimes.com/2010/02/19/tech nology/19china.html.

19. James Glanz and John Markoff, "Vast Hacking by a China Fearful of Web," *New York Times*, December 4, 2010, www.nytimes.com/2010/12/05/world/asia /05wikileaks-china.html?_r=1.

20. Andrew Jacobs and Miguel Helft, "Google, Citing Attack, Threatens to Exit China," *New York Times*, January 12, 2010, www.nytimes.com/2010/01/13/world /asia/13beijing.html?mcubz=1.

21. Hillary Clinton, "Remarks on Internet Freedom," The Newseum, Washington, DC, January 21, 2010, https://2009-2017.state.gov/secretary/20092013clinton/rm/2010/01/135519.htm.

22. "Shi Tao's Case: Yahoo! Knew More Than They Claimed," *RConversation*, July 29, 2007, rconversation.blogs.com/rconversation/2007/07/shi-taos-case-y.html.

23. US House Subcommittee on Africa, Global Human Rights and International Operations, *The Internet in China: A Tool for Freedom or Suppression?* February 15, 2008, Opening statement by Congressman Chris Smith, R-NJ, chrissmith.house.gov/news/documentsingle.aspx?DocumentID=56325.

24. "Yahoo Criticized in Case of Jailed Dissident," *New York Times*, November 7, 2007, www.nytimes.com/2007/11/07/technology/07yahoo.html.

25. US Commission on the Intelligence Capabilities of the United States Regarding Weapons of Mass Destruction, *Report to the President of the United States*, March 31, 2005, fas.org/irp/offdocs/wmd_report.pdf, 471–472.

26. "Transcripts—The National Security Division at 10."

27. "Bush Speaks After Signing Patriot Act," *Washington Post*, March 9, 2009, www.washingtonpost.com/wp-dyn/content/article/2006/03/09/AR2006030901294.html.

28. US Department of Justice, Office of the United States Attorneys, "9-90.000—National Security," www.justice.gov/usam/usam-9-90000-national-security

29. McAfee Foundstone Professional Services and McAfee Labs, "Global Energy Cyberattacks: 'Night Dragon,'" McAfee, February 10, 2011, www.mcafee.com/hk/resources/white-papers/wp-global-energy-cyberattacks-night-dragon.pdf.

30. Diane Bartz, "Chinese Hackers Infiltrated Five Energy Firms: McAfee," *Reuters*, February 10, 2011, www.reuters.com/article/us-energy-cyber-china/chinese-hackers-infiltrated-five-energy-firms-mcafee-idUSTRE7190XP20110210.

31. Riva Richmond, "The RSA Hack: How They Did It," *New York Times*, April 2, 2011, bits.blogs.nytimes.com/2011/04/02/the-rsa-hack-how-they-did-it/.

32. Michael Riley and Dune Lawrence, "Hackers Linked to China's Army Seen from EU to D.C.," *Bloomberg*, July 26, 2012, https://web.archive.org/web/201503191 44923/https://www.bloomberg.com/news/articles/2012-07-26/china-hackers-hit-eu-point-man-and-d-c-with-byzantine-candor.

33. US Office of the National Counterintelligence Executive, "Foreign Spies Stealing U.S. Economic Secrets in Cyberspace: Report to Congress on Foreign Economic Collection and Industrial Espionage, 2009–2011," Office of the Director of National Intelligence, October 2011, www.dni.gov/files/documents/Newsroom/Reports%20 and%20Pubs/20111103_report_fecie.pdf, B-2 (28).

34. Dmitri Alperovitch, "Revealed: Operation Shady RAT," McAfee, 2011, www.csri.info/wp-content/uploads/2012/08/wp-operation-shady-rat1.pdf.

35. US Office of the National Counterintelligence Executive, "Foreign Spies Stealing U.S. Economic Secrets in Cyberspace."

36. Siobhan Gorman, "China Singled Out for Cyberspying," *Wall Street Journal*, November 4, 2011, www.wsj.com/articles/SB100014240529702037162045770155 40198801540.

37. Barack Obama, "Taking the Cyberattack Threat Seriously," *Wall Street Journal*, July 19, 2012, www.wsj.com/articles/SB10000872396390444330904577535492693 044650.

38. Aram Roston, "DOJ Plans to Indict State-Sponsored Cyber Attackers," *Defense News*, December 19, 2011, www.thecre.com/fisma/?p=4315.

CHAPTER 4

1. For more on this period, see David Crist's excellent book, *The Twilight War*.

2. US Department of Justice, Office of Public Affairs, "Five Individuals Indicted in a Fraud Conspiracy Involving Exports to Iran of U.S. Components Later Found in Bombs in Iraq," Department of Justice, October 25, 2011, www.justice.gov/opa/pr /five-individuals-indicted-fraud-conspiracy-involving-exports-iran-us-components -later-found.

3. US Department of Justice, Office of Public Affairs, "Manssor Arbabsiar Sentenced in New York City Federal Court to 25 Years in Prison for Conspiring with Iranian Military Officials to Assassinate the Saudi Arabian Ambassador to the United States," Department of Justice, May 30, 2013, www.justice.gov/opa/pr /manssor-arbabsiar-sentenced-new-york-city-federal-court-25-years-prison-conspiring -iranian.

4. David Ignatius, "Stopping Terror Plots Will Require More Than Luck," *Washington Post*, October 18, 2011, 19 www.washingtonpost.com/opinions/stopping-terror -plots-will-require-more-than-luck/2011/10/18/gIQAg4BlyL_story.html?utm _term=.bd54ce7f8763.

5. Collin Anderson and Karim Sadjadpour, *Iran's Cyber Threat: Espionage, Sabotage, and Revenge*, Carnegie Endowment for International Peace, 2018, carnegieendow ment.org/files/Iran_Cyber_Final_Full_v2.pdf, 5.

6. Ibid., 12.

7. Eva Galperin, Seth Schoen, and Peter Eckersley, "A Post Mortem on the Iranian DigiNotar Attack," Electronic Frontier Foundation, September 13, 2011, www.eff.org /deeplinks/2011/09/post-mortem-iranian-diginotar-attack.

8. Josephine Wolf, "How a 2011 Hack You've Never Heard of Changed the Internet's Infrastructure," *Slate*, December 21, 2016, www.slate.com/articles/technology /future_tense/2016/12/how_the_2011_hack_of_diginotar_changed_the_internet _s_infrastructure.html.

9. Tony Bradley, "Hackers Target Google, Skype with Rogue SSL Certificates," *InfoWorld*, March 24, 2011, www.infoworld.com/article/2623620/firewall -software/hackers-target-google--skype-with-rogue-ssl-certificates.html.

10. "Black Tulip: Report of the Investigation into the DigiNotar Certificate Authority Breach," Fox-IT, August 13, 2012, https://www.researchgate.net/publication /269333601_Black_Tulip_Report_of_the_investigation_into_the_DigiNotar _Certificate_Authority_breach.

11. Wolf, "How a 2011 Hack You've Never Heard of Changed the Internet's Infrastructure."

12. See Black Hat, "How to Implement IT Security After a Cyber Meltdown," *YouTube*, December 29, 2015, www.youtube.com/watch?v=WyMobr_TDSI; Nicole Perlroth, "In Cyberattack on Saudi Firm, U.S. Sees Iran Firing Back," *New York Times*, October 23, 2012, www.nytimes.com/2012/10/24/business/global/cyberattack-on -saudi-oil-firm-disquiets-us.html?mcubz=3; Chris Kubecka, "How to Implement IT Security After a Cyber Meltdown," *Black Hat*, www.blackhat.com/docs/us-15/materials /us-15-Kubecka-How-To-Implement-IT-Security-After-A-Cyber-Meltdown.pdf; and Jose Pagliery, "The Inside Story of the Biggest Hack in History," CNN, August 5, 2015, money.cnn.com/2015/08/05/technology/aramco-hack/index.html.

13. See [Arabic website] https://www.tech-wd.com/wd/2012/08/15/aramco -hacked/.

14. Symantec Security Response, "The Shamoon Attacks," *Symantec Official Blog*, Symantec, August 16, 2012, www.symantec.com/connect/blogs/shamoon-attacks.

15. Zain Shauk, "Amid Oil Boom, Saudi Aramco Urges Resilience," *Fuel Fix*, March 5, 2013, fuelfix.com/blog/2013/03/05/amid-oil-boom-saudi-aramco-looks -to-renewables/.

16. Jennifer Rizzo, "Cybersecurity Bill Fails in Senate," CNN, August 2, 2012, www .cnn.com/2012/08/02/politics/cybersecurity-act/index.html.

17. Qassamcyberfighters, "Bank of America and New York Stock Exchange Under Attack Unt," Pastebin, September 18, 2012, pastebin.com/mCHia4W5.

18. Antone Gonsalves, "Banks Can Only Hope for Best with DDoS Attacks," *CSO*, September 26, 2012, www.csoonline.com/article/2132304/malware-cybercrime /banks-can-only-hope-for-best-with-ddos-attacks.html.

19. Ellen Nakashima, "Iran Blamed for Cyberattacks on U.S. Banks and Companies," *Washington Post*, September 21, 2012, www.washingtonpost.com/world/national -security/iran-blamed-for-cyberattacks/2012/09/21/afbe2be4-0412-11e2-9b24 -ff730c7f6312_story.html?utm_term=.13f6cc06f2ef; and Nicole Perlroth and Quentin Hardy, "Bank Hacking Was the Work of Iranians, Officials Say," *New York Times*, January 8, 2013, www.nytimes.com/2013/01/09/technology/online-banking-attacks -were-work-of-iran-us-officials-say.html.

20. US Department of Defense, Press Operations, "Defending the Nation from Cyber Attack," Speech delivered by Leon Panetta before Business Executives for National Security, October 11, 2012, archive.defense.gov/speeches/speech.aspx?speech id=1728.

21. Antone Gonsalves, "Bank Attackers More Sophisticated Than Typical Hacktivists, Experts Say," *CSO*, September 28, 2012, www.csoonline.com/article/2132319 /malware-cybercrime/bank-attackers-more-sophisticated-than-typical-hacktivists -expert-says.html.

22. "DDoS Attack Definitions: itsoknoproblembro," Radware, security.radware .com/ddos-knowledge-center/ddospedia/itsoknoproblembro/.

23. Ronen Atias, "Under the Hood of the DDoS Attack on U.S. Banks," Imperva, January 8, 2013, www.incapsula.com/blog/cyber-attack-us-banks.html.

24. "Dissection of 'itsoknoproblembro,' the DDoS Tool That Shook the Banking World," *InfoSecurity*, January 4, 2013, www.infosecurity-magazine.com/news /dissection-of-itsoknoproblembro-the-ddos-tool/.

25. Perlroth and Hardy, "Bank Hacking Was the Work of Iranians."

26. Noah Shachtman, "Bank Hackers Deny They're Agents of Iran," *Wired*, November 27, 2012, www.wired.com/2012/11/bank-hackers-deny-theyre-agents-of-iran/; see also https://pastebin.com/E4f7fmB5.

27. "Lessons Learned from the U.S. Financial Services DDoS Attacks," Arbor Networks, December 13, 2012, www.arbornetworks.com/blog/asert/lessons-learned-from-the-u-s-financial-services-ddos-attacks/.

28. Joseph Berger, "A Dam, Small and Unsung, Is Caught Up in an Iranian Hacking Case," *New York Times*, March 25, 2016, www.nytimes.com/2016/03/26/nyregion/rye-brook-dam-caught-in-computer-hacking-case.html?mcubz=1.

29. "Lessons Learned from the U.S. Financial Services DDoS Attacks."

30. "Iranian Hacker: We Work in Cooperation with the Regime," *Memri Iranian Media Blog*, September 14, 2010, web.archive.org/web/20100914153250/http://www.thememriblog.org/iran/blog_personal/en/21039.htm.

31. "Behrouz Kamalian," Foundation for Defense of Democracies, accessed May 29, 2018, www.defenddemocracy.org/behrouz-kamalian/.

32. "Experts: Software Theft Shows Threat of Mercenary Hackers," ABC News, July 26, 2017, abcnews.go.com/amp/Technology/wireStory/experts-vermont-hack-shows-threat-mercenary-hackers-48866906.

33. US District Court for the District of Vermont, *United States of America v. Mohammed Saeed Ajily and Mohammed Reza Rezakhah*, April 21, 2016, www.justice.gov/opa/press-release/file/982106/download.

34. US Department of Justice, Office of Public Affairs, "Two Iranian Nationals Charged in Hacking of Vermont Software Company," Department of Justice, July 17, 2017,www.justice.gov/opa/pr/two-iranian-nationals-charged-hacking-vermont-software-company.

35. "Experts: Software Theft Shows Threat of Mercenary Hackers."

36. Ragip Soylu, "Turkey Extradites Hacker to US, Readies to Officially Demand Gulen's Extradition," *Daily Sabah*, February 25, 2015, www.dailysabah.com/politics/2015/02/25/turkey-extradites-hacker-to-us-readies-to-officially-demand-gulens-extradition.

37. US Department of Justice, US Attorney's Office, District of Vermont, "Man Pleads Guilty to Facilitating Computer Hacking of Vermont Company," Department of Justice, December 2, 2015, www.justice.gov/usao-vt/pr/man-pleads-guilty-facilitating-computer-hacking-vermont-company.

38. Gil Ronen, "Khamenei: 'Crush Adelson's Mouth,'" *Israel National News*, March 11, 2013, www.israelnationalnews.com/News/News.aspx/173558.

39. Benjamin Eligin and Michael Riley, "Now at the Sands Casino: An Iranian Hacker in Every Server," *Bloomberg Business*, December 12, 2014, https://www.bloomberg.com/news/articles/2014-12-11/iranian-hackers-hit-sheldon-adelsons-sands-casino-in-las-vegas.

40. Jim Mulder, "Mimikatz Overview, Defenses and Detection," SANS Institute InfoSec Reading Room, February 18, 2016, https://www.sans.org/reading-room/whitepapers/detection/mimikatz-overview-defenses-detection-36780; and gentilkiwi/mimikatz, https://github.com/gentilkiwi/mimikatz.

41. Eligin and Riley, "Now at the Sands Casino: An Iranian Hacker in Every Server."

42. Howard Stutz, "Website Owned by Las Vegas Sands' Casino Taken Down After Being Attacked," *Las Vegas Review-Journal*, March 2, 2014, web.archive.org /web/20140302001152/https://www.reviewjournal.com/news/websites-owned -las-vegas-sands-casinos-taken-down-after-being-hacked.

43. Eligin and Riley, "Now at the Sands Casino: An Iranian Hacker in Every Server."

44. Howard Stutz, "Las Vegas Sands: Websites Still Down, but Core Systems Not Affected," *Las Vegas Review-Journal*, February 12, 2014, web.archive.org/web /20140302093547/https://www.reviewjournal.com/business/las-vegas-sands-websites -still-down-core-systems-not-affected.

45. Matt Assad, "Sands Casino Websites Hacked," *Morning Call*, February 12, 2014, articles.mcall.com/2014-02-12/news/mc-bethlehem-sands-website-hacked-20140211 _1_las-vegas-sands-sands-bethlehem-sands-corp.

46. Howard Stutz, "Purported Hackers of Las Vegas Sands Websites Surface, Taunting," *Las Vegas Review-Journal*, February 18, 2014, web.archive.org/web/2014 0220202754/https://www.reviewjournal.com/business/purported-hackers -las-vegas-sands-websites-surface-taunting.

47. Ibid.

48. Hannah Dreier, "Las Vegas Sands Now Says Hacking Went Deeper Than Previously Realized," *Las Vegas Sun*, February 18, 2014, lasvegassun.com/news/2014 /feb/18/las-vegas-sands-hacking-went-deeper-previously-ack/.

49. Howard Stutz, "Customer Data Stolen from Las Vegas Sands' Casino in Pennsylvania," *Las Vegas Review-Journal*, February 28, 2014, www.reviewjournal.com /business/customer-data-stolen-from-las-vegas-sands-casino-in-pennsylvania/.

50. Assad, "Sands Casino Websites Hacked."

51. US Senate Committee on Armed Services, "Hearing to Receive Testimony on Worldwide Threats," Alderson Reporting Company, February 26, 2015, www.armed -services.senate.gov/imo/media/doc/15-18%20-%202-26-15.pdf, p. 11.

CHAPTER 5

1. Ellen Nakashima, "U.S. Said to Be Target of Massive Cyber-Espionage Campaign," *Washington Post*, February, 10 2013, www.washingtonpost.com/world/national -security/us-said-to-be-target-of-massive-cyber-espionage-campaign/2013/02/10 /7b4687d8-6fc1-11e2-aa58-243de81040ba_story.html?utm_term=.9f56fcfabf23.

2. Michael S. Schmidt and Nicole Perlroth, "Obama Order Gives Firms Cyberthreat Information," *New York Times*, February 12, 2013, www.nytimes.com/2013/02/13 /us/executive-order-on-cybersecurity-is-issued.html.

3. US Office of the Press Secretary, "Remarks by the President in the State of the Union Address," February 12, 2013, obamawhitehouse.archives.gov/the-press -office/2013/02/12/remarks-president-state-union-address.

4. "APT1: Exposing One of China's Cyber Espionage Units," Mandiant, February 19, 2013, www.fireeye.com/content/dam/fireeye-www/services/pdfs/mandiant-apt1 -report.pdf.

5. David E. Sanger, David Barboza, and Nicole Pelroth, "Chinese Army Unit Is Seen as Tied to Hacking Against U.S.," *New York Times*, February 8, 2013, www .nytimes.com/2013/02/19/technology/chinas-army-is-seen-as-tied-to-hacking -against-us.html.

6. US House Committee on Energy and Commerce, Subcommittee on Oversight and Investigations, *Cyber Espionage and the Theft of U.S. Intellectual Property and Technology*, July 9, 2013, docs.house.gov/meetings/IF/IF02/20130709/101104/HHRG -113-IF02-Wstate-WortzelL-20130709-U1.pdf, 9.

7. Shane Harris, "Exclusive: Inside the FBI's Fight Against Chinese Cyber-Espionage," *Foreign Policy*, May 27, 2014, www.foreignpolicy.com/2014/05/27 /exclusive-inside-the-fbis-fight-against-chinese-cyber-espionage/.

8. US Department of Defense, Office of the Secretary of Defense, "Annual Report to Congress: Military and Security Developments Involving the People's Republic of China 2013," archive.defense.gov/pubs/2013_China_Report_FINAL.pdf.

9. David E. Sanger, "U.S. Blames China's Military Directly for Cyberattacks," *New York Times*, May 6, 2013, www.nytimes.com/2013/05/07/world/asia/us-accuses -chinas-military-in-cyberattacks.html?mcubz=1.

10. Jonathan Tepperman, "Beijing's Brand Ambassador: A Conversation with Cui Tiankai," *Foreign Affairs*, May 27, 2013, www.chinausfocus.com/foreign-policy /beijings-brand-ambassador-a-conversation-with-cui-tiankai.

11. Lesley Stahl, "The Great Brain Robbery," *60 Minutes*, CBS News, January 17, 2016, www.cbsnews.com/news/60-minutes-great-brain-robbery-china-cyber-espionage/.

12. US Department of Justice, Office of Public Affairs, "Sinovel Corporation and Three Individuals Charged in Wisconsin with Theft of AMSC Trade Secrets," June 27, 2013, www.justice.gov/opa/pr/sinovel-corporation-and-three-individuals-charged-wisconsin -theft-amsc-trade-secrets.

13. Lesley Stahl, "The Great Brain Robbery."

14. Del Quentin Wilber, "How a Corporate Spy Swiped Plans for DuPont's Billion-Dollar Collar Formula," *Bloomberg*, February 4, 2016, www.bloomberg.com /features/2016-stealing-dupont-white/.

15. US Department of Justice, Office of Public Affairs, "Two Individuals and Company Found Guilty of Conspiracy to Sell Trade Secrets to Chinese Companies," March 5, 2014, www.justice.gov/opa/pr/two-individuals-and-company-found-guilty -conspiracy-sell-trade-secrets-chinese-companies.

16. US Office of the National Counterintelligence Executive, *Foreign Spies Stealing U.S. Economic Secrets in Cyberspace: Report to Congress on Foreign Economic Collection and Industrial Espionage, 2009–2011*, Office of the Director of National Intelligence, October 2011, www.dni.gov/files/documents/Newsroom/Reports%20and%20Pubs /20111103_report_fecie.pdf, 12.

17. Daniel Golden, *Spy Schools: How the CIA, FBI, and Foreign Intelligence Secretly Exploit America's Universities* (Henry Holt, 2017), ii.

18. Ibid., 5.

19. Evan Osnos, *Age of Ambition: Chasing Fortune, Truth, and Faith in the New China* (Farrar, Straus and Giroux, 2014), 67.

20. Golden, *Spy Schools*, 38.

21. David Zweig and Huiyao Wang, "Can China Bring Back the Best?: The Communist Party Organizes China's Search for Talent," *China Quarterly*, no. 215, September 2013, www.sosc.ust.hk/community_corner/pdf/David%20Zweig%20Working%20Paper%20May%202012.pdf.

22. This isn't universal. The two authors note that China continues to have trouble recruiting the "very best and the very brightest." As they said, "The very talented who have numerous options both at home and abroad, are likely to opt for an environment that allows for free thinking, debating and writing, and whether this can be achieved in China without significant political liberalization remains a major question."

23. US Department of Justice, Office of Public Affairs, "Chinese Professors Among Six Defendants Charged with Economic Espionage and Theft of Trade Secrets for Benefit of People's Republic of China," Washington, DC, May 19, 2015, www.justice.gov/opa/pr/chinese-professors-among-six-defendants-charged-economic-espionage-and-theft-trade-secrets.

24. "SolarWorld and Coalition of U.S. Solar Manufacturers Petition to Stop Unfair Trade by China's State-Sponsored Industry," SolarWorld, October 19, 2011, www.solarworld-usa.com/newsroom/news-releases/news/2011/domestic-solar-manufacturers-petition-to-stop-unfair-trade-by-china.aspx.

25. Shane Harris, "Exclusive: Inside the FBI's Fight Against Chinese Cyber-Espionage," *Foreign Policy*, May 27, 2014, foreignpolicy.com/2014/05/27/exclusive-inside-the-fbis-fight-against-chinese-cyber-espionage/.

26. US Department of Justice, Office of Public Affairs, "U.S. Charges Five Chinese Military Hackers for Cyber Espionage Against U.S. Corporations and a Labor Organization for Commercial Advantage," Washington, DC, May 19, 2014, www.justice.gov/opa/pr/us-charges-five-chinese-military-hackers-cyber-espionage-against-us-corporations-and-labor.

27. Mark Wilcox, "The National Security Council Deputies Committee: Engine of the Policy Process," *InterAgency Journal*, vol. 5, no. 1, 2014, www.thesimonscenter.org/wp-content/uploads/2014/03/IAJ-5-1Winter-2014-22-32.pdf.

28. Charlie Mitchell, *Hacked: The Inside Story of America's Struggle to Secure Cyberspace* (Rowman & Littlefield, 2016), 198.

29. US Department of Justice, US Attorney's Office, Southern District of New York, "Co-Creator of 'Blackshades' Malware Pleads Guilty in Manhattan Federal Court," February 18, 2015, www.justice.gov/usao-sdny/pr/co-creator-blackshades-malware-pleads-guilty-manhattan-federal-court; US Department of Justice, Federal Bureau of Investigation, "International Blackshades Malware Takedown: Coordinated Law Enforcement Actions Announced," May 19, 2014, www.fbi.gov/news/stories/international-blackshades-malware-takedown-1; and US Department of Justice, US Attorney's Office, Southern District of New York, "Swedish Co-Creator of 'Blackshades' Malware That Enabled Users Around the World to Secretly and Remotely Control Victim's Computers Sentenced to 57 Months in Prison," June 23, 2015, www.justice.gov/usao-sdny/pr/swedish-co-creator-blackshades-malware-enabled-users-around-world-secretly-and-remotely.

30. US Office of the Press Secretary, "Remarks by President Obama and Prime Minister Abbott of Australia After Bilateral Meeting," June 12, 2014, obamawhite

house.archives.gov/the-press-office/2014/06/12/remarks-president-obama-and
-prime-minister-abbott-australia-after-bilate.

31. Nicole Perlroth, "2nd China Army Unit Implicated in Online Spying," *New York Times*, June 9, 2014, www.nytimes.com/2014/06/10/technology/private-report
-further-details-chinese-cyberattacks.html.

32. Blair Gable, "China Hack Cost Ottawa 'Hundreds of Millions,' Documents Show," *Globe and Mail*, March 30, 2017, www.theglobeandmail.com/news/national
/federal-documents-say-2014-china-hack-cost-hundreds-of-millions-of-dollars
/article34485219/.

33. Ellen Nakashima, "Confidential Report Lists U.S. Weapons System Designs Compromised by Chinese Cyberspies," *Washington Post*, May 27, 2013, www.washing
tonpost.com/world/national-security/confidential-report-lists-us-weapons-system
-designs-compromised-by-chinese-cyberspies/2013/05/27/a42c3e1c-c2dd-11e2
-8c3b-0b5e9247e8ca_story.html?utm_term=.5411b61a86ae.

34. Colin Freeze, "Chinese Soldiers Implicated in U.S. Military Hacking Case," *Globe and Mail*, January 18, 2016, www.theglobeandmail.com/news/national/chinese
-entrepreneur-living-in-canada-implicated-in-us-military-hacking-case/article28253148/.

35. "'We Only Came to Help': Canadian Couple Imprisoned in China, Accused of Spying," CBC, December 8, 2016, www.cbc.ca/radio/thecurrent/the-current-for
-december-8-2016-1.3885770/we-only-came-to-help-canadian-couple-imprisoned
-in-china-accused-of-spying-1.3885918.

36. Dan Levin, "2 Canadians Investigated in China over Spying Claims," *New York Times*, August 5, 2014, www.nytimes.com/2014/08/06/world/asia/china-inves
tigating-canadian-couple-on-suspicion-of-espionage.html.

37. Dan Levin, "Couple Held in China Are Free, but 'Even Now We Live Under a Cloud,'" *New York Times*, January 1, 2017, www.nytimes.com/2017/01/01/world
/canada/canadian-couple-china-detention.html?mcubz=1.

38. Ellen Nakashima, "Business Admits Helping Chinese Military Hackers Target U.S. Contractors," *Washington Post*, March 23, 2016, www.washingtonpost.com
/world/national-security/businessman-admits-helping-chinese-military-hackers
-target-us-contractors/2016/03/23/3e74e4a4-f136-11e5-85a6-2132cf446d0a
_story.html?utm_term=.c38104fb617b.

CHAPTER 6

1. Jim Heintz, "A Look at Russian Hacking," ABC News, www.abcnews.go.com
/Technology/story?id=119291&page=1.

2. Benjamin Bidder, "Russian Hackers Target Political Opposition," *Spiegel*, July 30, 2007, www.spiegel.de/international/world/under-fire-from-internet-mercenaries
-russian-hackers-target-political-opposition-a-497841.html.

3. Mark Galeotti, "Why Are Russians Excellent Cybercriminals?" *Moscow News*, November 21, 2011, web.archive.org/web/20120107121032/http://themoscow
news.com/siloviks_scoundrels/20111121/189221309.html.

4. Vladimir Shlapentokh, "Russian Crime, Corruption Give New Meaning to 'Roof,'" *Christian Science Monitor*, March 8, 1996, www.csmonitor.com/1996/0308/08191.html.

5. Joseph Menn, *Fatal System Error*, 204.

6. Tim Maurer, *Cyber Mercenaries: The State, Hackers, and Power* (Cambridge, 2018), books.google.com/books?id=rKpCDwAAQBAJ&pg=PA97&lpg=PA97&dq=maga zine+Khaker&source=bl&ots=SYjoG5pWmU&sig=6Rc2LttzSOv-dNWob8KQkpsn NTI&hl=en&sa=X&ved=0ahUKEwjz1LLHqcnYAhUDct8KHQY3CYQQ6 AEIQzAG#v=onepage&q=magazine%20Khaker&f=false.

7. Menn, *Fatal System Error*, 202.

8. Art Jahnke, "Alexey Ivanov and Vasiliy Gorshkov: Russian Hacker Roulette," *CSO*, January 1, 2004, www.csoonline.com/article/2118241/malware-cybercrime/alexey -ivanov-and-vasiliy-gorshkov--russian-hacker-roulette.html.

9. Tim Johnson, "U.S. Sweeping Up Russian Hackers in Broad Global Dragnet," *Miami Herald*, March 31, 2017, www.miamiherald.com/news/nation-world/world /article141998499.html.

10. Robert Gates, *Duty: Memoirs of a Secretary at War* (Knopf, 2014), books .google.com/books?id=lYzZAAAAQBAJ&q=illegals#v=onepage&q=exfiltration& f=false, 410–411.

11. Michael Riley, "How Russian Hackers Stole the Nasdaq," *Bloomberg*, July 21, 2014, www.bloomberg.com/news/articles/2014-07-17/how-russian-hackers-stole-the -nasdaq.

12. Ibid.

13. Details about the GameOver Zeus case are adapted from and based on Garrett M. Graff, "Chasing the Phantom: Inside the Hunt for Russia's Most Notorious Hacker," *Wired*, April 2017, www.wired.com/2017/03/russian-hacker-spy-botnet/.

14. US Department of Justice, Office of Public Affairs, "Ensuring Botnets Are Not 'Too Big to Investigate'," November 22, 2016, www.justice.gov/archives/opa /blog/ensuring-botnets-are-not-too-big-investigate.

15. United States for the Northern District of California, *United States of America v. Dmitry Dokuchaev*, Indictment, Department of Justice, February 28, 2017, www.justice .gov/opa/press-release/file/948201/download.

16. Andrew Kramer, "Hacker Is a Villain to Russia and the United States, for Different Reasons," *New York Times*, March 16, 2017, www.nytimes.com/2017/03/16 /world/europe/russian-hacker-fsb-agent-dmitry-dokuchaev.html?_r=0.

17. Joseph Goldstein and Michael Schwirtz, "Indictment Details Collusion Between Cyberthief and 2 Russian Spies," *New York Times*, March 15, 2017, www .nytimes.com/2017/03/15/us/politics/indictment-collusion-cyberthief-russian -spies-yahoo.html.

18. Kramer, "Hacker Is a Villain to Russia and the United States, for Different Reasons."

19. "Four Men Charged with Hacking 500M Yahoo Accounts," *Krebs on Security*, March 15, 2017, www.krebsonsecurity.com/2017/03/four-men-charged-with -hacking-500m-yahoo-accounts/#more-38562.

20. Thomas Fox-Brewster, "The Hacker History of Alexsey Belan, a Latvian Accused of Yahoo for Russian Spies," *Forbes*, March 20, 2017, www.forbes.com /sites/thomasbrewster/2017/03/20/alexsey-belan-yahoo-fbi-hacker-allegations /#34e8d2ab76f2.

21. Ibid.

22. Chris McNab, "Alexsey's TTPs," *Medium*, March 20, 2017, medium.com /@chrismcnab/alexseys-ttps-1204d9050551.

23. Goldstein and Schwirtz, "Indictment Details Collusion Between Cyberthief and 2 Russian Spies."

CHAPTER 7

1. Mark Seal, "An Exclusive Look at Sony's Hacking Saga," *Vanity Fair*, February 4, 2014, www.vanityfair.com/hollywood/2015/02/sony-hacking-seth-rogen-evan-gold berg; see also Peter Elkind, "Inside the Hack of the Century," *Fortune*, June 27, 2015, http://fortune.com/sony-hack-part-1/.

2. "Sony C.E.O. on How the Hack Changed Business—Full Conversation," *Vanity Fair*, October 8, 2015, video.vanityfair.com/watch/sony-ceo-how-the-hack-changed -business.

3. Sean Gallagher, "Sony Pictures Hackers Release List of Stolen Corporate Files," *Ars Technica*, November 26, 2014, arstechnica.com/information-technology/2014 /11/sony-pictures-hackers-release-list-of-stolen-corporate-files/.

4. Ibid.

5. Mike Fleming Jr., "Sony Hackers Paralysis Reaches Day Two—Update," *Deadline*, November 25, 2014, www.deadline.com/2014/11/sony-computers-hacked-skull -message-1201295288/.

6. Fleming Jr., "Sony Hackers Paralysis Reaches Day Two—Update"; and Seal, "An Exclusive Look at Sony's Hacking Saga."

7. "Sony C.E.O. on How the Hack Changed Business—Full Conversation."

8. Kevin Roose, "Hacked Documents Reveal a Hollywood Studio's Stunning Gender and Race Gap," *Splinter*, December 1, 2014, www.splinternews.com/hacked -documents-reveal-a-hollywood-studios-stunning-ge-1793844312.

9. Kim Zetter, "Sony Got Hacked Hard: What We Know and Don't Know So Far," *Wired*, December 3, 2014, www.wired.com/2014/12/sony-hack-what-we-know/.

10. Brooks Barnes and Nicole Perlroth, "Sony Films Are Pirated, and Hackers Leak Studio Salaries," *New York Times*, December 2, 2014, www.nytimes.com/2014/12/03 /business/media/sony-is-again-target-of-hackers.html?_r=0.

11. Andrea Peterson, "Hackers Gave Sony Pictures Entertainment a Major Headache Thanksgiving Week," *Washington Post*, December 1, 2014, www.washingtonpost .com/news/the-switch/wp/2014/12/01/hackers-gave-sony-pictures-entertainment -a-major-headache-thanksgiving-week/?utm_term=.70765d438fcc.

12. Seal, "An Exclusive Look at Sony's Hacking Saga."

13. Jim Easterhouse, "With 'The Interview' Controversy Brewing, North Korea Tests Missiles," *Los Angeles Times*, June 26, 2014, www.latimes.com/entertainment /movies/moviesnow/la-et-mn-north-korea-tests-the-interview-20140626-story.html.

14. Seal, "An Exclusive Look at Sony's Hacking Saga."

15. Jenny Jun, Scott LaFoy, and Ethan Sohn, "North Korea's Cyber Operations: Strategy and Responses," Center for Strategic and International Studies, Washington, DC, 2015, 27.

16. Ibid., 28.

17. Andrea Stricker, "Case Study—United States Busts Likely North Korean Trans-shipment Scheme," Institute for Science and International Security, May 24, 2013, isis-online.org/isis-reports/detail/case-study-united-states-busts-likely-north-korean -transshipment-scheme/; US Department of Justice, Federal Bureau of Investigation, "Taiwanese Father and Son Arrested for Allegedly Violating U.S. Laws to Prevent Pro-liferation of Weapons of Mass Destruction," May 6, 2013, archives.fbi.gov/archives /chicago/press-releases/2013/taiwanese-father-and-son-arrested-for-allegedly -violating-u.s.-laws-to-prevent-proliferation-of-weapons-of-mass-destruction.

18. Jason Meisner, "Taiwan Businessman Admits Violating Ban on Exporting Machinery," *Chicago Tribune*, October 10, 2014, www.chicagotribune.com/news/ct -weapons-mass-destruction-met-20141010-story.html.

19. US Department of Justice, US Attorney's Office, Northern District of Illi-nois, "Taiwan Businessman Sentenced to 24 Months for Conspiring to Violate U.S. Laws Preventing Proliferation of Weapons of Mass Destruction," March 16, 2015, www.justice.gov/usao-ndil/pr/taiwan-businessman-sentenced-24-months-conspiring -violate-us-laws-preventing.

20. Martyn Williams, "How the Internet Works in North Korea," *Slate*, Novem-ber 28, 2016, www.slate.com/articles/technology/future_tense/2016/11/how_the _internet_works_in_north_korea.html.

21. David E. Sanger and Nicole Perlroth, "North Korea Loses Its Link to the Inter-net," *New York Times*, December 23, 2014, www.nytimes.com/2014/12/23/world /asia/attack-is-suspected-as-north-korean-internet-collapses.html?_r=0.

22. Jun, LaFoy, and Sohn, "North Korea's Cyber Operations: Strategy and Responses," 53.

23. Martyn Williams, "One IP Address for All of PUST." *North Korea Tech*, August 20, 2012, www.northkoreatech.org/2012/08/20/one-ip-address-for-all-of-pust/.

24. Jun, LaFoy, and Sohn, "North Korea's Cyber Operations: Strategy and Responses," 3.

25. David E. Sanger, David D. Kirkpatrick, and Nicole Perlroth, "The World Once Laughed at North Korean Cyberpower. No More," *New York Times*, October 15, 2017, www.nytimes.com/2017/10/15/world/asia/north-korea-hacking-cyber-sony.html?_r=0.

26. Jun, LaFoy, and Sohn, "North Korea's Cyber Operations: Strategy and Responses," 5.

27. Nate Thayer, "American Spy Chief Secret Meeting with the Head of North Korean Cyber Warfare," Nate Thayer—Journalist, January 9, 2015, www.nate-thayer.com /american-spy-chief-secret-meeting-with-head-of-north-korean-cyber-warfare/.

28. Ashley Rowland, " 'Dangerously Uncertain' Times in Korea, Thurman Tells Congress," *Stars and Stripes*, March 29, 2012, www.stripes.com/news/dangerously -uncertain-times-in-korea-thurman-tells-congress-1.172961.

29. Jun, LaFoy, and Sohn, "North Korea's Cyber Operations: Strategy and Responses," 38.

30. "Just How Formidable Are North Korea's Hackers?" *Ask a Korean!*, March 29, 2013, www.askakorean.blogspot.com/2013/03/just-how-formidable-is-north-koreas .html.

31. Sangwon Yoon, "North Korea Recruits Hackers at School," *Al Jazeera*, June 20, 2011, www.aljazeera.com/indepth/features/2011/06/201162081543573839.html.

32. Jun, LaFoy, and Sohn, "North Korea's Cyber Operations: Strategy and Responses," 42.

33. Yoon, "North Korea Recruits Hackers at School."

34. Sanger, Kirkpatrick, and Perlroth, "The World Once Laughed at North Korean Cyberpower. No More."

35. Kim Zetter, "Logic Bomb Set Off South Korea Cyberattack," *Wired*, March 21, 2013, www.wired.com/2013/03/logic-bomb-south-korea-attack/.

36. Lucian Constantin, "New Disk Wiper Malware Linked to Attacks in South Korea, Researchers Say," *ComputerWorld*, IDG, June 28, 2013, www.computer world.com/article/2498277/malware-vulnerabilities/new-disk-wiper-malware -linked-to-attacks-in-south-korea--researchers-say.html.

37. Choe Sang-Hun, "Computer Networks in South Korea Are Paralyzed in Cyber-attacks," *New York Times*, March 20, 2013, www.nytimes.com/2013/03/21/world /asia/south-korea-computer-network-crashes.html?pagewanted=all&_r=0.

38. Matthew J. Schwartz, "South Korea Changes Story on Bank Hacks," *Dark-Reading*, March 22, 2013, www.darkreading.com/attacks-and-breaches/south-korea -changes-story-on-bank-hacks/d/d-id/1109211.

39. Sang-Hun, "Computer Networks in South Korea Are Paralyzed in Cyberattacks."

40. Jeremy Kirk, "South Korean Cyberattacks Linked to Known Gang," *PCWorld*, IDG, June 26, 2013, www.pcworld.com/article/2043102/south-korean-cyberattacks -linked-to-known-gang.html.

41. Dmitry Tarakanov, "The 'Kimsuky' Operation: A North Korean APT?" *Secure-List*, Kaspersky Lab, September 11, 2013, securelist.com/the-kimsuky-operation -a-north-korean-apt/57915/.

42. Ibid.

43. Thayer, "American Spy Chief Secret Meeting with the Head of North Korean Cyber Warfare."

44. "Channel 4 Green Lights North Korean Political Thriller Opposite Num-ber," Channel 4, August 21, 2014, www.channel4.com/info/press/news/channel -4-green-lights-north-korean-political-thriller-opposite-number.

45. James Cox, "Cyber Drama: Channel 4 Axe North Korea Thriller Opposite Numbers After Being Attacked by Hackers," *Sun*, October 17, 2017, www.thesun.co.uk /news/4700350/channel-4-axe-north-korea-drama-opposite-number-after-being -targeted-by-hackers/.

46. "Sony C.E.O. on How the Hack Changed Business—Full Conversation."

47. US Department of Justice, Office of Public Affairs, "National Security Divi-sion Announces New Senior Leadership Hires and Restructuring of Counterespio-nage Efforts," October 21, 2014, www.justice.gov/opa/pr/national-security-division -announces-new-senior-leadership-hires-and-restructuring.

48. Aruna Viswanatha, "U.S. National Security Prosecutors Shift Focus from Spies to Cyber," *Reuters*, October 21, 2014, www.reuters.com/article/us-usa-justice -cybersecurity/u-s-national-security-prosecutors-shift-focus-from-spies-to-cyber -idUSKCN0IA0BM20141021.

49. Lisa Monaco, "Remarks as Prepared for Delivery by Assistant to the President for Homeland Security and Counterterrorism Lisa O. Monaco Strengthening Our Nation's Cyber Defenses," Wilson Center, Washington, DC, February 11, 2015, obamawhitehouse.archives.gov/the-press-office/2015/02/11/remarks-prepared -delivery-assistant-president-homeland-security-and-coun.

50. James Comey, "Addressing the Cyber Security Threat," International Conference on Cyber Security, Fordham University, New York, January 7, 2015, www.fbi .gov/news/speeches/addressing-the-cyber-security-threat.

51. Ibid.

52. Steve Ragan, "FBI Memo Warns of Malware Possibly Linked to Hack at Sony Pictures," CSO, December 1, 2014, www.csoonline.com/article/2853893/disaster -recovery/fbi-memo-warns-of-malware-possibly-linked-to-hack-at-sony-pictures.html.

53. Zetter, "Sony Got Hacked Hard: What We Know and Don't Know So Far."

54. James Marchio, "'If the Weathermen Can...': The Intelligence Community's Struggle to Express Analytic Uncertainty in the 1970s," Studies in Intelligence, vol. 58, no. 4, December 2014, www.cia.gov/library/center-for-the-study-of-intelligence/csi-publications/csi-studies/studies/vol-58-no-4/pdfs/If%20 the%20Weatherman%20Can.pdf.

55. "Words of Estimative Probability," Sherman Kent and the Board of National Estimates: Collected Essays, Central Intelligence Agency, March 19, 2007, www.cia.gov/library /center-for-the-study-of-intelligence/csi-publications/books-and-monographs/sherman -kent-and-the-board-of-national-estimates-collected-essays/6words.html.

56. Michael Morell, "Intelligence, Trump, Putin, and Russia's Long Game," The Cipher Brief, January 4, 2017, www.thecipherbrief.com/column/expert-view /intelligence-trump-putin-and-russias-long-game-2.

57. US National Intelligence Council, Iran: Nuclear Intentions and Capabilities, Office of the Director of National Intelligence, November 2007, www.dni.gov/files /documents/Newsroom/Reports%20and%20Pubs/20071203_release.pdf.

58. Mike Fleming, "Hollywood Cowardice: George Clooney Explains Why Sony Stood Alone in North Korean Cyberterror Attack," Deadline, December 18, 2014, www .deadline.com/2014/12/george-clooney-sony-hollywood-cowardice-north-korea -cyberattack-petition-1201329988/.

59. Aaron Sorkin, "The Sony Hack and the Yellow Press," New York Times, December 14, 2014, www.nytimes.com/2014/12/15/opinion/aaron-sorkin-journalists-shouldnt -help-the-sony-hackers.html?_r=0.

60. Andrea Peterson, "Sony Pictures Hackers Invoke 9/11 While Threatening Theaters That Show 'The Interview,'" Washington Post, December 16, 2014, www .washingtonpost.com/news/the-switch/wp/2014/12/16/sony-pictures-hackers-invoke -911-while-threatening-theaters-that-show-the-interview/?utm_term=.03964ef97e6a.

61. Brent Lang, "Sony Cancels Theatrical Release for 'The Interview' on Christmas," Variety, December 17, 2014, www.variety.com/2014/film/news/sony-cancels -theatrical-release-for-the-interview-on-christmas-1201382032/.

62. Christopher Rosen, "Sony Cancels Plans to Release 'The Interview,'" Huffington Post, December 17, 2014, www.huffingtonpost.com/2014/12/17/sony-cancels-the -interview_n_6343926.html.

63. Timothy B. Lee, "Judd Apatow and Jimmy Kimmel Blast 'Cowardice' of The-ater Owners Who Pulled *The Interview*," *Vox*, December 17, 2014, www.vox.com /2014/12/17/7411901/judd-apatow-says-pulling-the-interview-was-disgraceful.

64. Federal Bureau of Investigation, National Press Office, "Update on Sony Inves-tigation," December 19, 2014, www.fbi.gov/news/pressrel/press-releases/update-on -sony-investigation.

65. US Office of the Press Secretary, "Remarks by the President to the Busi-ness Roundtable," December 19, 2014, obamawhitehouse.archives.gov/the-press -office/2014/12/19/remarks-president-year-end-press-conference.

66. Eric Brander, "Obama: North Korea's Hack Not War, but 'Cybervandalism'," CNN, December 24, 2014, www.cnn.com/2014/12/21/politics/obama-north-koreas -hack-not-war-but-cyber-vandalism/index.html.

67. David Robb, "The Sony Hack One Year Later: Just Who Are the Guard-ians of Peace?" *Deadline*, November 24, 2015, www.deadline.com/2015/11/sony -hack-guardians-of-peace-one-year-anniversary-1201636491/.

68. Ju-min Park and Meeyoung Cho, "South Korea Blames North Korea for Decem-ber Hack on Nuclear Operator," *Reuters*, March 17, 2015, www.reuters.com/article /us-nuclear-southkorea-northkorea/south-korea-blames-north-korea-for-december -hack-on-nuclear-operator-idUSKBN0MD0GR20150317.

69. David Brunnstrom, "N. Korea Has Internet Outage; Hacking May Be to Blame—U.S. Expert," *Reuters*, December 22 2014, www.reuters.com/article /sony-cybersecurity-northkorea/n-korea-has-internet-outage-hacking-may-be-to -blame-u-s-expert-idUSL6N0U63DM20141222.

70. Ellen Nakashima, "Why the Sony Hack Drew an Unprecedented U.S. Response Against North Korea," *Washington Post*, January 15, 2015, www.washington post.com/world/national-security/why-the-sony-hack-drew-an-unprecedented-us -response-against-north-korea/2015/01/14/679185d4-9a63-11e4-96cc-e858eba91ced _story.html?utm_term=.982757b04a07; and Ted Bridis, Josh Lederman, and Tami Abdollah, "AP Sources: US Did Not 'Hack Back' Against North Korea," Associated Press, January 9, 2015, apnews.com/d0c286a7ff7541d888fa054d4c1b147b.

71. David E. Sanger and Michael S. Schmidt, "More Sanctions on North Korea After Sony Case," *New York Times*, January 2, 2015, www.nytimes.com/2015/01/03 /us/in-response-to-sony-attack-us-levies-sanctions-on-10-north-koreans.html.

72. US Department of the Treasury, Press Center, "Treasury Imposes Sanctions Against the Government of the Democratic People's Republic of Korea," Department of the Trea-sury, January 2, 2015, www.treasury.gov/press-center/press-releases/Pages/jl9733.aspx.

73. US National Security Agency, "Fordham University's Fifth International Conference on Cyber Security (ICCS 2015)," May 3, 2016, www.nsa.gov/news -features/speeches-testimonies/speeches/fordham-transcript.shtml.

CHAPTER 8

1. David Robb, "The Sony Hack One Year Later."

2. "2015 Executive Orders Signed by Barack Obama," US National Archives, www .archives.gov/federal-register/executive-orders/2015.html.

3. Michael Daniel, "Our Latest Tool to Combat Cyber Attacks: What You Need to Know," The White House, President Barack Obama, August 1, 2015, obamawhitehouse.archives.gov/blog/2015/04/01/our-latest-tool-combat-cyber-attacks-what-you-need-know.

4. Ibid.

5. FireEye, *Redline Drawn: China Recalculates Its Use of Cyber Espionage*, June 2016, www.fireeye.com/content/dam/fireeye-www/current-threats/pdfs/rpt-china-espionage.pdf, 5.

6. Paul Mozur, "Warm West Coast Reception for China's Web Czar (Chillier in Washington)," *New York Times*, December 8, 2014, bits.blogs.nytimes.com/2014/12/08/a-trip-to-california-for-chinas-internet-czar/.

7. Kelsey D. Atherton, "China's Cyber Censors Have a Theme Song," *Popular Science*, February 12, 2015, www.popsci.com/china-sings-song-cyber-censors.

8. Bruce Sterling, "Boss of Chinese Cyberspace Administration Gets Purged," *Wired*, February 19, 2018, www.wired.com/beyond-the-beyond/2018/02/boss-chinese-cyberspace-administration-gets-purged/.

9. "Annual Highlights 2014," Federal Trade Commission, www.ftc.gov/reports/annual-highlights-2014.

10. Ross Kerber, "Banks Claim Credit Card Breach Affected 94 Million Accounts," *New York Times*, October 24, 2007, www.nytimes.com/2007/10/24/technology/24iht-hack.1.8029174.html.

11. Ellen Nakashima, "Consumer Data Breach Began in 2005, TJX Says," *Washington Post*, February 22, 2007, www.washingtonpost.com/wp-dyn/content/article/2007/02/21/AR2007022102039.html.

12. Kim Zetter and Kevin Poulsen, "Government Stops Shielding Corporate Breach 'Victims,'" *Wired*, March 30, 2017, www.wired.com/2010/03/sunshine/.

13. Nicole Perlroth, "Target Struck in the Cat-and-Mouse Game of Credit Theft," *New York Times*, December 19, 2013, www.nytimes.com/2013/12/20/technology/target-stolen-shopper-data.html.

14. "Lessons from Our Cyber Past: The First Cyber Cops: Transcript 5/16/12," Atlantic Council, https://web.archive.org/web/20120826235220/http://www.acus.org:80/event/lessons-our-cyber-past-first-cyber-cops/transcript.

15. Courtney Perkes, "Personal Data Accessed on Blue Cross Website," *Orange County Register*, June 24, 2010, www.ocregister.com/2010/06/24/personal-data-accessed-on-blue-cross-website/.

16. "Identity Theft Resource Center Breach Report Hits Record High in 2014," Identity Theft Resource Center, January 12, 2015, www.idtheftcenter.org/ITRC-Surveys-Studies/2014databreaches.html.

17. Reed Abelson and Matthew Goldstein, "Anthem Hacking Points to Security Vulnerability of Health Care Industry," *New York Times*, February 5, 2015, www.nytimes.com/2015/02/06/business/experts-suspect-lax-security-left-anthem-vulnerable-to-hackers.html?_r=0.

18. "FBI Liaison Alert System: #A-000049-MW," Krebson Security, n.d., www.krebsonsecurity.com/wp-content/uploads/2015/02/FBI-Flash-Warning-Deep-Panda.pdf.

19. Abelson and Goldstein, "Anthem Hacking Points to Security Vulnerability of Health Care Industry."

20. Michael Riley and Jordan Robertson, "Chinese State-Sponsored Hackers Suspected in Anthem Attack," *Bloomberg*, February 5, 2015, www.bloomberg.com/news/articles/2015-02-05/signs-of-china-sponsored-hackers-seen-in-anthem-attack.

21. Ibid.

22. "Obama Blocks Chinese Purchase of Small Oregon Wind Farm Project," Associated Press, September 28, 2012, www.oregonlive.com/environment/index.ssf/2012/09/oregon_wind_farm_purchase_by_c.html.

23. David Fahrenthold, "Sinkhole of Bureaucracy," *Washington Post*, March 22, 2014, www.washingtonpost.com/sf/national/2014/03/22/sinkhole-of-bureaucracy/?utm_term=.c8923571c17e.

24. US Committee on Oversight and Government Reform, "The OPM Data Breach: How the Government Jeopardized Our National Security for More Than a Generation," US House of Representatives, 114th Congress, September 7, 2016, https://oversight.house.gov/wp-content/uploads/2016/09/The-OPM-Data-Breach-How-the-Government-Jeopardized-Our-National-Security-for-More-than-a-Generation.pdf, p. 75.

25. Billy Mitchell, "How the OPM Breach Was Really Discovered," *Cyberscoop*, May 27, 2016, https://www.cyberscoop.com/how-the-opm-breach-was-really-discovered/.

26. US Committee on Oversight and Government Reform, "The OPM Data Breach," 83.

27. Ibid., 97.

28. US Committee on Oversight and Government Reform, "Memorandum: Committee Investigation into the OPM Data Breach," US House of Representatives, 114th Congress, September 6, 2016, https://democrats-oversight.house.gov/sites/democrats.oversight.house.gov/files/documents/2016-09-06.Democratic%20Memo%20on%20OPM%20Data%20Breach%20Investigation.pdf, 3.

29. US Committee on Oversight and Government Reform, "The OPM Data Breach," 165.

30. "OPM Breach Analysis," *ThreatConnect*, June 5, 2015, https://www.threatconnect.com/blog/opm-breach-analysis/.

31. US Committee on Oversight and Government Reform, "The OPM Data Breach," 103.

32. US Committee on Oversight and Government Reform, "The OPM Data Breach," vii.

33. US Committee on Oversight and Government Reform, "The OPM Data Breach," 86.

34. Ellen Nakashima, "Security Firm Finds Link Between China and Anthem Hack," *Washington Post*, February 27, 2015, www.washingtonpost.com/news/the-switch/wp/2015/02/27/security-firm-finds-link-between-china-and-anthem-hack/?utm_term=.6666697773f6.

35. US Committee on Oversight and Government Reform, "The OPM Data Breach," 82.

36. Ibid., 59.

37. Ibid., 61.

38. US Committee on Oversight and Government Reform, "Memorandum: Committee Investigation into the OPM Data Breach," 6.

39. US Committee on Oversight and Government Reform, "The OPM Data Breach," 51.

40. US Committee on Oversight and Government Reform, "Memorandum: Committee Investigation into the OPM Data Breach," 10.

41. Brendan I. Koerner, "Inside the OPM Hack: The Cyberattack That Shocked the US Government," Wired, October 23, 2016, www.wired.com/2016/10/inside-cyber attack-shocked-us-government/.

42. US Committee on Oversight and Government Reform, "The OPM Data Breach," 78.

43. David Perera and Joseph Marks, "New Disclosed Hack Got 'Crown Jewels'," Politico, June 12, 2015, www.politico.com/story/2015/06/hackers-federal-employees -security-background-checks-118954.

44. James Clapper, Facts and Fears: Hard Truths from a Life in Intelligence (Viking, 2018), 295.

45. Ibid., 298.

46. US Committee on Oversight and Government Reform, "The OPM Data Breach," vii.

47. Julienne Pepitone, "China Is 'Leading Suspect' in OPM Hacks, Says Intelligence Chief James Clapper," NBC News, June 15, 2015, www.nbcnews.com/tech /security/clapper-china-leading-suspect-opm-hack-n381881.

48. "The Anthem Hack: All Roads Lead to China," ThreatConnect, February 27, 2015, www.threatconnect.com/the-anthem-hack-all-roads-lead-to-china/.

49. Ellen Nakashima, "U.S. Developing Sanctions Against China over Cyber-thefts," Washington Post, August 30, 2015, www.washingtonpost.com/world/national -security/administration-developing-sanctions-against-china-over-cyberespionage /2015/08/30/9b2910aa-480b-11e5-8ab4-c73967a143d3_story.html?utm_term= .01cfd4d81bdc.

50. Julie Hirschfeld Davis, "Obama Hints at Sanctions Against China over Cyber-attacks," New York Times, September 16, 2015, www.nytimes.com/2015/09/17/us /politics/obama-hints-at-sanctions-against-china-over-cyberattacks.html?mcubz=1.

51. Ellen Nakashima and Adam Goldman, "In a First, Chinese Hackers Are Arrested at the Behest of the U.S. Government," Washington Post, October 9, 2015, www.washingtonpost.com/world/national-security/in-a-first-chinese-hackers-are -arrested-at-the-behest-of-the-us-government/2015/10/09/0a7b0e46-6778-11e5 -8325-a42b5a459b1e_story.html?utm_term=.90fb7cb8bd15.

52. "Full Transcript: Interview with Chinese President Xi Jinping," Wall Street Journal, September 22, 2015, www.wsj.com/articles/full-transcript-interview-with -chinese-president-xi-jinping-1442894700.

53. US Office of the Press Secretary, "Fact Sheet: President Xi Jinping's State Visit to the United States," The White House, President Barack Obama, September 25, 2015, obamawhitehouse.archives.gov/the-press-office/2015/09/25/fact-sheet-president -xi-jinpings-state-visit-united-states.

54. Ellen Nakashima, "World's Richest Nations Agree Hacking for Commercial Benefit Is Off-Limits," *Washington Post*, November 16, 2015, https://www.washingtonpost.com/world/national-security/worlds-richest-nations-agree-hacking-for-commercial-benefit-is-off-limits/2015/11/16/40bd0800-8ca9-11e5-acff-673ae92ddd2b_story.html.

CHAPTER 9

1. Lorenzo Vidino and Seamus Hughes, "ISIS in America: From Retweets to Raqqa," Program on Extremism, George Washington University, December 2015, cchs.gwu.edu/sites/cchs.gwu.edu/files/downloads/ISIS%20in%20America%20-%20Full%20Report.pdf.

2. Ibid., 22.

3. Dustin Volz and Mark Hosenball, "White House, Silicon Valley to Hold Summit on Militants' Social Media Use," *Reuters*, January 7, 2016, www.reuters.com/article/us-usa-security-tech/white-house-silicon-valley-to-hold-summit-on-militants-social-media-use-idUSKBN0UL2H320160107.

4. Jim Acosta, "First on CNN: Government Enlists Tech Giants to Fight ISIS Messaging," CNN, February 25, 2016, www.edition.cnn.com/2016/02/24/politics/justice-department-apple-fbi-isis-san-bernardino/index.html.

5. Ibid.

6. Sheera Frenkel, "Inside the Obama Administration's Attempt to Bring Tech Companies into the Fight Against ISIS," *Buzzfeed*, February 25, 2016, www.buzzfeed.com/sheerafrenkel/inside-the-obama-administrations-attempt-to-bring-tech-compa?utm_term=.faW5rKMj6V#.ppbN2XMv4e.

7. Max Fisher and Jared Keller, "Syria's Digital Counter-Revolutionaries," *Atlantic*, August 31, 2011, www.theatlantic.com/international/archive/2011/08/syrias-digital-counter-revolutionaries/244382/.

8. Ibid.

9. "Speech of H. E. President Bashar al-Assad at Damascus University on the Situation in Syria," *SANA*, June 23, 2011, web.archive.org/web/20110623151403/http://www.sana.sy/eng/337/2011/06/21/353686.htm.

10. Fisher and Keller, "Syria's Digital Counter-Revolutionaries."

11. Jillian C. York, "Syria's Electronic Army," *Al Jazeera*, August 15, 2011, www.aljazeera.com/indepth/opinion/2011/08/201181191530456997.html.

12. E. B. Boyd, "Anonymous Goes Old-School, Attacks Egypt with Faxes," *Fast Company*, January 18, 2011, www.fastcompany.com/1721846/anonymous-goes-old-school-attacks-egypt-faxes.

13. York, "Syria's Electronic Army."

14. "Reuters Blogging Platform Hacked, False Syria Blog Posted," *Reuters*, August 3, 2012, www.reuters.com/article/reuters-syria-hacking/reuters-blogging-platform-hacked-false-syria-blog-posted-idUSL2E8J37CR20120803.

15. Max Fisher, "Syria's Pro-Assad Hackers Infiltrate Human Rights Watch Website and Twitter Feed," *Washington Post*, March 17, 2013, www.washingtonpost.com

/news/worldviews/wp/2013/03/17/syrias-pro-assad-hackers-infiltrate-human
-rights-watch-web-site-and-twitter-feed/?utm_term=.ee5e2fee7a20.

16. Jeff Goldman, "Human Rights Watch Hacked by Syrian Electronic Army," *eSecurity Planet*, March 18, 2013, www.esecurityplanet.com/hackers/human-rights-watch
-hacked-by-syrian-electronic-army.html.

17. "Trade Sanctions Cited in Hundreds of Syrian Domain Seizures," *Krebs on Security*, May 8, 2013, www.krebsonsecurity.com/2013/05/trade-sanctions-cited-in
-hundreds-of-syrian-domain-seizures/.

18. "AP Warned Staffers Just Before @AP Was Hacked," April 23, 2013, www.jim
romenesko.com/2013/04/23/ap-warned-staffers-just-before-ap-was-hacked/.

19. Edmund Lee, "AP Twitter Account Hacked in Market-Moving Attack," *Bloomberg*, April 24, 2013, www.bloomberg.com/news/articles/2013-04-23/dow
-jones-drops-recovers-after-false-report-on-ap-twitter-page.

20. @acarvin, "@Max_Fisher Apart from accessing so many news orgs' sites and accts at one point or another," *Twitter*, April 23, 2013, 11:39 a.m., twitter.com/acarvin
/status/326767288420298752.

21. Gerry Shih and Joseph Menn, "New York Times, Twitter Hacked by Syrian Group," *Reuters*, August 27, 2013, www.reuters.com/article/net-us-newyork
times-hacked/new-york-times-twitter-hacked-by-syrian-group-idUSBRE97Q11
J20130828.

22. See *US District Court for the Eastern District of Virginia, US v. Ahmad Umar Agha and Firas Dardar*, Case #1:14-MJ-292, 15, www.justice.gov/opa/file/834271
/download.

23. US Department of Justice, Office of Public Affairs, "Computer Hacking Conspiracy Charges Unsealed Against Members of Syrian Electronic Army," March 22, 2016, www.justice.gov/opa/pr/computer-hacking-conspiracy-charges-unsealed-against
-members-syrian-electronic-army.

24. US Department of Justice, Office of Public Affairs, "Syrian Electronic Army Hacker Pleads Guilty," September 28, 2016, www.justice.gov/opa/pr/syrian-electronic
-army-hacker-pleads-guilty.

25. See, for instance, DHS Assistant Secretary Jeanette Manfra in interview with NBC News, "We saw a targeting of 21 states and an exceptionally small number of them were actually successfully penetrated," in Cynthia McFadden, William M. Arkin, and Kevin Monahan, "Russians Penetrated U.S. Voter Systems, Top U.S. Official Says," NBC News, February 7, 2018, www.nbcnews.com/politics
/elections/russians-penetrated-u-s-voter-systems-says-top-u-s-n845721.

26. Garrett M. Graff, "A Guide to Russia's High Tech Tool Box for Subverting US Democracy," *Wired*, August 13, 2017, www.wired.com/story/a-guide-to
-russias-high-tech-tool-box-for-subverting-us-democracy/.

27. Michael McFaul, *Cold War to a Hot Peace* (Houghton Mifflin Harcourt, 2018), 269.

28. Bill Whitaker, "When Russian Hackers Targeted the U.S. Election Infrastructure," *60 Minutes*, CBS News, July 17, 2018, www.cbsnews.com/news
/when-russian-hackers-targeted-the-u-s-election-infrastructure/.

29. "Foreign Affairs Issue Launch with Former Vice President Joe Biden," Council on Foreign Affairs, January 23, 2018, www.cfr.org/event/foreign-affairs-issue-launch-former-vice-president-joe-biden.

30. Clapper, *Facts and Fears*, 350.

31. Kailani Koenig, "Denis McDonough: McConnell 'Watered Down' Russia Warning in 2016," NBC News, March 4, 2018, www.nbcnews.com/politics/politics-news/denis-mcdonough-mcconnell-watered-down-russia-warning-2016-n853016.

32. Selena Larson, "The Hacks That Left Us Exposed in 2017," CNN Tech, December 20, 2017, www.money.cnn.com/2017/12/18/technology/biggest-cyberattacks-of-the-year/index.html.

33. Patrick Howell O'Neill, "NotPetya Ransomware Cost Merck More Than $310 Million," *Cyberscoop*, October 27, 2017, www.cyberscoop.com/notpetya-ransomware-cost-merck-310-million/.

34. Warwick Ashford, "NotPetya Attack Cost up to £15m, Says UK Ad Agency WPP," ComputerWeekly.com, September 25, 2017, www.computerweekly.com/news/450426854/NotPetya-attack-cost-up-to-15m-says-UK-ad-agency-WPP.

35. Charlie Osborne, "NotPetya Ransomware Forced Maersk to Reinstall 4000 Servers, 45000 PCs," ZDNet.com, January 26, 2018, www.zdnet.com/article/maersk-forced-to-reinstall-4000-servers-45000-pcs-due-to-notpetya-attack/.

36. Natasha Turak, "US Will Impose Costs on Russia for Cyber 'Acts of Aggression,' White House Cybersecurity Czar Says," CNBC.com, February 16, 2018, www.cnbc.com/2018/02/16/us-will-impose-costs-on-russia-for-cyber-aggression-says-cybersecurity-czar.html.

37. Sarah Marsh, "US Joins UK in Blaming Russia for NotPetya Cyber-Attack," *Guardian*, February 15, 2018, www.theguardian.com/technology/2018/feb/15/uk-blames-russia-notpetya-cyber-attack-ukraine.

38. Clapper, *Facts and Fears*, 350.

EPILOGUE

1. Garrett M. Graff, "How a Dorm Room *Minecraft* Scam Brought Down the Internet," *Wired*, December 13, 2017, www.wired.com/story/mirai-botnet-minecraft-scam-brought-down-the-internet/.

2. Jack Corrigan, "Air Force Pays Out Government's Biggest Bug Bounty Yet," *NextGov*, December 18, 2017, www.nextgov.com/cybersecurity/2017/12/air-force-pays-out-governments-biggest-bug-bounty-yet/144640/.

3. Sophia Chen, "Why This Intercontinental Quantum-Encrypted Video Hangout Is a Big Deal," *Wired*, January 20, 2018, www.wired.com/story/why-this-intercontinental-quantum-encrypted-video-hangout-is-a-big-deal/.

4. US Department of the Treasury, "Treasury Targets Supporters of Iran's Islamic Revolutionary Guard Corps and Networks Responsible for Cyber-Attacks Against the United States," September 14, 2017, www.treasury.gov/press-center/press-releases/Pages/sm0158.aspx.

5. Thomas P. Bossert, "It's Official: North Korea Is Behind WannaCry," *Wall Street Journal*, December 18, 2017, www.wsj.com/articles/its-official-north-korea -is-behind-wannacry-1513642537.

6. US Department of Justice, Office of Public Affairs, "Deputy Attorney General Rod J. Rosenstein Delivers Remarks at the Aspen Security Forum," Aspen, Colorado, July 19, 2018, www.justice.gov/opa/speech/deputy-attorney-general-rod-j-rosenstein -delivers-remarks-aspen-security-forum.

Index

Credit: Andrew Propp

JOHN P. CARLIN is the former Assistant Attorney General for National Security under Barack Obama, where he worked to protect the country against international and domestic terrorism, espionage, cyberthreats, and other national security threats. A career federal prosecutor and graduate of Harvard Law School, John has spent much of the last decade working at the center of the nation's response to the rise of terrorism and cyberthreats, including serving as national coordinator of the Justice Department's Computer Hacking and Intellectual Property (CHIP) program, as an Assistant United States Attorney for the District of Columbia, and as chief of staff to FBI Director Robert Mueller. Today, Carlin is the chair of the Aspen Institute's Cybersecurity & Technology Program. He also is the global chair of the risk and crisis management practice for the law firm Morrison & Foerster and is a sought-after industry speaker on cyber issues as well as a CNBC contributor on cybersecurity and national security issues.

GARRETT M. GRAFF is an award-winning journalist who has spent nearly a decade covering national security. Today, he serves as executive director of the Aspen Institute's Cybersecurity & Technology Program and is a contributor to *Wired* and CNN. He is the former editor of two of Washington's most prestigious magazines, *Washingtonian* and *POLITICO Magazine,* and the author of multiple books, including, most recently, *Raven Rock: The Story of the U.S. Government's Secret Plan to Save Itself—While the Rest of Us Die,* as well as *The Threat Matrix: Inside Robert Mueller's FBI.*

PublicAffairs is a publishing house founded in 1997. It is a tribute to the standards, values, and flair of three persons who have served as mentors to countless reporters, writers, editors, and book people of all kinds, including me.

I. F. STONE, proprietor of *I. F. Stone's Weekly*, combined a commitment to the First Amendment with entrepreneurial zeal and reporting skill and became one of the great independent journalists in American history. At the age of eighty, Izzy published *The Trial of Socrates*, which was a national bestseller. He wrote the book after he taught himself ancient Greek.

BENJAMIN C. BRADLEE was for nearly thirty years the charismatic editorial leader of *The Washington Post*. It was Ben who gave the *Post* the range and courage to pursue such historic issues as Watergate. He supported his reporters with a tenacity that made them fearless and it is no accident that so many became authors of influential, best-selling books.

ROBERT L. BERNSTEIN, the chief executive of Random House for more than a quarter century, guided one of the nation's premier publishing houses. Bob was personally responsible for many books of political dissent and argument that challenged tyranny around the globe. He is also the founder and longtime chair of Human Rights Watch, one of the most respected human rights organizations in the world.

•   •   •

For fifty years, the banner of Public Affairs Press was carried by its owner Morris B. Schnapper, who published Gandhi, Nasser, Toynbee, Truman, and about 1,500 other authors. In 1983, Schnapper was described by *The Washington Post* as "a redoubtable gadfly." His legacy will endure in the books to come.

Peter Osnos, *Founder*